The Politics of Competence

Using decades of public opinion data from the US, UK, Australia, Germany and Canada, and distinguishing between three concepts – issue ownership, performance and generalised competence – Green and Jennings show how political parties come to gain or lose 'ownership' of issues, how they are judged on their performance in government across policy issues, and how they develop a reputation for competence (or incompetence) over a period in office. Their analysis tracks the major events that lead people to re-evaluate party reputations and the costs of governing, and cause electorates to punish parties in power. They reveal why, when and how these movements in public opinion matter to elections. The implications are important for long-standing debates about performance and partisanship, and reveal that public opinion about party and governing competence is, to a great extent, the product of major shocks and predictable dynamics.

Jane Green is Professor of Political Science at the University of Manchester and a co-director of the British Election Study, the UK's leading source of election data since 1964.

Will Jennings is Professor of Political Science and Public Policy at the University of Southampton.

The Politics of Competence

Parties, Public Opinion and Voters

Jane Green
University of Manchester

Will Jennings
University of Southampton

CAMBRIDGE
UNIVERSITY PRESS

CAMBRIDGE
UNIVERSITY PRESS

University Printing House, Cambridge CB2 8BS, United Kingdom

One Liberty Plaza, 20th Floor, New York, NY 10006, USA

477 Williamstown Road, Port Melbourne, VIC 3207, Australia

4843/24, 2nd Floor, Ansari Road, Daryaganj, Delhi – 110002, India

79 Anson Road, #06–04/06, Singapore 079906

Cambridge University Press is part of the University of Cambridge.

It furthers the University's mission by disseminating knowledge in the pursuit of education, learning, and research at the highest international levels of excellence.

www.cambridge.org
Information on this title: www.cambridge.org/9781107158016
DOI: 10.1017/9781316662557

First published 2017

Printed in the United Kingdom by Clays, St Ives plc

A catalogue record for this publication is available from the British Library.

ISBN 978-1-107-15801-6 Hardback

To Bruce and Natalie

Contents

List of Tables		*page* viii
List of Figures		xii
Acknowledgements		xv
1	Introduction	1
2	Conceptual Problems and Solutions	27
3	Three Concepts of Issue Competence	47
4	Explaining Issue Ownership Change	94
5	Government Performance and Oppositions	137
6	Generalised Competence and the Costs of Governing	167
7	Ownership, Performance, Generalised Competence and the Vote	197
8	Conclusion	234
	Appendices	257
	Bibliography	294
	Index	306

Tables

2.1 Concepts, operationalisation and measures   *page* 45
3.1 Classification of issue categories   51
3.2 Issue ownership and ownership change, US Republican Party   58
3.3 Issue ownership and ownership change, US Democratic Party   59
3.4 Issue ownership and ownership change, UK Conservative Party   60
3.5 Issue ownership and ownership change, UK Labour Party   61
3.6 Issue ownership and ownership change, Australian Liberal Party   62
3.7 Issue ownership and ownership change, Australian Labor Party   63
3.8 Issue ownership and ownership change, German Christian Democratic Union   64
3.9 Issue ownership and ownership change, German Social Democratic Party   65
3.10 Ranking of US President George W. Bush evaluations by Republican and Democratic Party identifiers   71
3.11 Ranking of UK Conservative Party evaluations by Conservative and Labour identifiers   73
3.12 Persistence in performance evaluations, US President George W. Bush   78
3.13 Persistence in performance evaluations, candidates for the Republican and Democratic Party nomination for the US presidency   80
3.14 Persistence in performance evaluations, Labour government and Conservative opposition, UK, 2004–2010   80
3.15 Summary statistics for macro-competence in the United States, the United Kingdom, Germany, Canada and Australia   84
3.16 Granger causation tests between macro-competence and macro-partisanship, US   89

3.17	Granger causation tests between macro-competence and macro-partisanship, UK	90
3.18	Granger causation tests between macro-competence and macro-partisanship, Germany	90
4.1(a)	Changes in issue ownership, US, 1976–2013	105
4.1(b)	Changes in issue ownership, UK, 1970–2015	112
4.1(c)	Change in issue ownership, Australia, 1987–2013	117
4.1(d)	Changes in issue ownership, Germany, 1972–2013	118
4.2	Cases of no change in issue ownership	127
5.1	Measures of policy outcomes in the US, the UK and Germany	142
5.2	Summary table of logistic regression models of vote choice in 2005, 2010 and 2015, UK	162
5.3	Summary table of logistic regression models of presidential vote choice in 2000, 2008 and 2012, US	164
6.1	Governing party competence as function of outgoing party competence	180
6.2	The average length of honeymoon period for governing parties	182
6.3	Macro-competence and governing party vote (negativity bias and accumulation)	187
6.4	'Coalition of minorities' and governing party vote	191
7.1	Effect of events on dynamic conditional correlation with party support, Republican Party, US, 1956–2012	227
7.2	Effect of events on dynamic conditional correlation with party support, Conservative Party, UK, 1968–2012	230
8.1	Summary of concepts, measures, theory and implications	246
A3.1	Summary statistics for issue handling, US Democratic Party	257
A3.2	Summary statistics for issue handling, UK Conservative Party	257
A3.3	Ranking of ratings of Hillary Clinton by party identifiers, non-partisans and rival partisans	258
A3.4	Ranking of ratings of John Edwards by party identifiers, non-partisans and rival partisans	258
A3.5	Ranking of ratings of Barack Obama by party identifiers, non-partisans and rival partisans	258
A3.6	Ranking of ratings of Rudy Giuliani by party identifiers, non-partisans and rival partisans	258
A3.7	Ranking of ratings of John McCain by party identifiers, non-partisans and rival partisans	259

A3.8 Ranking of ratings of Mitt Romney by party identifiers, non-partisans and rival partisans   259

A3.9 Ranking of ratings of Fred Thompson by party identifiers, non-partisans and rival partisans   259

A5.1 Time series regression model of subjective and objective economic performance effects on handling of the economy, US, 1990–2013   260

A5.2 Time series regression model of subjective and objective economic performance effects on handling of the economy, UK, 2003–2015   260

A5.3 Time series regression model of Labour and Conservative Party support, UK, 2004–2010   261

A5.4 Logistic regression model (odds ratios) of party vote choice, British Election Study, 2005   262

A5.5 Logistic regression model (odds ratios) of party vote choice, British Election Study, 2010   262

A5.6 Logistic regression model (odds ratios) of party vote choice, British Election Study, 2015 (Internet Panel Study, Wave 4 and Wave 6)   263

A5.7 Logistic regression model (odds ratios) of party vote choice, British Election Study, 2015 (face-to-face survey)   263

A5.8 Logistic regression model (odds ratios) of presidential vote choice, American National Election Study, 2004   264

A5.9 Logistic regression model (odds ratios) of presidential vote choice, American National Election Study, 2008   264

A5.10 Logistic regression model (odds ratios) of presidential vote choice, American National Election Study, 2012   265

A6.1 31 countries used for analysis of costs of governing in aggregate-level vote intention in legislative elections   265

A7.1 Time series error-correction model of competence effects upon party support, US, 1956–2012   266

A7.2 Time series error-correction model of competence effects upon party support, UK, 1968–2012   268

A7.3 Logistic regression model (odds ratios) of vote choice, US, 2000–2012   270

A7.4 Logistic regression model (odds ratios) of vote choice, UK, 2005–2015   271

A7.5 Logistic regression model (odds ratios) of vote choice, UK, 2015   272

A7.6 Autoregressive distributed lag model of dynamic conditional correlations, Republican Party, US, 1956–2012   274

A7.7 Autoregressive distributed lag model of dynamic conditional
        correlations, Democratic Party, US, 1956–2012   277
A7.8 Autoregressive distributed lag model of dynamic
        conditional correlations, Conservative Party, UK,
        1968–2012   280
A7.9 Autoregressive distributed lag model of dynamic
        conditional correlations, Labour Party, UK, 1968–2012   282

Figures

1.1 Issue-handling reputations of a fictional party on seven
    issues   *page* 14
3.1 Public opinion about issue handling for the
    US Democratic Party, 1980–2013   52
3.2 Public opinion about issue handling for parties
    in the US, UK, Australia and Germany   53
3.3 Republican and Democrat identifier ratings of President
    George W. Bush on issues   71
3.4 Conservative and Labour identifier ratings of the UK
    Conservative Party on issues   73
3.5 Box plot of issue ratings of the US Republican Party, by year   75
3.6 Scatter plot of standard deviation of issue ratings against
    rank (within election cycle)   77
3.7 Macro-competence and macro-partisanship,
    US Democratic Party   85
3.8 Macro-competence and macro-partisanship,
    US Republican Party   86
3.9 Macro-competence and macro-partisanship, UK
    Conservative Party   86
3.10 Macro-competence and macro-partisanship, UK Labour
    Party   87
3.11 Macro-competence and macro-partisanship, German
    Social Democratic Party   87
3.12 Macro-competence and macro-partisanship, German
    Christian Democratic Union   88
4.1 A theory of ownership change   101
5.1 Performance evaluations and policy outcomes, US,
    1940–2013   145
5.2 Performance evaluations and policy outcomes, UK,
    1952–2012   147
5.3 Performance evaluations and policy outcomes, Germany,
    1961–2013   148

5.4 Subjective and objective economic performance and party handling, governing and opposition parties, US, 1990–2013   151

5.5 Subjective and objective economic performance and party handling, governing and opposition parties, UK, 2003–2015   152

5.6 Subjective evaluations and party handling, governing and opposition parties, UK, 2004–2010   154

5.7 Subjective evaluations and party handling, by party identification, Labour government, UK, 2004–2010   156

5.8 Subjective evaluations and party handling, by party identification, Conservative opposition, UK, 2004–2010   157

5.9 Subjective evaluations of policy conditions and party vote choice, Labour and Conservative parties, UK, 2004–2010   160

6.1 Vote intention for governing parties by length of time in government   169

6.2 Macro-competence rating of governing parties by length of time in government   174

6.3 Marginal effect of outgoing government party competence on incoming government party competence   181

6.4 The curvilinear effect of blame on vote choice   188

7.1 Competence effects upon governing party support, aggregate level, US, 1956–2012   206

7.2 Competence effects upon opposition party support, aggregate level, US, 1956–2012   207

7.3 Competence effects upon governing party support, aggregate level, UK, 1968–2012   209

7.4 Competence effects upon opposition party support, aggregate level, UK, 1968–2012   210

7.5 Competence effects upon governing party support, individual level, US, 2000–2012   213

7.6 Competence effects upon opposition party support, individual level, US, 2000–2012   214

7.7 Competence effects upon governing party support, individual level, UK, 2005–2015   215

7.8 Competence effects upon opposition party support, individual level, UK, 2005–2015   216

7.9 Competence effects upon governing party (Conservative) support, individual level, UK, 2015   218

7.10 Competence effects upon opposition party (Labour) support, individual level, UK, 2015   220

7.11 Dynamic conditional correlations between vote choice and measures of competence, US, 1956–2012   223

7.12 Dynamic conditional correlations between vote choice and
       measures of competence, UK, 1968–2012   225
A3.1 Public opinion about issue handling for the US Democratic
       Party, 1980–2013   284
A3.2 Public opinion about issue handling for the US Republican
       Party, 1980–2013   284
A3.3 Public opinion about issue handling for the UK Labour
       Party, 1980–2015   285
A3.4 Public opinion about issue handling for the UK
       Conservative Party, 1980–2015   285
A3.5 Public opinion about issue handling for the Australian
       Labor Party, 1989–2014   286
A3.6 Public opinion about issue handling for the Australian
       Liberal Party, 1989–2014   286
A3.7 Public opinion about issue handling for the German Social
       Democratic Party, 1980–2013   287
A3.8 Public opinion about issue handling for the German
       Christian Democratic Union, 1980–2013   287
A3.9 Macro-competence, US Democratic Party, 1945–2013   288
A3.10 Macro-competence, US Republican Party, 1945–2013   288
A3.11 Macro-competence, UK Labour Party, 1945–2012   289
A3.12 Macro-competence, UK Conservative Party, 1945–2012   289
A3.13 Macro-competence, Australian Labor Party, 1989–2014   290
A3.14 Macro-competence, Australian Liberal Party, 1989–2014   290
A3.15 Macro-competence, Canadian Liberal Party, 1945–2001   291
A3.16 Macro-competence, Canadian Progressive Conservatives,
       1945–2001   291
A3.17 Macro-competence, German Social Democratic Party,
       1961–2013   292
A3.18 Macro-competence, German Christian Democratic Union,
       1961–2013   292
A6.1 Vote intention for governing parties by length of time in
       government   293

Acknowledgements

The idea of issue ownership was first introduced to us by Laura Stoker. The challenge to think about what ownership is – and is not – inspired a PhD, subsequent research papers and this book. Laura also inspired the ambition to think more carefully about concepts and measures and the validity of argument, concepts and findings. Our book would also not exist without the inspiration and contributions of Jim Stimson. Our interest in long-term dynamics and context for understanding public opinion, and most of our thinking about the nature and nuances of public opinion, owes in very large part to Jim and his extraordinary generosity of ideas, data and methods. We are also both fortunate in being inspired by Christopher Wlezien, whose drive and quality of scholarship continues to challenge and motivate us. And we are lucky to have been taught by Christopher Hood while we were graduate students at Oxford. We hope to do justice to his example of thoughtfulness, originality and scholarliness. We would like to give credit to Donald Stokes, and to all those people whose work we continually return to, and whose contributions established the standard to which the political science community responds. If we have succeeded in combining novel analysis with political relevance and understanding, there is David Butler's guidance in these pages.

Many brilliant and generous people have kindly given us comments on drafts. The book has benefitted from great comments at many conferences and seminars over the years. Thank you especially to Jim Adams, John Bartle, Shaun Bevan, Ian Budge, Patrick Egan, Bob Erikson, Matt Golder, Eitan Hersh, Mark Kayser, Luke Keele, Kathleen Knight, Matt Lebo, Michael Lewis-Beck, Johannes Lindvall, Thomas Meyer, Caitlin Milazzo, Pippa Norris, Sergi Pardos, Mark Pickup, Henrik Seeberg, Jim Stimson, Laura Stoker, Zeynep Somer-Topcu, Marcus Wagner, Stefaan Walgrave, Christopher Wlezien, and to Rob Johns and Hugh Ward and the reviewers of the *British Journal of Political Science*. We are very grateful to the reviewers of our book proposal and manuscript, and to Cambridge University Press for supporting it. Giving one's time, ideas and commitment to someone else's project is one of those unsung commitments made by people who prioritise other people's work above their own. The reviews to our proposal and manuscript genuinely helped us make the book far better than it would have been otherwise. We really do appreciate it.

The analyses in this book draw on tens of thousands of individual survey items. We are indebted to the support of many generous people who provided and helped us access data. Thank you to Michael Alvarez, John Bartle, Eric Belanger, Harold Clarke, Luke Keele, Paul Kellstedt, Matt Lebo, Roger Mortimore, David Sanders, Stuart Soroka, Jim Stimson and Steffen Weiss. Thank you also to Lee Bentley, Stefanie Doebler, Tom Loughran, Emma Kilheeney, Mackenzie Merk, Wasel bin Shadat, Benjamin Tallis and John Jennings for various research assistance throughout the years, and to the Roper Centre and Lois Timms-Ferrara, to Hart Research Associates and Jeff Horwitt, the British Election Study team past and present, the Annenberg Election Study and to the US National Election Study teams.

This project began a long time ago with a seed funding grant from the University of Manchester, and then an Economic and Social Research Council small grant which we used for gathering data, and subsequently support from the Centre for Citizenship, Globalization and Governance at the University of Southampton. These grants have been invaluable for investing in a huge data-gathering project. Our institutions at Manchester and Southampton have, in a variety of ways, facilitated the freedom to focus on our research and address questions and projects we most believe in.

Our thanks go to Mike Addelman, who not only provided much-valued help on the British Election Study along with very timely moral support and encouragement, but who also designed our book cover. Thank you also to Tracy and Derek Willis for making it possible to finish writing.

With the publication of this book comes an opportunity to thank the people who have made our academic careers possible. From the earliest point, thank you to Gary and Janet Streeter, Sam and Mark Graves, Charlie Colchester, David Plummer, Tim and Hannah Davy, Tim Montgomerie and Mark Lancaster. That simple line of thanks doesn't do justice to how much of life's course was changed, but it is good to be able to print it. And for support throughout the years, our fondness and thanks to Jim Adams, Frank Baumgartner, John Curtice, Bob Erikson, Geoff Evans, Ed Fieldhouse, Christopher Hood, Bryan Jones, Martin Lodge, Pippa Norris, Colin Rallings, Graham Smith, Zeynep Somer-Topcu, Jim Stimson, Gerry Stoker, Laura Stoker and Christopher Wlezien.

We are very grateful to John Haslam and Cambridge University Press for being so patient with our manuscript. The writing spanned a general election and a referendum on European Union membership, which gave us fascinating but nevertheless very big disruptions of time on the book.

Our most important thanks go to Bruce Strouts, who kindly, quietly and steadfastly supports an erratic lifestyle and who brings much-needed balance and normality. And to Natalie Jennings for her endless patience and good humour faced with the disruption caused by long and unsociable working hours in front of Stata.

1 Introduction

Political science has given considerable attention to the spatial competition that occurs between parties on matters of policy. But as Donald Stokes observed in 1963, political evaluations and voting decisions are not just about policy distances and disagreements. They often turn on management, delivery, trust, good government: on competence. Indeed, elections are always partly about these things, and sometimes fundamentally about them. Competence is a necessary condition of electability.

'Governments can't afford to mess with competence. Once they are seen as incapable of running the country, the game is up. The political argument stops being about direction of travel, and centres on whether the government can even start the engine.'[1]

No self-respecting politician will waste an opportunity to attack the competence and trustworthiness of his or her opponent. No party will fail to claim credit for its performance in office, and no government will fail to avoid – or try to avoid – embarrassment and blame. Parties develop reputations for trust on certain policy issues and they develop associations with certain issues. There are consequences that arise from those associations – or from 'issue ownership' (Petrocik 1996): parties are expected to benefit electorally when issues on which they are considered most competent are also important to electoral choice. This leads to expectations of ownership-based framing and priming strategies in campaigns. These aspects of politics are well known and widely researched. What is far less well understood and researched is the public opinion side to the politics of competence. Understanding the politics of competence requires a focus on mass publics, as well as on political elites. This book responds to that gap.

In the study of competence, the concepts, measures, theories and evidence for public opinion about policy competence are less advanced and integrated than in the study of spatial voting and party competition.

---

[1] Jonathan Freedland, *The Guardian* newspaper, 1 April 2012.

The competence literature uses concepts of issue ownership, valence, performance, economic voting and partisanship as a running tally of performance. These are often contested and loosely defined and they are commonly only analysed in isolation. This has resulted in a mismatch of evidence and a myriad of different definitions of what does – and what does not – constitute evaluations of competence, and how and why these matter. This book clarifies and integrates concepts about policy competence in public opinion.

We propose that public opinion about competence is characterised by three main concepts:

(i) Issue ownership – defined as the representation by parties of different issue-publics and constituencies and a positive handling reputation, measured as the relative advantages a party has across the issue agenda;

(ii) Issue performance – defined as the degree to which a policy is going well or going badly for the party in office, measured as the change in evaluations of party handling of a given policy or perceptions of whether a policy area is going well or badly;

(iii) Generalised competence – defined as the degree to which parties are trusted or otherwise across the policy agenda, measured as the latent factor in public opinion about party competence.

Each of these concepts has an application in individual-level and aggregate-level analyse. We focus on both levels in this book.

Our concepts are not exhaustive, but they have construct validity and clear causes and consequences. The book proceeds to test the implications of our three concepts. By so doing, it addresses some of the major theoretical and empirical puzzles in the literature about issue competence. We reveal how greater clarity in theory, concepts and measurement offers new insights into some of the important questions about competence in political science. These questions include: how frequent are major changes in party strengths and weaknesses on issues, and what explains these changes? Are parties rewarded and punished for their performance on issues, and to what degree does this occur for governments and oppositions? Why do governments tend to lose support over the period their party is in power, and in such a predictable way? What is the contribution of a competence-based explanation to voting? When and under what conditions does competence matter for party support? This book offers answers to these questions, and more.

We analyse the three concepts alongside the concept of partisanship. By so doing we resolve some of the puzzles about competence and partisanship to understand when these concepts overlap and when they are distinct. This gives us a better understanding of public opinion about competence on issues, and also a better understanding of partisanship and its characteristics and consequences.

This book is about public opinion regarding competence on *issues*. This aspect of public opinion is distinct to public opinion about leader strengths and weaknesses, to the concept of partisanship (as a political identity), and complementary to economic evaluations. We purposefully extend the range of policy domains on which public opinion dynamics are theorised and about which implications are understood.

Competence is not perfectly distinct to position, neither in conceptual nor empirical terms. When we talk of competence we assume there is a positional aspect to competence. A voter shouldn't trust a party if they disagree with the party on an issue. We take these overlapping concepts into account in our conceptualisation and analysis.

The book's contributions are made possible by amassing thousands of survey items on public opinion about issue competence and handling in five countries (the United States, the United Kingdom, Australia, Canada and Germany). These data cover up to seven decades in aggregate-level public opinion about party competence on issues and span multiple issue topics in each country. Specifically, we collated responses to 11,004 survey questions about party handling of multiple policy issues going back to the 1940s. These data are a unique resource which makes possible a range of new insights into public opinion. We combine findings from these aggregate data with insights from individual-level data. To our quantitative analysis we also add in-depth qualitative comparative analysis of cases. The result is, to the best of our knowledge, the most comprehensive coverage of issues, time and countries for which data are available.

The State of the Literature

We highlight here the main tensions and important puzzles in existing research about competence in public opinion, party competition and vote choices.

Confusion about Issue Ownership

The concept of 'issue ownership' relates to party reputations on specific policy issues (Petrocik 1996), but in reality we lack a really clear idea of what 'ownership' actually constitutes and how it should be measured. The public tends to rate parties as better on some issues relative to other issues, with some degree of predictability and stability over time, but the degree of stability is questionable. Parties are expected to be more successful in elections when their owned issues are also important – or 'salient' – to voters. All things being equal, parties seek to prime or frame election choices to be about issues they own (Robertson 1976; Budge and Farlie 1983). As argued by Walgrave et al. (2015), however, issue ownership is a multidimensional concept; it is more complex than often assumed.

Petrocik combined two concepts in his theory of issue ownership: the concept of long-term party-constituency issue ownership and the concept of short-term issue ownership lease. The former relates to representation and commitment to issues and issue publics over the long term. It clearly has a spatial dimension as well as a commitment dimension, although the spatial element is absent in Petrocik's definition. The latter (short-term ownership lease) relates to performance. The two concepts can be differentiated by their assumed stability (long-term ownership) versus their potential for change (short-term lease). Petrocik (1996: 827) said, 'Party constituency ownership of an issue is much more long-term (although it can change and occasionally exhibits fluctuation) because its foundation is (1) the relatively stable, but different social bases, that distinguish party constituencies in modern party systems and (2) the link between political conflict and social structure.' By contrast, 'short-term' ownership is a positive competence or handling 'lease': 'The record of the incumbent creates a handling advantage when one party can be blamed for current difficulties ... wars, failed international or domestic policies, unemployment and inflation, or official corruption can happen at any time and provide one party with a "lease" – short-term ownership – of a performance issue' (Petrocik 1996: 827).

In this book we argue that the former concept of party-constituency ownership should be called 'ownership', whereas the latter concept points to a distinct characteristic of public opinion, namely short-term changes in party ratings on issues. One is issue ownership (though questions still remain concerning how to measure issue ownership and what its characteristics are), the other might be a source of a change in issue ownership and may also occur alongside stability in issue ownership. That is to say, parties have reputational strengths and weaknesses on issues (ownership) but there is also important over-time variation in public opinion about party competence within a party's relative issue strengths. Sometimes, those short-term changes may alter issue ownership but these instances should be relatively rare. Separating these longer term and shorter term properties of public opinion offers a clearer way to study causation and effects. It also helps to solve the following difficulties in the ownership literature that arise from the conflation of long- and short-term 'issue ownership'.

The first difficulty in the issue ownership literature is the debate about whether ownership is stable or volatile. Petrocik described the changing issue agenda as the point of between-election variation, but issue-handling reputations and the voters' bias towards the party advantaged by issues as 'critical constants'. Separating ownership from short-term performance enables us to examine the degree to which ownership – measured in a way consistent with a relative issue reputation – is indeed a constant. Our analyses in Chapter 4 reveal that this is far from true, with fascinating implications for explanation and effects. We also gain insights into the fundamental characteristics of public opinion about competence with respect to persistence and fluctuation. Issue ownership is, by definition, an evaluation structured in time, more enduring than transitory. The short-term nature of performance evaluations, however, is more transitory, returning more rapidly to an equilibrium state.

The second but related difficulty concerns operational definitions and measurement of issue ownership. Using average ratings of parties on issues, for example, combines a definition of long-term ownership and short-term performance. It ignores the contrasting time series dynamics of stability and change. Using the lead of one party over another on an issue inflates partisan bias in competence evaluations; partisans will tend to rate their party higher, and other parties lower, meaning that it is not always possible to disentangle a party's issue ownership from its popularity overall. Separating these concepts allows for empirical precision and the analysis of distinct empirical dynamics and consequences. One party's ownership loss does not have to be another party's ownership gain. This is only possible to detect using a measure of ownership that compares issue ratings within parties rather than between parties. It gives us novel, intuitive and important insights into public opinion about party reputations on issues. We outline the concepts and their measurement in detail in Chapter 2, and we reveal their different properties and characteristics in Chapter 3.

The third difficulty relates to whether ownership is fundamentally a concept about competence and handling or whether it is about spatial competition and proximity, representation and association (Stubager and Slothuus 2013; Walgrave et al. 2015, 2016). The notion of issue ownership has combined various aspects of a party's reputation and the representation of policy positions and constituencies. Separating 'ownership' from performance allows us to explicitly recognise the representational and associational aspect of ownership and a competence and policy handling aspect of performance, although acknowledging that the two cannot be separated entirely. This book responds by analysing the degree to which ownership change results from both positional and competence aspects of politics and by seeking to parse out issue position effects from issue competence.

Debates about Endogeneity

One of the famous debates in political behaviour has been between those who argue that partisanship is a measure of performance, representing a running tally of performance assessments (Fiorina 1981; MacKuen et al. 1989; Clarke et al. 2004, 2009; Whiteley et al. 2013), and those who argue that partisanship is the lens through which competence (and other) assessments are formed (Campbell et al. 1960; Gerber and Green 1998; Bartels 2002; Green et al. 2004). Given how important partisanship is to politics, and to the implications of a perceptual screen and a selection mechanism which filters out opposing voices, this debate continues to have central importance. At its extremes, partisanship becomes either a competence measure (see Whiteley et al. 2005; Clarke et al. 2004, 2006, 2009; Sanders et al. 2011) or at the other end of the debate competence assessments have little or no independent influence on the outcome of vote choices (see the debate between Evans and Chzhen 2016, and Whiteley et al. 2016, and a helpful response by Wlezien 2016a). The implications have been examined quite widely in relation to economic voting and recently applied to a broader concept of 'valence', or competence (Wlezien et al. 1997; Green et al. 1998; Evans and Andersen 2006; Evans and Pickup 2010; Evans and Chzhen 2016). We respond to the question of endogeneity in public opinion about competence in three ways.

The first is to argue for clearer concepts in public opinion about competence and to analyse their behaviour alongside measures of partisanship. The distinctions we bring to the concept of competence allow for assessment of when and how partisanship interacts with each one. We analyse relative party strengths and weaknesses on issues among partisans, rival partisans and independents, showing that these issue strengths and weaknesses cut through partisan biases, whereas overall level differences reveal expected partisan divides. Using a measure of ownership as a relative strength of a party across issues therefore eliminates the bias towards a party in terms of the level of its ratings on competence, and the bias in its lead in ratings over other parties (see also Stubager and Slothuus 2013), and enables us to show how even rival partisans rank a party's relative strengths and weaknesses in the same order as partisans. We also analyse our concepts of performance and generalised competence alongside party identification. There is substantial performance updating among partisans but less long-term updating of party ratings among non-partisans. Our concept of generalised competence has prior temporal ordering to partisanship, much more than the other way around.

The second way we respond to the question of endogeneity is by creating new over-time measures of public ratings of parties on competence. The competence literature has suffered from the absence of continuous measures of public opinion about party handling and performance. It has meant that measures of partisanship have been used as a proxy for performance updating, and the same measures have been used as a measure of a partisan lens. The distinction then comes down to the properties and characteristics, causes and consequences of this same measure. We amassed thousands of survey items across time and across countries. Using these data we analyse the interrelationship between public opinion about competence and measures of party identification. We find evidence consistent with an exogenous impact of competence on partisanship (a running tally), although not only in this causal direction.

The third way is to control for the degree to which competence effects are influenced by partisanship in our models, allowing for the endogeneity in party competence evaluations and taking a conservative approach to the estimation of competence effects. We also take into consideration, wherever possible, the contribution of survey question wording to the particular problem of endogeneity. Survey measures provide imperfect instruments to assess perceptions of competence. They can conflate competence and position, such as the question 'which party is *best* on issue x' (see Therriault 2015). They can also easily prime survey respondents to heavily draw on their partisan biases and affiliations in their answers 'how well has party x handled issue y'/'how well would party x handle issue y'. For this reason we use a variety of different measures.

Valence and Competence: Valence as a Fuzzy Empirical Concept

Stokes (1963, 1992) famously distinguished between position issues and valence issues, defining position issues as 'those that involve advocacy of government actions from a set of alternatives over which a distribution of voter preferences is defined' (Stokes 1963: 373) and valence issues as 'those that merely involve the linking of the parties with some condition that is positively or negatively valued by the electorate' (Stokes 1963: 373). Since Stokes, the concept of 'valence' has been used widely in political science and increasingly so. Yet the term 'valence' has become rather nebulous – such that we argue that it should be used and applied very cautiously. We differentiate the term 'valence' from a narrower concept of 'issue competence', but our book applies directly to analyses of 'valence' and how we should theorize about them.

Stokes' argument was a response to the spatial model of Downs (1954). Stokes (1963: 374) argued that not all political evaluations are over an 'ordered set of alternatives' needed for the spatial model to work. Sometimes the more important electoral evaluation is about competence, or valence. According to Stokes, among the symbolic components of valence, success or failure are most important, and 'valences' are learnt by the electorate 'from its experiences with the parties and the leaders, and the results they achieve, over time' (Stokes 1992: 150). 'Parties may be unequally linked in the public's mind with the universally approved conditions of good times, and the universally disapproved conditions of bad times' (Stokes 1992: 144). If the condition has passed, the evaluation focuses on credit or blame for past performance. If the condition is a future or current state, the 'argument turns on which party, given possession of the government, is the more likely to bring it about' (Stokes 1963: 373).

There are four common mistakes in uses of the term 'valence issues' in empirical political science if we take a close and careful reading of the argument put forward by Stokes (we discuss problems in formal theoretical uses later). These arise from researchers treating issues as falling into discrete categories as either valence or positional, as if those categories are permanent and exclusive. Simply labelling an issue 'a valence issue' is invariably the wrong thing to do.

When Stokes defined a valence issue, he highlighted how issues *become* about competence when the politics of the time makes them so. Issues are only valence issues when the terms of political debate and public evaluations become about management, trust, delivery and competence.

The first mistake is therefore to label issues as valence issues or position issues without recognition that the same issue could be more valence- or position-oriented over time. Issues can be transformed from valence to position issues if parties take opposing positions on any end goal. Position issues can be transformed into valence issues if the relevant evaluation concerns which party can deliver. The key for Stokes is whether the electorate is making a decision on the basis of valence or on the basis of position, depending on how the particular issue becomes contentious – in either valence or position terms – in mainstream political debate.

The second mistake is to ignore the possibility that the relevant measure could be more valence- or position-oriented depending on how a question about the same issue is asked, whether about ends (valence) or means (position) (see Fiorina 1981). Stone and Simas (2010: 372) touch on the distinction between ends and means, where they say: 'political outcomes often turn on which party is associated with valued outcomes such as virtue in government, peace, and low unemployment. It is true that position issues relate to how best to achieve these valued outcomes, but election outcomes are sometimes more dependent on which party is associated with such outcomes (or blamed for their opposites) than on which party is closer to the electorate on how best to achieve them.' The same issue can be asked about in a valence way ('have healthcare services got better or got worse?') or in a positional way ('should there be more or less privatisation of healthcare services?'). This has implications for survey questions that seek to measure public opinion about issues.

The third mistake is to assume that an issue (and a measure) cannot include both valence and positional components. As argued by Egan (2008: 3), 'it is sensible that on valence issues, voters evaluate candidates with regard to both position (that is, the solution they propose to a particular public policy problem) and valence (the likelihood that they and their party will enact the solution should they be elected)'. Even an issue like the economy cannot be viewed in a discrete category of valence (Sanders and Gavin 2004; Lewis-Beck and Nadeau 2011). Voters will evaluate a government on its economic approach from an ideological perspective, and also its success or failure. And a party's position on an issue may be inextricably linked with its valence. As argued by Ansolabehere and Snyder (2000: 333), 'the issue positions that parties or candidates take depend on their relative advantages on the valence issue.' And as Stokes (1963: 373) said, position issues 'lurk behind' many valence issues.

The final mistake is to ignore conditions and to focus only on valence *issues*. 'Valence issues' may denote good times and bad times, or good economic times and hard times, war, national prestige abroad, low levels of crime, economic growth, and success or failure in government (Stokes 1963, 1992). As Clark (2009; see also Clark 2014) highlighted, for Stokes, valence issues include both policy characteristics (such as economic prosperity) and non-policy characteristics (the absence of corruption). These combinations have continued in definitions of valence issues, including, for example, the ability to deliver on policy, commitment and/or managerial competence on an issue, a nation safe from external enemies, a clean environment, a well-educated citizenry (Egan 2007), peace, prosperity or virtue in government (Stone and Simas 2010), prosperity, scandal-free administration and the absence of inflation (MacDonald and Rabinowitz 1998). Valence issues can be policy-based and non-policy-based depending on the issue, goal or end in question. While we focus on issue competence in this book, we also analyse the impact of events, shocks and conditions which make vote choices more dependent on evaluations of competence. We reveal the importance of a generalised notion of competence, inspired by Stokes, in addition to specific issue competence and also the notion of issue ownership.

Finally, it is worth noting that there are some issues that are so dominantly about position that they might deserve a category of their own: they are attitudes which indicate long-standing ideological *values* and orientations. Egan (2007: 2–3) states that, 'Pure position issues are those on which citizens disagree over desired outcomes: should abortion be legal? Should gun ownership be restricted?' Preferences over abortion, as well as gay rights, women's rights, censorship in the media and in schools, and euthanasia represent issues on which preferences relate to concepts of right and wrong in ways of living. While these are political issues, a person's beliefs also relate to underpinning value orientations in liberal authoritarian or small 'c' conservative terms. The valence element of these 'issues' or 'values' may be less important, but not necessarily absent altogether.

Valence as Everything and Nothing

There is an additional problem with how the term 'valence' is treated in the formal theoretical literature. The term 'valence' has been used as a catch-all term for almost any positive asset of a candidate or party that isn't a spatial term in a formal theoretic model. It highlights the risks to empirical political science of using the term 'valence' too loosely. To demonstrate some of these difficulties,[2] we offer a list of studies applying the term 'valence'.

We have seen authors defining valence as a valence dimension or a party valence score (MacDonald and Rabinowitz 1998; Ansolabehere and Snyder 2000; Groseclose 2001), a candidate's character or strategic advantage (Stone and Simas 2010; Adams et al. 2011), a leader advantage or disadvantage (Schofield 2004), the ability to manage a strong economy (Ansolabehere and Snyder 2000), a strategic advantage (Bruter et al. 2010), candidate quality (Schofield 2004), candidate experience, reputation (Fenno 1978; also see Burden 2004), education and income or the lack thereof (Galasso and Nannicini 2011), party activism or the level of activist support (Schofield 2004), candidate spending (Zakhorov 2009; Serra 2010), and the reputation of candidates, scandals and corruption (or their absence) in political parties and corruption at the level of candidates (Hollard and Rossignol 2008). To this list we can add incumbency (Zakharov 2009), the degree of uncertainty associated with candidates' locations on positional issues (e.g.

---

[2] See also Green and Jennings (2017b).

Enelow and Hinich 1981; Bernhardt and Ingberman 1985; Austen-Smith 1987; Hinich and Munger 1989, 1995; Ingberman 1992) or simply 'the personal vote' (Ansolabehere and Snyder 2000). Valence has been used to denote high levels of name recognition and goodwill among electorates (Mayhew 1974; Fiorina 1977), charisma, name recognition and greater campaign funds (Kim 2005; Serra 2010), superior character or intelligence (Groseclose 2001), the skills, assets and resources that candidates need for campaigning (Serra 2011), campaign spending on advertising (Zakharov 2009), negative campaigning (Curini and Paolo Martelli 2010) and even better handshaking skills (Hollard and Rossignol 2008)! Some authors define valence as honesty and integrity (Wittman 2005), or the knowledge and reputation of a party's staff and activists (Enelow and Hinich 1982). Buechler (2008) proposes five dimensions to any candidate valence term; two associated with honesty (susceptibility to influence and personal integrity), and three associated with competence (policy expertise, legislative skill and managerial competence). From the precise to the general, valence has been defined as the variation in popularity of each candidate in the electorate (Schofield 2003), 'the candidate advantage where one candidate is more popular than the other' (Bruter et al. 2010: 157), a dimension orthogonal to policy; a non-policy attribute of candidates (Serra 2010) and a 'non-policy advantage' (Grose and Globetti 2008). We trust this list makes our point!

To the degree that this book is about 'valence' it is about the competence aspects of issues, with consideration also of how competence and position are inextricably linked, especially in issue ownership. We distinguish between policy competence and those existing variables which have an element of performance, or 'valence'. Our book examines public opinion about competence on the economy *and* on the wider set of issue domains for which survey data are available. It analyses issue competence alongside leadership evaluations, economic conditions and partisanship, but specifically distinguishes them, to isolate their dynamics, explanations and impacts. It also analyses all of these concepts alongside spatial measures of public opinion, mindful of the way in which ideological positions and evaluations interact with these concepts, not just with issue competence and ownership.

Finally, this book takes the view that 'valence' is a contextual phenomenon. We test the argument made by Stokes which was never actually tested, to our knowledge: that valence voting occurs when major events heighten the relevance of competence. This argument and evidence occurs later on in the book, in Chapter 7.

A New Approach: Three Concepts of Public Opinion about Issue Competence

We suggest there are three main kinds of public opinion about competence that matter: (i) public opinion about reputations on issues; those issues a party is considered relatively best on due to long-term representation and reputation, a party's owned issues; (ii) public opinion about how well parties-in-government are handling individual policy issues in terms of short-term fluctuations; and (iii) public opinion about how parties and governments are judged overall in terms of competence on issues; or 'generalised competence'. The three concepts we put forward here are not all new. They represent a new reading of the insights of the existing literature on issue ownership, performance and valence, which is reviewed and discussed in greater detail in Chapter 2. The need for these three separate concepts becomes evident when considering the following scenario.

Imagine a president or a party presiding over a succession of high, low and then high numbers of military casualties of war over a period of months. Public opinion about the incumbent's handling of war will fluctuate. However, it is not obvious that the president's party or governing party will lose a long-term reputation as being more trusted on the issue of defence. It is also not obvious that this over-time variation in policy handling and outcomes will result in an indictment of the administration overall. Nevertheless, the individual-level variation in an evaluation of a government's handling of casualties of war will be tremendously important. Regions or electoral districts with high military populations may weigh military casualties more heavily than others. Doves may weigh them more heavily than hawks. The over-time variation in the importance of war – and the public salience of military casualties – will be important for variation in presidential approval and in electoral preferences. The party may retain its 'issue ownership' of the issues of foreign affairs and defence, but meaningful volatility in public opinion can still exert an impact on the governing party's approval.

Imagine now that our president or incumbent also presides over a major scandal in public spending. Perhaps a high-profile resignation occurs and major political figures begin to apportion blame in conflicting directions, leading to questions of unity and party control. Media and opposition party attention detects the government is in trouble, seizes on that opportunity and public awareness grows. These kinds of difficult political periods happen frequently. Yet the two concepts which are commonly applied to understanding public opinion about competence, that of the relatively stable reputations different parties have on issues and short-term policy handling on specific policy issues, would not explain this ebb and flow of positive and negative party competence. A government that has lost public trust will lose public trust across the policy agenda. 'A rising tide lifts all boats' (and an outgoing tide lowers all boats). We need a concept of issue competence that is general, capturing overall gains and losses in perceived party and government policy competence over time. And we need a concept of policy evaluations on specific issues and a concept of issue-specific advantages that parties tend to carry over time. Sometimes those short-term evaluations may indeed alter issue ownership, but we do not know how frequently this occurs, if it does, or the conditions that make this more or less likely. These are questions we take up in Chapter 4.

The three concepts we argue for are as follows:

(i) Long-Term Reputations: *Issue Ownership*

For a party to gain 'ownership' of an issue, it should be closer to the preferences of a particular issue public that cares about this issue, it should take (or have taken) a greater interest in the issue than another party and it should be recognised as the party most likely to handle the issue well and deliver on it. This reputation and issue association is faithful to Petrocik's (1996) definition of 'party-constituency issue ownership' based upon long-term constituency representation. We know that parties are better trusted on some issues compared to others due to reputations they come to hold over a long time period. These reputations tend to be relatively stable (although how much is questionable) and lead the average rating of a party on an 'owned' issue to be higher than its rating on other issues, and higher than those of another party.

(ii) Variation in Issue-Specific Handling: *Policy Performance*

Every party-in-government may be judged more positively on its handling of an issue (perhaps because a policy statement is made which voters agree with, or a positive outcome is noticed or felt by voters) and it may be judged more negatively on its handling of an issue (due to deteriorating policy outcomes, or a successful criticism by a non-partisan group, or a party's rivals). We recognise the positional and performance nature of judgements about handling and competence. These short-term changes are not the same as issue ownership; they do not denote a long-term reputational advantage, and they can exhibit meaningful variation on an owned issue and meaningful variation on other issues as well.

(iii) General Evaluations about Party Competence: *Generalised Competence*

The third concept relates to the generalised way in which parties and governments come to be rated more positively or negatively – on average – on all policy issues. If a party is rated more positively across the policy agenda, its owned issues will still remain better rated than others, but the mean evaluation of the party will be higher overall. There may still be important issue-specific variance, as parties are judged better or worse on individual issues. But the general mood of an electorate about the party-in-government (or a party-in-opposition) will exhibit meaningful variation in its average rating across issues.

The concepts are represented in the following graph. Figure 1.1 depicts the issue-handling ratings of a fictional party on seven issues over time: the economy, healthcare, education, foreign affairs, transport, immigration and the environment. The ratings on the y-axis indicate the percentage of the public who consider the party as best able to handle a given issue.[3] Each

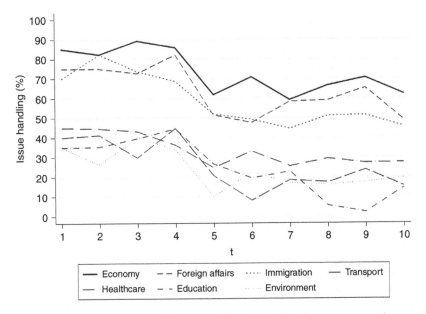

Figure 1.1 Issue-handling reputations of a fictional party on seven issues

---

[3] These fictional data were created by first setting the intercept of each issue at a different level, to indicate its underlying relative strength or weakness for the party (these values ranged from 25 to 85). We then added random noise to each series

line exhibits issue-specific variation. As voters recognise changes in the state of the health system, or the number of immigrants, or economic growth, they ascribe more positive or more negative evaluations to the party in question. However, this party always tends to be more trusted on the issues of the economy, foreign affairs and immigration (we would assume our fictional party is a right-of-centre party). Whilst those issues exhibit fluctuation, the mean level of these evaluations tends to be higher. Finally, our fictional party suffers a shock to its competence evaluations in year 5. From this point, the average competence evaluation on all issues experiences a negative shock. While the party still retains relative ownership of 'its' issues, and while there continues to be issue-specific variation in perceived handling and performance, there is an overarching loss of competence in public opinion we would need to explain. Each feature of public opinion may have an independent consequence.

We see large competence shocks as a type of performance effect. In this sense, performance can be a cause of ownership loss (or gain).[4] In Figure 1.1 there is a shock at year 5. Here there is no change in 'ownership'; the same issues are more (and less) positive for our fictional party, just less so across the issue agenda. A major performance shock could, however, alter ownership of an issue, which we theorise in detail in Chapter 4. Importantly, shocks in performance can have an independent effect, resulting in a change in party handling on one issue, they can result in a deterioration (or improvement) in generalised competence across all issues, and they can also, under certain conditions, impact on a party's ownership of an issue.

These fictional phenomena are based on trends we observe in a wealth of aggregate-level survey data on public opinion that we have collected in five countries: the United States, the United Kingdom, Australia, Canada and Germany. The level differences (ownership), fluctuations (performance) and average competence declines and increases (generalised competence) are found in all five countries, where traditions of over-time opinion polling make these analyses possible.

from a normal distribution with a mean of zero and a standard deviation of 6 (this value was somewhat arbitrarily chosen, but importantly was intended to be greater than might be expected from sampling error alone). Finally, we subtracted 20 points from each series in year 5 and all subsequent years, to capture the lasting drop in competence evaluations. This can be represented as $P_i = a_{0i} - k_{t \geq 5} + \varepsilon_t$ where i is the issue, k is the effect of an external shock at $t = 5 \ldots t = n$ and ε is the random noise component.

[4] Whether it results in a temporary 'lease' or realignment of an issue for one party or another (to a new equilibrium) is an empirical question we address in Chapter 4.

Puzzles in Political Science

The clarification of concepts makes it possible to tackle new theoretical questions.

How Stable Is 'Long-Term Ownership', and What Explains Changes in Issue Ownership?

We know very little about where ownership comes from, or what explains variation in a party's reputations on different issues. The latter puzzle may have arisen because scholars have assumed long-term ownership to be invariant. We show that this is not the case. Using a conservative measure of ownership change, which makes it difficult for us to find substantial movement in parties' relative issue reputations, we reveal frequent and long-lasting changes in issue reputations, even on issues which might be thought of as classic issues of parties on the left, and issues of parties on the right. Taking a long time frame is key here. Taking a narrower one binds us into assumptions rooted in a particular period. We provide a theory and evidence to understand and explain the causes of issue ownership change and in its absence the causes of stability. This addresses a significant gap in the literature and has implications for parties' electoral fortunes, and their strategies. Our response appears in Chapter 4.

Does Policy Performance Matter, and If So, for Which Parties?

It may be assumed that voters and electorates notice government performance on a range of issues, but to what extent is this actually the case? It may alternatively be true that the economy is a 'super issue', but that attention on other issues is less intense. If that were the case, governments may have a license to govern poorly on non-economic policy issues. If voters notice government performance, however, across policy issues, there are stronger potential accountability mechanisms at work. One of the classic folk theories in politics is that oppositions do not win elections, governments lose them. To what extent are opposition parties the beneficiaries of performance ratings of governments in terms of (a) enhanced evaluations of their own performance capabilities and (b) the consequences of performance ratings on party choice? These are the questions we address in Chapter 5.

Why Do Governing Parties Regularly Lose Support?

The concept of generalised competence, and its estimation at the aggregate level, offers an over-time measure of subjective evaluations of parties on competence. This has been the 'missing link' in efforts to explain the phenomenon of declining levels of support for parties over a period in office. Why do governments so regularly appear to lose public support over a period in office? Why does blame seem to be more acute towards the end of a period in government, but less severe at the beginning? We account for these time-based trends in a theoretical and empirical manner, moving beyond offering an ad-hoc explanation for their existence. In Chapter 6 we present a theory and evidence, building on the implications of the idea of 'grievance asymmetry' (Nannestad and Paldam 2002), that take us closer to an answer of why parties in government so regularly experience costs of ruling.

How and When Does Competence Matter in Elections?

Political parties have incentives to prime competence and incentives to avoid it and will sometimes be successful and sometimes less so. The exogenous environment will make some issues – and some evaluations – important in such a way that it would be strange to think that it is parties alone that can shape, prime or frame the political agenda, or even do any more than to respond to it (see Green-Pedersen and Mortensen 2010). It is important to ask, therefore: when is competence more important to party support, and when is it not? What factors shape the relevance of competence, and which are less likely to do so? Is the effect of competence (ownership, performance and generalised competence) constant, or are there systematic predictors of a stronger and weaker association over time? These questions are central to understanding when – and under what conditions – scholars should focus more on a competence explanation of vote choices (and party competition) and when they should focus more on other factors. We provide our answers to those questions in Chapter 7.

How Much Agency Do Parties and Governments Have?

It is often assumed that parties and governments are the shapers of politics. Politics is, after all, the art of the exercise of power. Our book has implications for a fundamental question of how much parties and governments are actually responding to the broader political and policy environment over which they have limited immediate control. We put forward a range of ways in which parties are the principals, rather than the agents, of public opinion about competence and when public opinion about competence matters.

One reading of issue ownership theory is that parties are able to influence the issues that decide elections. Parties are also expected to enhance their reputations on policy issues via their commitment to those issues, to electoral constituencies and via attention to issues in office. Spatial models assume that parties compete strategically by adjusting their policy offerings to voters. Riker's (1986) theory of heresthetics, for example, assumes that governments can shape the dimensions on which competition is based, not just at election time, but also between elections. Governments use their power to establish legislative priorities and to determine the direction of policies. To some degree, we see a strategic element to changes in issue ownership. In Chapter 4 we detail the positional strategies that coincide with changes to party reputations on issues. However, with every change in issue ownership we identify a major 'shock' in performance or competence, and many of these shocks are exogenous. There are periodically major events in political life – landmark policies, economic crises, policy failures, military campaigns, corruption scandals, changes of leadership. Those events are drivers of public opinion about parties, and they shape their decisions and strategies. While not always exogenous, they often are, and they have a major impact on electorates and their opinions. They shape the dynamics of public opinion about competence.

We analyse the degree to which evaluations of government issue handling are products of policy performance. Not all policy performance is a strategic response. It can also be driven by events. Our focus on the 'costs of governing' phenomena also points to a pattern of governing party support that is so regular and predictable that it begs the question of whether and under what conditions governments can ever strategically buck the trend of declining support over their time in office. When analysing the impact of events and shocks on competence voting, we find a consistent pattern that it is these 'exogenous' shocks which determine the importance of issue ownership, performance and generalised competence for explaining electoral choice.

Our book does not claim that parties and governments have no control over their reputations, over the issue agenda or over the basis of what matters in elections. Our findings do, however, strongly challenge the extent to which this is always true, or should always be a guiding assumption of political strategies. This calls for a re-focusing of attention on the degree to which parties and governments, their strategies, emphases and priorities, are responders to their environment, rather than the architects of it. We stress the limits of political power in shaping public opinion, and the power of public opinion in shaping politics.

Our Analytic Approach

The aim of this book is to assess long-term factors in public opinion, the importance of political context, government cycles, events, major policy changes, performance shocks and the interrelationship between public opinion and the exogenous policy environment, and with partisanship. Our approach is therefore to assess variation over time, across parties, periods of government, countries and policy issues. We briefly highlight the value of this approach.

Over Time

An explanatory model of the effects of issues, the economy, leaders, ideological preferences, indeed of any variable, can rarely – if ever – be generalised across all elections. 'We should explore longer time series where possible and not assume that our contemporary context reflects a constant' (Brasher 2009: 74). The context in which an election is fought can fundamentally alter the salience and relevance of any one or more explanatory factor(s). The economy will matter more to electoral choice when economic conditions are negative rather than positive (Paldam 1991; Soroka 2006, 2014), or when the proportions of partisans in the electorate are low (Kayser and Wlezien 2011). Ideology will matter more to electoral outcomes when parties and voters are divided on issues than when politics is consensual (Stokes 1963; Green 2007; Green and Hobolt 2008). Such a focus upon context is particularly important when considering the consequences of competence. Voters are more likely to make a vote choice based upon competence when things are going badly than when they are going well. This is something we consider in various chapters in this volume, finding support for negativity bias in public opinion and its effects (see Nannestad and Paldam 2002; Soroka 2006, 2014).

The time dimension is crucial if we are to separate institutional variation from party alternation, or to compare the effects of significant policy events, or to analyse the decline (or incline) of competence ratings for governments across electoral cycles. We need variation on periods in which parties are responsible for handling public policy issues and when they are not; when they form governments and when they are in opposition.

Across Country Context and Institutional Differences

We present data on the largest number of countries possible for each theoretical question considered. Where we can address a question using survey data on vote intention, we present our analysis for 31 countries over 116 periods of government. Where we can answer a theoretical question using our time series measure of generalised competence, we analyse its dynamics in the United States, the United Kingdom, Australia, Canada and Germany. These countries are those in which sufficient traditions in opinion polling and national election studies make possible the collection of sufficient data for reliable time series analysis.

In some of our analyses, the need for equivalent covariates means we focus more closely on the United States and the United Kingdom. Here we have aggregate-level measures of partisanship, public policy mood, presidential or prime ministerial approval, trust in government, economic evaluations and other indicators, and also salient events. These countries also give us individual-level data that are comparable for our purposes. The in-depth analysis of two countries, one presidential and one parliamentary, one with a clear tradition of strongly partisan two-party politics and one having experienced a period of partisan dealignment and party system fragmentation (see Green and Prosser 2016), means that we can provide as much evidence as possible to give greater confidence that our findings are generalisable, and not confined to a single country.

Aggregate and Individual Levels

Much of the focus in this book considers the dynamic nature of aggregate-level public opinion as part of our understanding of the macro-polity. We are careful to develop theories of electorates rather than of individual voters when we test our research questions at the macro-level. Our research questions concern how parties respond to the long term and general nature of public opinion: how they are rated on average and in general, one issue to another, rather than within segments of the electorate. This in no way implies that parties and individual politicians are not eagerly aware of the segmentation and heterogeneity of the electorate, and will not target their campaigns and messages to these different groups. Yet the priorities of a government are national, and the outcome of an election is governed by the aggregation of a myriad of electoral concerns. Our conceptual development of the three concepts of competence uses both individual and aggregate data in the United States and the United Kingdom, where comparable questions are asked. When we develop a combined model of vote choice in Chapter 7, we demonstrate the implications using aggregate-level data, as well as individual-level data.

We combine a wealth of quantitative evidence together with in-depth qualitative analysis of cases. In Chapter 4 we present a comparative analysis of cases of issue ownership change drawing on extensive exploration of a range of contextual data in the histories of the United States, the United Kingdom, Australia and Germany, and also of issue ownership stability.

Implications and Applications

This book tackles questions including but also moving beyond a focus upon elections.

Understanding Party Competition

Average issue-handling ratings of parties confuse three concepts, as highlighted earlier: the relative strengths of a party on a given issue in relation to strengths on other issues; the way in which evaluations of parties fluctuate on individual issues; and the general direction in public opinion about competence which causes those issue-handling ratings to increase together and decrease together. These insights have different implications for the issue-based competitive strategies of candidates and parties.

The first implication is that issue ownership effects might be better understood by thinking of different kinds of advantages across concepts. For example, a party may have a positive rating on the issue of healthcare, and that issue may be its 'best' issue over time. Even a loss of positive ratings on healthcare would result in that issue remaining the 'best' among all issues, and an issue on which the party retains a lead over its opponent, even if narrow. But another issue – law and order – may have become more positive for the party, perhaps due to falling crime levels, investment in policing and so on. This may not be an 'owned' issue in the sense that it is consistently positive for the party over time, but the issue becomes positive for a relevant electoral period. Here a focus on the relative ratings of the party on an issue would denote a campaign focus on crime. Instances where parties and candidates do not appear to campaign on their 'owned' issues might therefore be explained by the party's relatively positive ratings in the shorter term. Allowing for this variance in relative issue evaluations may lead to greater explanatory power.

The concept of generalised competence reveals how parties face different strategic contexts according to their popularity and public confidence, and it serves as a contextual variable. In periods when parties are more trusted on a range of policy issues, their issue agenda might be broader. Such contexts may be characterised by a stronger focus on competence, trust, handling and delivery, whereas alternative foci in periods of competence losses might be on a limited number of issues, on positional advantages, on uncertainty and risk over the competence of an alternative government, and perhaps more negative campaigning. When a government lacks strong generalised competence, we can expect the rival party's attention, and the attention of the media, to be strongly focused on competence. These are empirical questions beyond the scope of this book, but they are hypotheses which can be tested in light of it.

Scholars have tackled a range of questions concerning the relationship of a valence advantage or disadvantage to the moderate or extreme positions of candidates and parties. Those implications may be evaluated according to individual policy issues, both in terms of change in ratings and in terms of relative issue-based strengths, and in relation to the more positive or negative context in which candidates and parties compete.

Understanding Electoral Choice

There is a growing body of scholarship revealing how competence evaluations have an important and influential effect upon vote choice. However, the effects of competence have not been widely or consistently estimated. One reason for this is the absence of consistent and comparative measures. The opinion polling industry has been far more focused upon issue-handling variation over time than the electoral studies community, and so have candidates and political parties themselves – clues, of course, to the strategic importance of analysing public opinion about the competence of candidates and parties on issues. This book highlights the importance of issue competence effects by demonstrating the nature of variance in public opinion about issue competence, and by delineating the concepts which explain unique variance in vote choice models. Crucially, we reveal that competence effects are not constant; they vary in response to the political relevance of competence following different exogenous and political events, and matter in some elections more than others.

The concept of generalised competence offers a way to explain a variety of electoral questions. Does ideology matter more to vote choices when party competence is higher, or lower? Do voters use competence as a heuristic more under contexts of stronger partisan conditions or in contexts of partisan dealignment? Does the ideological blurring common in Western party democracies strengthen the influence of competence (see Green 2007; Green and Hobolt 2008), or is competence more important within the polarised politics of countries such as America? Does competence matter more in times of crisis and upheaval? These questions, and more, can be answered and further investigated in future work using over-time and comparative measures of competence made available and described in this book.

Understanding the Macro-Polity

This book makes a contribution to the broader understanding of the macro-polity via two substantive implications of competence evaluations at the macro-level. We reveal how variation in generalised competence explains aggregate-level changes in voting preferences, and how variation in generalised competence explains the comparative evidence of losses in electoral support for parties over a period in government.

The measurement of generalised competence ('macro-competence') can be applied to the analysis of the macro-polity more widely. It will be possible to further address the question of whether macro-partisanship is a running tally of these evaluations. Researchers, using our measure, will be able to assess how different presidents and prime ministers contribute to, and benefit from (or are harmed by), the competence evaluations of their parties. We can calculate the impact of major political events, of leader evaluations and partisan attachments and the effects of generalised competence on electoral preferences over time (see Green and Jennings 2012a). Realigning elections may exist for competence, as well as for partisanship, such that shocks to competence have a long-lasting and fundamentally important effect upon political evaluations in some elections, but a lesser effect in others. There may also be fascinating inter-relationships between generalised competence evaluations and the loss of relative issue reputations which affect issue ownership.

Public Policy Processes and Outcomes

There is little question that the quality of government – its effectiveness, management and policy outcome successes and their measurement – has enormous implications for public policy and public management. The performance and competence of governments, through perception and reality, will impact upon public management reform, priorities and actions.

Our contribution in this area is to better understand the nature of electoral responsiveness to government performance, and to reveal how public opinion responds to a government over time. As governments lose a reputation for competence over a period in office, the incentives for performing better may become stronger, or they may weaken. An important puzzle will be resolving the likelihood that administrations do better over a period in office (Dewan and Myatt 2012) and the reality of the regularity of decline in public perceptions. We can imagine a vicious circle, whereby a loss in reputation for competence leads to factionalism and disunity, with different factions apportioning blame and proposing competing solutions. It is therefore of interest to explore whether performance incentives within administrations are influenced by the responsiveness of the public to different issues.

The literature on risk and blame management suggests that policymakers have enhanced incentives to avoid blame (Hood 2002, 2011). Our work confirms the presence of a negativity bias in competence effects upon vote choices. As argued by Weaver (1986), politicians may tend to be more blame averse than they are credit-seeking. Obtaining measures of policy competence – and doing so for issues in addition to the economy – provides an insight into the degree to which the public is attentive and responsive to policy performance across a range of policy issues. This can have a range of implications for theories of blame avoidance. While theories assume that delegated policy areas result in less blame attribution to national governments, the consistency of responsiveness to policy performance points to a more complex model in which these strategies are either unsuccessful or the beliefs of their potential success are misguided.

The implications and applications represent literatures which have thus far been unconnected. None have hitherto been able to draw upon a systematic understanding of how competence reputations are won and lost, how voters formulate opinions about party competence, how they differ by incumbents and oppositions and the degree to which they are stable over time. We actually know relatively little about public opinion regarding competence. This book bridges this gap.

Book Outline

The remainder of the book is organised as follows.

Chapter 2 argues for the three concepts of competence, drawing on a re-reading of Petrocik's definitions of issue ownership and reflecting on the wider literature about reputations, ownership, valence issues and competence. It outlines the concepts, how we operationalise them and how we measure them.

Chapter 3 offers an empirical validation of the concepts using the broadest range of public opinion data available, illustrating similarities and differences in our country cases: the United States, the United Kingdom, Australia, Canada and Germany. For each concept we systematically explore the relationship with partisanship, revealing the degree to which the concepts are not coterminous and offering insights into how partisanship relates to competence.

Chapters 4, 5 and 6 each take one of the concepts of competence and explore new theoretical implications and explanations.

Chapter 4 analyses cases of issue reputation losses and gains. We put forward a theory to explain why parties gain and lose ownership of issues. The theory is based on symbolic politics; those policy changes and performance signals which reshape partisan evaluations and alter the make-up of partisan constituencies, subject to the necessary conditions of salience and party supply. Cases are drawn from four countries and the theory is evaluated against a range of primary empirical data and secondary sources.

Chapter 5 analyses the nature and implications of short-term evaluations of performance. Taking the assumption that short-term fluctuations arise mainly from the actions of the government, this chapter examines the association between policy outcomes and indicators and fluctuations in public evaluations of government performance on issues. It evaluates the responsiveness of public evaluations of policy performance on ratings of the party-in-power and the main opposition party, exhibiting asymmetry in the degree of responsiveness and change. Finally, the chapter examines how performance evaluations exert a similar effect on governing and opposition vote choices.

Chapter 6 reveals how electorates come to evaluate a party more negatively for its competence the longer it governs. There is a degree to which generalised competence evaluations are cyclical and behave in similar ways to declines in governing party support. These cycles offer an explanation for incumbent vote losses – the 'costs of ruling' or 'costs of governing', allowing for their relationship with partisanship, leader approval and the economy. We put forward a time-varying theory of blame attribution, revealing how honeymoon periods arise from the discounting of new incumbent performance, how negative shocks to competence evaluations are more heavily weighted and how they accumulate against a government over its period of office, up to a saturation point beyond which accumulation effects weaken.

In Chapter 7 we integrate the three concepts to reveal how each provides explanatory power when analysing electoral choice. Controlling for partisanship and other variables, we demonstrate the effects of a combined competence model of vote choice, at both the aggregate and individual levels. We also reveal how competence effects are contextual; much less than offering a constant explanation over time, the effects of ownership, performance and generalised competence vary in systematic ways following performance shocks and events, and elections in which competence is particularly salient.

Chapter 8 considers the findings and the implications of issue competence as issue ownership, performance and generalised competence, and directions for future research.

Conclusion

The study of issue competence has been concerned with its influence on vote choices when parties' owned issues are salient in elections, and with understanding the basis of party competition. Scholars have debated the degree to which issue ownership is stable and whether ownership is therefore a long-term asset of a party, or whether this asset is more temporary. Alongside these debates, the literature on performance, competence and 'valence' has been muddled. It has lacked precise definitions and agreements on what is – and what is not – ownership or competence.

In this book we differentiate between issue ownership, performance and generalised evaluations of competence. We focus on the mass-level characteristics of public opinion about competence to (i) clarify the concepts and measures of issue competence, (ii) analyse the relationships between public opinion about competence and partisanship and (iii) open up new lines of analysis to tackle important theoretical and empirical questions. The remainder of this book delves into those questions and provides our answers. Before doing so, Chapter 2 reviews the literature on competence, clarifying the concepts and gaps, offering a solution, and Chapter 3 examines the construct validity of our three concepts of ownership, performance and generalised competence.

2 Conceptual Problems and Solutions

This chapter reviews the literature on issue ownership and competence, and offers a response. It navigates the theories and evidence from which we construct our argument for the three concepts of issue competence used in this book: issue ownership, performance and generalised competence. At the end of the chapter we outline these concepts and the operationalisations we use in our analyses.

Issue Ownership: Confusing Long-Term Reputation and Short-Term Lease

The issue ownership theory of Petrocik (1996; Petrocik et al. 2003) built upon the issue saliency theory of Budge and Farlie (1977, 1983). They argued that parties' issue reputations lead parties and candidates to try to increase the salience of their best issues in campaigns and downplay the relevance of issues on which they do not have an advantage (see also Robertson 1976). This theory of public opinion 'finds a campaign effect when a candidate successfully frames the vote choice as a decision to be made in terms of problems facing the country that he is better able to "handle" than his opponent' (Petrocik 1996: 826). Parties are expected to do better in elections when the issues they own are the issues that are also salient to voters.

The implication of issue ownership theory is that there should be selective emphasis of issues in campaigns – parties should not emphasise the same issues. This is because ownership of an issue is held only by one party, rather than shared across them. In reality, campaigns are much more complex than this, and the expectation of selective emphasis is far from clear-cut (see Budge 2015, for a review). While Spiliotes and Vavreck (2002) found patterns in US House, Senate and gubernatorial candidate television advertising consistent with the notion of selective emphasis, Simon (2002) found issue dialogue (i.e. convergence) in almost every election studied. Damore (2005) reported that the incidence of issue convergence in campaign advertising was quite common,

27

although divergence was, on average, more frequent. Sides (2006) revealed that parties engage in competition on the same issues, but rival parties campaign on an opponent's owned issues by framing the issue in different ways. Damore (2004, 2005), investigating the factors influencing issue trespassing or convergence, found that the candidate's competitive standing, their partisanship, the importance of the issue for the electorate and the campaign message tone were all associated with candidates' decisions to address issues owned by their opponent's party.

Parties have to respond to each other, and they also have to respond to issues that are salient in the electorate, irrespective of whether they happen to own a salient issue. The saliency of an issue can force parties and candidates to engage in competition on the same issues, even if one party is seen to have a clear disadvantage (Ansolabehere and Iyengar 1994; Holian 2004; Sides 2006). 'The actual state of the world may make certain issues unavoidable' (Budge and Farlie 1983: 129). In fact, Budge and Farlie (1983) acknowledged that candidates could be expected to campaign similarly on performance issues, such as foreign relations and government record, since 'such issues are not permanently owned by any party, but may be annexed temporarily ... hence, most direct argument and confrontation will be focused in this area' (Budge and Farlie 1983: 42). Sides (2006) differentiates between a deterministic theory of issue ownership (one whereby parties can be expected to diverge towards their best issues) and a probabilistic theory, whereby there is some expectation of divergence. Nevertheless, and in spite of these contrary findings on selective emphasis, it is widely assumed that parties benefit when their owned issues are salient in an election.

Issue ownership theories can also be seen alongside a longer term strategic goal of focusing political debate and competition on issues and dimensions which advantage a party. This is consistent with the idea of 'heresthetics' (Riker 1986, 1993). Heresthetics predicts that dominant parties strategically shape the dimensions of the debate around new conflicts that win them votes. Like issue ownership or saliency theories, the purpose of campaign agenda shaping is not to engage other parties in debate or dialogue but to increase the salience of issues over which the party is perceived to be credible.

Ownership: Stable or Changing?

The theory of issue ownership has been extensively tested and applied to a range of research questions. Across all of these, the operationalisation and interpretation of issue ownership differ according to whether emphasis is placed on ownership as a stable feature of party reputations – and whether this is therefore the explanatory power of the concept – or whether there is greater emphasis on shorter term variation in party reputations. These differences stem from the combination of two concepts in the notion of 'issue ownership', described as the long-term and short-term sources. 'The first is the long term factor, originated from the policy interests of the party electoral bases to which parties respond and which they represent. The second, on the other hand, is a more temporal inter-election specific factor: it refers to the parties' reputation for problem solving and, mainly, to the record of the incumbent party, its performance in government' (Bellucci 2006: 550).

Defined as a long-term stable reputation, Petrocik (1996: 826) explained that ownership is 'the ability to resolve a problem of concern to voters. It is a reputation for policy and program interests, produced by a history of attention, initiative and innovation toward these problems, which leads voters to believe that one of the parties (and its candidates) is more sincere and committed to doing something about them.' As highlighted in Chapter 1, Petrocik (1996) described the changing issue agenda as the point of between-election variation, but issue-handling reputations and the voters' bias towards the party as 'critical constants'. However, Petrocik (1996: 827) noted, 'Party constituency ownership of an issue is much more long-term (although it can change and occasionally exhibits fluctuation).' According to Petrocik, even long-term ownership can change and exhibit fluctuation, even if it is only 'occasionally'.

Petrocik also referred to 'short-term' ownership where the definition of ownership is a positive competence or handling 'lease'. 'The record of the incumbent creates a handling advantage when one party can be blamed for current difficulties ... The challenger acquires an advantage, a performance-based ownership of the issue, from this irrefutable demonstration that the incumbent party cannot handle the job' (Petrocik 1996: 827). Thus, insofar as ownership is a 'critical constant', it is only a constant within an election, rather than a between-election constant which might be inferred by the long-term association of a party with an issue.

The implication of Petrocik's long-term and short-term issue ownership has to be that evaluations can be stable *and* volatile. And even stable evaluations can change sometimes. However, there has been considerable debate about whether and how much issue ownership can fluctuate.

For Petrocik (1996; Petrocik et al. 2003) and Holian (2004), an issue is either owned or not owned, most likely due to relatively clear ownership of issues by the Republican and Democrat parties, on which the studies are based. Hence a short-term performance shock changes a party's rating on an issue; this only affords a rival a temporary 'lease'. The implication is that issue ownership is an equilibrium state and short-term shocks have effects that will return to this ownership equilibrium.

The long-term definition of issue ownership has gained ground in recent research. Smith (2010: 1478) summarised: 'certain parties are seen as a voice for certain interests within society shaping the perception of the electorate as to how parties will handle different problems' (see also Blomquist and Green-Pedersen 2004). Bélanger (2003: 540), following this definition, reported that 'a party's reputation is thus generally established for long periods of time and changes very little because it is usually driven by the interests of the party's relatively stable traditional constituency and grounded in the issues and cleavages that initially underlay their birth'.[1] Seeberg (2016a) analysed ownership evaluations across multiple countries and time periods and found ownership to be much more stable than changeable. Given that a party's interests are relatively stable, and these interests lead to commitment and ownership, Egan (2013) found that issue ownership is consistent with and explained by 'partisan priorities' (Egan 2013). A party's owned issues tend to be those which elites prioritise over time, particularly in law-making. Egan (2013) argued that issue ownership arises primarily through selective commitment, rather than position or performance.

Bélanger and Meguid (2008) illustrated the degree to which scholars have confused Petrocik's notion of ownership to denote only the 'critical constant' and 'objective' notion of ownership: 'A cursory examination of the survey data presented in several analyses of issue ownership, including Petrocik's seminal, 1996 article, reveals that all issue handling reputations are contested, with many being awarded to a party on the basis of less than 50% of survey responses. Thus, with even research on American issue ownership challenging the "objective" reputation concept of ownership first articulated by Budge and Farlie (1983) and Petrocik (1996)' (Bélanger and Meguid 2008: 483).

Some researchers have highlighted the dynamic nature of public opinion about party issue competence. Lanz and Sciarini (2016) analysed 'short-term dynamics in issue ownership', identifying the effects of changes at the individual level in evaluations of a party best on a given issue. Nadeau and Blais (1990: 325) highlighted a 'dual pattern of stability and change' in Canadians' perceptions of party competence at the aggregate level. 'This suggests that a strong element of inertia characterises perceptions in that Canadians only slowly modify their assessment

---

[1] Note that Bélanger (2003) also discusses the varying aspects of opinion about competence, discussed below.

of party competence on an issue. As well, it shows that a party's performance on a given question can sometimes alter seemingly well-established distinctions' (Nadeau and Blais 1990: 325). The observation that performance alters 'well-established distinctions' suggests that ownership does not necessarily return to equilibrium. Aggregate-level changes will indicate a more significant change in party reputations, but some individual-level changes (and measurement error leading to these changes) – will be inevitable.

The remainder of this discussion concerns stability and change in ownership at the level of electorates or populations, not individuals.

Sides (2006) found that the US Democrats were consistently ranked the best party on the issues of social security and Medicare, education, the environment, and healthcare, but there was less consistent evidence of Republican issue ownership in the period (1990 to 1998) and fluctuation in party advantage on the budget deficit, crime, taxation, national defence and foreign affairs. Likewise, Damore (2004), Holian (2004) and Kaufmann (2004) all reported that the ownership of issues varies across the two main American parties over time. Brasher (2009) went as far as to argue that party issue associations are dynamic rather than enduring. Using Gallup opinion poll data spanning a period from 1952 to 2004, Brasher's analysis revealed that neither US party had a consistent or enduring advantage on two of the most important issues in American electoral politics: prosperity, and war and peace. These issues would fall into Budge and Farlie's (1983: 42) classification of 'performance issues', which might be expected to be owned by neither party. But Brasher's observation runs counter to many assumptions about stability in US party advantages, at least on these issues.

Kiewiet (1981) noted that the Democrats are generally associated with being able to handle the issue of unemployment and the Republicans are generally associated with being able to handle the issue of inflation, but beliefs about the abilities of different parties to handle inflation and unemployment fluctuate, and parties' economic ratings change from election to election. Bélanger (2003) highlighted significant variation in issue competence level for each issue by each party in Canada, and also a switching of the overall best party following two periods in Canadian politics (during the fall of two unpopular Conservative governments).

It is only if we assume that ownership is a stable and enduring concept that we see volatility in issue ownership as something surprising. Recall that Petrocik noted a stable element of issue ownership (which could change under certain conditions) and also a short-term potential for change, or a 'lease' in issue ownership. There are three things at work here: (i) the tendency of a party to have a relative advantage on an issue;

(ii) the possibility that performance shocks can disturb these ratings – either temporarily affording a rival a 'lease' or causing a re-equilibrating effect on a change in issue ownership; and (iii) volatility in public opinion about party competence on any issue, including on 'owned' issues. Each of these 'sources' of issue ownership is confused when scholars expect ownership either to be stable or volatile. There are two different concepts – long-term ownership and short-term performance. Performance shocks may cause short-term or more permanent changes in 'ownership'. Volatility in public opinion about competence runs alongside a more stable notion of issue ownership.

Measurement Problems

Following the debate over stability and change, there are different operationalisations of ownership. These mean that researchers refer to different aspects of opinion about competence (and position and association) within the same literature. They find different results but with measures that are not comparable.

Petrocik (1996; and Petrocik et al. 2003) measured ownership by the percentage of respondents rating the Republicans or Democrats best on a given issue, capturing long-term reputations and short-term performance. Bélanger (2003) used an individual-level measure and an aggregate measure, taking first a score for each individual for whether they considered a party the best party on each given issue, and then the aggregate mean competence differential for an issue over time, subtracting the popularity of the party from its aggregate 'best party' competence score. Ownership is then operationalised as the mean competence of a party on an issue across a period of time (from 1953 to 2001 for the longest running issue series and 1988 to 2011 for the shortest time period). This is possibly the most long-term operationalisation of aggregate-level issue ownership. Damore (2004, 2005) used the assignment of owned issues used by Petrocik (1996), employing the assumption that the owned issues of the US parties published by Petrocik (1996) and Petrocik et al. (2003), using data between 1960 and 1992, remain sufficiently stable to employ these assumptions between 1976 and 1996. These assumptions were also used by Dulio and Trumbore (2009) in their analysis of the 2006 midterm elections (years for which data were not analysed by Petrocik (1996) or Petrocik et al. (2003). Benoit and Airne (2005) likewise assumed that education, healthcare, jobs/labour, poverty and the environment were Democratic issues, and the issues of national defence, foreign policy, government spending/deficit, taxes and illegal drugs were Republican issues. Petrocik himself noted that long-term ownership could change. Making a long-term assumption about ownership is therefore rather risky.

Other scholars use a more dynamic measure of issue ownership but they incorporate concepts of stability and change in their measures as well. Sides (2006) subtracted the percentage ranking the Republicans as the best party across available issues (twelve in total) from the Democratic percentage, a measure similar to that used by Seeberg (2016a) but for multiple parties. Egan (2007) calculated the party with a greater percentage of respondents ranking that party best on each issue as the issue owner. Druckman et al. (2010) calculated which US party gained the overall 'best party' percentage advantage on an issue, giving each party an 'ownership score' for the three years they analysed, 2002, 2004 and 2006 – the difference between the best ranked and second ranked party, or the 'partisan advantage'; the percentage rating of the highest rated party minus the percentage rating of the competitor party. Bélanger and Meguid (2008) used an individual-level measure of ownership allowing for no party to own an issue, where respondents were coded as equal to one if they thought a given party was most competent (or 'best'), equal to minus one if the respondent considered another party best and equal to zero if the respondent considered no party best.

Combining the two explanations of ownership means that the measurement of issue competence conflates stability and change. Scholars who use the mean or percentage rating of a party on an issue to denote ownership will be picking up long-term level differences between parties as well as short-term performance fluctuations. The same will be true using the lead of one party on an issue over another party, or the distance between the proportion of citizens rating the party positively above the party's underlying electoral support. These measures pick up the partisan effects of one party's supporters thinking their party is better able to handle the issue, and rival partisans the opposite. A researcher wishing to isolate a party's long-term issue reputations will not be able to use these measures. Simply assuming that public opinion about party competence on issues is stable will also miss important and meaningful variance.

These distinctions lead us to suggest that we should separately conceptualise and measure long-term issue ownership and short-term performance, and distinguish between the two concepts in our understanding of public opinion dynamics and stability. We can allow a performance shock to be a cause of a change in issue ownership (or otherwise) and analyse performance fluctuations distinctly. This means that we should separately consider explanations or sources of issue ownership and sources of public evaluations of short-term performance.

Different Implications of Long-Term and Short-Term Competence

The empirical and theoretical implications of ownership as long-term party constituency ownership are different to the implications of short-term fluctuations in public opinion about policy performance.

Implications of Party Constituency Issue Ownership

A long-term explanation of issue ownership points to a specific set of empirical and theoretical consequences. It is a definition of ownership as association, with a positive competence or handling reputation as a consequence of long-term policy representation, innovation and initiative.

We should expect change in party constituency-based associations to be relatively rare. Parties change their attention to issues over the long term as they alter their representation of electoral constituencies. But such is the significance of the latter that we term them electoral realignments or realigning elections to denote periods in which the social cleavage underlying party support undergoes significant change (see Evans and Norris 1999). These kinds of realignments may result in ownership realignment or 'issue evolution' (Carmines and Stimson 1989). A party rejecting its social base will be judged more harshly on issues its prior supporters were most concerned about, perhaps when another party exists to continue to represent those interests. Think of social democratic parties in Western Europe competing at the political centre rather than looking to their declining left-wing working class bases (Przeworksi and Sprague 1988). Those parties may eventually lose a reputation for trust and handling of issues such as unemployment, social security and public services. Petrocik et al. (2003: 602) explained, 'Issue-handling reputations are not eternal or even invariant. A party can lose an advantage on a constituency-based issue when major shifts occur in the party coalitions.' If a party has a reputation for ownership of an issue that it appears to be moving away from, there may be a considerable lag in the updating of evaluations, especially if no other party is a likely available owner of the issue.

Long-term issue ownership should most closely reflect 'partisan priorities' (Egan 2013) because ownership arises via the representation over time of partisan constituencies. Egan discovered that a party's long-term owned issues corresponded to the issue priorities of electoral elites and party activists. We should therefore expect the effects of long-term ownership to be evident in legislative attention and executive-level policy-making and bureaucracies, because a party gains ownership via a history of 'initiative and innovation' (see Egan 2013; Green and Jennings 2017a). The combination of ownership as 'partisan priority' and 'ownership as long-term attention' points to the prevalence of long-term issue ownership incentives on the pursuit of partisan priorities in legislation. These effects may also influence policy decisions of executives. Palmer and Whitten (2000) found that right-wing governments are more sensitive to inflation performance in terms of precipitating calling an election, while left-wing governments are more sensitive to the level of unemployment. These incentives may arise because governments are sensitive to the electoral benefits arising from long-term issue associations.

The notion of party-constituency ownership has implications for reward and blame. Kiewiet (1981) found that the Democrats did better under periods of high unemployment and among voters affected by it, a finding explained by the Democrats being seen as the better party to handle the issue of unemployment. In a study by Kinder and Kiewiet (1979) on which Kiewiet (1981) based his hypothesis, eighteen out of nineteen election unemployment effects benefited the Democrats. In a related finding, Bélanger and Gélineau (2010) found that issue ownership of the economy acted as a mediating factor on the effects of economic conditions on vote choice. They reported, 'an incumbent party that enjoys a good economic policy reputation should see its vote share less affected by the macroeconomic situation than one that lacks such reputation, or worse, that has a negative reputation' (Bélanger and Gélineau 2010: 86). This finding underlines the strategic importance to a party of issue ownership, or its reputation on an issue for other reasons. Its long-term reputation may help insulate the party in government against failures in performance.

If ownership denotes long-term party-constituency association, its explanation may be more closely tied to ideological position, which is also more glacial (in terms of change) than short-term policy decisions and announcements. It will certainly arise from policy positions (see Stubager and Slothuus 2013) and from the perception of an association of a party with an issue, as argued by Walgrave et al. (2012, 2015) and Tresch et al. (2013). Although Petrocik (1996; Petrocik et al. 2003) referred to ownership as competence, trust and handling, it must clearly be the case that a voter evaluating a party as 'best' on an issue will be drawing on policy preferences and perceptions of party policy positions and constituencies, as well as their evaluation of competence (Therriault 2015). Petrocik et al. (2003: 603) indeed noted that, 'Constituency pressures within and between the parties, constant party rhetoric, and recurring policy initiatives reinforce issue reputations and keep them intact over long periods of time.' Long-term constituency ownership should arise from agreement with a party's policies, and the perception of constituency representation, as well as a perception of competence. A voter is unlikely to think a party is handling – or would handle – an issue well if they disagree with the party's position.

Wagner (2012) argued that parties have incentives to emphasise more extreme positions in order to be clearly identified with an issue; 'a Liberal party – for example in Germany or in the Netherlands – would be relatively extreme on matters of economic liberalism but would also be particularly identified with that topic and seen as competent on it' (Wagner 2012: 68). These definitions might be particularly applied to niche party competition. Niche parties are associated over time with a narrow set of issues. Single-issue or niche parties may be the definition of parties campaigning only on 'owned issues' (Meguid 2005, 2010; Smith 2010) where this ownership is defined via party constituency ownership. Mass parties in government, on the other hand, will also experience more short-term 'leasing' of issues and ownership via legislative attention, innovation and commitment.

Implications of Short-Term Issue Competence

The definition of ownership as performance lease is different to the above definition of party constituency ownership. Each could afford a party a positive handling reputation, but one is the handling reputation itself – won or lost via performance in office – and one is a long-term association which results in a handling reputation. It is unclear whether a party can gain long-term ownership of an issue via short-term performance. These distinctions are significant, and together they inform our conjecture that long-term constituency ownership should be defined as issue ownership, whereas short-term fluctuations should be defined distinctly as perceptions of performance. The implications of these short-term evaluations are as follows.

The first conceptual implication is that short-term 'ownership' can be explained by a period of government, and is therefore a definition applicable to governing parties, with a lease to an opposition. It implies that an opposition party will gain an issue if a governing party loses it, and that the attribution of blame results in credit to a rival. The combination of long-term constituency ownership and shorter term performance issues led Petrocik (1996) to argue that opposition parties had greater incentives to focus on issues on which the incumbent had performed badly, and that this incentive would increase as things became more difficult for the incumbent. This is not easily applied to multi-party systems, or to niche parties (unlike constituency-based ownership). Niche parties may not be afforded a lease, and they cannot lose ownership unless they help form a government (and then only if blame is attributed to them in coalition). In multiparty systems, ownership may overlap where there are more than two major parties and other parties may not own any issues at all (Blomquist and Green-Pedersen 2004). It would seem, therefore, that the two definitions of ownership apply well in two-party systems, but not to party systems where some parties can be judged on delivery and performance, and some other parties cannot.

The second implication is that parties could have many issues on which they have a temporary advantage or disadvantage. A party cannot be expected to have long-term party constituency ownership on a broad array of policy issues, but a successful governing party, or a lucky party in opposition, could have a temporary lease on any number of policy issues, depending on the political context. 'Competence can be based or expressed (and perceived) also on issues outside the traditional policy preferences of parties. Parties can indeed be associated with any problem' (Bellucci 2006: 551). Public opinion moves in predictable ways, and a governing party that has lost public confidence on one issue will likely lose confidence on others too. This is a concept we return to later (and analyse in detail in Chapter 6), but for now we note that the idea of short-term 'ownership' will not be confined to individual issues on which a party's reputation insulates it from short-term performance fluctuations.

Further to this, the third implication is that only significant perfor-mance failures will shake a party's long-term ownership, but short-term performance signals will alter short-term assessments (on the latter point see Stubager and Seeberg 2016). It must also follow that there can be short-term fluctuations in performance issues on those constituency issues a party traditionally owns. Even the most stable definition of ownership must allow for some volatility in party handling assessments. The variation in levels of the 'best party' to handle particular issues occurs, as shown by Bélanger (2003: 550), 'even in the case of well-established ownerships'.

Fourth, if handling reputations are more volatile than implied by party constituency ownership, parties should be able to gain a more positive rating on an issue via their strategic actions. Bellucci (2006), for example, assumes that short-term competence can vary over time, as parties choose to emphasise or de-emphasise certain issues. Researchers have suggested that office-holders can use their positions to 'steal' another party's issue via strategic issue emphasis. Holian (2004) analysed presidential remarks in public and Congressional hearings, and identified how a president is able to use issue framing and rhetoric to neutralise an opponent's ownership of an issue and gain a relative issue advantage. Sulkin (2005) revealed how individual Congressmen/women take up issues in Congress to neutralise an opponent's issue advantage. These alterations in party reputations may not constitute changes in perceived constituency representation or long-term ownership, but instead a shorter term lease or reputational softening, with important strategic causes and consequences.

Finally, a short-term change in issue-handling ratings should be more consistent with short-term policy announcements and high-profile policy failures than the association of party constituency ownership with longer term ideological positions. A party may win short-term advantages on issues by announcing popular policy decisions or hand over a lease to an opposition party if their policies are visibly unpopular or unsuccessful. Voters will consider a party better able to handle an issue if they agree with the handling strategy being adopted. This again emphasises the interrelationships between trust and proximity assessments. Candidates and parties hold relatively stable ideological positions, but they also regularly make policy announcements in government, vote on issues in the legislature and make policy promises in their speeches and campaigns. These vary in the level of public attention they receive, but these short-term policy announcements might be expected to be associated with short-term changes in issue competence, though perhaps not a 'lease' to another party.

Separating Issue Ownership and Performance

The above discussion highlights the benefits of conceptualising ownership and short-term performance separately. It would provide conceptual clarity, measurement clarity and more meaningful and important theoretical implications that can be tested. We therefore argue that 'ownership' should be reserved for the relative (within-party) strengths and weaknesses in public opinion a party holds across issues over time. There is something long term about the notion of issue ownership but it need not be entirely stable, even when separated from the short-term evaluations of parties on performance. The concept of short-term performance should be reserved for exactly that: short-term adjustments in public opinion about party performance.

Major shocks to performance may alter issue ownership. If a performance shock alters ownership it is likely to be enduring and long-lasting (rather than a 'lease'). It should reorganise public perceptions of a party's reputation on a policy issue, and therefore be resistant (if not impervious) to further updating. If citizens are reluctant to update their evaluations of political parties, whether due to partisanship, other pre-existing biases and decisions about which party should be trusted, or due to the costs of acquiring new information, then a performance shock that alters party strengths and weaknesses on issues (ownership) should be big enough to cut through those biases and be clear enough to be visible, received and accepted (Zaller 1992). It will result in a new equilibrium of issue ownership.

If performance has a short-term impact, its impact on public opinion is likely to return to the previous equilibrium. It may be sufficient to alter voters' opinions about a political party and cause them to adjust their evaluations of performance at a particular moment in time, but it may not cut through partisan biases, reach a majority of voters or cause a reorganisation of the issue-party associations held by electorates.

When distinguishing between ownership and performance, we are assuming that ownership is more than the sum of short-term changes in performance, agreeing with the scholars mentioned earlier who point to the associative element of ownership (see Walgrave et al. 2012; Tresch et al. 2013), the constituency-based element of ownership (Petrocik 1996; Egan 2013) and a positional and performance aspect of ownership.

By referring to short-term fluctuations in public opinion about party competence on issues as 'performance' we are agreeing with Petrocik's assumption that these short-term fluctuations are primarily caused by the performance of parties in government. But we test (and find support for) this assumption in Chapter 4. Where we depart from Petrocik is by accepting the idea of an 'ownership lease'. This concept of a lease in ownership is far from clear. We take it to assume that a party could have strength on an issue for one period, but not have that strength in another.

In empirical terms, we think of ownership as the relative strengths and weaknesses a party tends to have on different policy issues: its reputation across multiple issues. If we study relative issue strengths for each party (not between parties) we remain faithful to the idea of association, to commitment to those issues over time, and to reputations, but we allow public opinion to move for one party and not necessarily the other. Ownership change can be asymmetric, and ownership does not have to be a zero-sum game. We think this is far more reflective of the ways in which public opinion can update for one party without updating for another. This also overcomes the problems of partisan conflation of one party's lead over another. These relative ownership strengths tend to be *relatively* stable. They tend to be stable within an election cycle, but they are by no means stable over the longer term. Issue ownership refers to the relative strengths of any party on issues; those issues the party is best on within a given period, compared to those it is considered worst on. A helpful way to think about ownership in measurement terms is the ranking of a party across different policy issues. If health is always a party's top-ranked issue, this reveals that the party is associated with, and owns, the issue.

On the other hand, we think of public opinion about performance as change in the issue-specific ratings of parties over shorter time periods, such as updated evaluations over months or years. This idea extends the concept of reward and punishment voting applied to economic improvements and deteriorations ('is the economy getting better or worse?'; 'Has your household income got higher or lower?') and extends its application to the longer list of policy domains: healthcare, immigration, crime, education, defence, welfare and so on. Issue performance relates to the within-issue change in public opinion on an issue that can mean a party's rating on an owned issue can become more positive, or it can deteriorate, but that issue can remain one of that party's best (or worse) issues overall. Sometimes there may be a shock to performance that is large enough to change the relative evaluations of parties on their owned issues. In this sense, performance and issue ownership can be interlinked. But in conceptual terms and measurement terms, we can distinguish between these concepts.

The differences are summarised as follows:

Ownership   Relative strengths of parties on issues (within-party rank)
Performance Change in public opinion about party competence (within-issue change)

Thinking about issue competence as a combination of issue (re) alignments and short-term fluctuations has important consequences for the sorts of patterns that we might observe over time. If short-term fluctuations are transitory, then these processes should, in time series language, be 'stationary' processes. That is, most shocks to performance evaluations will be quickly forgotten, as they revert to their long-term mean. As Mackuen (1983: 170) observes: 'an evaluation of simple competence ought to be subject to rather quick reevaluation ... simply because those views can only be sustained by further success or failure. If the president does nothing at all, even if he does it well, a single positive reaction can be expected to wither away in the face of the ordinary reequilibration forces. For example, a "competence" evaluation depressed by an ordinary presidential failure ought to return to normal if that failure is not repeated.' This is because public reactions to specific events tend to be visceral (e.g. MacKuen 1983; Ostrom and Simon 1985; Ostrom and Smith 1992), though the impact of some events will still be more persistent than others. As we argue in Chapter 4, a significant symbolic failure could lead to an issue ownership loss or gain, or an issue ownership realignment (a switch from one party to another). Public opinion about party competence may therefore be characterised by 'structural breaks', as parties infrequently lose or gain their stable long-term advantage on a given issue. These different concepts will produce different sorts of temporal dynamics and the time window of observation may influence the sorts of inferences that scholars draw: if one looks over a short time period it might appear that issue ownership is highly stable, but over several decades there might be more frequent losses, gains and realignments in party issue competence.

Valence and Issue Transfer

In the midst of debates over the stability or volatility of issue ownership, and also the definition of what is – and what isn't – a valence issue, a broader perspective on public opinion about party competence on issues has been overlooked.

Throughout the discussions of different literature in this book, another concept has been alluded to: the concept of 'valence', which extends beyond just one policy issue. Some of the factors listed by Petrocik (1996) as leading to a handling lease would not be expected to only influence a rating on a single policy issue. Petrocik (1996: 827) listed wars, failed international or domestic policies, unemployment and inflation, or official corruption. While an opposition party might gain an advantage on the issues of unemployment and inflation, blame for these other major difficulties would not lead to distrust on one issue alone. They will signify a lack of trust and competence in general. Petrocik et al. (2003: 602) further discussed, 'Short-term circumstances can change the advantage on performance issues when, for example, foreign policy failures or economic downturns occur. Candidates or parties can even lose control of their issues in the short term because dissatisfied voters will be inclined to deny the party or candidate with whom they are unhappy any redeeming qualities.' If dissatisfied voters deny a party or candidate *any redeeming qualities*, it is more likely that this results in a drop in competence evaluations of the focal party or candidate in general, rather than on any one performance issue, per se.

The economy provides an example. Some economic shocks may be relatively short-lived, moving issue-handling judgements in the short term. Other shocks may introduce considerable persistence into ratings of issue competence and offer voters information about competence on other issues. The Exchange Rate Mechanism crisis in Britain in September 1992 cost the Conservative Party its reputation for economic competence for more than a decade (Green 2011), and the run on the Northern Rock bank in September 2007 and subsequent financial crisis had a similar impact on the reputation of the Labour Party for economic management. The issue-handling ratings of both parties declined across the issue agenda in the aftermath of these economic crises (Green and Jennings 2012a, 2012b). Such 'extraordinary' events can have fundamental consequences for competence evaluations (Ostrom and Smith 1992).

A serious mishandling of policy, mismanagement of a crisis or disaster, or occurrence of a damaging scandal can lead voters to adjust their opinions about a candidate or party *overall*. Competence can therefore be understood as a generalised reputation – a widespread belief about the fitness of a candidate or party for office and government. Generalised variance in competence evaluations means that losses in confidence or trust can result in losses across a range of issues. Bellucci (2006: 555) outlines a similar notion of party competence, defined as 'people's perception of party handling capacity *across* issues, that is to conceive it as a "general ruling competence", the capacity to pursue policies effectively'. These examples provide reasons to expect that a substantial component of parties' reputations for competence will reflect a general judgement on their performance across policy issues.

Forming reliable judgements about specific issue and policy performance, delivery and likely handling of different parties places high cognitive demands upon voters. As Peffley and Sigelman (1987: 103) said, 'the average citizen is unlikely to have an informed working knowledge of the national political and economic situation'. When asked to evaluate the incumbent on different policy areas it must be questionable whether voters always answer with respect to performance and success on a specific issue, or whether they also rely upon other heuristics and cues. This is particularly applicable for opposition parties or candidates, where handling judgements are based upon hypothetical evaluations of the future or performance in the past (Fiorina 1981). As Popkin (1995: 31) notes, 'An incumbent president deals with "real" events; the challenger can be judged only by those he "manufactures."'

We suggest two routes through which competence judgements are formed which give rise to a shared variance in public opinion on issue competence or generalised competence (Green and Jennings 2012a, 2012b). First, we expect that experience with an issue and performance of the government will guide voters on some issues, but these experiences and judgements can also be transferred to expectations and ratings on others. Transfer of competence judgements may occur when salient events or economic shocks alter public perceptions of party or candidate competence. A major event such as an economic crisis or an unpopular military conflict will introduce performance ratings into the public's mind, providing a heuristic to judge the party on other issues. Second, we expect that these ratings accumulate with time in office, and so the costs of governing will accentuate the effect of heuristics for the incumbent party or candidate. Heuristics represent the short-cuts or cues voters use to overcome cognitive burdens of information. Zaller and Feldman (1992: 609) note, 'the making of these judgements requires an aggregation of one's feelings across frequently diverse concerns'. Heuristics may be particularly useful for evaluating performance. While voters have informed experiences and perceptions of policy outcomes, it must be doubted whether voters possess sufficient information to evaluate government or potential party performance across all areas of policy, or instead whether evaluations also represent 'an aggregation of one's feelings' about a party's ability to govern.

A major performance shock may therefore trigger two major changes in issue competence evaluations. It may alter a party's issue ownership on a particular issue, since this is one of the causes of an expected change in issue ownership. It may also cause deterioration in a party's reputation (its average rating) on all issues. We therefore add a third concept to the concepts of issue ownership and performance: the concept of generalised competence.

Generalised competence   Shared variation in public opinion about party competence (across issues)

Because shocks to at least some issues will persist (while they may decay quickly for other issues), generalised party reputations should be characterised by greater persistence and stability than the short-term fluctuations that are observed in issue-specific performance. Variation in evaluations across issues and individuals means that over-time measures of party competence may carry forward past shocks (see Granger 1980; Granger and Joyeux 1980; Box-Steffensmeier and Smith 1996).

Generalised competence ratings will not be entirely distinct to issue performance ratings and issue ownership. If a governing party exhibits a major failing on a particular issue, we expect that failing to influence perceptions of overall competence. And voters will still hold issue-specific evaluations of a generally competent party – or of an incompetent party. If a party loses ownership of an issue on which it is trusted, it could be more severely rated on other issues as well. And it is unlikely that a party will gain ownership of an issue unless it is credible and perceived to be competent, as we argue in Chapter 4.

Three Concepts and Measurement

Recall above that ownership is defined as the relative strengths of parties on issues (the rank), and performance is defined as the change in public opinion about competence on individual issues (change in level). Generalised competence is defined as the shared variation in public opinion about party competence. We operationalise this generalised competence as a latent factor in public opinion.

It is necessary to conceptualise and provide measures at the individual and aggregate levels because each has relevance and explanatory power.

Issue ownership is generally thought to be a property of parties, and of party systems, and measured and analysed at the aggregate level. When we conceive of ownership as a party characteristic, this is appropriate. But ownership at the aggregate level also implies that the relative ranking of a party on issues has implications for the individual voter. That voter is expected to vote for a party if the owned issue is more salient to their calculation. Hence we use an aggregate (rank) measure of ownership throughout the analyses in this volume, and also, where appropriate, a measure of ownership for the individual; as the evaluation of a party on the issue most important to the respondent. Similarly, we expect performance to be a characteristic of a party but for perceptions of improvement or deterioration on specific issues to also have explanatory power for voters as individuals.

Finally, our concept of generalised competence is a concept that has been primarily conceptualised at the aggregate level; as a 'mood' in public opinion about competence that can add understanding to our broader analysis of the macro-polity (see Green and Jennings 2012a). But this concept is also theorised at the level of the individual who uses heuristics to transfer ratings of a party on one issue to formulate their trust and confidence of the same party on other issues. Hence we measure generalised competence as 'macro-competence' at the aggregate level, and as a latent factor at the individual level.

Table 2.1 summarises the concepts, their operationalisations and the measures we use for them.

Table 2.1 *Concepts, operationalisation and measures*

Concept	Operationalisation	Measures
Ownership	Relative strengths of parties on issues	*Individual level*: Party considered best on issue most salient to voter
	Within party (rank)	*Aggregate level*: Rank ordering of perceived issue strengths and weaknesses of parties
Performance	Change in public opinion about party competence	*Individual level*: Subjective evaluations of changing policy conditions in specific domains
	Within issue (level)	*Aggregate level*: Short-term fluctuations (change) of issue-specific handling evaluations
Generalised competence	Shared variation in public opinion about party competence on issues	*Individual level*: underlying factor in party competence evaluations across issues
	Across issues	*Aggregate level*: generalised competence of parties (shared variance over time)

Conclusion

The concept of 'issue ownership' (Petrocik 1996; Petrocik et al. 2003) should be divided into two empirical concepts: longer term issue reputations and fluctuations in performance. This reflects the original causal explanations of ownership by Petrocik, who differentiated between short-term performance-based 'lease' of issues and long-term constituency-based issue-associations. Others have identified these two sources of ownership, but until now both concepts have been called 'issue ownership'. This means that we miss the empirical distinction between causes and consequences of long-term ownership, and causes and consequences of fluctuations (with performance potentially being one cause of changes in ownership).

Researchers have subsequently debated the degree of fluctuation but also stability in party issue ratings. Debates remain unresolved about how to measure 'issue ownership', resulting from the mixture of long-term and short-term changes in public opinion about competence. The confusion can be resolved if only the concept of long-term reputation represents issue *ownership*, and if performance fluctuations are understood and explained distinctly. This has implications for the measurement of issue performance and issue ownership.

The third concept comes from our work highlighting how public opinion about party competence exhibits common increases and decreases in evaluations of competence across issues (Green and Jennings 2012a, 2012b). Electorates tend to think a party is generally more – or less – competent across all issues, with meaningful variation in this generalised evaluation over time. The important point made in this chapter is that these generalised evaluations are different to long-term, issue-specific reputations (ownership), and to short-term fluctuations in performance evaluations on specific issues. A party can be thought to be generally less competent over time but still have relative strengths on its owned issues, and still display some issue-specific performance information on individual policy issues.

We propose three measures of public opinion about issue competence: (i) issue ownership, where this is defined as relatively stable reputations of parties on issues. The mean ratings of those issues can fluctuate, but the important explanatory component relates to the tendency of some issues to be best, and others to be worse (ranking). This is a within-party not between-party measure, allowing one party's reputation to change while another's remains stable, also minimising problems of partisanship that may drive the gap between parties; (ii) performance-based issue fluctuations, which are best measured by variations in performance ratings of parties over time (change); and (iii) generalised evaluations of party competence across issues, measured by the combination or latent dimension of issue evaluations at the individual or aggregate level (shared variance). The following chapter provides an empirical demonstration of these characteristics of public opinion about competence, their properties and their relationships with partisanship.

3   Three Concepts of Issue Competence

This chapter provides evidence for the three concepts of competence. We highlight the degree of stability of a party's top-rated issues (issue ownership) over time and the frequency of instances of issue ownership loss, gain and realignment – (the latter where ownership moves from one party to another). We identify frequent changes (within the time span of the data) in issue reputations in the United States, the United Kingdom, Australia and Germany, covering eight political parties. The data allow us to examine how much within-issue volatility also exists in issue competence or handling evaluations across time and across countries. We reveal how changes in party ratings on issues display unique variation, and how changes in performance evaluations are as great on a party's owned issues as on non-owned issues; ownership of an issue does not denote greater stability in performance updating. Furthermore, this chapter examines how much shared variance there is in competence evaluations. The analyses show how public opinion about issue competence exhibits common variation over time, such that broad shifts are observed where a party's ratings move on all issues together, resulting in a mood in public opinion about competence, or in 'generalised competence' – an underlying tendency in how voters perceive the issue handling of parties.

For each concept, we consider the interrelationship with partisanship.

We show that the *relative* strengths of parties on issues (issue ratings within parties, not between parties) cut through partisan biases. Partisans, rival partisans and independents tend to attribute parties with the same relative strengths and weaknesses on issues, although the levels are – of course – different. This finding is important for measuring issue ownership and for understanding its importance; ownership is more than a product of partisan bias.

Our analyses suggest that performance assessments are also more than simply a product of partisanship. Examining the degree to which partisans, rivals and independents update their assessments of performance, and the degree to which performance shocks persist in future performance evaluations, we find that it is partisans who respond to information about performance by updating their evaluations of party handling. Our analysis of independent voters, by contrast, shows no evidence of shocks having lasting impacts on public opinion about performance.

Our measures of generalised competence are not explained only by partisanship. Furthermore, in models of 'Granger causation' we find evidence that generalised competence tends to lead partisanship to a greater degree than lags it. This finding reveals that competence has the potential to offer an important predictor of party support and offers evidence consistent with the concept of partisanship as a running tally (Fiorina 1981) (while not ruling out the concept of partisan lens).

Public Opinion Data over Time and across Countries

This chapter draws on public opinion data spanning more than sixty years in the United States, the United Kingdom and Canada, over fifty years in Germany and some twenty-five years in Australia. This comprises a total of 10,920 individual survey items relating to issue competence. These aggregate data are collected from a range of sources.

Our US data were compiled from the database of survey data held by the *Roper Center for Public Opinion Research*. Our UK data are drawn from a combination of Gallup polls, as reported in King and Wybrow's (2001) *British Political Opinion 1937–2000*; the online archives of the polling firms Ipsos MORI, YouGov and Populus; a dataset compiled as part of the *Continuous Monitoring Survey* (CMS) between 2004 and 2013; and surveys of the British Election Study between 1963 and 2010. The Australian survey data are from the online archives of Newspoll. The Canadian data were compiled from Bélanger (2003) and original monthly reports of the *Canadian Gallup Index* held at McGill University. Our data for Germany come from a combination of the GESIS archive holdings of German Election Studies and Forschungsgruppe Wahlen's monthly *Politbarometer* from 1977 to 2013, supplemented with additional data from the online archives of Forschungsgruppe Wahlen.

Survey questions aimed at measuring public evaluations on party handling of issues take a range of forms. Common formulations ask respondents 'which party' would handle issue X 'best', or 'would do a better job' handling issue Y, or which would 'you trust to do a better job on'.

I am going to read out a list of problems facing the country. Could you tell me for each of them which political party you personally think would handle the problem best? Education and schools

With Britain in economic difficulties, which party do you think could handle the problem best – The Conservative Party or the Labour Party?

Do you think the Republican Party or the Democratic Party would do a better job of dealing with each of the following issues and problems?

Which political party, the Democrats or the Republicans, do you trust to do a better job handling ... the economy?

Which one of the (ALP, Liberal and National Party Coalition or someone else) do you think would best handle welfare and social issues?

There are cross-national and within-country variations in question wording but all relate to some aspect of handling, competence, performance, effectiveness, trust or delivery. These tend to tap citizens' evaluations of party competence in similar ways. A typical question format in the United States asks respondents 'Who do you trust to do a better job of handling the economy: the Democrats or the Republicans?' or 'Do you think the Democratic Party or the Republican Party can do a better job in ... reducing the crime rate ... or don't you think there's any difference between them?' The most common question format in the United Kingdom asks respondents 'I am going to read out a list of problems facing the country. Could you tell me for each of them which political party you personally think would handle the problem best?' In Germany, a variant of these asks, 'Welche Partei ist Ihrer Meinung nach am besten geeignet, neue Arbeitsplätze zu schaffen?' [Which party is best, in your opinion, at creating new jobs?].[1] In Canada, the question is posed along the lines of 'Which federal political party do you think can best handle the problem of social security?' In Australia, pollsters ask 'Which one of the (ALP, Liberal and National Party Coalition or someone else) do you think would best handle national security?' The survey items, therefore, typically relate to which party is best able to handle or deliver on a particular issue, relative to other parties.

Due to the extended time span of the data, these consist of a variety of survey modes (face-to-face, telephone, online panels). Most refer to all voting-age adults. While the US data does include some items with registered or likely voter filters, this is not the norm. The sample sizes can also vary, but they are typically in the region of 1,000 or more, with just a few instances where polling firms use split samples to ask about competence across a greater number of issues (such as for the NBC/Wall Street Journal poll series regarding party issue handling).

In an ideal world we would use survey data collected using a consistent weighting and sampling strategy, but in the absence of this luxury the data provide the best available measures of how each party is perceived as capable of handling a particular issue at any given point in time. To the

---

[1] Ratings of the CDU typically include evaluations of its Bavarian sister party, the Christian Social Union (CSU).

extent that weighting and sampling impacts on these measures it serves to introduce error – and thus, if anything, our analyses will understate the importance of issue competence.

One option for analysing these data would be to examine issue evaluations recorded by a single source (e.g. the same polling house over an extended period of time) where ratings of parties across issues should be expected to be most similar (respondents often rate parties across a range of issues in the same survey and so the influence of partisanship and of satisficing in survey answers will be maximised). Another is to evaluate survey data gathered across a range of different sources, examining greater amounts of data on more issues and over a longer time period with fewer gaps. We opt for the latter approach, taking the average ratings of parties on issues over multiple survey items in a given year. We aggregate our data within particular issue topics so that trends can be compared over time and across countries. Survey questions on issue handling are often fielded irregularly and infrequently by polling organisations and national election studies. We develop a classification scheme, adapted from the Comparative Agendas Project, consisting of thirteen issues. These are issues that attract the attention of mass publics, media, parties and governments; the major issues on the public agenda. Most correspond directly to specific domains of public policy, such as the economy, health, defence and education. The classification scheme is outlined in Table 3.1, with corresponding examples for each issue category. Managing public spending, reducing taxes and balancing the budget are classified as economic issues. Dealing with pensions and social security are welfare issues. National security and terrorism are defence issues. The exception is our thirteenth topic, morality, which relates to moral standards and promotion of family issues, another focus of parties and publics (see Engeli et al. 2012).

This approach to classification enables us to consider how evaluations of issue-handling change or remain stable over time. It also allows for comparative insights. It does mean that evaluations of parties on these aggregate issues might fluctuate due to the evolution of the issue topic – for example, as the focus of defence changes from being about the Cold War to preoccupation with terrorism. Likewise, the historical focus of rights and minorities on civil rights and race relations, in the United States, has more recently incorporated rights as they relate to same-sex marriage and gender. To study ownership, performance and generalised competence over time we have to allow that the underlying mix of issues can adapt and change. By aggregating across survey items, we expect substantial changes in issue competence to therefore represent meaningful change; not simply change that cancels out within issue categories.

Table 3.1 *Classification of issue categories*

Category	Examples
1: Economy, Business & Trade	Economy, business, inflation, prices, interest rates, unemployment rate, exchange rates, taxation, foreign investment, balance of payments, financial stability, keeping the country prosperous, business depression, protecting industry against foreign competition, cost of living, balancing the budget, fiscal responsibility.
2: Rights & Minorities	Civil rights, promoting racial equality, race relations, democracy, freedom of speech, privacy, women's rights/issues, native/aboriginal rights.
3: Health	Healthcare, health system (e.g. National Health Service, Medicare).
4: Labour & Employment	Jobs, job situation, strikes, industrial disputes, labour relations, trade unions, employment, industrial relations.
5: Education	Education, schools, improving education, universities, education system.
6: Environment	The environment, climate change, global warming, protecting the environment.
7: Law & Order	Law and order, crime, disorder, death penalty, reducing the crime rate, policing, the crime problem, delinquency.
8: Welfare & Housing	Pensions, social security, welfare, benefits, homelessness, housing, shortage of affordable housing, building more houses, housing market, reducing poverty, helping the poor, prescription drugs for the elderly, reforming welfare, housing construction.
9: Defence	Defence, national security, military conflicts (e.g. Iraq, Afghanistan, Vietnam), nuclear weapons, terrorism, ensuring a strong national defence, war on terrorism.
10: Foreign Affairs	Foreign affairs, foreign policy, relations with other countries, world peace, European Union, keeping out of war.
11: Government	Can better manage the federal government, dealing with the issue of corruption in government, standing up to lobbyists and special interests, reforming government in Washington, governs in a more honest and ethical way, dealing with ethics in government, constitution/devolution.
12: Immigration	Immigration, controlling immigration, illegal immigration, asylum seekers.
13: Morality	Creating a more moral society, encouraging high moral standards and values, upholding traditional family values, commitment to family, promoting strong moral values, improving morality in this country, abortion, family issues.

Public Opinion about Party Competence

We begin our analysis by displaying data on public evaluations of the major parties from our dataset.

In Figure 3.1, we display aggregate-level data on the public's evaluations of the US Democratic Party on the thirteen issues for which we have data over time, and in Figure 3.2 for selected parties in the United States, the United Kingdom, Australia and Germany for a smaller subset of issues. This enables closer visual inspection of trends in evaluations of party handling of individual issues.[2] There are not enough survey data for Canada to enable inspection of party issue competence for individual issues, and for Germany we have only four issues with sufficient data. The figures cover the periods for which the data are richest (and thus most informative) between 1980 and 2013 in the United States, between 1980 and 2015 in the United Kingdom, between 1989 and 2014 in Australia and between 1980 and 2013 in Germany.

The trends in Figure 3.1 exhibit three immediately clear features. The first is that the Democrats have no issues that are clearly and stably

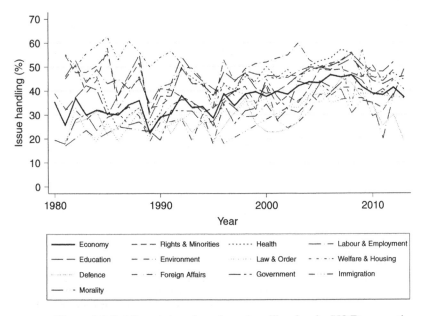

Figure 3.1 Public opinion about issue handling for the US Democratic Party, 1980–2013

---

[2] Data for all issues are presented in the Appendix, Figures A3.1 to A3.8.

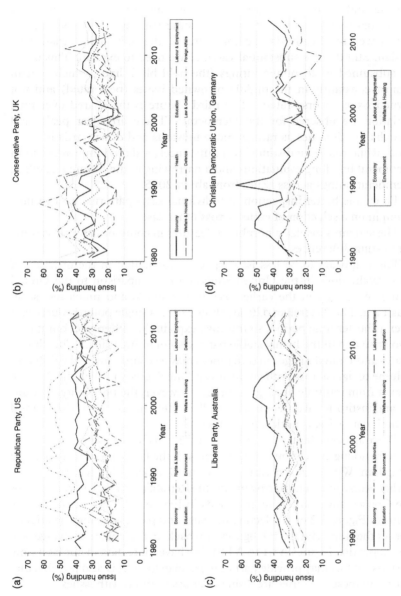

Figure 3.2 Public opinion about issue handling for parties in the United States (a), the United Kingdom (b), Australia (c) and Germany (d)

owned over time. Their best issue in the earlier time period is welfare and housing, but this is later replaced by the environment (in around 2000). The second feature is the amount of noise and variation in ratings on individual issues. Note that by aggregating sub-topics into issue categories we are already dampening some of the noise and variance by design. Still there is substantial variance we need to explain. This is not all subsumed in economic ratings (the bold black line), which remain almost constantly in the middle of owned issues (best rated) and not owned issues (worse rated). The third feature is the shared over time variation we observe for the Democrats. There are clear peaks and troughs for all issues as ratings move upwards and downwards in common, while retaining distinct level differences, a shared improvement in Democrat handling evaluations and a narrowing in the distance between Democrat ratings across issues from about 2005.

To enable better inspection of individual issue patterns, we can now zoom in on a selection of issues across other cases.

These figures display a number of features in common, as well as some interesting differences.

There appears to be less issue-specific fluctuation in the ordering of issue evaluations in the United Kingdom in comparison to the United States, especially in the earlier part of the series, and much less so in Australia. The Australian data are drawn from a single polling source and over a shorter time period, so this may explain this difference, but it may also arise due to the highly stable party system in Australia.[3] The United States and United Kingdom differences may also arise due to the different volume of data across both countries and the degree to which the data are drawn from multiple or single sources. However, the possibility of country and institutional differences, as well as differences over the time period in both countries, is noticeable in Figure 3.2.

There are some hints in Figures 3.1 and 3.2 of increasing homogeneity of issue-handling evaluations over time in both the United States and United Kingdom. We see greater variation for the Democrats in Figure 3.1 in the earlier years, and some narrowing for the Republicans and less variance for the Conservatives in the latter periods in Figure 3.2. Given that we only focus in Figure 3.2 on a selection of issues and parties, we may be missing part of the story. But the full figures also back up this apparent change (see the Appendix, Figures A3.1 to A3.8). We have more data in our later time periods, so this may provide part of the explanation. It is also possible that parties in these countries are losing clear associations with issues.

---

[3] The Australian data are from 1989 to 2014 and all data are drawn from the regular Newspoll series.

There is a more complex picture in the data revealed in Figures 3.1 and 3.2 than explained by the traditional notion of issue ownership as a stable feature of party reputations. Each party has a set of issues that tend to be better rated for a period, and some issues that tend to be worse. However, there is also over-time variability on the top issues and bottom issues. In addition to the Democrats' gain of the environment (and apparent loss of welfare and housing), the Republican ownership of defence in Figure 3.2 appears to substantially weaken by 2010. The same loss can be seen for the UK Conservative Party, but on the issue of foreign affairs. Even the issue of healthcare for the Conservatives becomes less of a clear liability for the party at this point than the issue was between 1980 and 2000. Whereas we see stability of ownership in Australia in Figure 3.2, even only using four issues in Germany we find evidence of ownership change. The German right-of-centre Christian Democratic Union (CDU) seems to gain the issue topic of labour and employment relative to their earlier ratings on this issue. Note that by presenting all issues by party, not between party, we capture variance that is overlooked by examining the lead of one party over another.

In addition to a notion of issue ownership, Figures 3.1 and 3.2 reveal a considerable amount of over-time variation in the average levels at which the public rates each party on issues. Much of this will be random noise, but much will not. The data also reveal that these changes sometimes alter the overall ranking of a party across issues. This point is clearly demonstrated in the Republican ratings on defence in Figure 3.2. Here we see the Republicans retain a relative lead (over other issues) on this issue through-out the period until around 2005 but the party secures significant gains in its ratings in different time points, and incurs significant losses too. This issue-specific variation should be highly important as a party considers how it is evaluated entering an election, or as voters who consider that issue important decide whether to stick with the party or defect.

In addition to relatively stable differences in level, and in addition to issue-specific differences in change, the data in Figures 3.1 and 3.2 reveal that there is a degree to which the public updates its ratings of parties on issues in common. As discussed, the US Democratic Party is evaluated more positively for a time between 2000 and 2010; the party is evaluated more positively on all issues: on higher ranked and lower ranked issues alike. This common shift is not a simple partisan story, as is clear in Figure 3.2. If we ignore the Republicans' best issue (defence) for much of the series, and its worst issue (environment), there is some indication that the Republicans' ratings on many other issues have moved in a more positive direction over the entire period, whereby the ratings on issues such as 'labour and employment', education, 'welfare and housing', morality and 'rights and minorities' all climb in common. The common variation is apparent for the UK Conservative Party too. There is a clear structural break in the data which coincides with 1993; this was the year following the events of the infamous 'Black Wednesday', in which the Conservatives lost their reputation for economic competence over the ERM crisis. That period also coincided with party disunity, which further affected the party's reputation for governing, under then Prime Minister John Major. Figure 3.2 makes clear that this reputational damage translated to ratings across policy issues. The party begins to improve its ratings on all issues in common between 2000 and 2010, but the data also reveal some shared peaks in competence: in 1997 and in 2000. The Australian Liberal Party experienced a downward shift in common across issues in 2008 to 2009, a time at which the party was divided over policy (specifically over its response to the Rudd government's proposed emissions trading scheme) and changed leader twice in a period of just over a year.

Each of these graphs reveals the three concepts we argued for in Chapters 1 and 2. They show how each party has issues on which it tends to be better rated over time and how these within-party better or worse issues can change. Taking the mean of any of these issues, or the lead of one party over another, as measures of 'ownership' would confuse two further characteristics: (i) the degree to which every issue exhibits specific variation in some time points or in all and (ii) the degree to which there is a shift in the average ratings across issues for a party, which runs alongside ownership of issues and specific issue volatility. It would also force issue ratings and changes to be, in essence, symmetric, when our data reveal that this assumption is not accurate.

The remainder of this chapter focuses in greater detail on the properties of each of three concepts in turn.

The Characteristics of Issue Ownership

Substantively, issue ownership theory accounts for (a) those issues on which a party should prefer to focus election campaigns and election choices upon, and (b) the relationship between voting behaviour and the salience of issues on which a party is considered the 'issue owner'. This can explain the focus on the mean level of, or the lead in, positive competence ratings as the empirical focus of attention, since votes will be associated with positive/higher ratings – whether those arise from long-term reputation and representation or whether they arise from short-term fluctuations. However, this operationalisation cannot help us with different theoretical and empirical questions. We seek to explain how issue ownership arises, and how reputations on issues are lost. For this, it is much more meaningful to examine ownership as the long-term reputation of a party for strength and competence on an issue relative to other issues, rather than relative to another party's rating on an issue.

We propose that ownership is operationalised and measured according to the rank ordering of a party's issues. This allows us to determine which issues a party should view as its assets, since assets will always be relative to overall performance. It allows one party's reputation to be damaged on an issue without another party's reputation being automatically enhanced. It provides insight into important variation in the loss, gain and stability of a party's 'best', 'worst' or neutral issues. And, as we show below, it provides a measure that is less susceptible to the problem of endogeneity in ratings of preferred and rival parties on issues.

Taking our dataset of aggregate survey items on issue competence, we create a variable where an issue is the top ranked issue for a party (i.e. it receives a higher score, on average, than every other issue), second ranked issue, third ranked issue, fourth ranked issue and so on, through to the bottom ranked issue (from the n of issues for which survey items are available). We calculate the average score and a ranking by election cycle to ensure that our rankings are not based on too large a number of missing cells (a possibility evident from the incomplete coverage of issues for earlier time periods, before the 1970s, in the United States and the United Kingdom), and also to reflect a long-term notion of ownership which should not change due to measurement error and noise. Such a measure of issue ownership could be calculated for any defined unit of time (such as by year).[4]

Tables 3.2 to 3.9 present the within-party ranking of each party's issue competence over the longest time period for which data are available for the United States, the United Kingdom, Australia and Germany. Additionally, we highlight issues that are in the top-, middle- and bottom-third of a party's issues depending on how many issues our survey data cover overall (with middle-ranked issues marked in grey text). This summarises each party's best and worst issues. Having identified each party's relative issue strengths and weaknesses, we then classify cases of gains, losses or realignments (switching) of ownership, and indicate those in Tables 3.2 to 3.9. Our criteria are as follows.

Table 3.2 presents our cases of ownership and ownership change for the US Republican Party. Table 3.3 follows for the US Democratic Party, Table 3.4 for the UK Conservative Party, Table 3.5 for the UK Labour Party, Table 3.6 for the Australian Liberal Party, Table 3.6 for the Australian Labor Party, Table 3.8 for the German Christian Democrats and Table 3.9 for the German Social Democrats.

---

[4] It could also be calculated at the individual level, with sufficient coverage of ratings across issues.

Table 3.2 *Issue ownership and ownership change, US Republican Party*

Election cycle	1st Issue	2nd Issue	3rd Issue	4th Issue	5th Issue	6th Issue	7th Issue	8th Issue	9th Issue	10th Issue	11th Issue	12th Issue	13th Issue
1940–1944	Economy	Labour & Employment	Government	Foreign Affairs	Defence								
1944–1948	Labour & Employment	Economy	Welfare & Housing	Government	Foreign Affairs	Health	Education	Defence					
1948–1952	**Government* (+3)**	**Defence* (+6)**	Economy	Labour & Employment* (−3)	Foreign Affairs	Rights & Minorities							
1952–1956	**Foreign Affairs* (+4)**	Economy	Rights & Minorities										
1956–1960	Foreign Affairs	Economy	Rights & Minorities	Foreign Affairs	Economy								
1960–1964	Foreign Affairs	Economy	Rights & Minorities	Government									
1964–1968	Law & Order	Economy	Foreign Affairs	Defence	**Rights & Minorities* (−2)**	Labour & Employment							
1968–1972	Foreign Affairs	Economy	Defence	**Law & Order* (−3)**									
1972–1976	Foreign Affairs	Economy	Health	Government	Morality								
1976–1980	**Government* (+3)**	Economy	Defence	Foreign Affairs	Health	Labour & Employment	Law & Order	Education	Environment				
1980–1984	Economy	Defence	Foreign Affairs	Morality	Government	Law & Order	Labour & Employment	Welfare & Housing	Education	Rights & Minorities	Health	Environment	
1984–1988	Defence	Economy	Foreign Affairs	Government	Law & Order	Labour & Employment	Morality	Health	Environment	Welfare & Housing	Education	Rights & Minorities	Environment
1988–1992	Defence	Foreign Affairs	Government	Economy	Morality	Law & Order	Labour & Employment	Education	Rights & Minorities	Health	Welfare & Housing	Environment	
1992–1996	Defence	Foreign Affairs	Economy	Morality	Immigration	Labour & Employment	Welfare & Housing	**Government* (−5)**	Law & Order	Education	Health	Rights & Minorities	Environment
1996–2000	Defence	Morality	Economy	Foreign Affairs	Law & Order	Government	Education	Welfare & Housing	Rights & Minorities	Labour & Employment	Health	Environment	
2000–2004	Defence	Foreign Affairs	Morality	Immigration	**Economy* (−2)**	Law & Order	Government	Labour & Employment	Education	Welfare & Housing	Health	Rights & Minorities	Environment
2004–2008	Defence	**Labour & Employment* (+6)**	Foreign Affairs	Morality	Law & Order	Economy	Education	Immigration	Welfare & Housing	Government	Health	Rights & Minorities	Environment
2008–2012	**Economy* (+5)**	Labour & Employment	Law & Order	Foreign Affairs	Morality	Health	Immigration	**Defence* (−7)**	Education	Welfare & Housing	Government	Rights & Minorities	Environment
2012–2013	Economy	Labour & Employment	**Health* (+3)**	Defence	Welfare & Housing	Immigration	Education	Law & Order	**Foreign**	Government	Morality		

Election cycle	1st Issue	2nd Issue	3rd Issue	4th Issue	5th Issue	6th Issue	7th Issue	8th Issue	9th Issue	10th Issue	11th Issue	12th Issue	13th Issue
1940–1944	Defence	Labour & Employment	Foreign Affairs	Government	Economy								
1944–1948	Defence	Health	Education	Foreign Affairs	Economy								
1948–1952	Rights & Minorities	Economy* (+3)	Labour & Employment	Foreign Affairs	Defence* (−4)	Government	Labour & Employment	Welfare & Housing					
1952–1956	Economy	Rights & Minorities	ForeignAffairs	Foreign Affairs	Rights & Minorities	Government							
1956–1960	Economy	Health	Labour & Employment	Foreign Affairs	Rights & Minorities								
1960–1964	Economy	Rights & Minorities* (+3)	Foreign Affairs	Government									
1964–1968	Law & Order	Labour & Employment	Economy* (−2)	Defence	Rights & Minorities	Foreign Affairs							
1968–1972	Economy	Foreign Affairs	Defence	Law & Order* (−3)									
1972–1976	Health	Economy	Government	Foreign Affairs	Morality								
1976–1980	Rights & Minorities* (+4)	Labour & Employment	Welfare & Housing	Foreign Affairs	Economy	Environment	Defence	Health* (−7)	Education	Government	Law & Order		
1980–1984	Welfare & Housing	Rights & Minorities	Labour & Employment	Health	Environment	Education	Economy	Foreign Affairs	Defence	Government	Law & Order	Morality	
1984–1988	Welfare & Housing	Rights & Minorities	Environment	Labour & Employment	Education	Economy	Foreign Affairs	Health	Defence	Government	Law & Order	Morality	
1988–1992	Welfare & Housing	Labour & Employment	Health* (+5)	Education	Rights & Minorities* (−3)[5]	Environment	Morality	Economy	Government	Foreign Affairs	Law & Order	Defence	
1992–1996	Environment* (+4)	Labour & Employment	Education	Health	Welfare & Housing* (−4)	Rights & Minorities	Economy	Morality	Law & Order	Government	Foreign Affairs	Defence	Immigration
1996–2000	Environment	Health	Welfare & Housing	Labour & Employment	Education	Rights & Minorities	Economy	Foreign Affairs	Law & Order	Government	Morality	Defence	
2000–2004	Environment	Labour & Employment	Health	Welfare & Housing	Education	Economy	Rights & Minorities	Immigration	Government	Morality	Law & Order	Defence	
2004–2008	Health	Environment	Education	Labour & Employment	Welfare & Housing	Rights & Minorities	Economy	Morality	Government	Defence	Foreign Affairs	Immigration	Law & Order
2008–2012	Education	Rights & Minorities	Health	Environment	Labour & Employment	Welfare & Housing	Government	Economy	Law & Order	Immigration	Morality	Defence	Foreign Affairs
2012–2013	Education	Morality	Health	Government	Labour & Employment	Welfare & Housing	Economy	Immigration	Law & Order	Defence	Foreign Affairs	Foreign Affairs	

[5] While 'rights and minorities' drops three places, we do not classify this as an ownership loss. The fall is due to the emergence of women's rights as an issue in the underlying data. Because neither party has a strong standing on this nascent issue, the decrease in the overall Democrat ratings is not due to deterioration on civil rights.

Table 3.4 *Issue ownership and ownership change, UK Conservative Party*

Election cycle	1st Issue	2nd Issue	3rd Issue	4th Issue	5th Issue	6th Issue	7th Issue	8th Issue	9th Issue	10th Issue	11th Issue	12th Issue	13th Issue
1939–1945	Welfare & Housing												
1951–1955	Foreign Affairs	Welfare & Housing											
1955–1959	Foreign Affairs	Rights & Minorities	Economy										
1959–1964	Defence	Economy	Foreign Affairs										
1964–1966	**Foreign Affairs*** (+2)	Economy	Rights & Minorities	Education	Defence	Immigration	Labour & Employment	Welfare & Housing	Health	Law & Order			
1966–1970	Economy	Immigration	Foreign Affairs	Welfare & Housing	Labour & Employment								
1970–1974	Defence	Education	Foreign Affairs	Labour & Employment	Immigration	**Economy*** (−5)	Health						
1974–1979	**Law & Order*** (+9)	**Immigration*** (+2)	Welfare & Housing	Education	Foreign Affairs	Defence	Economy	Rights & Minorities	Health	Labour & Employment			
1979–1983	Defence	Law & Order	Immigration	Foreign Affairs	Education	**Welfare & Housing*** (−3)	Labour & Employment	Economy	Rights & Minorities	Health			
1983–1987	Defence	Law & Order	**Labour & Employment*** (+4)	Foreign Affairs	Economy	Welfare & Housing	Education	Environment	Health				
1987–1992	Defence	Labour & Employment	Foreign Affairs	Law & Order	Economy	Education	Rights & Minorities	Welfare & Housing	Health	Environment			
1992–1997	Defence	Labour & Employment	Foreign Affairs	Law & Order	Economy	Education	Morality	Government	Rights & Minorities	Welfare & Housing	Environment		
1997–2001	Immigration	Defence	Law & Order	Economy	**Foreign Affairs*** (−2)	**Labour & Employment*** (−4)	Morality	Education	Welfare & Housing	Government	Health	Environment	
2001–2005	Immigration	Law & Order	Economy	Foreign Affairs	**Defence*** (−3)	Health	Education	Welfare & Housing	Government	Labour & Employment	Environment		
2005–2010	Law & Order	Immigration	Economy	Education	Health	Defence	Welfare & Housing	Foreign Affairs	Environment	Government			
2010–2015	Law & Order	Immigration	Economy	Education	Welfare & Housing	Health	Foreign Affairs	Environment					

Table 3.5 *Issue ownership and ownership change, UK Labour Party*

Election Cycle	1st Issue	2nd Issue	3rd Issue	4th Issue	5th Issue	6th Issue	7th Issue	8th Issue	9th Issue	10th Issue	11th Issue	12th Issue	13th Issue
1939-1945	Welfare & Housing												
1951-1955	Economy	Welfare & Housing	Foreign Affairs										
1955-1959	Health	Labour & Employment	Welfare & Housing	Economy	Defence	Foreign Affairs	Rights & Minorities	Law & Order					
1959-1964	Welfare & Housing	Labour & Employment	Economy	Defence	Foreign Affairs								
1964-1966	Health	Labour & Employment	Welfare & Housing	Education	Economy	Foreign Affairs	Immigration	Rights & Minorities	Defence	Law & Order			
1966-1970	Welfare & Housing	Foreign Affairs	Labour & Employment	Economy	Immigration								
1970-1974	Health	Labour & Employment	Education	Economy	Foreign Affairs	Defence	Immigration						
1974-1979	Labour & Employment	Health	Welfare & Housing	Economy	Education	Rights & Minorities	Foreign Affairs	Defence	Law & Order	Immigration			
1979-1983	Health	Welfare & Housing	Labour & Employment	Economy	Rights & Minorities	Education	Foreign Affairs	Defence	Law & Order	Immigration			
1983-1987	Health	**Education* (+4)**	Welfare & Housing	Economy	**Labour & Employment* (-2)**	Foreign Affairs	Defence	Environment	Law & Order				
1987-1992	Health	Welfare & Housing	Education	Rights & Minorities	Economy	Labour & Employment	Foreign Affairs	Law & Order	Environment	Defence			
1992-1997	Health	Welfare & Housing	Education	Rights & Minorities	Economy	Labour & Employment	Morality	Government	Law & Order				
1997-2001	Education	**Economy* (+3)**	**Morality* (+4)**	Health	Labour & Employment	Welfare & Housing	Law & Order	Foreign Affairs	Government	Immigration	Defence	Environment	
2001-2005	Health	Economy	Welfare & Housing	Education	Labour &Employment	Defence	Law & Order	Foreign Affairs	Immigration	Government	Environment		
2005-2010	Health	Economy	Education	Welfare & Housing	Law & Order	Foreign Affairs	Environment	Government	Defence	Immigration			
2010-2015	Health	Education	Welfare &Housing	**Economy* (-3)**	Law & Order	Foreign Affairs	Immigration	Environment					

Table 3.6 *Issue ownership and ownership change, Australian Liberal Party*

Election cycle	1st Issue	2nd Issue	3rd Issue	4th Issue	5th Issue	6th Issue	7th Issue	8th Issue	9th Issue
1987–1990	Economy	Immigration	Welfare & Housing	Labour & Employment	Environment				
1990–1993	Immigration	Economy	Health	Labour & Employment	Welfare & Housing	Rights & Minorities	Environment		
1993–1996	Economy	Immigration	Health	Labour & Employment	Welfare & Housing	Environment	Rights & Minorities		
1996–1998	Economy	Immigration	Labour & Employment	Health	Welfare & Housing	Environment	Rights & Minorities		
1998–2001	Defence	Economy	Immigration	Health	Education	**Labour & Employment**	Welfare & Housing	Environment	Rights & Minorities
2001–2004	Defence	Economy	Immigration	Labour & Employment	Education	Health	Welfare & Housing	Rights & Minorities	Environment
2004–2007	Defence	Economy	Immigration	Health	Education	Welfare & Housing	Labour & Employment	Rights & Minorities	Environment
2007–2010	Economy	Defence	Immigration	Health	Labour & Employment	Education	Rights & Minorities	Welfare & Housing	Environment
2010–2013	Defence	Economy	Immigration	Labour & Employment	Health	Education	Environment		

Table 3.7 *Issue ownership and ownership change, Australian Labor Party*

Election Cycle	1st Issue	2nd Issue	3rd Issue	4th Issue	5th Issue	6th Issue	7th Issue	8th Issue	9th Issue
1987–1990	Labour & Employment	Welfare & Housing	Economy	Environment	Immigration				
1990–1993	Labour & Employment	Health	Welfare & Housing	Rights & Minorities	Environment	Economy	Immigration		
1993–1996	Labour & Employment	Health	Welfare & Housing	Rights & Minorities	Economy	Immigration	Environment		
1996–1998	Labour & Employment	Health	Welfare & Housing	Rights & Minorities	Immigration	Economy	Environment		
1998–2001	Labour & Employment	Welfare & Housing	Health	Education	Rights & Minorities	Environment	Economy	Immigration	Defence
2001–2004	Health	Labour & Employment	Welfare & Housing	Education	Rights & Minorities	Economy	Immigration	Environment	Defence
2004–2007	Labour & Employment	Welfare & Housing	Education	Health* (−3)	Rights & Minorities	Immigration	Environment	Economy	Defence
2007–2010	Welfare & Housing	Education	Labour & Employment	Health	Rights & Minorities	Economy	Environment	Defence	Immigration
2010–2013	Labour & Employment	Education	Health	Economy	Environment	Defence	Immigration		

Table 3.8 *Issue ownership and ownership change, German Christian Democratic Union*

Election cycle	1st Issue	2nd Issue	3rd Issue	4th Issue	5th Issue	6th Issue	7th Issue	8th Issue	9th Issue
1957–1961	Education	Foreign Affairs	Defence	Welfare & Housing	Economy	Labour & Employment			
1961–1965	Foreign Affairs	Economy	Welfare & Housing	Education	Economy	Health	Environment	Rights & Minorities	
1969–1972	Defence	Foreign Affairs	Education	Law & Order					
1972–1976	**Law & Order* (+3)**	Economy	Labour & Employment	**Foreign Affairs* (−2)**					
1976–1980	Law & Order	Welfare & Housing	Labour & Employment	Economy	Foreign Affairs	Environment			
1980–1983	Law & Order	Economy* (+2)	Welfare & Housing	Labour & Employment	Foreign Affairs	Environment			
1983–1987	Economy	Law & Order	Welfare & Housing	Foreign Affairs	Labour & Employment	Defence	Environment		
1987–1990	Economy	Welfare & Housing	Labour & Employment	Environment					
1990–1994	**Foreign Affairs* (+3)**	Economy	Immigration	Defence	Law & Order	Labour & Employment	Welfare & Housing	Environment	
1994–1998	**Defence* (+3)**	Immigration	Law & Order	Economy	Welfare & Housing	Labour & Employment	Environment		
1998–2002	**Labour & Employment* (+5)**	Economy	Welfare & Housing	Environment					
2002–2005	Labour & Employment	Economy	Welfare & Housing	Environment					
2005–2009	Economy	Labour & Employment	Welfare & Housing						
2009–2013	Economy	Labour & Employment	Welfare & Housing						

Table 3.9 *Issue ownership and ownership change, German Social Democratic Party*

Election cycle	1st Issue	2nd Issue	3rd Issue	4th Issue	5th Issue	6th Issue	7th Issue	8th Issue	9th Issue
1957–1961	Labour & Employment	Economy	Welfare & Housing	Foreign Affairs	Defence	Education			
1961–1965	Education	Welfare & Housing							
1969–1972	Rights & Minorities	Economy	Foreign Affairs	Education	Defence	Health	Environment	Law & Order	
1972–1976	Foreign Affairs	Labour & Employment	Economy	Law & Order					
1976–1980	Foreign Affairs	Economy	Welfare & Housing	Labour & Employment	Environment	Law & Order			
1980–1983	Foreign Affairs	Welfare & Housing	Environment	Economy* (−2)	Labour & Employment	Law & Order			
1983–1987	Foreign Affairs	Defence	Environment	Welfare & Housing	Labour & Employment	Economy	Law & Order		
1987–1990	Environment* (+2)	Labour & Employment	Welfare & Housing	Economy					
1990–1994	Welfare & Housing* (+2)	Environment	Labour & Employment	Economy	Immigration	Law & Order	Foreign Affairs* (−6)	Defence	
1994–1998	Environment	Welfare & Housing	Immigration	Labour & Employment	Law & Order				
1998–2002	Economy	Welfare & Housing	Labour & Employment	Environment* (−3)		Economy	Defence		
2002–2005	Welfare & Housing	Economy	Labour & Employment	Environment					
2005–2009	Welfare & Housing	Labour & Employment	Economy						
2009–2013	Welfare & Housing	Labour & Employment	Economy						

(1) Gains are where an issue moves *at least two places* from the middle-third of a party's issues into the top-third and it remains there for at least two election cycles (where data are available). This criterion requires that there has to be more than a minor change in ranking and that this change has to persist for a meaningful period of time. This means we do not count cases where a party briefly improves its rankings – perhaps due to a short-term change in evaluations or due to noise in the underlying survey data.

(2) Losses are where an issue moves at least two places from the top-third of a party's issues into the middle- or bottom-third, remaining there for at least two election cycles. Again this requires the change in ranking to be consequential in its order and persistence.

(3) Lastly, issue ownership realignments are where an issue moves from the top-third of a party's issues into the bottom-third, or moves from the bottom-third of a party's issues into the top-third, remaining there for at least two election cycles, and at the same time the issue moves to the top-third or the bottom-third of its opponent's issues.

Issue ownership gains and losses are indicated by the issues in bold font, with a number reported denoting the number of rankings the issue has moved either positively (e.g. +3) or negatively (e.g. −3).[6]

The first thing to note from Tables 3.2 to 3.9 is that there is a considerable amount of variance in issue ownership, even applying our criteria that a change should be a change of at least two rankings and move from a top issue to a middle or bottom issue (or the reverse for a gain), and remain so for two election cycles. Note also that these changes are exhibited in data that have been aggregated across sub-topics and which take an average rating at each period. We are making it difficult to detect a change, and yet we still find considerable variation in party reputations on issues. This is true for the findings in the United States, the United Kingdom and Germany, though not for Australia. This variance is not just seen in issue ownership losses and gains but also in the *extent* of reputational change. In many instances, an issue moves from being one of a party's best issues to its worst. An example of this is the issue category of 'government' (this includes survey items that refer to running the government efficiently, reforming government and delivering on public services) for the Republicans. It moves from being the party's top-ranked issue in 1976–1980 to its eleventh-ranked issue in 2008–2012. Another example

---

[6] We do not assign issues as being lost, gained or realigned in earlier election cycles in the United States, the United Kingdom and Germany due to the relative scarcity of data for these periods.

is the issue of foreign affairs for the Democratic Party, which was the party's fourth-ranked issue in 1976–1980 but its thirteenth best issue in 2008–2012. The Conservative Party's rating on 'labour and employment' moves from second place (between 1987 and 1997) to tenth place in 2001–2005.

The second thing to note is that few of the changes in ownership are instances where one party's loss of an issue results in another party's gain. The Republicans lose the issue of 'government', for example, by 1992. This issue only enters the top four issues for the Democrats during the 2012 to 2016 election cycle (and note this data point is sparse and incomplete due to the time of writing). Likewise, the issue category of 'morality' is lost by the Republicans by 2008–2012, and only becomes a Democratic strength (ranked second) when it is a bottom-ranked issue for the Republicans by 2012–2013. In the United Kingdom, labour and employment was the Labour Party's top-ranked issue in 1974–1979, and its third best in 1979–1983, but by 1983–1987 had become the Conservative Party's third-ranked issue and then its second best in 1987–1992 and 1992–1997. By 1997–2001, however, the Conservatives had lost ownership of the issue and by 2001–2005 it was as low as tenth. Apart from these examples, there are no instances where one party loses an issue and another party gains it: there are no sudden and permanent realignments. It might be the case that there is a considerable lag between the loss of an issue and the gain of an issue by another party (i.e. one spanning beyond our final data points), but the absence of a clear realignment in issue ownership is indicative of the nature and basis of ownership. It is not possible for a party to own an issue just because another party does not. We suggest that ownership is earned rather than conferred by the relatively poor rating of another party. This is an important reason to use a within-party measure of ownership. It makes possible the observation that reputations on issues are not symmetric and enables better understanding, therefore, of the causes of these relative shifts.

There is an interesting additional observation we can draw from Tables 3.2 and 3.3, where we see that two parties can be ranked relatively highly on the same issues, but one party can lose ownership. It is difficult to draw too much from the earliest period when the number of issues is smallest, but it appears that both the Republicans and Democrats were ranked best on the issues of the economy, defence and foreign affairs. These issues are later lost by the Democrats, after the mid-1970s, and retained as the Republican's best issues, with the exception of a dramatic loss in foreign affairs rating for the Republicans during the 2012 to

2013 period. This highlights that voters do not necessarily always associate any party with an issue, i.e. there may be certain issues where many voters are unsure who is best, and thus both parties in a system receive low ratings.

The next observation from Tables 3.2 to 3.9 is that when an owned issue is 'lost' it appears to be lost irrevocably. Of course, the data do not last indefinitely, and issues could become owned by a party in the future. But Tables 3.2 to 3.9 only reveal a few instances where an issue moves out and then in from the list of top-ranked issues. One such instance is the category of 'rights and minorities' for the Democrats, which covers civil rights and race relations. This appears to be an issue that tends to be owned by the Democrats, but it is lost for two periods (becoming a middle-ranked issue); in the 1950s to 1960s (during the 1956–1960 and 1964–1968 election cycles) and then again from 1988 onwards (only then becoming a second-ranked issue during the 2008–2012 cycle). This might be an issue set that the Democrats have a *propensity* to be rated best on, but this does not insulate them from a loss of reputation. Indeed, inspection of the underlying poll data (for the earlier period not reported in Figure 3.2) indicates that while the Democrats still held a considerable lead on the issue of rights and minorities over the Republicans during the 1950s and 1960s, the party's ratings declined relative to other issues. The issue of immigration offers a similar pattern for the Conservative Party in the United Kingdom. This issue is an owned issue which switches quite significantly from being second-ranked (1966–1970) to fifth (1970–1974), to second again (1974–1979). Again, this reveals how an issue for which a party has a very strong reputation can still cease to be an owned issue in certain cases, even if it later returns to being an issue asset. Another example comes in the form of foreign affairs for the German Christian Democrats. This high-ranking issue for the party (placed second or third between 1957 and 1972) is lost to a middle-ranked issue between 1972 and 1987, but becomes the top-ranked issue for the CDU during the 1990–1994 election cycle after reunification.[7]

The final point to note from Tables 3.2 to 3.9 is that the contestable notion of ownership is again apparent. While we reveal within-party rankings of issue competence ratings and classify a drop in rankings as a loss of 'ownership', a range of other nuances are evident. For example, we might think of ownership as a *tendency* for a party to be rated positively

---

[7] Note that the poll data are sparser in Germany and the issue isn't included in our data after 1994, making inferences about stability particularly difficult.

on an issue; in such cases the return of an issue into a party's most highly ranked issues, some years later, might suggest its reputation is more durable over a long time period. Another might be the loss of a positively ranked issue that an opposing party never comes to own. This conceptualisation would not, however, allow for explanation of the many losses and gains in issue reputations that so rarely result in realignments or switches of issue ownership. Most importantly, we reveal important and substantial variation in issue reputations across issues, parties and countries. These require explanation, and they relate to the concept of issue ownership – as it has been understood to date. However, they challenge a notion that ownership is always relative to a rival party. In our data, an issue can be 'lost' even if there is the possibility the party may still have a higher rating on the issue than its rival.

Issue Ownership and Partisanship

If issue ownership relates to long-term reputations of parties on issues, then it may be less prone to a problem of endogeneity than other evaluations in public opinion. This follows from the explanation of ownership resulting from long-term commitments to issues and from the representation of constituencies. These are characteristics which may be recognised and credited to the party by a majority of voters, rather than only the natural supporters of the party. It also follows from an explanation of ownership loss arising from a major and symbolic policy failure, which causes voters to re-evaluate and assess a long-standing view of the party as more committed to and trusted on an issue. Such a reputational loss may be recognised by supporters of the party, cutting through favourable partisan perceptions.

This may help to define the basis of issue ownership. If a party has a lead on an issue over other issues, it is likely to be the better rated party by a majority of the electorate; attracting the support on the issue from its own supporters, from floating voters or independents, and perhaps even from the supporters of rival parties. If the Republican Party is evaluated on a Democratic-owned issue, it will mainly be Republicans who rate it as best on that issue. But if the Republican Party is evaluated on an owned issue, their reputation for better handling will most likely extend beyond their partisan base. This does not mean that a party will be assigned positive evaluations on any issue by a rival party supporter, but that a party's reputations on issues will follow the same ordering among rival supporters.

We cannot break down our aggregate data in Figures 3.1 to 3.5 and Tables 3.2 to 3.9 by partisanship. This requires individual-level data with consistent and repeated questions about issue handing.

The rolling cross-sectional survey of the National Annenberg Election Study (NAES) allows us to compare how US partisans (and independents) evaluated the incumbent George W. Bush and prospective party nominees (Hillary Clinton, John Edwards, Barack Obama, Rudy Giuliani, John McCain, Mitt Romney, Fred Thompson) for the 2008 presidential election for their handling of issues in the pre-primary season, between September and December 2007. The question asked on presidential issue handling was: 'Do you approve or disapprove of the way George W. Bush is handling this issue: [... the economy]?' The question asked on candidates was, 'Are there any candidates who you think would do a particularly good job of handling [the nation's economy]?' These presidential/candidate issue-handling evaluations are not direct measures of party reputation, but it is reasonable to expect that candidates are evaluated at least partially on the basis of the issue-handling reputations of their parties.

The following graph compares the average issue-handling scores for President George W. Bush on seven issues, covering a period of 16 weeks in total. We expect (a) Republicans to rate George W. Bush with higher mean ratings than Democrats, but (b) the ranking of issues to be similar. We can analyse this by presenting the mean issue evaluations by Republican Party identifiers (respondents who indicated that they are either strong, weak or lean Republican) and the mean issue evaluations by Democratic Party identifiers (strong, weak or lean Democrat) over time. This is presented in Figure 3.3. We also compare the ranking of George W. Bush on each issue for Republican Party identifiers, Democratic Party identifiers and non-identifiers,[8] taking the mean rating over the time period. These rankings are presented in Table 3.10.

The differences in Figure 3.3 are striking. They reveal the way in which mean presidential handling evaluations are strongly associated with partisanship. If we use the average evaluations of candidates (or parties), or the lead of one party over another, we can expect strong effects of party identification, either leading to party identification or arising – endogenously – because of party identification.

However, Table 3.10 reveals that the *relative* issue reputations of George W. Bush are largely the same, revealing very little or no systematic partisan bias or influence. This pattern is consistent whichever candidate for the party presidential nomination we analyse using the NAES rolling cross-sectional data for the period between October and December 2007. In fact, where we have fewer issues available (four), we find exactly the same rankings (in evaluations of issue handling for Hillary Clinton, John

[8] Non-identifiers are not presented in Figure 3.3 for clarity of presentation.

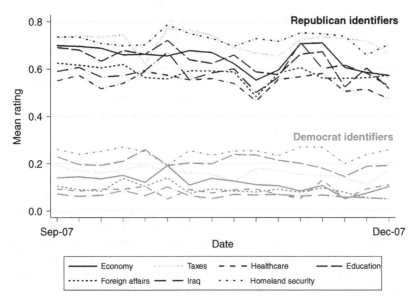

Figure 3.3 Republican and Democrat identifier ratings of President George W. Bush on issues

Table 3.10 *Ranking of US President George W. Bush evaluations by Republican and Democratic Party identifiers*

Rank	Republican partisans	Non-partisans	Democrat partisans
1	Homeland security	Homeland security	Homeland security
2	Taxes	Education	Education
3	Economy	Taxes	Taxes
4	Education	Healthcare	Economy
5	Iraq	Iraq	Foreign affairs
6	Foreign affairs	Economy	Healthcare
7	Healthcare	Foreign affairs	Iraq

Edwards, Barack Obama, Rudy Giuliani, John McCain) and almost identical rankings (Mitt Romney, Fred Thompson). (See the Appendix, Tables A3.3 to 3.9.)

We can also check to see whether these consistent rankings are unique to the United States and to evaluations of presidential (candidate) handling, and further whether they remain consistent assessed over a longer time period and using survey questions with different question stems and response options.

In Britain, the CMS provides the most useful data, asking respondents to evaluate the handling of issues by governing parties, rather than candidates. Specifically, for the incumbent Labour Government it asked 'How well do you think the present government has handled the National Health Service?', and for the opposition Conservative Party 'How well do you think a Conservative government would handle the crime situation in Britain?' The data can be disaggregated by party identification for the same issues (with handling of the financial crisis added to the set of issues in October 2008) over time.

The CMS data run over a substantially longer time period than the NAES. This offers a total of 71 monthly cross-sectional observations over the period between April 2004 and April 2010.[9] We examine average party issue-handling evaluations (where the scale runs from 0 being equal to 'very badly' to 4 equal to 'very well') across respondents who identify (either very strongly, strongly or not very strongly) with the Conservatives or with Labour, and for people with no party identification. With these data it should be harder to find consistent relative issue-handling rankings across partisans and independents.

Figure 3.4 reveals the mean scores for each issue for Conservative identifiers and Labour identifiers, and Table 3.11 presents the rankings.

Figure 3.4 reveals partisan differences in mean levels that are substantively identical to those shown for President George W. Bush in Figure 3.3. The mean evaluations are strongly associated with the partisanship of respondents, as we would expect. However, as with the US data, Table 3.11 reveals substantial similarity between Conservative and Labour party identifiers in the average rankings of party issue evaluations over the period. There is slightly weaker correspondence across all issues than evident in the NAES for presidents and candidates, which could arise from the longer time period (which allows for more variation), the evaluation of parties rather than candidates, the different question wordings or from country differences. However, Table 3.11 reveals – with the exception of one issue, terrorism – that the same issues feature in the top, middle and bottom rankings for Conservative partisans and for Labour partisans.

---

[9] We do not include issue-handling evaluations from the CMS after May 2010 for two reasons. First, the set of issues addressed in the CMS was altered to reflect the increased salience of new issues (with 'the number of immigrants' replacing 'asylum seekers' and 'government debt' replacing 'Britain's railways'). Second, restricting analysis to the period before May 2010 keeps the question stem consistent ('how well do you think a Conservative government would handle'). After this point in time, 'the present government' included both the Conservatives and Liberal Democrats ruling together in coalition.

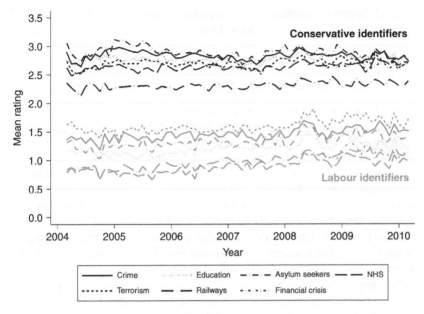

Figure 3.4 Conservative and Labour identifier ratings of the UK
Conservative Party on issues

Table 3.11 *Ranking of UK Conservative Party evaluations by
Conservative and Labour identifiers*

Rank	Party identifiers	Non-partisans	Rival partisans
1	Asylum Seekers	Terrorism	Terrorism
2	Crime	Crime	Crime
3	Education	Education	Asylum Seekers
4	Terrorism	Asylum Seekers	Education
5	Financial Crisis	Financial Crisis	Financial Crisis
6	NHS	NHS	Railways
7	Railways	Railways	NHS

From these analyses, we suggest that the ranking of parties on issues
provides a measure that is far less susceptible to partisan bias or partisan
effects than the mean level or the between-party lead.

Figures 3.1 and 3.2 earlier showed how parties tend to have issues on
which they are consistently stronger or weaker, how public opinion fluctuates on each issue and how public opinion also moves in a common

general direction across issues, indicative of generalised assessments of competence. We now consider evidence for issue-specific performance fluctuations.

The Characteristics of Performance Fluctuations

Here we assess whether changes in issue ratings are distinct to issue ownership by considering whether there is greater, lesser or an equal amount of variation or volatility in public evaluations of parties on issues, irrespective of whether an issue is owned or not owned. This is examined by comparing the variance of public assessments of performance on individual issues to their rank. If issue ownership is conceptually distinct to the fluctuations in public opinion about competence we should expect a similar amount of volatility in public opinion on a party's 'best' issues relative to worse. This would tell us that ownership, as a relative ranking, is the more stable concept, but that ongoing fluctuations and change in assessments should be conceptualised independently.

We display box plots in Figure 3.5 of mean ratings of the Republican Party on all issues over the entire period 1939 to 2013. The box area indicates the interquartile range, while the line that intersects it denotes the median value of mean issue-handling ratings. The 'whiskers' that protrude from the top and bottom of the box indicate the minimum and maximum values (with any outliers marked with a dot).[10] We are interested in whether variation in public assessments of performance on individual issues reflects the relative strength (or weakness) of parties on an issue. We would find evidence of lesser variance on owned issues if the range were lower around issues exhibiting higher mean values. As shown in Figure 3.5, this does not appear to be the case.

In the figure, we see variation in the median level of issue competence for the Republicans across issues, for example being viewed more positively on defence than on the environment. There are also differences in the size of the interquartile range across issues, with a much wider spread of values for defence than immigration. However, the figures reveal no systematic relationship between higher rated issues and wider or narrower ranges of values. Indeed, we observe high means with large ranges more often than we observe high means with small ranges, or low means with high ranges. That is to say, there appears to be no systematic variation between mean and range which would be consistent with higher rated issues exhibiting less short-term variability.

---

[10] Values that exceed the lower or upper quartiles by more than one-and-a-half times are considered to be outliers.

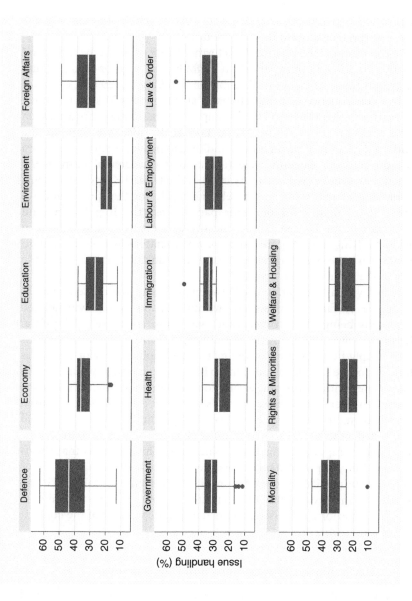

Figure 3.5 Box plot of issue ratings of the US Republican Party, by year

To ensure these findings are not party-specific we examined the same relationships focusing on the US Democrats, the UK Conservative Party and the UK Labour Party. In none of those box plots did we find a clear relationship between the overall mean level of public opinion and the degree of variance around those estimates.

We can examine the relationships further by focusing on the mean and variance for different time periods. It might be the case, for example, that the greater range of values of Republican handling of defence, above, is partly a consequence of being observed at different points over a much longer time period (1940 to 2013) compared to handling of an issue such as the environment (1979 to 2011). To test this idea, we compare the standard deviation of mean issue-handling ratings for a party on a given issue during each election cycle (a four-year presidential term in the United States and a parliamentary cycle in the United Kingdom) against the ranking of that issue in that election cycle for that party, and we display those figures for our four party cases (the Republicans and Democrats in the United States, and the Conservatives and Labour in the United Kingdom). Figure 3.6 displays the scatter plots of the standard deviation of issue-handling ratings against the ranking of that issue for the party in the same election cycle.

We find virtually no difference between high- and low-ranked issues in the degree of variation observed (within election cycle), with all the R-squareds being close to zero and with little structure to the data. The slight upward slope for the Republicans, Conservatives and Labour might simply be a function of the fact that sampling error of surveys is a function of the sample proportion, so higher mean ratings would tend to be associated with slightly more variation simply as a product of statistical theory. However, even if these upwards slopes are due to greater variation in public opinion, we note that this is in the opposite direction than would be expected if there were greater stability on issues on which a party has its most positive reputation, or issue ownership. This confirms that short-term variability of performance assessments is not tied to long-term ownership of issues, or if there is a relationship, it is extremely weak (and in the direction of more variability on best rated issues). There is meaningful variation in performance assessments that is independent of the concept of long-term ownership.

Performance Fluctuations and Partisanship

Earlier we revealed how the relative rankings of parties on issues were held consistently by partisans as well as by non-partisans and rivals. Here we examine whether performance evaluations are likely to provide

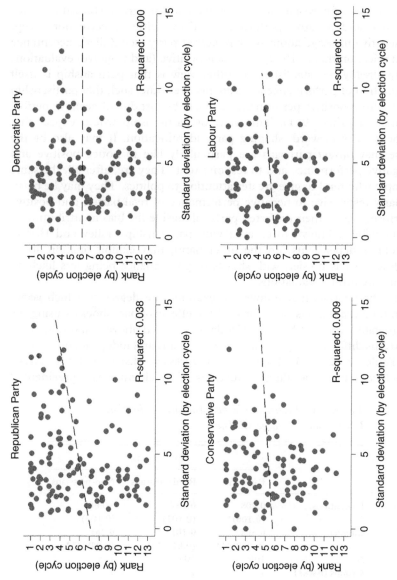

Figure 3.6 Scatter plot of standard deviation of issue ratings against rank (within election cycle)

explanatory power above and beyond the tendency of partisans to evaluate a party more positively, i.e. whether partisans update evaluations of preferred parties and rivals on performance. One view of partisanship may be that partisans are too biased to notice positive and negative performance. They neither receive nor accept a negative message about their preferred party (see Zaller's acceptance and rejection theory 1992), and their positive (and negative) evaluations may already be established. Another view is that partisanship is itself a function of performance assessments over time, such that partisanship arises from positive performance and can be lost due to negative performance (Fiorina 1981). This view of partisanship would expect that shocks carry forward, shaping party identification. It may also be the case that *current* partisans are particularly like to notice positive and negative performance and to respond to it. They are, after all, the same people who tend to give greater attention to politics. They may be particularly responsive to negative performance of rival parties and positive performance of their preferred party, alongside the bias in attribution of responsibility known to co-exist with partisanship (Tilley and Hobolt 2011). Independents, on the other hand, may exhibit opinion about politics that is noisier, with shocks to performance being less likely to structure future evaluations.

In the analysis that follows we examine the degree to which issue-handling evaluations carry forward the effects of past shocks – using the aggregate level NAES and CMS data discussed above – and how these patterns differ across partisans, rival partisans and independents.

Tables 3.12 to 3.14 report autoregressive distributed lag (ADL) models of issue-handling evaluations of President Bush, presidential

Table 3.12 *Persistence in performance evaluations, US President George W. Bush*

	Evaluations$_{it}$		
	Partisans	Rival partisans	Non-partisans
Evaluations$_{it-1}$	0.208	0.137	−0.087
	(0.106)*	(0.101)	(0.103)
Intercept	0.508	0.101	0.261
	(0.070)***	(0.014)***	(0.049)***
N	105	105	105
Groups (issues)	7	7	7
Overall R-squared	0.69	0.88	0.11

* $p<0.05$; ** $p<0.01$; *** $p<0.001$ (standard errors in parentheses)

nomination candidates and parties (pooling data across issues by president/candidate/party). The ADL takes the form $Y_{it} = a_0 + a_1 Y_{it-1} + \beta_i + \varepsilon_t$, where Y_{it} refers to the competence evaluation at time t for a given issue i, and Y_{it-1} refers to the competence evaluation on the same issue in the previous time period. We include issue-fixed effects (β_i) to control for variation in the average handling rating by issue. In this model specification, the parameter a_1 indicates the rate of autoregression. That is, the degree to which current competence evaluations are a function of competence evaluations in the previous period.[11] Of key interest is the strength of the autoregressive process which takes a value between 0, where no portion of past evaluations are carried forward, and 1, where all shocks to performance evaluations are remembered. Analysing this autoregressive process for each group reveals the extent to which the persistence of performance evaluations varies across partisans, rival partisans and non-partisans.

In Table 3.12, we consider performance evaluations of President George W. Bush across seven issues on a week-by-week basis over the 16-week period using data from the NAES. These are the best data we have disaggregated by partisan identity for the United States.

These results reveal that non-partisans and rival partisans exhibit much more short-term fluctuation in their issue competence assessments than partisans, who were much more inclined to update their evaluations of George W. Bush in response to shocks. The coefficient of the autoregressive term (Evaluations$_{t-1}$) is equal to 0.2 ($p<0.001$) for partisans but not significant for rival partisans or non-partisans. The goodness-of-fit of the model, as measured with the overall R-squared, is 0.7 for partisans and 0.9 for rival partisans (perhaps revealing the highly persistent attitudes that Democrats held towards George W. Bush by this period), but equal to 0.1 for non-partisans.

We see a similar pattern for performance evaluations of prospective party presidential nominees in Table 3.13, but here we find a similar autoregressive process for partisans as for rival partisans. The pattern is of significantly greater persistence among partisans and rival partisans compared to non-partisans. Note that the R-squared for non-partisans is much lower than that for the models for partisans and rivals. This indicates that past competence shocks provide far less information about current evaluations for non-partisans.

---

[11] We also estimate these models with an AR(1) process, which produces similar results in terms of the degree of persistence and the same inferences.

Table 3.13 *Persistence in performance evaluations, candidates for the Republican and Democratic Party nomination for the US presidency*

	Evaluations$_{it}$		
	Partisans	Rival partisans	Non-partisans
Evaluations$_{it-1}$	0.287	0.271	−0.115
	(0.057)***	(0.056)***	(0.065)
Intercept	0.317	0.051	0.163
	(0.026)***	(0.005)***	(0.015)***
N	336	336	336
Groups (candidates* issues)	28	28	28
Overall R-squared	0.97	0.96	0.66

* $p<0.05$; ** $p<0.01$; *** $p<0.001$ (standard errors in parentheses)

The differences we observe between Tables 3.12 and 3.13 – that of substantial updating for rival partisans for candidates, but only for the partisans of the president's party for presidential handling – may arise due to the highly partisan and competitive period in which presidential candidate data are asked: the candidate campaigns for each party's presidential nominee.

Table 3.14 *Persistence in performance evaluations, Labour government and Conservative opposition, UK, 2004–2010*

	Evaluations$_{it}$		
	Partisans	Rival partisans	Non-partisans
Evaluations$_{it-1}$	0.662	0.644	0.259
	(0.027)***	(0.026)***	(0.033)***
Intercept	0.957	0.521	1.100
	(0.078)***	(0.039)***	(0.056)***
N	852	852	852
Groups (parties* issues)	14	14	14
Overall R-squared	0.97	0.93	0.63

* $p<0.05$; ** $p<0.01$; *** $p<0.001$ (standard errors in parentheses)

The analysis is again repeated using the UK data, in Table 3.14. This uses performance evaluations of the Labour government and Conservative opposition across seven issues over the period between April 2004 and

April 2010.[12] These data provide monthly units of analysis rather than weekly, which might be expected to exhibit higher rates of persistence.

In Table 3.14, we find stronger persistence for non-partisans in the United Kingdom than we found for the United States and stronger rates of persistence overall: for partisans and rivals. However, once again we find that partisans are much more likely to exhibit updating, in terms of persistence, than are independents. On a month-by-month basis, partisan and rival partisan performance evaluations are substantially autoregressive, with the coefficient of around 0.65 in both cases ($p<0.001$), whereas non-partisan evaluations are more weakly dependent, with a coefficient of closer to 0.3 ($p<0.001$). The R-squared is again much lower for non-partisans compared to partisans and rival partisans.

These UK and US differences may arise due to the stronger party system in Britain, which results in stronger party-based assessments across the board, or the differences between evaluations of individuals (presidents and candidates) and parties, but more likely and most simply, probably arises as a consequence of using the monthly unit of aggregation instead of weekly observations. However, we again find much weaker persistence among non-partisans than among partisans, consistent with the US findings. And as in Table 3.13, our results demonstrate persistence in evaluations among partisans and rival partisans alike.

Our analyses confirm that evaluations of performance by partisans or rival partisans are subject to long-term accumulation of short-term performance shocks, whereas evaluations of non-identifiers are only temporarily affected by recent events or performance, exhibiting little 'memory' of past shocks and fluctuating noisily. Partisans notice and respond to past information, exhibiting more performance updating than non-partisans. To the degree, therefore, that performance fluctuations matter, they should matter just as much, if not more, for people who identify with a party than for people with no partisan affiliation.

The Characteristics of Generalised Competence

As highlighted earlier in Figures 3.1 and 3.2, there are periods where we can discern a shift in public opinion about the competence of parties where those translate across policy issues. Crucial to understanding these periods is whether these are simply a function of increasing or decreasing popular support for a party, which has the effect of increasing or decreasing issue-handling evaluations (whether generalised shifts in competence are endogenous to popularity). Another reason might be the transfer of

---

[12] We see a similar pattern for the June 2010 to April 2013 data from the CMS.

competence ratings from one issue to another, such that a party that is seen to fail significantly on an issue, or conversely to demonstrate significant success, might be judged more negatively – or positively – for its competence on other issues. This is the notion behind our work on 'macro-competence' (Green and Jennings 2012a), which reveals how common variance exists in public opinion about competence.

The idea behind macro-competence is that voters use heuristics to assess the competence of political parties. This allows low-information voters to make boundedly rational judgements about party competence; drawing on small amounts of information to update their assessments of performance by transferring evaluations across issues or using a generalised sense of the performance of parties.

We reveal here how much shared variance exists in public opinion about competence in countries for which we have sufficient aggregate level survey data over time: the United States, United Kingdom, Canada, Germany and Australia. Stimson's (1991; Stimson et al. 1995) 'dyad ratios algorithm' is used to extract the underlying dimensions of citizens' evaluations of party competence across all available survey items. This method builds on the idea that ratios of aggregate-level survey responses to the same question, asked at different points in time, provide meaningful information about the relative state of public opinion (see Stimson 1991 and Bartle et al. 2011 for an extended discussion of the method). Aggregate competence evaluations can be scored either as the raw percentage of respondents naming a party as most competent/trusted on an issue in a survey (e.g. 55 per cent rating the Republicans as best on defence), or as an index of the relative proportion of respondents naming either of the main parties as the most competent/trusted (e.g. the ratio between 55 per cent rating the Republicans as best on defence and 35 per cent rating the Democrats as best on the issue, so calculated $0.55 / (0.55 + 0.35) = 0.61$). We use the former measure here since it allows party competence evaluations to vary due to changing levels of respondent uncertainty and favouring of other parties (or 'none of the above').

Each survey item can be expressed as the ratio of competence evaluations at two points in time, i.e. a 'dyad'. The ratio provides an estimate of the relative perceived competence of a party, on a given issue, in years $t+i$ and $t+j$:

$$C_{ij} = \frac{X_{t+i}}{X_{t+j}}$$

This enables recursive estimation of the competence index for each survey item for each time period (i.e. years or quarters) based on all data available for that time period (and other time periods). There are multiple overlapping estimates of these separate competence indices and each one is not an equivalent indicator of the underlying construct. To solve this, the dyad ratios algorithm iteratively estimates the squared correlation of each series with the latent dimension and uses this to weight the series, proportional to their indicator validity (Bartle et al. 2011: 269).[13] The method extracts the central tendency of all survey items relating to evaluations of party issue competence, analogous to a principal components approach. Note that these measures do not parse out the influence of electoral popularity or partisanship (see Green and Jennings 2012a: 335), and we turn to those relationships later. They simply reveal how much common variance exists across the time period and the parties for which we have data. This is derived from 5,436 survey items for the United States, 3,536 for the United Kingdom,[14] 1,120 for Germany, 752 for Australia and 160 for Canada (consisting of 11,004 items in total).

Table 3.15 reports the proportion of variance loading onto the first and second dimensions of the extracted measure of macro-competence, and the mean and standard deviation of each dimension.

Table 3.15 reveals particularly high proportions of variance loading onto the first dimension, or 'macro-competence'. This first dimension represents the greatest proportion of common variance in competence evaluations across all issues. It is interpretable as the central tendency in the public's evaluations of the issue-handling capabilities of parties. Higher values of macro-competence indicate that the public views a party more positively in its handling across a range of issues. Lower values indicate that the public tends to view a party as handling issues poorly, in common. The remainder of variance explained – approximately 35 per cent in the United States, 30 per cent in the United Kingdom, 15 per cent in Germany and 25 per cent in Australia – provides an assessment of the unique variation that is specific to individual issues; i.e. the part that can be explained by issue-specific changes in public

---

[13] The separate estimates, x_{tk}, are weighted according to their degree of indicator validity, u_i^2, with the equation denominator being the average validity estimate (i.e. communality) across all items, of series length k, for N years (where k is always less than N). The formal expression of the equation, as derived in Bartle et al. (2011: 269), is therefore:

$$C_t = \frac{\sum_{k=1}^{N} h_i^2 x_{tk}}{h^2 N}$$

[14] Note that the number of survey items that is used to estimate macro-competence for the United Kingdom is slightly greater than that for our earlier analysis of ownership (3,452) because we also include items that relate to the handling of issues by just one party.

Table 3.15 *Summary statistics for macro-competence in the United States, the United Kingdom, Germany, Canada and Australia*

	Start	End	N	First dimension	Second dimension	Mean (1ˢᵗ D)	SD (1ˢᵗ D)
United States							
Democratic Party	1939	2013	75	54.9	11.5	38.2	3.4
Republican Party	1939	2013	75	54.5	14.5	33.7	3.4
United Kingdom							
Labour Party	1945	2012	68	57.1	15.9	32.3	3.9
Conservative Party	1945	2012	68	65.1	10.1	31.7	4.4
Germany							
SPD	1961	2013	53	76.9	10.1	33.0	6.3
CDU	1961	2013	53	78.2	9.5	33.2	5.8
Canada							
Conservatives	1945	2001	57	89.6	3.8	30.5	8.3
Liberal Party	1945	2001	57	80.7	6.5	47.9	6.2
Australia							
ALP	1989	2014	26	63.1	10.8	34.1	4.1
Liberal/National Party	1989	2014	26	66.5	12.8	34.7	3.9

opinion about performance.[15] The first and second dimensions together show very high proportions of shared variance.

The amount of shared variance is an important observation in its own right; it suggests that generalised competence assessments provide an additional and substantively important concept in the understanding of public opinion about competence. A generalised concept of competence is distinct to the concept of issue ownership, and it is distinct to measures of issue-specific fluctuations in policy performance. This common variation may also indicate a strong partisan component, such that the common variation is driven by shifts in party attachments and popularity. This is also an important insight, insofar as a small but still very significant proportion of variation in public opinion about competence is *not* shared across issues.

---

[15] The comparability of the amount of variance explained is compromised by the lack of comparability in the number of survey items or range of data sources, but for our purposes it is helpful to conclude that the amount of shared variation in public opinion on competence far outweighs the unique variance that arises from issue-specific volatility in public opinion.

Generalised Competence and Partisanship

Here we address the question: to what extent are generalised competence evaluations a function of partisanship, and to what extent do generalised competence evaluations shape changes in partisanship? We assess these questions in two ways. First, we visually present the relationship between macro-competence and partisanship over time. We have aggregate-level data on partisanship ('macro-partisanship') in the United States, United Kingdom and Germany, and so time series for these variables are displayed for those countries. Second, we assess the temporal relationships between macro-competence and partisanship using tests of 'Granger causation' (Granger 1969).

Figures 3.7 to 3.12 display the macro-competence and macro-partisanship series for each party by country. The macro-partisanship series represent the percentage of respondents indicating political affiliation to a particular party (e.g. the Democratic Party in the United States or the Social Democrats in Germany). In the United States and United Kingdom, we have multiple sources of survey data concerning party identification, so we again use Stimson's dyad ratios algorithm to create a single index (following Erikson et al. 2002). For Germany, we have

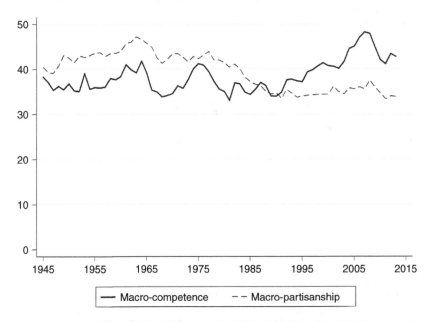

Figure 3.7 Macro-competence and macro-partisanship, US Democratic Party

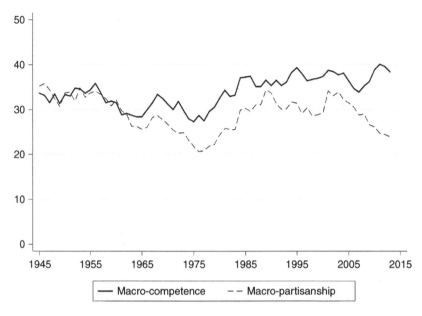

Figure 3.8 Macro-competence and macro-partisanship, US Republican Party

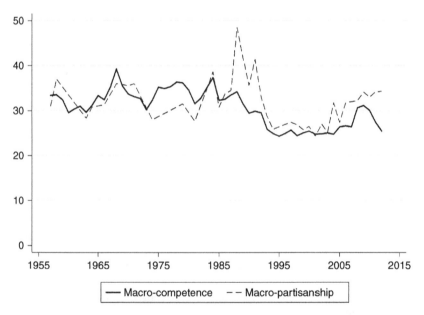

Figure 3.9 Macro-competence and macro-partisanship, UK Conservative Party

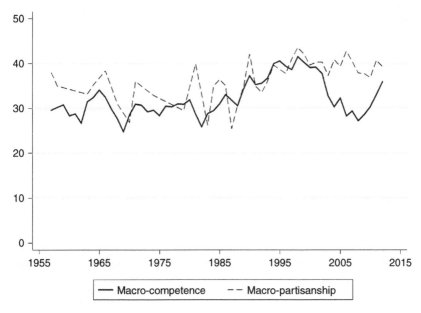

Figure 3.10 Macro-competence and macro-partisanship, UK Labour Party

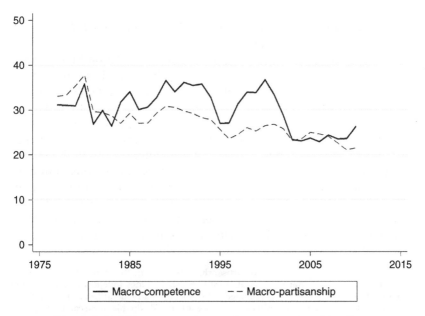

Figure 3.11 Macro-competence and macro-partisanship, German Social Democratic Party

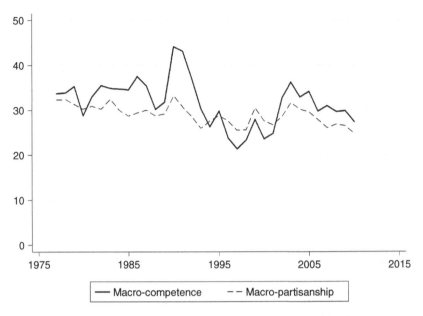

Figure 3.12 Macro-competence and macro-partisanship, German
Christian Democratic Union

a single data source, Forschungsgruppe Wahlen's monthly *Politbarometer*,
so we simply take the average percentage using these data.[16]
It is not possible to assess the precise temporal relationships between
macro-competence and macro-partisanship by visual inspection of the
figures alone, but it is evident that while there are clear parallels between
the measures there is also a substantial degree of difference. In the United
States, for example, we see that macro-competence and macro-
partisanship have tended to move together over time, but have diverged
for both Republicans and Democrats since around 2000. In the United
Kingdom, the series have also tended to track one another, but have
diverged at points in time. While the macro-competence of the Labour
Party declined after 1997, its macro-partisanship remained relatively
stable. In Germany, macro-competence tends to fluctuate rather more
than partisanship, which has declined since the 1970s. Thus, while it is

---

[16] Note that this version of macro-partisanship differs from that typically used for the
United States (e.g. MacKuen et al. 1989), which excludes independents and 'don't
know' responses, where the percentage of Democratic Party identifiers is divided by the
total of Democratic and Republican Party identifiers. We do this so we can compare the
most comparable measure of macro-partisanship to macro-competence.

evident that generalised evaluations of party competence and partisan attachments are related, they are not synonymous in their levels or variances.

Next we examine the temporal interrelationship between the series. This helps us establish whether changes in macro-competence tend to precede changes in macro-partisanship (performance-based updating) or whether changes in macro-partisanship tend to lead changes in macro-competence (partisan conditioning). Specifically, tests for Granger causation (Granger 1969) determine whether past values of a variable x improve prediction of another variable y, relative to prediction from y from past values of itself alone. This is not a test of causation in the strictest sense, but evidence of the predictive content and the temporal ordering of one measure in relation to another (Granger 1988). If macro-partisanship shapes macro-competence (and if macro-competence were endogenous to macro-partisanship), we would at least expect the temporal ordering between the variables to tend to be stronger in the direction from macro-partisanship to macro-competence than from macro-competence to macro-partisanship.

Tables 3.16 to 3.18 reveal the tests for Granger causation between macro-competence and macro-partisanship (and vice versa) for each party, country and period where we have quarterly data series, which enable a more fine-grained examination of the dynamics of each of the

Table 3.16 *Granger causation tests between macro-competence and macro-partisanship, US*

	Democratic Party	Republican Party
Macro-competence Granger-causes macro-partisanship		
χ^2 test statistic	13.201***	9.393**
p-value	0.001	0.002
Macro-partisanship Granger-causes macro-competence		
χ^2 test statistic	1.939	13.224***
p-value	0.379	0.000
AIC	5.537	5.806
Durbin-Watson d-statistic	1.987	1.953
Lag, selected according to AIC criteria	2	1
Start	1956 Q4	1956 Q4
End	2013 Q2	2013 Q2
N	227	228

* $p \leq 0.05$, ** $p \leq 0.01$, *** $p \leq 0.001$
Note: Granger causation test in first differences

Table 3.17 *Granger causation tests between macro-competence and macro-partisanship, UK*

	Labour Party	Conservative Party
Macro-competence Granger-causes macro-partisanship		
χ^2 *test statistic*	11.646**	15.082***
p-value	0.003	0.001
Macro-partisanship Granger-causes macro-competence		
χ^2 *test statistic*	1.314	0.682
p-value	0.518	0.771
AIC	9.160	9.973
Durbin-Watson *d*-statistic	1.978	1.950
Lag, selected according to AIC criteria	2	2
Start	1979 Q4	1979 Q4
End	2012 Q3	2012 Q3
N	132	132

$* p \leq 0.05$, $** p \leq 0.01$, $*** p \leq 0.001$

Note: Granger causation test in levels; party identification series is interpolated for missing values, with uncertainty added to the interpolated series as a function of the standard deviation of raw values of party identification for each party.

Table 3.18 *Granger causation tests between macro-competence and macro-partisanship, Germany*

	Christian Democrat Union	Social Democratic Party
Macro-competence Granger-causes macro-partisanship		
χ^2 *test statistic*	3.956*	6.505†
p-value	0.047	0.089
Macro-partisanship Granger-causes macro-competence		
χ^2 *test statistic*	0.302	3.775
p-value	0.583	0.287
AIC	8.252	8.923
Durbin-Watson *d*-statistic	1.908	1.989
Lag, selected according to AIC criteria	1	3
Start	1978 Q2	1978 Q4
End	2010 Q4	2010 Q4
N	131	129

$† p \leq 0.1$, $* p \leq 0.05$, $** p \leq 0.01$, $*** p \leq 0.001$

Note: Granger causation test in levels.

measures than we can obtain using annual data. Using shorter (quarterly) time intervals provides more information for analysis of the predictive content of lagged values of macro-competence and macro-partisanship: not only does this provide a larger N but it also reduces the likelihood that meaningful variation will be aggregated away (see Granger 1969: 427). It does, however, mean that we are limited in analysis of Granger causation for periods where the data underlying the macro-competence and macro-competence series are quite thick.[17]

These Granger causation tests reveal that macro-competence tends to lead macro-partisanship to a greater extent than macro-partisanship leads macro-competence. In just one instance – for the Republican Party in the United States – there is evidence of Granger causation in both directions. The estimated χ^2 test statistic considers whether macro-competence Granger-causes macro-partisanship or whether macro-partisanship Granger-causes macro-competence, such that where the χ^2 test statistic is significant there is Granger-causation between the variables. For example, in the case of the US Democratic Party, the χ^2 test statistic provides support for the hypothesis that macro-competence Granger-causes macro-partisanship (13.2), significant at the 99.9 per cent confidence level. In contrast, the χ^2 test statistic in the opposite direction (1.9) is not statistically significant at the 95 per cent level.

Our findings, on Granger causality, suggest that partisanship is *not* strongly exogenous to competence evaluations, but the temporal ordering is consistent with 'running tally' expectations of party attachments. This does not mean that party identification is not also acting as a perceptual screen. What we find here, and in previous analysis (Green and Jennings 2012a), is that generalised competence evaluations are informative about subsequent changes in party identification, arguably as voters incorporate perceptions of competence into their affective orientations towards parties. In our previous work (Green and Jennings 2012a), we found evidence that there is a strong and substantively large effect of macro-competence on vote intention, controlling for macro-partisanship and other variables. Our evidence suggests that macro-competence is far from purely endogenous to partisanship. Our later analysis (in Chapter 7) also bears this out, with more comprehensive models of competence. The concept of generalised competence evaluations provides a new and important addition to our understanding of public

---

[17] We test for Granger causation of the variables in either first differences or levels depending on the results of Dickey-Fuller tests for stationarity of the time series. These reject the null hypothesis of the presence of unit root for parties in the United States and United Kingdom, but not Germany. The lag order is selected according to the Akaike information criterion (AIC).

opinion about competence, and one which is conceptually and empirically distinct to partisanship.

Conclusion

There are three distinct empirical concepts to public opinion about competence: (1) The relative strengths and weaknesses of parties on different issues: issue ownership. These 'level differences' exhibit stability but also important variation, as exhibited in this chapter using decades of public opinion data from the United States, United Kingdom, Germany and Australia. The loss and gain of issue ownership is a topic that requires much more investigation, but it is only made possible by careful and accurate conceptualisation of the key variance that needs to be explained. The next chapter offers a theory and evidence to account for these losses and gains. (2) Fluctuations in public opinion about party competence on specific issues. These short-term *changes* in issue-based ratings are independent of within-party ownership rankings; owned and non-owned issues exhibit similar amounts of variance over time. (3) Generalised competence evaluations, which account for the largest proportion of variation in public opinion about competence and which represent the large shifts in direction in overall competence across the issue agenda. These three concepts are empirically and conceptually distinct.

This chapter also dealt with the relationship of each of the three concepts with partisanship. In each case we revealed how the concept is distinct to party identification.

Following our measurement of issue ownership as the ranking of better to worse within-party evaluations, we are able to overcome some potential problems arising from endogeneity. Partisans are more likely to rate their party higher on all issues, but the within-party ranking is broadly equivalent, irrespective of partisanship. Reputations are reputations, and they cut through the potential for a partisan bias or lens. We are concerned about measures of issue ownership that rely on the average of issue-handling evaluations for parties, or the gap between parties. As revealed here, there is a very strong relationship between party identification and mean party or candidate ratings on issues, which we assume reflect partisan conditioning to a large degree. However, a measure of issue ownership which uses party reputations as its basis, and which analyses the relative issue-handling strengths and weaknesses of a party, provides consistent evidence which is far less sensitive to partisanship or not sensitive to partisanship at all.

With respect to performance fluctuations, we identified strong effects of past ratings on partisans' ratings of political parties for competence, but a much weaker autoregressive tendency in the views of non-partisans. That is to say, we believe performance fluctuations reflect meaningful updating among those people who have a prior partisan attachment.

There is a close correspondence between macro-competence and macro-partisanship but these concepts are by no means synonymous. Testing for the temporal ordering of both concepts across countries reveals that generalised competence assessments more commonly lead partisanship than vice versa. The implications may be important for our understanding of partisanship as a running tally of performance and they suggest that macro-competence is not simply the sum of over-time movements in partisanship.

The literature has been inconsistent in the use of terms and concepts in the study of issue ownership, competence and valence. This chapter demonstrates three ways forward in understanding public opinion about competence and in measuring meaningful and consequential concepts: issue ownership, issue-specific performance fluctuation and generalised assessments of competence.

What are the implications of three distinct concepts in public opinion about party competence? The answers to this question are sought in the remaining chapters of this volume. Given the frequency and potential significance of changes in within-party issue ownership, we set out a theory to explain these changes. This is the subject of Chapter 4. In Chapter 5 we examine the way fluctuations of performance assessments correspond to the performance of governments, and therefore relate to governing party vote choices much more than oppositions'. Chapter 6 analyses the concept of macro-competence in much greater detail, revealing the systematic trends in these generalised competence evaluations and how those cycles offer an explanation for the 'costs of governing' experienced so regularly by incumbents. Chapter 7 draws the three concepts together and reveals how each exerts an independent effect upon party choice, as well as considering when competence is more – and when it is less – strongly associated with party support.

4 Explaining Issue Ownership Change

There are two major gaps in current understanding of issue ownership. The first relates to the question of how much and when issue ownership changes. The previous chapter (Tables 3.2 to 3.9) revealed that within-party issue ownership change is frequent, even taking a cautious and conservative definition of change which requires ownership change to persist over two election cycles, across at least two ranks in the average issue ratings of a party, and for the average rating calculated over an election cycle. The second gap relates to the absence of a tested theory of issue ownership change. While we have some ideas from the literature about what may cause ownership change, some examination of isolated cases and some indicators of predictors of ownership (all discussed below) there has been no systematic test – until now – of why parties lose and gain reputations on issues. We provide such a test in this chapter, providing cross-national over-time evidence in support of a theory of issue ownership change. Such a theory is important, since issue ownership has been found to shape election campaigns, presidential rhetoric, legislative and elite priorities and ultimately the outcomes of elections. Issue ownership change relates to fundamental realignments of party reputations and potentially the issue publics which correspond to them. Understanding the forces that determine these changes in issue ownership provides an explanation for a central concept in party competition and political behaviour.

Existing Accounts

Petrocik (1996), who coined the term 'issue ownership', referred to long-term ownership as, 'produced by a history of attention, initiative and innovation toward these problems' (1996: 826), and to short-term ownership as arising 'when one party can be blamed for current difficulties' (Petrocik 1996: 827). These descriptions offer potential explanations for ownership change, but they were untested by Petrocik and have remained largely untested since.

94

Existing research on ownership has examined particular instances of ownership change. Holian (2004) analysed presidential remarks in public and Congressional hearings on the issue of crime, identifying how a president (Bill Clinton) could use framing and rhetoric to neutralise an opponent's ownership of an issue. Sulkin (2005) revealed how individual Congressmen/women take up issues in Congress to neutralise an opponent's issue advantage, but Sulkin did not examine multiple cases of ownership loss or gain. Using our alternative measure (within-party rank), the US cases of ownership neutralisation examined by Holian and Sulkin do not appear in our cases of ownership gains, losses or realignments in Chapter 3. Holian was referring to *neutralising* of an issue, but the issue of crime was neither a clearly Republican-owned issue, nor did it become a Democrat issue during this period, according to Table 3.2 in Chapter 3. In that table, we revealed that law and order moved from sixth- to fifth-ranked issue for the Republicans between the 1988–1992 and 1996–2000 presidential administrations (though it fell to 9th in 1992–1996), and from 11th to 9th for the Democrats. There is consequently a set of cases where parties come to have less strong associations on issues, or less weak associations. In these cases, changes in the issue associations of parties are less clear. We do not focus on these relatively slight changes in this chapter. Instead we focus on clear cases of ownership change in terms of within-party losses, gains or realignments. These changes will likely have significant electoral impact, and they are the least equivocal cases we can identify in our extensive datasets. Subtle changes are difficult to verify with public opinion data that are subject to noise. Nevertheless, the analysis of ownership neutralisation suggests there is potentially a rhetorical basis to ownership change.

Other research has examined individual-level evaluations of issue ownership and factors associated with those evaluations. Tresch et al. (2013) examined whether campaign messages alter issue associations with parties, using online experimental methods instead of actual cases of losses or gains. Walgrave et al. (2012) examined associations between survey questions about position and competence evaluations on ratings of parties on issues, indicating a relationship between the two. This research suggests that there is a policy position, competence and associative aspect to issue ownership which may account for ownership losses and gains (see also Wagner and Zeglovits 2014).

None of these studies takes a comparative approach, either across issues or across countries and institutional contexts. Furthermore, none offers a general test of a theory of ownership change, and the explanations offered by Petrocik for ownership change have not been subjected to empirical validation. It remains possible that major performance changes will influence issue ownership: that policy shifts, constituency representation and commitments will also influence ownership. There may be contextual explanations that become clear when we examine instances of issue ownership change over multiple policy domains, over multiple time periods and in a number of countries.

A Theory of Issue Ownership Change

Ownership change should occur when something happens that is so clear a signal, and so symbolic, that widely held beliefs about political parties are thrown into question. Issue ownership relates to ratings of competence and also to the notion of positional representation and commitment. Therefore, for a substantial reputation change to occur, we argue that either a major performance shock or a major symbolic policy change should take place.

Throughout this book we have highlighted the interaction between partisanship and competence. Within-party ownership is important because it transcends partisan biases. Partisans and rival partisans tend to see the ordering of a party's best and worst issues as the same (with the average rating being what differs), as revealed in Chapter 3. Partisans and rival partisans should in general be resistant to updating ratings of parties on issues that are reputational and defining. A re-ordering of party strengths among a party's existing supporters and its rivals should therefore occur only when events and actions are sufficiently strong to cause a substantial reappraisal.

As highlighted already, Petrocik (1996) referred to short-term ownership arising due to blame for current difficulties (e.g. failed policies, economic conditions) providing another party with a lease. As will be clear by now, we differentiate the idea of a short-term lease from the concept of issue ownership, and we do not expect short-term switches in ownership from one party to another. But it remains possible that major performance shocks could result in the loss, or the gain, of an issue. Also, if issue ownership is caused by positional competition – the representation by a party of a side or direction in policy which causes people who agree with the party to confer a sense of association, representation and trustworthiness (and competence), or a policy shift away from the position of voters in the case of an ownership loss – then a major ideological shift or a major change in commitment and representation of a position could result in an ownership change. A minor shift in policy should not cause a major re-evaluation of a party in terms of the issues it is trusted on and associated with. But a major ideological shift could do this.

A perceived party ideological shift could occur due to a symbolic change in policy. Consider Tony Blair's ideological repositioning of the UK Labour Party, which was helped by removal of a clause in the party's constitution supporting 'common ownership of the means of production, distribution and exchange' (Clause IV). An ideological shift could occur due to a major change in spending or state ownership of public assets (a party may advocate a new belief in privatisation or a major disinvestment of public funds), a legislative commitment (e.g. giving greater or less support to trade unions or business interests) or it could result from a major and symbolic change in rhetorical emphasis. A policy shift could therefore be directional or it could be one based on emphasis; due to legislation, spending or rhetoric. This policy change, or emphasis, should be politically symbolic for a change in ownership to occur; it should challenge preconceptions of party issue associations. Otherwise a party may change its policy or spending commitments and the change may not be recognised. Even an observed change might not be substantial but rather a minor change or one which confirms existing reputations. Where a change is significant it can lead to an ownership shift. A symbolic performance shock or policy change will be one which is sufficient to re-order the reputation of a party on that issue, either unintentionally or intentionally.

Policy shifts towards majority opinion or towards the median opinion of an issue public should result in ownership gains, while shifts away should conversely result in losses. Public opinion could also, in theory, move towards a party, resulting in a gain in issue ownership.

Note that when we refer to a policy commitment, we do not mean an increase in emphasis during an election campaign or a single political speech or announcement. Something so fundamental and meaningful in public opinion as issue ownership (within-party reputations on issues) should not be open to influence simply by one party deciding to emphasise that issue in an election campaign, over the short-term.[1] Its emphasis should signify a major commitment. It might denote prioritising an issue above all else over a sustained period, investing heavily in a policy area via legislation and spending, and/or symbolically tying a party's character and priorities to one issue above others.

In reality, performance and position factors may always go hand in hand. If a party is in power and suffers a major reputational shock in terms of performance, an opposing party may respond by proposing an alternative policy direction. If a party in government changes its policy over

---

[1] This may not always hold in the event of exceptional elections. If something symbolic and realigning occurs for a party's reputation, such as nomination of Donald Trump as candidate for the Republicans in the 2016 US presidential election, for example, a party may lose its traditional issue associations via an election campaign, or gain new issues.

time, disinvesting in an area of policy in public spending and prioritisation, that issue may become 'up for grabs', switching the issue owner when a new governing party is perceived to handle the issue well. We expect a handling change such as a major change in governing party performance to result in greater positional policy competition between different actors. The significance and salience of the issue opens up an opportunity for one or other party to gain a new advantage. Note that a substantial handling change should usually relate to a party-in-government, but a positional explanation could relate to an incumbent or challenger.[2]

We do not assume that it is the combination of a symbolic performance change and a symbolic position change that is a necessary or sufficient condition for issue ownership change to take place. Each could cause a shift in relative issue reputations for a given political party depending on the distribution of preferences. A position shift might cause an ownership change alone if a party comes to occupy a position held by the majority of voters, and if no other party holds that position, or if public opinion shifts in the existing direction of only one party: the new issue owner. A symbolic performance change alone might also be sufficient if parties are not differentiated on policy terms. But when both factors coincide, and if they are especially significant, we would expect issue ownership change to be more likely, and perhaps to be longer-lasting.

We refer here to symbolic performance shocks and to symbolic position shifts, meaning position (and salience) shifts representing changes in policy on a given policy dimension. Neither need be sufficient for a symbolic change in *constituency representation* to occur, though any major change in constituency representation would also be coupled with a change in policy.

The representation of different electoral or issue-based constituencies offers a further explanation of issue ownership change. It is, we contend, particularly useful in accounting for new issue ownership *formations* and the formation of new parties. This aspect of Petrocik's definition of ownership – 'the representation of constituencies' – is a highly important aspect in understanding issue ownership. A party may be the issue owner on the issue of labour and unemployment because it was born from the organised labour movement and, in the case of the UK Labour Party, that trade

---

[2] We do not extend our aggregate-level expectations to sub-national performance, though our expectations might vary for individuals nested within first and second order governments where the incumbent party differs at the first and second order level. In most cases, issue ownership relates to national parties and governments but the theory does not preclude application to a more complex structure of responsibility attribution and evaluation of policy positions.

union movement is integral to the party organisation. A party may be the issue owner of moral or cultural issues because it is a party traditionally associated with the established Church or an ethnic-linguistic group. Nationalist parties arise because they represent particular nationalist interests. Niche parties gain support because they represent specific issue-publics, such as those arising from the environmental movement, women's rights, opposition to immigration and so on. However, these party origins rarely involve a departure of a party from its foundational issue-public such that a party breaks with its electoral constituency, although this is certainly not impossible. A party may loosen its representation of a constituency, its advocacy and prioritisation weakening over time. We identify *changes* in constituency representation as infrequent events that result in changes in issue ownership – even a realignment of the issue from one party to another. But usually we expect constituency representation to be associated with the formations of political parties, with some overlap with the freezing hypothesis of Lipset and Rokkan (1967). Lipset and Rokkan argued, famously, that party systems became frozen through party formation around stable social cleavages. With that party-cleavage association we expect constituency representation-based issue ownership to find some parallels. But like the apparent unfreezing of party systems, there may also be a loss of traditional issue associations if parties no longer represent those traditional constituencies.

There should be two necessary pre-conditions for ownership change to occur.

If issue ownership denotes a major re-evaluation of a party's strengths and weaknesses, cutting through partisan allegiances and the general lack of attention of an electorate towards changes in performance and policy shifts, then a pre-condition for ownership change has to be public and political salience. Ownership change should only occur when either a political event causes the public to notice what the parties (and/or governments) are doing and saying (the performance shock or the policy shift is symbolic), or when an issue is so important to the public that it is attuned to the actions and the promises of elites.

Political significance and public salience will often go hand-in-hand. An issue may become a salient issue to the public because it is a primary issue of competition at a political level (and elites provide cues to voters) and vice versa. A major performance shock will also make an issue politically significant, and it may also make it a primary public concern. But a highly politically salient change could occur on a relatively low salience issue. In each case, it is the nature of that issue being highly relevant to the evaluations of the public at large that is necessary for an ownership change to occur.

There is another necessary pre-condition of issue ownership change; the availability of another party to challenge the issue owner: party supply. Imagine a party that fails to address an issue repeatedly, or fails to invest in a policy domain over a long period of time. That party will not necessarily lose its owned issue unless another party is perceived to be able to manage that issue better, or is expected to give the issue more investment or greater prioritisation. The pre-condition of party supply relates very closely to the condition of a change in constituency representation. Issue ownership change should only happen if another party comes to represent an otherwise 'neglected' constituency. This means that one explanation for ownership should not be that a party continually and consistently emphasises that issue and/or displays legislative and spending commitment to it. Rather, the gap opened up by a failure to nurture that reputation will be filled when there is another party to challenge or replace it. A party cannot gain an issue unless that party is able to offer a handling advantage, or able to offer a preferable policy position.

The implication of these arguments is that to avoid ownership loss to its competitor, a party should retain a commitment and investment in that issue, and a popular policy position, but only when there is potential competition on the issue. In the absence of competition over performance or position, a party might not cater to its issue reputations. In instances of greater party supply (for example, in multi-party systems) we might therefore expect ownership losses to become more frequent, or we might expect parties to be more committed to the issues they own; being more attentive to issues they might otherwise lose.

In summary, we expect that for ownership change to occur there should be a major – symbolic – performance and/or policy shift and for the issue to be salient to the public and/or in the political domain, drawing the attention of public opinion. We also expect that ownership occurs under conditions when another party is able to challenge or to become the issue owner: when there is party supply. Finally, in addition to a symbolic performance and/or policy shift, ownership change could occur when a party abandons a traditional constituency of supporters and another party represents it.

Our theory of ownership change is summarised in Figure 4.1.

When a substantial policy failure occurs, we also expect that issue to become salient, politically and electorally. A policy issue may also become salient and politically important *because* parties compete on an issue, or this may be why they compete on an issue. Furthermore, a large policy shift may reflect a change in constituency representation. While we separate these conditions above, we assume that they will also interact. However, it remains an empirical question whether – and to what degree – there is confluence of these factors, and whether they occur independently.

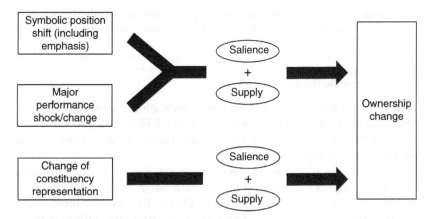

Figure 4.1 A theory of ownership change

Testing Our Theory

We use our US, UK, Australian and German data, which are sufficiently dense to allow for over-time variability and over-time within-country comparison of the relative ranking of issues for parties. Recall from Chapter 3, we calculate within-party issue ownership rankings using the average ratings of party issue handling within a given election cycle. This means that if there is a major shift in handling evaluations late in the cycle, it may not be fully observed until the subsequent time period (but it has to be substantial to be recorded either in the contemporaneous or later cycle). From all available survey data on the rank ordering of issue hand-ling in the previous chapter, we identify cases of within-party issue own-ership change. These are taken from the cases categorised as gains and losses in Tables 3.2 to 3.9 in Chapter 3.

As a re-cap of the selection of ownership losses and gains, in Chapter 3 we allocated all issues in the top-, middle- and bottom-third of a party's issues depending on how many issues the data cover overall in a given election cycle (i.e. in the data this ranges from one to 13 issues, though we focus on periods where there were at least four issues and usually more). We then identified gains, losses and realignments according to the following criteria:

An issue gain: an issue moves at least two places from the middle-third of a party's issues into the top-third, remaining there for at least two election cycles (where data are available).[3]

---

[3] We relax this criterion of lasting change in two scenarios. First, we report losses or gains in the final election cycle for which data is available. Second, we include cases where there are missing data for subsequent or intervening time periods if there is a large jump in the issue ranking.

An issue loss: an issue moves at least two places from the top-third of a party's issues into the middle- or bottom-third, remaining there for at least two election cycles.

An issue realignment: an issue moves from the top-third of a party's issues into the middle- or bottom-third and the issue moves for another party from the bottom- or middle-third into the top-third.

In order to have confidence in our classifications, we omitted earlier time periods in the United States, the United Kingdom and Germany where there are insufficient data to produce a convincing measure of issue strengths and weaknesses.

These criteria allow for certain phenomena. First, it is quite possible for a party to gain a reputation for strength on an issue and then lose it over the course of four election cycles. That is, by construction we may see an issue yo-yo in and out of a party's issue strengths, although these changes are far more substantial than between-election fluctuations in public opinion. Second, even after an issue realignment, a party's rating on an issue may eventually decline, but the realignment is observed in the fundamental reordering of the basis of political competition. We are not focused here on cases where a party's ratings on a middle-ranked issue decline further, or in cases where there is very slow, incremental change (e.g. from one rank position to another, and another, and so on).

It is not rare for issue ownership loss or gain to occur over two or three election cycles. Many of the cases we identify represent lasting changes within the period for which we have data. This is not to say they could not be reversed, only that we see no reversal by the end point of available data. It is also not the case that the majority of losses and gains represent shifts from middle to top issues, or top to middle issues. Our cases include major changes in public evaluations of parties: changes which should have an important bearing on the issues a party chooses to campaign upon in subsequent elections, and which should have significant consequences for party support.

Using these criteria we identify 37 changes in issue ownership in the periods covered by our data for the United States, the United Kingdom, Australia and Germany. To account for these cases, and to assess evidence against each of the explanatory factors summarised in Figure 4.1, we conduct an examination of available data and sources in the periods before and during the ownership change to identify which of the above theoretical explanations coincide with these cases.[4]

---

[4] We assess evidence during the period of ownership change because that change occurs across two election cycles in our data, and may therefore start in the first period of that

For data on issue salience, we use survey data on the 'most important problem' (MIP) or the 'most important issue' (MII) facing the country, drawn from the US and UK Policy Agendas Projects. We also review a series of official political accounts, documented in each case, to explore the political relevance of the particular issue in each period. Survey responses on the 'most important' issue, while useful, do not always capture the *importance* of a topic because they entail a forced choice between many important issues (Wlezien 2005). The economy, for example, could become 'the most important issue', but another issue (such as military interventions or immigration) could remain politically salient and important to the electorate but no longer appear to be the 'most' important issue.

For data on competence, we use indicators of policy outcomes (e.g. crime and immigration rates, days lost to labour disputes) and so on, and draw widely on academic and news accounts of the events taking place prior to and during each period.

Our data on party issue emphases and positional competition include data on issue emphasis in party platforms from the Manifesto Research on Political Representation (MARPOR) project, data on legislative policy agendas (such as from the Congressional Bills Project), data on executive speeches (such as the State of the Union Address in the United States and the Queen's Speech in the United Kingdom), and also official government statistics on public spending.

The criteria we apply for a change in constituency representation are the following: (a) the party's policy competition is concerned with capturing a new issue public that the party has not traditionally been supported by; (b) the party's policy competition is concerned with opposing an issue public the party has traditionally been associated with; and/or (c) there is a change – at the electoral level – in the alignment of an issue public with the party. By 'issue public' we mean a particular demographic associated with the party (e.g. race, social class), or a constituency defined by an issue (e.g. the environment).

For each of these explanatory factors, careful qualitative evaluations or judgment calls are involved in determining the presence and extent of each of our criteria. The data and evidence is provided alongside each case of issue ownership change.

We do not only select on the dependent variable of ownership change. The data allow us to examine periods in which there was *no* ownership change so that we can assess whether our explanatory variables are *absent* in those periods. To do this, we later take cases of no-ownership-change

cycle but be fully completed in the second period where mean issue-handling ratings are observed.

for a sample of issues, enabling us to determine whether the presence of particular conditions is associated with the occurrence or non-occurrence of changes in issue ownership.

Issue Ownership Change and Co-existing Factors

Our analysis of the contributing factors to ownership change involves the collation of a considerable amount of evidence, which is displayed for each country and party in the following tables. In Table 4.1(a) to (d) we provide an overview of all 37 cases of issue ownership change (gains, losses and realignments), by country, with evidence on each of the contributing factors summarised in turn. Table 4.1(a) presents the US cases, 4.1(b) the UK cases, 4.1(c) the Australian case and 4.1(d) the German cases.

Discussion of Ownership Change Cases

The evidence presented in the Tables 4.1(a) to (d) reveals that in every case of within-party issue ownership change we identify the pre-condition of public salience or of political salience, the presence of a symbolic performance shock or change, and the presence of a symbolic policy shift. We interpret a shift in the underlying electoral constituency represented by the party in only a small number of cases; for the environment in the United States (a Democrat gain under Clinton when the Democrats made gains, associated with having Al Gore on the ticket), and for the issue of foreign affairs in the United Kingdom, lost by the Conservative Party in a period where their electoral base fragmented strongly towards the UK Independence Party and other Eurosceptic alternatives.[5] These data suggest that changes in issue ownership mainly require public or

---

[5] The time frame of our analysis excludes the most famous case of realignment in constituency representation, the case of civil rights in the United States (see Carmines and Stimson 1989), where realignment on the issue led to the Democrats' loss of southern white voters and gains among northern liberals. In the data presented in Table 3.2, we see the Democrats first gain the issue of rights and minorities during the 1960–1964 election cycle, around the time of the passing of the Civil Rights Act. In May 1956, Gallup had asked which party 'can do the best job of handling segregation–that is, the relations between whites and negroes?' As it was currently framed, the parties were pretty level, with the Democrats holding a marginal 28 per cent to 26 per cent lead. By August 1964, after Johnson's signing of the historic civil rights legislation, a substantial gap had opened up on this question (with the reference to segregation dropped) 'Which political party . . . do you think will do the best job of handling relations between the whites and the Negroes?', and the Democrats now held a 50 per cent to 18 per cent lead. (Because of the sparseness of the data during this period, a change in the mix of survey items in the 1964–1968 cycle sees the Democrats briefly lose the issue, as both parties are rated lower on handling 'racial problems' (at a time of continued racial unrest) compared to evaluations based on 'relations' and 'seeing that everyone . . . have equal rights', as had been the focus of polls in the earlier period.)

Table 4.1(a) *Changes in issue ownership, US, 1976–2013*

Party	Issue	Time period	Type	Pre-conditions	Performance	Position	Constituency representation
Party experiencing a change in ownership (and government/opposition status)				*Symbolism of events/signals: high level of political/issue salience (i.e. political importance or public concern) and/or change in party supply (i.e. new entrant or reformed challenger).*	*Competence, relating to good or poor performance and policy outcomes. Performance shocks.*	*Emphasis, commitment (legislation, spending, symbolic rhetoric). Major ideological shifts in party policy and commitment.*	*Change in a party's constituency, disassociating itself from a particular group/public.*
Dem (Gov)	Rights & Minorities	1976–1980	Gain	Since height of political salience in mid-1960s under the Johnson administration, civil rights continued to be of major importance. (Increase in public salience of rights and minorities, MIP jumping to 11% in the third quarter of 1979 – coincides with ruling of Supreme Court in United Steelworkers of America v. Weber (June 27th), that the affirmative action plan in the case was lawful).	Carter administration secures passage of major civil service reform which includes equal opportunities and affirmative action provisions. Powers consolidated in the Equal Employment Opportunity Commission.	President Carter continues commitment of federal government to affirmative action (e.g. 1978 Civil Service Reform Act requires federal agendas to increase recruitment of under-represented groups). Substantial increase in attention of the Democratic Party to rights and equality in 1980 election platform. At the same election the Republican Party oppose government mandates on quotes for hiring of minorities.	Realignment of the US electorate: Democrat Party loses support among Southern Whites, gain African-Americans and liberals.

Table 4.1(a) (cont.)

Party	Issue	Time period	Type	Pre-conditions	Performance	Position	Constituency representation
Dem (Gov)	Health	1976–1980	Loss	Growing legislative attention to healthcare in the 1970s (in Congressional bills/statutes). Healthcare not a salient issue for the public in the 1970s, but became a priority for Jimmy Carter during 1976 Democratic nomination contest with Senator Edward Kennedy.	Carter pledged healthcare reforms in the 1976 campaign, but cooperation with Congress over health insurance legislation proved unsuccessful and proposals were eventually abandoned in 1980 due to budget constraints, as the economic situation worsened.	Increase in Democrat Party emphasis of 'welfare expansion' (including healthcare) in 1976 and 1980 party platforms. Carter pledge in presidential campaign in 1976 for comprehensive national health insurance program.	–
Dem (Opp)	Health	1988–1992	Gain	Sustained increase in salience of health. MIP rises to as high as 37% in the third quarter of 1989, and on average c.20% during the 1988–1992 period. Public concern with issue associated with the failed reform of Medicare.	Failure of the expansion of Medicare under the previous administration. From early 1990s, surge in healthcare spending due to rising costs (inflation measured by the medical price index exceeded the consumer price index).	President Reagan outlines proposals for the Medicare Catastrophic Coverage Act in the 1986 SOTU; passed by Congress in 1988, expands healthcare coverage but also increases monthly premiums and tax liability for the affluent. Proved to be unpopular, and is repealed by Congress in November 1989.	–
Dem (Gov)	Welfare & Housing	1992–1996	Loss	Welfare reform was a central plank of Clinton's election campaign in 1992 and of the Newt Gingrich Republican's 'Contract	Concern over long-term viability of social security. Pressure for reform. Increase in tax liability of social security benefits in	In 1992 presidential campaign, Bill Clinton pledges to 'end welfare as we know it'. Similar welfare reform agenda in Republican platform for 1994	–

Dem (Gov)	Environment	1992–1996	Gain	Environment of relatively low political salience typically but given greater prominence by the Clinton administration (in part reflecting influence of Vice President Gore). Not a very salient issue for public opinion, apart from in the second quarter of 1993, when MIP responses hit 11%.	Clinton appointments to key environmental positions in federal agencies (e.g. Bruce Babbitt as Secretary of the Interior and Carol Browner as Director of the Environmental Protection Agency), alongside Gore as Vice President. Series of accomplishments in this policy domain, such as setting new ozone standards and signing the Biodiversity Convention.	Democrats give greater emphasis to environmental issues in platforms from 1984 through 1992 – establishing lead on the issue. Clinton Administration takes a more pro-environmental position than its predecessors (increase in budget of the EPA). Clinton resisted Republican attempts to roll back environmental protections. In 1993, Clinton and Gore announce Climate Change Action Plan for voluntary reduction of emission of greenhouse gases by the US.
				with America' in the 1994 mid-term elections. Politically salient and also of concern for voters, with welfare/social security reaching around 10% in MIP responses at times.	1993 budget. Gingrich criticises President Clinton for delaying on welfare, having vetoed two Republican-sponsored bills on welfare reform. Following negotiation with Republican lawmakers, Clinton signs the 'Personal Responsibility and Work Opportunity Reconciliation Act of 1996' into law.	mid-terms. As a result of Republican control of Congress, Clinton under pressure to pass more conservative legislation (so a shift in position away from the Democrat preferred option).
						Provided partial representation of the environmental movement (inclusion of Al Gore on the ticket important in securing green voters).

Table 4.1(a) (cont.)

Party	Issue	Time period	Type	Pre-conditions	Performance	Position	Constituency representation
Dem (Opp)	Education	2004–2008	Gain	Education increasingly salient to the public from mid-1990s; reaches high of 11% in second quarter of 1999, peaks at 12% in first quarter of 2001.	Declining satisfaction among voters with quality of the education system and public schools (as shown in Gallup polling).	No Child Left Behind (NCLB) passed by President Bush in 2001. Initially proved popular with voters but support later faded. The Republicans increase emphasis of education in their 2004 election platform (though this is still at a lower level than the Democrats).	.
Rep (Opp)	Government	1976–1980	Gain	Trust in government a huge issue following Watergate scandal. Difficulties of Carter administration highly visible and politically significant. Of substantial importance to voters: MIP responses on the issue of government at times exceed 10% (reaches 13% in 1976 and 14% in 1977).	Carter set out to make government 'competent and compassionate' but was hit by economic/ energy crisis and Iran hostage crisis. Carter's 'Malaise' speech seen to have backfired (perceived as blaming the American people for the 'crisis of confidence'), and situation exacerbated by cabinet resignations.	Republican Platform in 1980 increases attention to cutting back the size of government (in particular cutbacks to social programs). Support for smaller government. Widening of positions on the role of government – between the Democrats and the Reagan Republicans.	
Rep (Opp)	Government	1992–1996	Loss	Government shutdown a highly salient political event (MIP on government reaches 9%). More widely public trust	Republican Party gains reputation for integrity/ ethics after house banking scandal and Congressional Post Office scandal. Steep	Group of freshmen Republicans in the House (the 'Gang of Seven'), on right of party, attack corruption scandals under Democratic leadership	–

				in government a significant issue since the 1970s, fuelled by scandals affecting both the presidency and Congress.	rise in Republican emphasis of party's fitness to govern (and lack of competence of opponents) in its 1992 platform (from 0% to 15%). Controls the House for first time 1954. Blamed for federal government shutdown in 1995/96 (WaPo/ABC). Party loses reputation for being able to manage government well.	of the House. Sets agenda for 'Republican Revolution' in 1994 mid-terms. Linked to new right agenda of reducing the size/power of government. Democrat and Republican parties adopt opposing positions on the government shutdown in 1995/96 (Republicans are blamed for not compromising).	–
Rep (Gov)	Economy	2000–2004	Loss	Economy is salient as usual, upward trend from 2000 to 2004, as economic situation deteriorates.	Rise in unemployment rate between 2001 and 2003, and decline in growth rate (GDP).	The 'Bush Tax Cuts' were a significant shift in federal policy, increasing tax relief to the wealthy, e.g. dividends (whereas Clinton had increased the tax rate for high-income individuals).	–
Rep (Gov)	Labour & Employment	2004–2008	Gain	Rise in MIP responses about labour and employment. Close to 12% in the second quarter of 2006. But decline in MIP responses on economy from 2003 until late 2007.	Unemployment declines from 2003–08 before financial crisis hits (Republicans have strong ratings on jobs during this period).	Republicans talk more about labour groups (positive) than Democrats in 2004 platform (and in 2008) for first time since 1976. President Bush gives slightly more attention to labour and employment in SOTU in 2004–2008 than 2000–2004 period.	–
Rep (Opp)	Economy	2008–2012	Gain	US sub-prime mortgage crisis and the global financial crisis predate	Economic stimulus package credited with ameliorating impact of global financial	The US economic stimulus (American Recovery and Reinvestment Act 2009)	–

Table 4.1(a) (*cont.*)

Party	Issue	Time period	Type	Pre-conditions	Performance	Position	Constituency representation
				Obama administration but political fallout dominates start of the presidency. Salience of the economy peaks once Obama is in office. Over 60% in 2009, and remains at around 50%.	crisis on the United States, but Obama administration criticised for continued rise in unemployment (high of 10.2% in October 2009); number of payroll jobs added only becomes positive in March 2010.	a Keynesian macroeconomic response to the economic crisis. Republican's take position favouring tax cuts and banking regulation. Clear differentiation between the parties in terms of policy.	
Rep (Opp)	Defence	2008–2012	Loss	Defence remains politically salient with ongoing military operations in Afghanistan and Iraq. Decline in proportion of MIP responses about defence after 2008 (for most of 2000s was >20%, falls to <10% under Obama).	Failure of US military campaigns in Iraq and Afghanistan under President Bush. Withdrawal of troops from Iraq completed in 2011 under President Obama. Ten years after 9/11, Osama Bin Laden is killed in Pakistan by US special forces in May 2011. Relative success of US defence policy under Obama compared to Bush years.	Republican Party emphasis of defence declines in its platform for the 2008 election, contrasted with increased Democrat attention to the issue. Clear differentiation of positions, with the Democrats supporting a programme for withdrawal from Iraq, and Republicans giving no timetable. Obama was not a Senator at time, so had not voted for military authorisation (unlike John Kerry the Democrat candidate in 2004. Republicans also divided on policy, between neoconservatives favouring interventionism and its libertarian wing who are opposed.	–

Rep (Opp)	Health	2012–2013	Gain	Highly politically salient and symbolic issue, central to the policy agenda of the Obama administration. Share of MIP responses about health jumps when Obamacare legislation is introduced in 2009.	Public approval of 2010 Affordable Care Act; gains 2010–12 but declines 2012–14 (see Pew Research). Initial problems with website. Between 2008 and 2013, percentage uninsured rises (starts to fall towards end of 2013). Obama struggles in securing Congressional support for bill, has to settle on compromise. Problems with Obamacare lead to questions about competence.	Intense opposition of Republican Party to Obamacare (multiple efforts in House to repeal/amend it). Congressional support for legislation is highly polarised. Large partisan gaps in public support for the Affordable Care Act, with Democrats tending to support and Republicans tending to oppose. Polarised attitudes on the government provision of healthcare (Pew Research).
Rep (Opp)	Foreign Affairs	2012–2013	Loss/ Realignment[+]	Foreign policy a major focus of party competition and news coverage, e.g. Arab Spring. The issue of foreign affairs of less salience to voters during the Obama presidency, compared to the Bush administration.	In part Republican loss of handling reputation partly due to no longer controlling the presidency. In 2012 presidential election campaign, the Democrats target weakness of Mitt Romney for his foreign policy inexperience and flip-flops (benefiting from performance successes such as the killing of Osama Bin Laden and the US withdrawal from Iraq).	Substantial increase in Democratic Party emphasis of (positive) internationalism in its 2008 platform, while the Republicans emphasise on *negative* internationalism. Cautious multilateralism of Obama increasingly diverges from Hawkish rhetoric of Republican party leaders (e.g. Romney emphasis of Russia as a geo-political threat).

Table 4.1(b) *Changes in issue ownership, UK, 1970–2015*

Party	Issue	Time period	Type	Pre-conditions	Performance	Position	Constituency representation
Con (Gov)	Economy	1970–1974	Loss	Economy highly salient (MIP remains >50%), with issue of unemployment increasingly important. Three-day week most politically important post-war economic 'event'.	Oil price crisis of 1973 and 'three-day week', added to industrial disputes over pay freezes and strike action; contributed to economic recession.	U-turns by Heath government on economic policy in 1971–2, bailing out failing industries, increasing public spending and resuming price controls.	–
Con (Opp)	Law & Order	1974–1979	Gain	Crime becomes salient issue to public (reaches a post-war high, at the time, of some 7% in October 1978). Increased political emphasis of problem of crime by parties, by Labour in government (Queen's Speech) and Conservatives in party manifestos.	Rising crime rates under incumbent Labour government (following post-war upward trend). Perceptions of disorder and lawlessness in 1970s, e.g. football hooliganism, 'mugging' and vandalism (see Hall et al. 1978).	Beginning of shift of the Conservatives away from post-war liberal consensus on crime and justice. (Change in policy only completed under Major government in the 1990s.) Thatcher talks tough on crime in opposition (including in final election broadcast of 1979 election).	–
Con (Opp)	Immigration	1974–1979	Gain	Moderately salient, averages 4% in MIP responses between 1976–1978, peaks at 10% in June 1976 *around time* of reading of Race Relations Bill; and 9% in February 1978, *just after* Thatcher statement in TV interview about fear of being 'swamped' by immigration.	Immigration relatively stable between 1974 and 1979 (net migration falls.) But rising immigration levels in 1960s and early 1970s.	Conservatives in opposition emphasise restrictive migration policy; infamous statement in TV interview by Thatcher (opposition leader) about people feeling 'swamped' by immigration. In longer-term, famous 'Rivers of Blood' speech by Enoch Powell in 1968 associates party with restrictive policy.	–
Con (Gov)	Welfare & Housing	1979–1983	Loss	Reforming agenda of Thatcher government on housing and welfare (e.g. sale of council	Rising spending on benefits (in real terms) due to high unemployment rates. Rise in number of low income	'Right to Buy' introduced under the 1980 Housing Act (council house sell off); Act also removed rights of private tenants. Benefits cuts	–

				housing) was controversial and politically salient.	families (increase in recipients of the Family Income Supplement). Fall in proportion of population in council housing.		('death by a thousand cuts' according to Paul Pierson, 1995).
Con (Gov)	Labour & Employment	1983–1987	Realignment	Symbolic defeat of the National Union of Mineworkers (NUM) by the Thatcher Government. MIP responses on strikes, labour relations, trade unions reach 32% in August 1984. Most politically significant issue in the period and major long-running news story.	Initial spike in numbers of working days lost to strikes (1984) but long-term reduction in industrial disputes. Conservatives demonstrate governing strength by pushing through planned pit closures.	Powers of unions restricted. Increase in attention in Conservative party platforms to trade unions (negative) in 1979 and 1983. Positional shift to confrontational stance on unions.	–
Con (Opp)	Labour & Employment	1997–2001	Loss	Strikes and unemployment of low political salience during this period. MIP responses on the issue of unemployment at lowest level since 1970s. But, introduction of minimum wage by Labour government in 1998 a popular, flagship policy.	Low level of industrial disputes and weakened power of the unions means the issue is no longer salient. Labour gain power and demonstrate relative competence handling the issue (i.e. industrial relations are managed well). Unemployment rate falls under the new Labour government. Minimum wage proves to be a success (does not lead to increases in unemployment as predicted by the CBI).	Conservatives do not campaign negatively on labour groups (i.e. unions) in 1997 (or thereafter). Issue neutralised by New Labour and its one member one vote reforms. Conservatives oppose popular national minimum wage policy.	–
Con (Opp)	Foreign Affairs	1997–2001	Loss	Foreign policy, and specifically Britain's relationship with Europe, remains a politically important issue in aftermath	Conservatives lose perceived strength on handling of EU, due to internal party divisions (particularly bad in the years	Sharp increase in negative emphasis of Europe in 1997 Conservative manifesto, plus a reduction in positive emphasis of the issue in	Precursor to later loss of Eurosceptics to UKIP (structural conditions in place well before 2014).

Table 4.1(b) (cont.)

Party	Issue	Time period	Type	Pre-conditions	Performance	Position	Constituency representation
				of signing of the 1992 Maastricht Treaty. Dominates internal debates within Conservative Party (even influencing leader selection). MIP/MII responses on Europe high during 1997–2001 level (MII averages 15% over four year period).	1992 to 1997). Possible loss of handling due to loss of office, and thereby control of foreign policy.	2001. Under William Hague, the Conservatives pursue a Eurosceptic agenda.	
Con (Opp)	Defence	2001–2005	Loss	Politically important issue in the post-9/11 era, due to global threat of Al-Qaeda and military operations in Afghanistan and Iraq. MII responses on defence/foreign affairs at very high level at points in 2001–2005 period.	Possible Conservative loss of handling reputation due to being out of office. Leading international role of Labour Prime Minister Tony Blair in response to 9/11 and the War on Terror, and UK involvement in operations in Afghanistan and Iraq.	Fall in defence spending under Conservative governments in 1990s. Reduced Conservative emphasis of defence in party platform in 2001 (and 1997) – contrast with increase in Labour (incumbent) emphasis. Blair Hawkish on War on Terror and War in Afghanistan and in Iraq. Conservatives support Iraq War under leader Michael Howard (unpopular position with the public).	–
Lab (Opp)	Education	1983–1987	Gain	Major legislation on education enacted (1986 Education (No. 2) Act) and large scale industrial action by teachers. Prime Minister Thatcher had previously been Secretary of State for Education (1970–1974).	In 1985–86, Conservative government hit by series of strikes by teachers over pay and proposals of performance-related pay (850,000 days lost to industrial action in education sector in 1985). Labour	Spending on education as a percentage of GDP continues downward trend that started in 1970s. Labour opposition emphasise education in 1983 manifesto (parties about level in 1979 and before). The 1979 Education Act passed by the	

					opposition criticises government over failure to resolve pay dispute.	Conservative government gave local education authorities rights over use of selection for secondary education, but proved unpopular locally.	—
Lab (Opp)	Labour & Employment	1983–1987	Loss	Symbolic struggle between unions and government (see above).	Labour leader Neil Kinnock critical of tactics of NUM leader Arthur Scargill (opposing picketing), but ineffective in criticising Thatcher government for its handling of the strike.	Labour gives higher levels of emphasis in pro-union content in election platform, gap widens in 1983 and 1987 manifestos. Party divided on handling of miners' strike (and handling of 'Militant' groups within Labour).	—
Lab (Gov)	Morality	1997–2001	Gain	Preceding period dominated by 'Tory sleaze' stories; a major political story in the earlier period. Some constituencies in 1997 election fought on 'anti-sleaze'.	In regards to lobbying, Blair argues that Labour government should be 'purer than pure' and 'not have any truck with anything that is improper in any shape of form at all'. Makes character/trustworthiness a key performance issue. Contrasted against ill-discipline of Conservative Party as opposition. (Does suffer one or two scandals, such as Bernie Ecclestone affair, but is largely unscathed during first term.)	Party attacks 'sleaze' of its predecessor during 1992–97 period (aided by a number of scandals involving MPs and ministers). Blair promotes importance of family values in first Labour conference as Prime Minister in 1997. Wider use of 'moral talk' by Blair as opposition leader and in government.	—
Lab (Gov)	Economy	1997–2001	Gain	Follows the ERM crisis in the previous election cycle, a major economic shock/event which damaged the Conservative incumbent. Symbolic first act of newly	Period of sustained economic growth. First-time Labour government presides over economic prosperity. Stick to initial spending plans (but	Labour Party moves to centre, rejecting Clause 4 and support for public/national ownership. Pledges to stick to spending plans of its Conservative predecessor for first two years of office.	—

Table 4.1(b) *(cont.)*

Party	Issue	Time period	Type	Pre-conditions	Performance	Position	Constituency representation
				elected Labour government is to grant Bank of England independence over monetary policy.	starts to increase spending on public services).		
Lab (Opp)	Economy	2010–2015	Loss	Global financial crisis in 2008, considered the most significant economic crisis since the 1930s. Public concern (MIP) about the economy grows throughout 2008, peaking in May 2010. Salience of the economy continues for several years.	Follows global financial crisis and subsequent economic downturn under Labour government in the previous cycle. Shift in performance ratings earlier, but becomes clearer in later time period. Memo from former Chief Secretary to the Treasury to his successor, 'Sorry, there's no money left' symbolically damaging. Labour accept some blame for the level of UK debt. Conservatives apportion blame to their predecessor.	Labour position in opposition is rejection of claims of over-spending. Divergence of parties on fiscal policy, in contrast to consensus up until 2007/8. (But main differentiation between parties is over performance.)	–

Table 4.1(c) *Change in issue ownership, Australia, 1987–2013*

Party	Issue	Time period	Type	Pre-conditions	Performance	Position	Constituency representation
ALP (Opp)	Health	2004–2007	Loss	Highly politically salient; major issue of the period given polarisation of competition. Around 80% of voters rate health and Medicare as 'very important' issue (Newspoll) over the 2004–07 period. Only education at a similar level of salience.	Liberal/National government of John Howard delivers increases in real spending on health (between 1996 and 2007). Performance in managing Medicare (despite privatisation of some elements) undercuts potential ALP opposition criticism of Liberals (loses performance advantage on a traditional issue strength).	In previous election cycle, ALP had campaigned against privatisation of Medicare (e.g. leader Mark Latham campaigned on GP rebates and 'bulk-billing'). Under Kevin Rudd, in 2007, the ALP reverses its opposition to Medicare 'safety net' (previously it had argued it was inequitable, favouring the well-off), moving policy to the right (described as a 'backflip' by opponents).	–

Table 4.1 (d) *Changes in issue ownership, Germany, 1972–2013*

Party	Issue	Time period	Type	Pre-conditions	Performance	Position	Constituency representation
CDU (Opp)	Economy	1980–1983	Gain	Economy considered the 'most important domestic problem' by around 65% of Germans (Anderson 1995).	SPD/FDP coalition in government (October 1980 to September 1982), presided over rising unemployment – from 3.6% to 7.2% (FDP then pulled out to form coalition with CDU/CSU).	CDU/CSU (and FDP) proposed monetarist policy as an alternative to expansionary Keynesian economics of the SPD and its Chancellor Helmut Schmidt. Substantial increase in CDU emphasis of 'economic orthodoxy' in 1983 manifesto (sizeable gap with SPD).	–
CDU (Gov)	Foreign Affairs	1990–1994	Gain	Wider context of major and defining political salience of German reunification. Foreign affairs moderately salient issue (German Election Study, GESIS Data Archive).	Initial success in the negotiation of reunification and integration of new Germany into NATO.	Substantial emphasis of internationalism and EU in CDU platform in 1990 (similar to 1987), far exceeding attention of SPD to the issue. CDU Chancellor Helmut Kohl plays a key role in signing the Maastricht Treaty in 1992.	–
CDU (Gov)	Defence	1994–1998	Gain	Moderately politically salient. In 1994 the federal Constitutional Court rules that German armed forces can participate in multilateral peace-keeping or crisis management operations.	Participation of German armed forces in UN-led peace-keeping operations in Somalia and Bosnia and Herzegovina. Handling of transition to multilateral (peace-keeping) interventionism of Germany's defence policy.	Party emphasis of the importance of external security and defence even in 1990; CDU/CSU give greater emphasis in 1994 (and more in 1998). In contrast, negative references to the military or use of military power are absent in the CDU platform in 1994.	–

CDU (Opp)	Labour & Employment	1998–2002	Gain	Extremely politically salient. Unemployment was the major issue of the 1998 federal election campaign; Gerhard Schröder (SPD) attacks incumbent Helmut Kohl (CDU) as 'the unemployment chancellor'. MIP responses on unemployment in the Forschungsgruppe Wahlen: Politbarometer series reach 73% in August 2001 and 85% in September 2002.	Unemployment levels fall slightly between 1997 and 2001, but start to rise in 2001/02, ahead of the next election. The SPD's plan for reducing unemployment 'Alliance for Jobs' unsuccessful.	Gerhard Schröder (SPD) makes a high-profile campaign pledge about reducing unemployment in 1998. Between 1998 and 2002, SPD/Green coalition reverses some of the labour market reforms introduced under the previous CDU government of Helmut Kohl (e.g. strengthening employment protections for employees in small firms). The parties adopt distinct positions on labour market reform during this period (CDU offering a more market-liberalising position compared to the SPD).
SPD (Gov)	Economy	1980–1983	Loss	(See case for CDU above.)		
SPD (Opp)	Environment	1987–1990	Gain	Environment salient in the 1987 election following the Chernobyl disaster (Greens won 8.7% of vote). Greens emerge as new electoral competitor.	Greens not seen as viable coalition partners during the federal election campaign (Pulzer 1987). SDP gain as potential 'handler' of environmental issues on back of Green-SDP coalitions at Länder (state) level.	SPD increased emphasis of environment at 1983 election, and in 1990 gave more attention to issue in its platform than the Green Party.
SPD (Opp)	Foreign Affairs	1990–1994	Loss	(See case for CDU above.)		
SPD (Opp)	Welfare and housing	1990–1994	Gain	Welfare state of major political and economic importance. Political salience increases due pressures on system due to reunification (and efforts of Kohl government	Reunification in 1990 increases the financial exposure of existing welfare state of West Germany, but does not bring corresponding growth in	Parties traditionally have taken distinct positions on welfare in general. Ahead of reunification and 1990 federal election, the CDU Government of Helmut

Table 4.1(d) (*cont.*)

Party	Issue	Time period	Type	Pre-conditions	Performance	Position	Constituency representation
				to reform some aspects of the system in 1989 prior to reunification).	receipts – increasing structural shortfall of the system.	Kohl seeks to introduce pension reforms in 1989 (taking effect in 1992) which link pension adjustments to net rather than gross wages and increase the retirement age. Legislation is passed with support of SPD opposition, who move to a more centrist policy position, accepting the need for support.	
SPD (Gov)	Environment	1998–2002	Loss	Just at time the Greens enter coalition, the environment had declined in public salience compared with the 1980s and early 1990s (Politbarometer, 1986–2000). Coalition situation changes the credit-blame context for the governing SPD.	In 1999, the SPD/Green coalition introduces the first stage of an 'eco-tax'. Rising fuel prices in 2000 prompt mass public protest. No reversal of policy, but adopts measures to compensate certain groups (i.e. commuters, low-income households).	SPD enter coalition with the Greens in 1998. Emphasis on environmental issues in SPD manifesto for federal elections in 1998 drops precipitously from 1994 (and falls further in 2002). SPD takes pro-environmental stance on nuclear energy, renewable energies and eco-taxation. In 2000, following mass protests, all-party support for eco-taxes breaks down and CDU oppose (calling for reversal of the policy).	–

political salience, symbolic performance changes and/or policy shifts. Only rarely do they require or co-exist with major changes in electoral constituencies.[6]

The data shown in Table 4.1(a) to (d) do not show any meaningful variation in contributing factors by country. Much more stability is observed in ownership in Australia, and quite considerable fluctuation in Germany, but the underlying conditions are similarly present in all cases, notwithstanding the lack of data points from which we can generalise in Australia.

At first glance, one might conclude that a combination of performance and policy shifts is required for a change in ownership to occur, but a number of nuances should be noted. The first is that we cannot disaggregate causation between each of the factors. The coarseness of our data, observed over an entire election cycle, means that we are unable to cleanly disentangle the order of events.

In some examples, we see policy shifts preceding performance shocks. The UK Conservative government under Edward Heath (1970–1974) attempted a number of policy initiatives to support failing industries and price controls prior to its performance difficulties of industrial action, the 'three-day week' and the oil price crisis in 1973. The US Democrats shifted to a more pro-environmental policy position before Bill Clinton made various inroads and accomplishments in appointments and environmental policy in office. The German CDU/CSU shifted their foreign affairs platform prior to the successful negotiation of reunified Germany's membership of NATO and the 1992 Maastricht Treaty.

In other cases, we see performance shocks preceding policy shifts. The Conservatives take a more authoritarian approach to law and order in the face of rising crime rates under the incumbent Labour government between 1974 and 1979. The US Democrats gain health in 1988–1992 following the aborted attempt to expand Medicare under the Republican administration and policy shifts by the Republicans. In Germany, the Chernobyl disaster in 1987, problems of acid rain in Europe and failed attempts of Green/SPD coalitions at state level (Hesse and Hamburg) precede a major environmental emphasis by the SPD on the environment, building on a smaller increase in emphasis beforehand.

The second point to note is that the association between a performance change and a policy change is often so close as to make differences between them very blurred. Indeed, drawing a simple distinction between

---

[6] It is possible that each ownership change *causes* an alternation in the basis of a party's support, a subject we cannot test in this book due to the lack of availability of panel data alongside the required survey items.

these concepts is as ill-advised as drawing a clear and unchanging distinction between position and valence issues. There is a positional and a valence aspect to issues which combine with high salience – and the supply of a viable party competitor – to lead to a change in issue ownership.

One way a positional aspect and a valence aspect interrelate is in the weighting of these dimensions in public opinion, and in the meaning of issue ownership. It is not necessary that there is always an equal weighting of a competence and policy component to ownership. In the UK case of labour and employment we see the Labour Party lose the issue during a period of industrial disputes and the very high salience miners' strikes, and the Conservatives gain the issue. Arguably, this arose because the Labour Party were the party that represented the trade unions and the working class, and were seen as having a preferable position vis-a-vis worker's rights and representation of this constituency. The Conservatives were able to gain the issue when *dealing* with the strikes and the confrontational tactics of the National Union of Mineworkers and dealing with unprofitable industries became most central to the evaluation of political parties on the issue.

Ownership could also change due to a change in the public's preferred position on an issue. Imagine two parties occupy stable positions at either end of a dimension of public opinion, but the majority public opinion moves from the left, which previously benefited one party, to the right, now benefitting the other. A performance shock might provide the conditions for such a repositioning of public opinion to occur. We know that as governments reduce (increase) spending in particular policy domains, the public tend to adjust their preference in favour of more (less) spending (Wlezien 1996; Soroka and Wlezien 2010). There may be a performance aspect to this change; the public may evaluate a policy as not working. In the US case of healthcare, gained by the Republicans in the most recent election cycle (drawing on data from 2012 and 2013), we note the initial negative public reaction to Obamacare and its implementation as a possible factor. Similarly on healthcare, the Australian Labor Party, while in opposition, lost its traditional strength on the issue, arguably due to the Howard government delivering increases in health spending between 1996 and 2007. Parties can lose issues in opposition because governing parties are able to neutralise them.

The pre-condition of public and/or political salience is met in every case, but it is worth noting that some of these are moderately salient and some are intensely salient. For example, when there is a change of ownership on the economy, the events and the issue's salience tend to be central to that period (unsurprisingly, given that voters typically consider that the economy is the 'most important issue'). We can think of the UK Conservatives' loss of the economy around the time of the oil price crisis and three-day week in 1973 and their later gain following the global financial crisis in 2008. We can also think of the US Republicans' loss of the economy in the early 2000s, and subsequently their regaining of the issue during the economic recession that followed the global financial crisis, and the gain of the economy for the CDU/CSU in Germany in 1980–1983, and later for 'labour and employment' in 1998–2002, both at times of rising concern over unemployment. Examples can be found for non-economic issues as well, such as healthcare in Australia during the 2000s. In other instances, an issue was important but not the main concern of the public during the period. This is the case for the UK Labour Party's gain of education between 1983 and 1987, the Democratic Party's gain of the environment between 1992 and 1996, and healthcare in the late 2000s in the United States, where we see a Republican gain. What seems to be decisive is not necessarily the proportion of the public who list an issue as being the 'most important' (in surveys), but the chances the parties' policy offerings and performance in office are noticed and recognised by the public; i.e. the political significance of the issue.

The pre-condition of supply is less easily evaluated, since in this respect we mean only that another party should provide sufficient competition for an issue owner to lose their issue, or for the rival party to gain the issue. In some instances, we see a party simply lose an issue apparently because another party is able to perform well, or offer a preferable policy position, but the new party does not come to own the issue. For example, the Republicans lose their owned issue of defence when President Obama takes office and successfully withdraws troops from Iraq as well as presiding over the killing of Osama bin Laden, but the Democrats do not become the issue owners of defence. We suggest that this erosion of ownership for the Republicans started prior to Obama's term of office, with the failure of US military operations in Iraq and Afghanistan under President George W. Bush. The same set of factors are present for the UK Conservative Party, whose association with defence gradually weakened since the heyday of the Thatcher government (and its role in the Falklands conflict and the end of the Cold War), but who only lost the issues of defence and foreign affairs after Tony Blair took office several years later. Despite major disinvestments in military spending before these new governments take office, the issues are lost only when a new incumbent is more effective and 'committed' (i.e. there are military interventions), whilst neither the Democrats nor the UK Labour Party become the issue owners. The UK Conservative Party's loss of foreign affairs (including the issue of Europe) is coupled with the emergence of a new supply party: the UK Independence Party (UKIP). This follows years of deteriorating Conservative ratings on foreign affairs – beset by party divisions over the EU since the 1990s – but the Conservatives retain ownership of the issue until the Referendum Party and later UKIP emerge as a threat (though the latter only become a major electoral force a decade later). On other issues, we see a switch in the issue owner, such as the two cases where we see a realignment; civil rights in the United States (prior to our period of analysis), and labour and employment in the United Kingdom, where in both cases competition over which party will deal with the issue better – and represent the issue public (in the case of the United States) provides the supply necessary for the issue owner to change.

Finally, the data in Table 4.1(a) to (d) reveal the importance of incumbency for changes in issue ownership. Parties appear to lose and gain issues in office and in opposition, but it is often the actions of a government and the event of the alternation of a party from power into opposition which forms an integral part of the explanation for the loss or gain of issue ownership. For example, we note how the economy is won or lost by the actions of the incumbent in office, and how oppositions gain (or lose) issues because of the performance and the policy decisions of governments. Some of these changes occur with high-profile symbolic policy statements and interventions by oppositions. The UK Conservative Party captures the issue of immigration in the late 1970s following rising public anxiety about immigration from the New Commonwealth under the Labour government. The US Republicans gain 'government' between 1976 and 1980 during the various troubles of the Carter administration and the Republican platform on reducing the size of government. However, many cases appear to occur simply due to performance of the incumbent, or indeed the party in control of the legislature – if the two are not the same. The UK Labour Party gain education between 1983 and 1987; the Republicans lose 'government' while not holding the White House between 1992 and 1996 after being blamed for the federal government shutdown; the Democrats gain education between 2004 and 2008 amid declining satisfaction with the education and public school system; and the CDU/CSU gain the economy off the back of the performance of the SPD coalition between 1980 and 1983, foreign affairs between 1990 and 1994 in office, then defence between 1994 and 1998 in office. Some changes occur after a period in office. The UK Conservative Party loses many of its issues after 1997, after leaving office, such as labour and employment, foreign affairs and defence. It is not simply sufficient to perform well or badly in office; a new incumbent does not always capitalise on performance success by gaining an issue (although an opposition may lose an issue), nor does a party in opposition always gain an issue because an incumbent performs badly, but these dynamics form a very important part of the explanation for the issue ownership losses and gains.

In summary, this evidence supports our explanation for issue ownership change. We see the confluence of highly significant political issues with both performance factors and positional factors, and the presence of a viable party supply.

Selecting on When Ownership Change Does Not Occur

In order to be more confident in our explanation of issue ownership change, we need to consider whether the explanatory factors we find support for while analysing cases of ownership change are also *absent* when issue ownership change does *not* occur. That is to say, we should not select only on the dependent variable of issue ownership change. The final empirical section of this chapter therefore focuses on cases for which we see no change in ownership.

We again examined the data presented in Chapter 3 and isolated a range of different issues – so that we do not also select on a single issue domain – across the four countries for which we could identify cases where ownership changed for neither of the parties in our dataset. The issues we identified were defence (1976–2008) and law and order (1976–2012) in the United States, environment (1983–2010) and health (1970–2012) in the United Kingdom, the economy (1987–2015) and immigration (1987–2013) in Australia, and welfare and housing in Germany (1990–2013). The seven issues in our sample comprise a total of 58 separate election cycles.

These cases differ from each other in important ways. Defence remains a Republican strength and a Democrat weakness between 1976 and 2008, but not beforehand or afterwards. Law and order is owned by neither party in the United States in any time period (for which we have data), but the Democrats are lower ranked on the issue throughout. In the United Kingdom, neither major party is rated positively on the environment; it is a low-ranking issue for both the Conservative and Labour parties in the available time periods. Health, on the other hand, remains a top-rated issue in our data for Labour, and bottom and later middle rated for the Conservatives. The Australian cases are more polarised; the Liberals are consistently rated positively and the Labor party is consistently rated negatively on both the economy and immigration. We have more volatility in ownership in Germany, but one issue topic – welfare and housing –

exhibits stability in ownership for the SPD, though only from the 1990–1994 cycle onwards (becoming a middle or bottom issue for the CDU). These differences alone highlight how ownership should not be considered a stable feature of political systems, except in a small number of issues and countries (health for the UK Labour Party, and economy and immigration for the Australian Liberal Party), and we should also not assume that one party's owned issue is a liability for another.

As with our analysis above, we present the cases in Table 4.2 alongside the evidence for our explanatory factors.

Discussion of No-Ownership-Change Cases

In terms of drawing causal inferences from Table 4.1(a) to (d) and Table 4.2, the first observation is that it is not the clear presence or absence of any one factor that appears to be what matters. We have cases of no ownership change where there is no clear performance change and cases where there is a significant performance change (in one or more election cycles), and cases where the parties' positions change (where there is new supply of a preferred policy position) and cases where they do not. In all cases, the issue is salient for at least part of the extended period of time, suggesting that issue salience is not a sufficient condition for issue ownership change to occur.

The second observation that can be drawn from Table 4.2 is that none of these cases of no-change exhibit the simultaneous combination of the three factors identified in our theory of ownership change (i.e. a symbolic performance shock associated with salience and supply, a symbolic policy shift associated with salience and supply or a constituency change associated with salience and supply). Nor is it the case that a performance shock *and* a policy change occur jointly in any of these cases, combined with political or public salience. This suggests that these factors must simultaneously be present for an ownership change to occur; causation is contingent on a combination of necessary conditions.

We cannot disentangle whether a performance shock plus salience and party supply is a sufficient condition, or whether a performance shock (and salience and supply) need to be combined with a symbolic policy change for a sufficient explanation of ownership change, but it seems plausible that either factor (performance or policy) is sufficient, with symbolic performance and policy shifts often running together, perhaps making an ownership gain or loss more substantial or long-lasting. In most of the election cycles comprising the cases in Table 4.2, there is no symbolic performance change or shock, and no symbolic policy shift, and no pre-condition of party supply. This gives us confidence that each

Table 4.2 *Cases of no change in issue ownership*

Country	Party	Issue	Time period (N of cycles)	Pre-conditions	Performance	Position	Constituency representation
UK	Con/Lab	Environment	1983–2010 (7)	*Present = not mainly* After emergence of the issue of the environment in the 1980s it is typically is of low political salience, with infrequent increases in legislative and public attention due to events or crises (e.g. ministerial conference on the Ozone layer in June 1990).	*Present = no* Few significant variations in policy performance on the environment across governments (i.e. moderate achievements in party handling of environmental issues but few major successes or failures for either party). No major performance 'shocks'.	*Present = no change* Relative positions/distance of the parties on the environment remains stable, with both parties increasing attention to the environment in their election platforms over time; and Labour slightly more pro-environmental but the Conservatives still adopting pro-environmental policies to reflect shifting public preferences.	*Present = no* No changes in party representation of social constituency. Environmentalists already tend to be associated with the Green Party, which means that ownership of the environment for the two major parties sees no change.
UK	Con/Lab	Health	1970–2012 (10)	*Present = yes* Healthcare and the NHS are of moderate to high political salience during the post-war period – receiving substantial (if intermittent) levels of attention from parties in and out of government. Public concern about the NHS varies (mean of 6% for MIP), periodically reaching high levels during the late 1980s, 1990s and early 2000s (up to 42% in 1988 and 46% in 2000).	*Present = yes, but reinforcing* NHS generally supported by both parties in government but experiences greater improvement under Labour governments and more symbolic deteriorations (waiting lists, funding shortfalls) under Conservative governments. No major sudden performance shocks (individual hospital failures not attributable to national governments).	*Present = no (stable)* Stable party positions on the NHS, with Labour associated with expansion of healthcare (e.g. coverage, spending) and Conservatives associated with reduction (e.g. privatisation). Public spending on health in real terms tends to rise under Labour governments and fall under Conservative governments; but Conservative party emphasises commitment to NHS throughout.	*Present = no* Stable representation of party constituencies in relation to health (e.g. Labour tends to represent, and be supported by, public sector workers).

Table 4.2 (cont.)

Country	Party	Issue	Time period (N of cycles)	Pre-conditions	Performance	Position	Constituency representation
US	Rep/Dem	Defence	1976–2008 (8)	*Present = yes* The Cold War is one of the key issues of US politics throughout the 1970s and 1980s. Political salience of defence declines after the end of the Cold War, but is revived in 2001 after the Al-Qaeda attacks on the US (MIP responses average 9% during the 1976 to 2008 period.)	*Present = yes, but reinforcing* Mixture of policy successes and failures (e.g. Reagan credited with contribution to end of Cold War, success of Gulf War under George H. Bush). No critical performance cases attributed to particular administration or party (e.g. failures of intelligence in lead-up to 9/11 not blamed on George W. Bush or to his predecessors).	*Present = no (stable)* Republicans consistently more hawkish on defence (e.g. pro-military emphasis in most party election platforms) than the Democrats. Bipartisan consensus around initial US response to 9/11, but parties later resume distinct positions on Iraq conflict.	*Present = no (stable)* Association of Republicans as party of the US military (party of Eisenhower, Reagan) is stable.
US	Rep/Dem	Law & Order	1976–2012 (9)	*Present = yes, but sporadically* Crime of some political salience throughout the period (figured in 1988 presidential election); and of more substantial public concern (MIP responses about crime average 9%).	*Present = no* Trend of rising crime rates up until the mid-1990s, but no major performance crises or incidents. Attributions of good and bad performance tend to focus on state/city outcomes (e.g. urban riots, success of policing tactics in NYC), rather than at federal-level.	*Present = no (stable)* Parties mainly retain distinct positions on law and order, with Republicans taking a more punitive approach (using 'tough on crime' rhetoric) and Democrats giving more emphasis to social causes of crime. Clinton seeks to neutralise issue with rhetoric, but the parties do not switch position (i.e. the Democrats adopt more punitive rhetoric aimed at depoliticising the issue).	*Present = no*

Aus	Lib/ALP	Economy	1987–2013 (9)	*Present = yes*	*Present = yes, but sporadic and reinforcing*	*Present = no (stable)*	*Present = no*
				Economy of high political salience, both as a focus of party competition and public opinion (frequently rating above 40% in MIP responses); especially in relation to interest rates, unemployment and the cost of living/inflation.	Delayed effects of the 1987 worldwide stock market crash on the Australian economy are felt in recession of early 1990s (hits in July 1990), with rises in unemployment continuing until 1992. This economic shock takes place under the ALP government of Bob Hawke, so only reinforces perception of handling competence of the Liberal Party (in opposition at the time). Australia enjoys a sustained period of economic growth between 1991 and 2013, but unemployment rises in 2009 following the global financial crisis (again coinciding with an ALP government).	Period of relative policy stability and consensus between the parties. Under Hawke/Keating in the 1980s, the ALP shift to a position supporting economic liberalisation. Few major ideological differences (or changes) in economic policies of the Liberals and the ALP over the 1987 to 2013 period.	

Aus	Lib/ALP	Immigration	1987–2013 (9)	*Present = yes*	*Present = yes, but sporadic*	*Present = no*	*Present = no*
				Immigration and asylum a recurring point of political concern. Issue prominent in election campaigns (e.g. 2001) and government (e.g. 'Pacific Solution' of the Howard government);	Mixture of policy outcomes during this period (under both Liberal and ALP governments). There is an upward trend in applications for asylum for much of the period (1992–2000 and 2005– onwards), but fall in between	Policy position of the Liberal Party on immigration is consistently to the right (i.e. more restrictive) than ALP (though ALP introduced mandatory detention in 1992 under Paul Keating). Takes a hard line stance on boat people and offshore processing	

Table 4.2 (cont.)

Country	Party	Issue	Time period (N of cycles)	Pre-conditions	Performance	Position	Constituency representation
				also of public salience at times.	2000 and 2005 under Howard. The numbers of boat arrivals were at low levels in late 1980s, first rising (temporarily) in 1994 and then reaching higher levels in 1999–2001 and 2008–2013. Overall, deterrent policy is considered to have been effective (but controversial in terms of human rights).	of asylum applicants. At times during this period the ALP has sought to neutralise the Liberals on the issue but typically has been reactive and weaker in its position. Party supply: One Nation party gained considerable support at the 1998 (8%) federal election, but this fell in 2001 (4%) and 2004 (1%).	
Ger	SDP/CDU	Welfare & Housing	1990–2013 (6)	*Present = yes* Welfare state of major political and economic importance, in West Germany and in unified Germany. Public social expenditure makes up a large proportion of total government outlays.	*Present = no* Reunification in 1990 imposed strain on the German Welfare state, with increased obligations but without equivalent growth in receipts (added to pressure of long-term demographic trends). Limited successes in policy reforms, but often unpopular with the public. Long-term pressures but no major performance shocks.	*Present = no (stable)* Relative stability in differentiated policy positions of parties. SPD tend to support welfare state expansion, overseeing growth in social expenditure in office (1969–1982) with greater emphasis in its election platforms, though later move to support reforms under Schroder (1998–2005). The CDU tend to pursue more conservative welfare state policies (e.g. unpopular reforms pursued by the Kohl government in 1997, cutting pensions, faced with rising fiscal pressure on the welfare state).	*Present = no* Growth in welfare state clienteles (recipients of pensions, disability, social assistance and unemployment benefits) between 1960s and 1980s (see Pierson 2001). Reinforces existing party constituency of SPD.

of these factors is important and necessary in accounting for the issue ownership changes we identified in Table 4.1.

The cases of no-ownership-change vary, as detailed above: in some (law and order in the United States and the environment in the United Kingdom) neither major party consistently has a clear lead. In others (defence in the United States, health in the United Kingdom, immigration and the economy in Australia) the issues are consistently best or very highly rated for one party with the other being at a consistent disadvantage. Welfare and housing in Germany is consistently a top-rated issue for the SPD and a mid-ranked issue for the CDU/CSU.

Having analysed the evidence in Table 4.2, we can offer two reflections about the factors which may be important in interpreting these cases.

It is plausible that the two cases for which we see neither party own the issue during the period may arise because there were no *symbolic* changes in performance or position (or constituency representation) and neither party offers the supply necessary for ownership change to occur. In each case there is stability in distinctive party policy positions and the issue becomes relatively salient for periods of time. In the United States, changes in performance are not clearly attributable to parties at the federal level. The focus of policing (and responsibility for policing) at state and city level may account for the lack of ownership in the United States by either party, such that neither major national party offers a performance 'supply' (in contrast to law and order in the United Kingdom, where we see an ownership gain for the Conservatives in 1974–1979). In the United Kingdom, there is little substantial change, especially contrasted with the Democrats under the Clinton administration between 1992 and 1996, which is one of the cases of ownership change listed in Table 4.1. If there is a supply argument for the environment in the United States, it is the Green movement's positional supply for ecological concerns among that particular issue public, and no major performance shock or supply of competence. These cases appear to give some support to our argument that performance and position has to be symbolic for ownership change to occur, and for there to be a party supply explanation for issue ownership change, or the presence of issue ownership. This is particularly true since the pre-condition of salience is present in each. The issues were important to the public, and yet in neither case did the parties manage to gain ownership of an important public and political issue.

Some of our no-change cases relate to consistent ownership of an issue for one party, and a consistently low ranking of the issue for the major party rival (defence in the United States, healthcare in the United Kingdom, immigration and the economy in Australia). In these cases, on the basis of the evidence in Table 4.2, we suggest that this constant ownership may arise from stable symbolic differences in performance and policy commitment to the issues, which means that there is no 'supply' present for ownership to change. Note that the issue of defence *does* change in the United States in a later period (after 2008), and so we are not arguing that these are immutable issues for the respective parties. It is possible for ownership to change, even on these issues (though arguably more difficult in Australia). For the US parties, the issue of defence remains an issue for which Republican incumbents are credited during and following the Cold War, and policy differences remain stable. There are no military interventions under the Democrat Clinton administration (when the Democrats could arguably offer a 'supply' of performance, and position), but when those occur, under Obama, ownership by the Republicans is lost. In the United Kingdom, our theory would predict that Labour would retain the NHS unless the Conservatives (or another party) provided the supply – in terms of performance or position – to make it possible for Labour to lose the issue. This does not happen. In real terms, the Conservatives invest less when they are in power and preside over performance deteriorations, and Labour invests more when they are in government. Labour's relative ranking may be buoyed up by this investment and commitment and the continuing policy differences between the parties, but we suggest that it is the failure of rival party supply on this issue that means ownership remains stable. In Australia, it is the performance of the two parties that appears to offer the explanation on the economy. The Australian economy experienced a severe recession under the ALP government of Bob Hawke in the early 1990s, and a period of high unemployment in its aftermath, whereas John Howard's Liberal government (from 1996 to 2007) coincided with an extended period of economic growth.[7] In contrast, the clearer explanation for the continued ownership of immigration for the Liberal Party appears to arise because of the lack of positional supply by the ALP, which is consistently more liberal on migration and refugee issues (with public opinion consistently restrictive throughout). At times, the ALP has sought to neutralise the issue, taking a tougher stance, but has been unable to match the Liberal's positional advantage. Support for Pauline Hanson's One Nation party at the 1998 federal election (and to a lesser extent at the 2001 election) led the Howard government to stress its restrictive credentials on boat arrivals and asylum processing. Again, it

---

[7] During the mid- to late 1980s high levels of inflation contributed to declining real wages, which preceded the Australian economy falling into recession in late 1990 (measured by two consecutive quarters of negative growth), with unemployment rising to above 10 per cent for an extended period (lasting up until mid-1994).

is the lack of supply that appears to explain the ongoing ownership of this issue, and again particularly in light of the high salience in periods for each of the issues. The opportunity for an ownership change might have existed had the parties been able and/or willing to successfully compete on these issues. A similar explanation appears to be in place for welfare and housing in Germany, which is consistently owned by the SPD in this period.

Overall, the comparison of cases of no-change – where we do not select on the dependent variable of change – supports our theoretical argument. While each of the cases exhibits high public and/or political salience for some if not all of the relevant periods, the lack of a symbolic performance change (in terms of the party associated with good or bad performance) and the lack of a symbolic policy shift coincide with the absence of a change in issue ownership. Perhaps the very presence of salience and stability in performance associations with parties, and policy positions, meant that these owned issues were more strongly held for each of these parties. A more systematic and deeper analysis of every single election cycle for which there is no change (which would entail many more null cases in terms of the contributing factors) may result in even clearer inferences. But it is reassuring that the evidence here runs in the expected direction and does not cause us to reject our explanations for the cases of ownership change.

Conclusion

This chapter has analysed the factors present when parties gain or lose ownership of issues. It has developed theoretically and empirically based explanations of why parties gained and lost issues over five decades in the US, UK, Australian and German politics, across a total of 37 cases of a change in issue ownership. For within-party ownership change to occur, we specify that the change should be observed across two or more election cycles, and represent a shift in ranking of issues in public opinion of two rankings or more. That is to say, ownership change must be a substantial change in reputation. The explanations we offer for these changes are the first to be applied across a range of cases, across time and across countries.

Our findings suggest that parties lose or gain reputations on issues when symbolic performance changes and/or policy shifts occur, which are salient in politics and/or salient among the public, and when another party is able to offer a preferable performance and/or position on the issue. These suggest that ownership change should be viewed from the perspective of conjunctive causation, when political opportunities arise (such as competence shocks making issues salient, or competence shocks occurring on salient issues) which political actors are then able to capitalise upon via policy competition, if there is party supply for this competition to take place. Only in a handful of cases do we find that a different electoral constituency is represented. When this does occur, a realignment in issue ownership tends to be witnessed. We also analysed seven cases where we observed no changes in ownership (across a total of 58 separate election cycles), which gave further support to our theory of issue ownership change. We cannot clearly infer whether either a symbolic performance shock or a symbolic policy shift is sufficient alone (with the pre-conditions of salience and supply). Our analyses suggest that it is the combination of the explanatory factors that is particularly powerful in accounting for instances of issue ownership gains or losses.

It remains possible that performance shocks tend to lead to policy shifts, and a performance shock is sufficient on its own to cause an ownership shift. Untangling this causation would only be possible if we were able to zoom in on a series of individual cases, perhaps observing changes at a monthly, or even weekly, level. However, more convincing to us is that the confluence of these factors is sufficient. Also, the greater their combined magnitude, the more significant the change in ownership: perhaps more deeply rooted in public opinion and resistant to subsequent change. All of these questions remain open for future research.

The data we provide in this chapter (and elsewhere in this volume) make it possible to distinguish between losses and gains (and realignments) in party reputations on issues and more subtle and diffuse neutralising of strengths and weaknesses. We note above that we do not focus on more moderate changes in issue strengths, or in the degree of a party's strength on an issue that may co-exist with a stable relative ranking. Those changes of degree may also be important. Goodwin and Milazzo (2015) show for the United Kingdom, for example, that while the Conservative Party remains the 'best party' on immigration over time, that strength has declined in magnitude, concurrent with an increase in the handling ratings for 'others'.

We could apply our theory in a deeper and more expansive way; selecting on the independent variables of performance shocks and policy shifts, rather than focusing on the dependent variable of the presence or absence of issue ownership change. We could also submit all of these data to alternative methods of analysis, for example using fuzzy set qualitative comparative analysis, enabling us to disaggregate explanatory factors, such as large and small policy shifts, high and more moderate issue salience, and so on. All of these steps are, however, made possible by the illumination of cases of ownership change via a long-term focus on public opinion and a conceptual distinction between the relative issue strengths and weaknesses of parties.

The implications of the findings in this chapter are important for understanding major changes in party issue strengths, and how party fortunes correspond to them. We are not aware of any other work which systematically evaluates the factors present when parties gain or lose their relative strengths on issues, either over time or across countries. Simply highlighting these cases is important for understanding the frequency and significance of changes in issue ownership. Understanding their likely causes provides insights for understanding public opinion, party competition and elections.

The first is that major performance 'events' will likely have long-term consequences in public opinion. These consequences will shape the issues that parties campaign upon in elections and the support a party receives via different issues which are consequential for electoral choice. Changes in issue ownership, caused by symbolic performance and/or policy shifts, will provide the campaign and election context for the factors shaping vote choices in subsequent elections.

The second implication is that parties need to nurture their issues over time, particularly if and when another party can perform well or position itself advantageously to cause competition over issue ownership. Issue ownership does not mean that parties can take 'their' issues for granted. This might be a fruitful area for the analysis of party priorities and strategies.

The third implication is the need to better understand the characteristics of party reputations on different policy issues. We have focused here on the rankings of party issue strengths as a measure of issue ownership. This allows a party to lose ownership of an issue, relative to other issues, and to gain new ownership of issues. These variations in party reputations on different policy issues might have important implications for political outcomes: for campaigns, voting behaviour, legislative priorities and others. They may also prompt us to refine our notion and perhaps our measures of issue ownership. For example, one new definition of issue ownership might be an issue that the issue owner can become worse rated on, but an opponent is never positively rated on. An alternative definition might be an issue that is never one of a party's worse-ranked issues. Or it could be an issue that a party tends to regain any loss of its positive rating for handling quickly, exhibiting a greater *tendency* to be a party's best issue relative to the ratings of an opponent. These definitions of issue ownership would each be difficult to measure without taking an over-time approach, and for the most part, even with seven decades of data, limiting scope for comparisons between them. What we can say, with confidence, is that the concept of issue ownership is a contested concept and therefore its measurement is contested. By analysing reputations over time, their alternation and behaviour, we gain greater insights into party reputations on issues, and issue ownership, than was possible before. The changes in within-party issue ownership in this chapter provide a wealth of important future opportunities for understanding how parties symbolically compete over time for ownership of issues, and how major unintended or unexpected performance events and changes can shape subsequent competition and election outcomes.

5 Government Performance and Oppositions

This chapter assesses how the public updates their evaluations of the issue handling of governing parties in response to policy performance. It explores our second concept – performance – following the short-term and more volatile aspect of public opinion referred to previously in studies of issue ownership. We know little about performance evaluations, how they vary and with what characteristics, with one exception: the economy. Understanding public opinion on a wider range of issues offers an important contribution. In addition, the argument by Petrocik discussed earlier in this book – that issue ratings respond to the performance of incumbents – has not been widely tested. It remains an open question whether opposition parties' ratings also respond to performance information in systematic ways. Petrocik assumes that one party's reputational loss is another party's reputational gain. This makes sense if ownership is a *zero-sum* asset; the issue owner's rating declines such that the rival party in turn gains a temporary lead over another party. But it also assumes that public opinion data exhibit symmetric alternations in performance ratings for incumbent and opposition parties alike, an assumption that – to the best of our knowledge – has not been tested. This chapter analyses the degree to which mass publics respond to government performance across a range of policy domains and how they make performance attributions about governing and opposition parties.

The chapter reveals, in a number of ways, asymmetry in the attribution for responsibility of incumbents versus oppositions. Public opinion updating about party issue handling across issues happens more for parties in power than it does for parties in opposition, although oppositions gain some credit for perceived governing party failures on policy issues. For the most part, our analyses show that publics assign responsibility to the party-in-government and are, in general, unlikely to trust an opposition party more on an issue as a result of a government failure in terms of policy performance.

We also show in this chapter, however, that asymmetric performance updating only sometimes results in asymmetric reward and punishment *voting.* Opposition parties frequently benefit at the ballot box from performance deteriorations under a rival party in government. The implications are important for understanding the dynamics of public opinion about performance and their electoral consequences. They suggest that performance models of vote choice should be broadened beyond economic voting alone, and applied to incumbent and opposition parties.

Governments and Oppositions

The economic voting literature assumes that economic credit or blame is laid at the door of the incumbent. There are electoral implications of economic conditions and perceptions for the party of the prime minister or president (e.g. Goodhart and Bhansali 1970; Norpoth 1987; Sanders et al. 1987; Lewis-Beck 1990; MacKuen et al. 1992; Powell and Whitten 1993; Lewis-Beck and Paldam 2000; Nadeau and Lewis-Beck 2001; Duch and Stevenson 2006; Bélanger and Gélineau 2010; Bélanger and Nadeau 2015). In most studies of economic voting, voters are believed to hold the incumbent responsible for perceived or actual improvements or deteriorations in the economy, broadly conceived at a national level or as changes to an individual's economic circumstances.

What does it mean for a voter to hold only an incumbent party responsible for a deterioration or improvement in economic conditions? Perhaps public opinion about the incumbent responds to a downturn or upturn in economic conditions, whereas a party in opposition gains no improvement or deterioration in their trust on the economy. It may alternatively be the case that opposition parties gain a reputation for better economic competence when governments lose a positive reputation for handling the economy, or even that previous incumbents (now parties in opposition) retain some blame for current performance-related conditions. Petrocik's (1996) notion of a 'performance lease' seems to make the assumption that a party in opposition may simply be better trusted on an issue because the party-in-power has lost trust on the same issue. Hence the notion that oppositions do not win elections, but governments lose them. We should therefore find symmetric dynamics in public opinion about performance and competence for parties in and out of power, if this is the nature of public opinion about performance.[1] We make five arguments to counter this expectation.

A rational public will update its evaluations on the basis of more reliable information following its experience of life under a governing party,

---

[1] This might be offset by a greater propensity of the public to punish rather than to reward (see Soroka 2014).

relative to less information on the expected performance of a challenger. Governing parties provide more information signals for updating of public opinion, whereas voters have less information about the potential performance of a challenger. There are strong asymmetries in the information voters have about the current and salient performance of incumbents (Fiorina 1977, 1981; Butt 2006; Green and Jennings 2012a) which should lead, simply, to less performance updating for oppositions than for incumbents.

There are several compelling pieces of research in the economic voting literature which point to the view that public evaluations of performance only relate to the party responsible: the incumbent. Electorates can distinguish between incumbents who have greater national domestic responsibility and governments whose economies are driven by globalised forces (Hellwig 2001; Hellwig and Samuels 2007). In cross-national analyses, Duch and Stevenson (2010) found that voters distinguish between economic shocks which are the result of incumbent competency or the result of exogenous shocks to the economy. Kayser and Peress (2012) revealed that electorates evaluate their domestic economy against expectations derived from the economic growth of neighbouring countries. This arises not from voter sophistication but from the benchmarking of economic evaluations in national media. At the individual level, the ability to identify parties forming the government is an important moderator of economic attribution (Duch and Stevenson 2013). These findings followed the seminal study by Powell and Whitten (1993), showing that economic voting is greater where signals for responsibility (across government type) are stronger. All serve to signify how credit and blame – and the attribution of responsibility – follow a rational, systematic pattern. Governments are judged on the basis of their responsibility or otherwise – broadly conceived – for economic outcomes.

A third argument can be briefly made following the above discussion of responsibility attribution in economic voting. The implication of work by Hellwig (2001), Hellwig and Samuels (2007), Duch and Stevenson (2010), and Kayser and Peress (2012) might simply be that performance updating – such that it occurs for incumbents – will only occur on issues where voters believe domestic government is responsible. This suggests two caveats to Petrocik's assumption. The first is that performance updating will only occur among citizens who can correctly identify the responsibility of an incumbent for a given policy outcome. The second is that performance updating should only occur on those issues for which domestic policy making and responsibility can be attributed to the government. Some policy issues might be ones where voters expect no party or government to be able to handle an issue well, or at all. Heath et al. (2001), for example, made the argument that attitudes on crime were not associated with British vote choices because voters thought no party could reduce the level of crime. Other policy issues might be the result of decisions made globally or exogenously to domestic policy, especially as globalisation has gathered pace. It is possible that governments are held accountable for terrorist incidents and their consequences (some research suggests that governments may even be held accountable for weather and natural disasters (see Gasper and Reeves 2011; Brechtel and Hainmueller 2011)), but it is equally possible that blame is attributed elsewhere.

Fourth, there is a possibility of symmetric performance updating, but in the opposite direction to that argued by Petrocik. On some occasions, rational voters may blame the opposition for performance outcomes, and/or they may blame both parties in equal measure. This would work in the opposite direction to Petrocik's notion of performance lease, since rather than gaining from performance failures, parties out of power may be blamed for them under new, recently elected incumbents. At the outset of a period of governing, a new incumbent party may not be held responsible for any given policy condition: voters may correctly assign responsibility to the previous party of government. This argument is advanced in greater detail in Chapter 6. It may even be the case that voters assign responsibility to a party of opposition (which has previously governed) long after a new government is in place. Fiorina (1977, 1981) suggested that the evaluation for a challenger is based upon retrospective evaluations of the opposition. Duch and Stevenson (2008) argued that (negative) economic voting can occur for oppositions too if they had some role in policy making, meaning that deterioration in conditions can impact on their vote, and economic voting is not always short term, or 'myopic'. We can imagine rival partisans of the incumbent party claiming their party is responsible for an improvement in a given policy condition (it was their party that made the decisive policy decision, change or investment in the past), or supporters of the government being more likely to hold the previous governing party responsible for deteriorations in a policy condition. As Hobolt and Tilley (2011) revealed, partisanship strongly conditions attributions of responsibility, indeed more so than it conditions evaluations of performance. Furthermore, as Duch and Stevenson (2013) argued, the economic vote is motivated by a coherent attempt to punish or reward parties that deserve it: that is, the party mostly responsible for choosing the policies that were implemented. This may be the outgoing party, rather than the party currently in office.

A final reason we might see symmetrical credit and blame would arise from a form of low information rationality (Popkin 1991), whereby citizens learn from the performance of a government that an issue cannot be handled well by any party, irrespective of responsibility for governing. A decline in trust for one party may simply result in a decline in trust for all parties on the issue. Some issues may become widely understood as intractable 'wicked' policy problems that no government can possibly solve (see Rittel and Webber 1973). The general sense of anti-mainstream politics we witness in many advanced industrialised democracies suggests that electorates increasingly distrust various parties of government to deliver on issues they most care about. These explanations for symmetrical performance updating (for incumbent and opposition parties alike) may therefore overlap with growing public disillusionment with politics and the belief that no party has the best policies or can be trusted to handle an issue.[2]

All together, we expect that public opinion updating about performance should be largely asymmetric but not completely so. The public will update its ratings of a government without conferring an advantage or a 'performance lease' to a party in opposition, and there is less likelihood of assessments of oppositions being the mirror image of government competence (Butt 2006; Green and Jennings 2012a). Hence, one of the important and distinct contributions of our concept of performance (as distinct from issue ownership) is that it is much more closely related to assessments of governing parties than it is to parties out of power. However, we also recognise limitations to the extent to which there will always be asymmetric performance updating for governments: either because performance updating will not be equally strong across all issues, because oppositions may be blamed for performance failures or because rational voters use information about the performance of one party to update handling evaluations of other parties.

Evidence of Asymmetric Performance Updating

We can assess whether public opinion moves in a way consistent with an incumbent performance-updating model by analysing the correspondence between public opinion about issue competence of governing parties and oppositions with exogenous indicators of policy performance on issues. We use objective data on policy outcomes so that any relation-

---

[2] Note that they further challenge the notion that ownership should be measured as which party is 'best'; since if public trust on issue declines for two or more parties, that decline is an important feature of public opinion that we should recognise and understand.

ship observed between policy outcomes and evaluations of party competence can be assumed to be causal. That is, it cannot be due to endogeneity in survey responses to questions about party handling.

Objective performance data are publicly available on policy outcomes through data such as the crime rate in a country, the homicide rate, the rate at which net immigration is increasing or decreasing, the number of strikes in a given year, the number of casualties of war and national performance on health outcomes, such as healthcare costs or the length of hospital waiting times. We compiled a series of measures of policy outcomes for the United States, United Kingdom and Germany stretching back to the 1940s. We focus on these countries because we have sufficiently long time series of available data on issue handling (as described in Chapter 3) and objective performance. We use economic data in our analyses too.

Table 5.1 *Measures of policy outcomes in the US, the UK and Germany*[3]

	Performance measure		
Evaluation	US	UK	Germany
Law & Order	Homicide rate	Crime rate	–
Economy	GDP	GDP	GDP
	Unemployment	Unemployment	Unemployment
	Inflation	Inflation	Inflation
	Misery Index	Misery Index	Misery Index
Defence/Foreign Affairs	Military Casualties	Armed Forces Deaths	–
Health	Healthcare Costs (CPI)	National Health Service Waiting Lists	–
Immigration	Immigration	Immigration	–
Labour & Employment	–	Days lost to strikes	–

Table 5.1 presents details of the annual time series data we compiled as indicators of objective conditions for the crime, economy, defence/foreign affairs, healthcare, immigration and labour, and employment policy domains. Compiling consistent and reliable measures of policy outcomes over an extended period is difficult, and for this reason our analysis is focused on these six policy domains.

[3] Source: For the United States: homicide rate is from FBI Uniform Crime Reporting statistics (1960–2009), GDP (percent change based on chained 2009 dollars) from Bureau of Economic Analysis (1948–2012), unemployment rate (LNU04000000) from US Department of Labor, Bureau of Labor Statistics (1944–2013), inflation (CPI-U) from US Department of Labor, Bureau of Labor Statistics (1945–1992), misery index is sum of the

If we find evidence of a relationship between objective performance measures and subjective evaluations of party issue handling, this is likely to be indicative of a stronger underlying relationship of competence with a broader set of indicators. None of these indicators should be expected to encapsulate *all* the information that may be relevant to a citizen's evaluations of a party or government on each issue. Measures of objective performance typically refer to a specific, incomplete aspect of policy. Ideally, we would have indicators that relate to the condition of the *whole* policy domain (Bevan and Hood 2006). The national crime rate will be a useful piece of information for judging a government's handling of crime, but citizens will also draw on local and personal experience, on the reputation of the police, whether news reporting exaggerates or understates the extent to which crime is a problem, and so on. The number of military casualties will be just one indicator of the success of a government's military action, while defence spending, negotiations with other countries (consider Barack Obama's Cuban foreign policy, Angela Merkel's role within the European Union), terrorist incidents, the rise of Islamic State and ongoing national crises will also contribute to assessments of handling of defence and foreign affairs. However, the above measures are helpful. They will not be contaminated by leadership evaluations or partisanship, or by subjective economic evaluations. Policy performance on one issue will not be associated with performance on another (unlike public opinion data where we expect common variance). We tested this assumption for our exogenous data by taking the mean of all policy outcomes (standardised within a governing cycle) and

unemployment and inflation rate (1943–2013), military casualties from Department of Defense Personnel and Procurement, *DoD Personnel and Military Casualty Statistics* (1981–2010), healthcare costs (CPI, CUSR0000SAM2) from US Department of Labor, Bureau of Labor Statistics (1983–2013), legal immigration from Department of Homeland Security, *Office of Immigration Statistics, Yearbook of Immigration* (1995–2012).

For the United Kingdom: total crime rate from Home Office, *Recorded Crime Statistics 1898–2005/06* and *Statistical Bulletin: Crime in England and Wales 2010/11* (HOSB: 10/11) (1977–2009), GDP (percent change based on chained 2009 pounds sterling, IHYP) from Office for National Statistics (1957–2012), unemployment rate (UNGBRM) from *Global Financial Database* (1977–2011), inflation (CPI, CPGBRM) from *Global Financial Database* (1953–2000), misery index is sum of the unemployment and inflation rate (1957–2011), armed forces deaths from Ministry of Defence, *UK Armed Forces Operational deaths post World War II* (1970–2009), inpatient total waiting list from Department of Health, Knowledge & Intelligence, *Statistical Information* (various) (1964–2009), total immigration from B.R. Mitchell, *British Historical Statistics* and Annual Abstract of Statistics (1964–2009), days lost to strikes (LABD01) from Office for National Statistics, *Labour market statistics* (1956–2000).

For Germany: GDP (percent change) from Federal Statistical Office, *National Accounts* (1961–2013), unemployment rate from Federal Statistical Office, *Registered Unemployed, Unemployment rate* (1976–2013), inflation (CPI) from www.inflation.eu (1961–2013), misery index is sum of the unemployment and inflation rate (1961–2013).

estimating whether there was an upward or downward trend over the course of a period in government. We found no evidence of governments increasingly improving on a set of policy issues in terms of objective indicators, or of government performance deteriorating in common over time, assumptions that might be consistent with ideas of public management improvement. We can therefore differentiate unique issue-shifts from the concept of generalised competence – whereby citizens use information about performance on one policy area to assess a party's handling on others. It also tells us that the broad shifts in performance evaluations reported in Chapter 6 are a characteristic of public opinion rather than a response to a characteristic of governing, and the quality of government.

We use the above objective measures of policy outcomes to assess the relationship between government performance and subjective evalua-tions of issue competence for parties in and out of power.

To avoid problems arising due to sparse data, the following scatter plots combine all available objective measures of performance (on the y-axis) and all subjective measures on the corresponding issues (on the x-axis).[4] These represent the mean or percentage level of the corresponding policy outcome measure in a given year and the mean issue-handling rating of a party in the same year. Values are standardised by governing cycle so they indicate whether or not a handling rating or policy outcome is higher or lower than the mean over the period of government in question, with the difference divided by the standard deviation of the variable.[5] We code the incumbent as the party of the president in the United States, the party-in-government in the United Kingdom (where there are no formal coalitions during the period covered by our data) and the party holding the chancellorship in Germany.[6] The scatter plots presented in Figure 5.1(a) and (b) show the relationship between these measures in the United States.

Figure 5.1(a) and (b) reveals a statistically significant association between objective performance and subjective evaluations for governing

---

[4] The relationships described here are similar, though slightly weaker, when economic issues are removed for the United States and United Kingdom (there are insufficient data on non-economic issues to test this in Germany); for governing parties the (positive) slope is steeper than the (negative/flat) slope for opposition parties. This confirms that our findings are not sensitive to the inclusion or exclusion of a particular issue or are simply the product of economic evaluations.

[5] This avoids the possibility of long-term trends in policy outcomes driving the results, or of changes in the level of handling outside the defined time period being associated with changes in policy outcomes within it.

[6] During the CDU/CSU-SDP grand coalition between 2005 and 2009 the CDU is coded as the incumbent, since Angela Merkel was Chancellor.

(a)

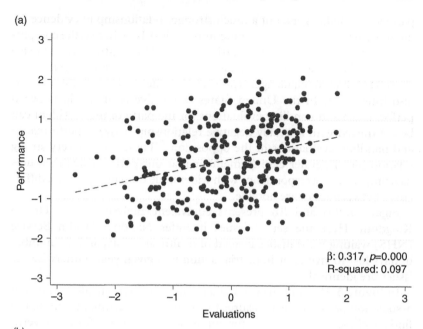

β: 0.317, p=0.000
R-squared: 0.097

(b)

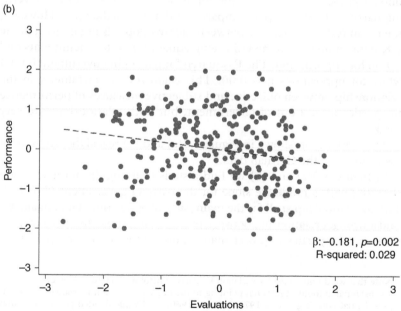

β: −0.181, p=0.002
R-squared: 0.029

Figure 5.1 Performance evaluations and policy outcomes, US,
1940–2013
    (a) Incumbent
    (b) Challengers

parties and challengers, but a much stronger relationship in evidence for incumbents. The R-squared for incumbents is 0.10, whereas the comparable R-squared for opposition parties is 0.03. These differences can also be seen in the slopes of the respective lines, being steeper for governments (β=0.316) than for challengers (β=−0.184). The direction of the slopes is also interesting. In the United States, a positive relationship between performance and handling evaluations for the party of the president can be contrasted with a weakly negative relationship between performance and handling evaluations of the opposition.[7] These are not very strong relationships in either case (remember that our performance measures have imperfect correspondence with wider issue domains), but the differences between them are notable.

Figure 5.2(a) and (b) presents equivalent analysis for the United Kingdom. Here the set of issues includes National Health Service (NHS) waiting list statistics instead of healthcare costs, and the number of days lost to strikes or industrial action in a given year. Otherwise the issues are identical.

In Figure 5.2(a) and (b) we find a positive and statistically significant association between the measures for parties in government, but do not find a significant relationship for oppositions. The slope for the governing party is clearly steeper compared to that for challengers. However, the magnitude of difference between the two slopes is not as great in the UK data compared to the US (being equal to 0.20 for incumbents and −0.06 for oppositions). The R-squared for parties in government is 0.04 while for oppositions it is 0.00. This again reveals asymmetry in the relationship between objective and subjective measures of performance for parties in and out of government, but both relationships are very weak.

The scatter plots shown in Figure 5.3(a) and (b) reveal the strengths of association for the German data.

In Figure 5.3(a) and (b) we find a statistically significant association (p<0.05) with a moderate slope for the party of government (β=0.180) and no relationship at all for the main party of opposition. Once again, we find a stronger relationship between objective and subjective performance measures for parties in power than we do for the parties in opposition.

---

[7] Note that we do not consider variation by party control of Congress. However, there is a substantial amount of research pointing to the impact of economic evaluations on the presidential vote (e.g. Tufte 1978; Erikson 1989), and while divided government may weaken attributions of responsibility in the US system, we expect that the party of the president will primarily be held responsible for good or bad performance – especially in the policy domains of the economy, law and order, defence and foreign affairs, labour and employment, and health, all of which are dominated by the executive.

(a)

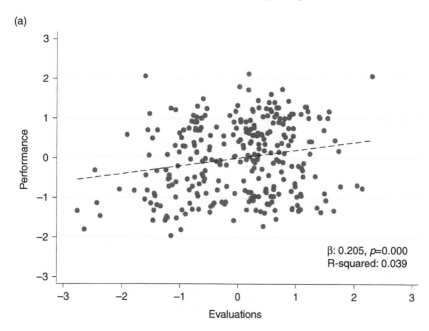

β: 0.205, *p*=0.000
R-squared: 0.039

(b)

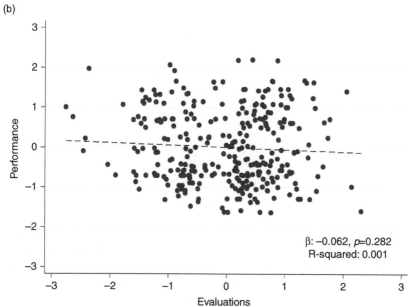

β: −0.062, *p*=0.282
R-squared: 0.001

Figure 5.2 Performance evaluations and policy outcomes, UK,
1952–2012
    (a) Incumbent
    (b) Challengers

(a)

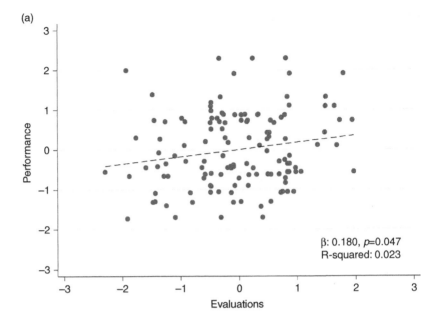

(b)

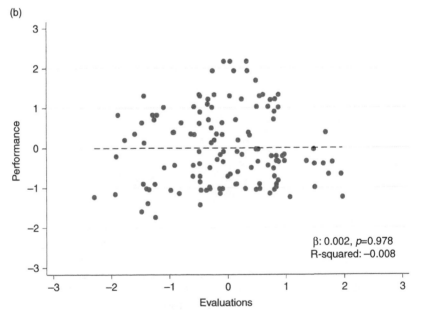

Figure 5.3 Performance evaluations and policy outcomes, Germany, 1961–2013
    (a) Incumbent
    (b) Challengers

The incumbent slope is weaker still for incumbents in Germany compared to the United States and United Kingdom. In Germany, coalition government results in shared policy responsibility, or weaker 'clarity of responsibility' (Powell and Whitten 1993). The weaker results may also arise from the sparser data (the set of issues is narrower than the United States or United Kingdom), but it is nevertheless a potential explanation deserving further exploration.

Jointly, the above analyses support two conclusions. First, there is a significant relationship between government policy performance and the subjective evaluations of governing parties, at an aggregate level. Given the availability of data, and the imperfect relationship assumed between available objective measures and subjective evaluations of handling, we suggest that the above relationships represent a very conservative test of the likely correspondence between performance and perceptions. Second, the relationships are significantly weaker or indeed absent when citizens evaluate the performance of parties that are not primarily responsible for governing. That there is some relationship suggests that with more data the relationship could be stronger, but we expect governing party ratings to be updated significantly more strongly than opposition party ratings in response to exogenous changes in policy outcomes. There is some evidence of symmetry in the US case, where a positive relationship for the incumbent contrasts with a negative relationship for the challenger. Nevertheless, the positive relationship is always stronger for the incumbent.

Further Evidence of Asymmetry

There are a number of difficulties in using objective performance data, not least the coarseness of our measures. Another problem is that publics are not necessarily aware of government performance on detailed policy outcomes, and/or they may only be aware when there are particularly strong deteriorations in policy. In this section we focus on one issue widely expected to be noticed by mass publics: the economy. This also enables us to draw out implications for the economic voting literature, discussed earlier. We expect that incumbent party economic handling measures will correspond more closely to economic evaluations and data than will opposition party economic handling measures. The economy provides an ideal way of testing the effects of (a) objective economic indicators and (b) subjective economic indicators. It is the only policy issue for which monthly over-time data is available on objective (the inflation and unemployment rate) and subjective policy outcomes (consumer confidence and economic perceptions).[8] Our analysis focuses first on the United States using aggregate-level data available for the period from 1990 to 2013, during which there were three alternations of the party controlling the White House.

We model changes in public evaluations of governing and opposition party handling (ΔHANDLING$_t$) of the economy as a function of changes in objective conditions, ΔMISERY$_t$ (that is, the 'misery index', which is the combined sum of the inflation rate and the unemployment rate) and changes in subjective economic evaluations, ΔICS$_t$ (consumer sentiment), with controls for the change of presidential administration (dummy variables indicating the election of Bill Clinton, George W. Bush and Barack Obama, respectively).[9] We first test the separate effect of objective and subjective conditions, and then include both variables in the full model. The time series regression model in first differences takes the form:

$$\Delta\text{HANDLING}_t = \alpha_0 + \beta_1 \Delta\text{MISERY}_t + \beta_2 \Delta\text{ICS}_t + \beta_3 \Delta\text{ADMIN}_{t-k} + \varepsilon_t$$

The coefficients for subjective and objective economic performance from our fully specified model are plotted in Figure 5.4 (estimates for all models are reported in the Appendix, Table A5.1). Here the variables are standardised[10] and the misery index is inverted so that positive values indicate better economic conditions. In the figure, the coefficient is indicated by a diamond, while the whiskers indicate the standard errors of the coefficients to show where the effects are statistically significant (where the error bars do not intersect the zero line), at the 95 per cent confidence level.

These results reveal a positive and significant relationship between consumer sentiment and the economic handling ratings of the incumbent party (the party of the president), but – interestingly – no similar effect for the misery index.[11] There is a striking absence of a statistically significant effect of consumer sentiment or the misery index on evaluations of the economic competence of the party that does not hold the White House. Handling evaluations for the incumbent party correspond to changes in subjective economic conditions, but this is not the case for parties in opposition. These models do not account for the potential that the

---

[8] Data on the consumer price index (series CUUR0000SA0) and unemployment rate (series LNS14000000) are from the US Bureau of Labor Statistics. The measure of consumer confidence is the Michigan/Reuters Index of Consumer Sentiment (ICS).

[9] The monthly measure of subjective evaluations of party economic handling is created using Stimson's (1991) dyad ratios algorithm, based on 673 survey items relating to party handling/performance in our US dataset.

[10] Calculated as the raw value minus the mean, divided by the standard deviation.

[11] Any effect of the misery index does not appear to be subsumed in consumer confidence; it makes no difference if both are added at the same time, or alone.

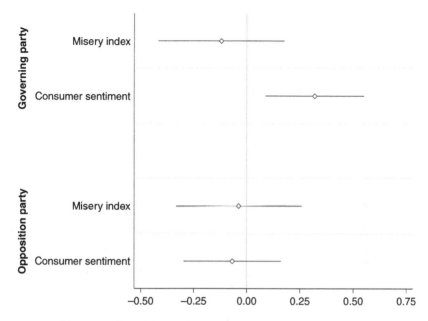

Figure 5.4 Subjective and objective economic performance and party handling, governing and opposition parties, US, 1990–2013

party in 'opposition' may control the legislature during periods of divided government. However, on the issue of the economy we expect the party of the president to primarily be held responsible. Our asymmetric results suggest that this is indeed the case.

The results in Figure 5.4 show that as consumers become more optimistic about the economy and their circumstances, the performance of the president's party on the issue is evaluated more positively. Our use of the measure of subjective economic evaluations leads us to refrain from inferring that any relationship between these series is causal: it could (plausibly) run in the other direction, from party economic evaluations to consumer confidence.

This asymmetry is further evident in the equivalent models for the United Kingdom using data available between 2003 and 2015. Here we use aggregate data on evaluations of party handling of the economy from YouGov and the CMS. We use objective (inflation and unemployment rates) and subjective (personal economic expectations) measures of the economy.[12]

---

[12] Data on both the consumer price index (series D7G7) and unemployment rate (series MGSX) are from the Office for National Statistics. The measure of subjective economic

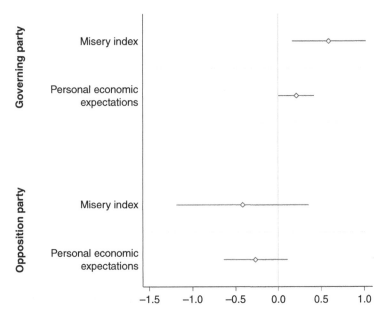

Figure 5.5 Subjective and objective economic performance and party handling, governing and opposition parties, UK, 2003–2015

We model changes in evaluations of governing and opposition party handling (ΔHANDLING$_t$) of the economy as a function of changes in objective conditions, ΔMISERY$_t$, and changes in subjective evaluations, ΔPEXP$_t$ (personal economic expectations), controlling for the change of government in 2010 (ΔPARTY$_t$).[13] The coefficient plots are presented in Figure 5.5.

These results reveal significant effects of the misery index on governing party handling evaluations in the United Kingdom, and also for consumer sentiment (prospective economic evaluations), but no significant effects for evaluations of the party in opposition.[14] These data again confirm the pattern of a public who selectively use observed policy conditions to update their evaluations of the party responsible (and vice versa).

evaluations is from the regular YouGov survey question 'How do you think the financial situation of your household will change over the next 12 months?', and consists of the percentage of respondents indicating 'better' in their response.

[13] The monthly measure of subjective evaluations of party economic handling is created using Stimson's (1991) dyad ratios algorithm, based on 263 survey items relating to party handling/performance in our UK dataset.

[14] Results for the fully specified model are plotted in Figure 5.5 with estimates for all the models reported in the Appendix, Table A5.2.

Asymmetry across the Issue Agenda

We have argued in this book that performance politics relates to issues beyond the economy alone. Here we use aggregate-level data for the 2004 to 2010 period in the United Kingdom (using CMS data) which are uniquely useful for the purpose of analysing the degree to which the asymmetry in performance updating on the economy applies to other policy issues, and the degree to which incumbent performance updating occurs across the issue agenda. The data include monthly observations of the handling ratings of both major UK parties over a period of six years – across a range of policy issues: asylum seekers, crime, the NHS, education, terrorism, the economy and railways. For these analyses we are no longer using objective measures of policy conditions. As noted earlier, those objective measures may be imperfect measures of the aspects of a policy the public notices. It may also be the case that while we find some asymmetric performance updating for governments using our objective data, the pattern is much more symmetrical in survey data, with implications for the inferences that can be drawn.

We use survey questions from the CMS that ask respondents, 'How well do you think the present government has handled each of the following issues?' and for the opposition 'How well do you think a Conservative government would handle each of the following issues?', listing a range of policy issues: 'Crime in Britain', 'Britain's education system', 'The number of asylum-seekers coming to Britain', 'The National Health Service', 'The condition of Britain's railways', 'The risk of terrorism to British citizens'. For the economy the survey asked the slightly different question 'If Britain were in economic difficulties, which party do you think would be able to handle the situation best – Labour or the Conservatives?' Alongside these questions, the CMS also asked about respondents' *perceptions* of the condition of each policy domain. For example, it asked 'Do you think that the crime situation in Britain these days is … ' with response options: 'A lot better', 'A little better', 'The same', 'A little worse', 'A lot worse'. For the economy we use a measure of personal economic retrospections: 'How does the financial situation of your household now compare with what it was 12 months ago?' with response options: 'Got a lot better', 'Got a little better', 'Stayed the same', 'Got a little worse', 'Got a lot worse'.

For our aggregate measures we use the proportion of respondents in each monthly cross section indicating that a party is handling, or would handle, a given issue 'very well' or 'well' and the proportion of respondents indicating that conditions have got 'a lot better' or 'a little better'. This enables us to test the effect of changes in the effect of subjective policy conditions (ΔCONDITIONS$_t$) on ratings of whether Labour (the incumbent) or the Conservatives (the opposition) are judged as being able to handle the issue well or badly (ΔHANDLING$_t$). We control for change in the proportion of party identifiers (ΔPID$_t$) to take into account any fluctuations due to partisanship. The time series regression model in first differences takes the form:

$$\Delta\text{HANDLING}_t = \alpha_0 + \beta_1\Delta\text{CONDITIONS}_t + \beta_2\Delta\text{PID}_t + \varepsilon_t$$

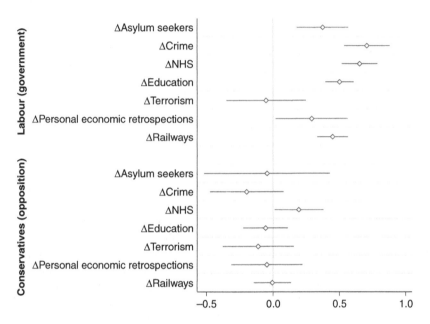

Figure 5.6 Subjective evaluations and party handling, governing and opposition parties, UK, 2004–2010

In Figure 5.6, we plot the coefficients (indicated by a diamond) for each issue for the effects of perceived changes in policy conditions on competence assessments of Labour (the governing party) and the Conservatives (the opposition). The whiskers in the plot again indicate the standard errors of the coefficients to show where these effects are statistically significant (i.e. where the error bars do not cross the zero line).

The findings presented in Figure 5.6 reveal no significant effects of evaluations of policy conditions on the handling ratings of the Conservative opposition between 2004 and 2010, except for a small, positive coefficient for the issue of the NHS. This indicates that both parties *gained* in their competence evaluations from perceptions of improvements in the performance of the NHS.[15] However, there was a significant positive coefficient for all policy issues upon handling evaluations of the incumbent Labour Party, the party-in-power, with the exception of the issue of terrorism. Even using subjective measures of how well different policy issues are going – whether they are getting worse or getting better – there is clear evidence of asymmetric performance updating for the party-in-power, not the party-in-opposition. These results could be due to the context in the United Kingdom and the political period. However, alongside evidence of asymmetric performance updating on the economy in the United States and the United Kingdom, and asymmetric performance updating across objective measures in the United States, United Kingdom and Germany, we are confident that we are able to identify a correspondence which tends to hold for evaluations of parties-in-power, but which is much less strong and consistent for parties in power, consistent with our expectations.

Exogeneity in Incumbent Evaluations

In Chapter 3, we systematically examined each of our three concepts (ownership, performance, generalised competence) alongside the concept of partisanship. Here we offer a further insight with respect to performance. One of the implications of asymmetric performance updating in public opinion is that we should expect there to be less endogeneity in handling evaluations of the governing party than for evaluations of the party-out-of-power. Put another way, rational performance updating based on perceived (and actual) changes in policy performance should be an important exogenous indicator of party support for the incumbent, but less so for the opposition.

We examine the degree to which perceived changes in policy performance result in updating of party handling evaluations for people who already hold a partisan attachment, and those who do not. We again use the UK case due to the richness of the repeated cross-sectional CMS data. This enables us to disaggregate public opinion by partisan identifiers of the governing (Labour) and opposition (Conservative) party, and rival partisans respectively, and by people who report having no partisan attachment in any given month. The analyses cover the period between

---

[15] One explanation may simply be that citizens saw the performance of the NHS improving during the latter part of this period (from early 2007 onwards) and perceived both parties as able to manage the NHS well, as the incumbent gained credit for an improving health service and the opposition was recognised as also better able to handle it. But to read too much into a small effect would be unwise.

2004 and 2010 when one party was in power (Labour) and in opposition (Conservatives). We replicate the time series regression models in first differences used for Figure 5.6 (it plots the coefficients of the effects of perceptions of policy condition variables on party handling) but estimate the effects from separate models for partisans, rival partisans and non-partisans for each of the seven policy issues.

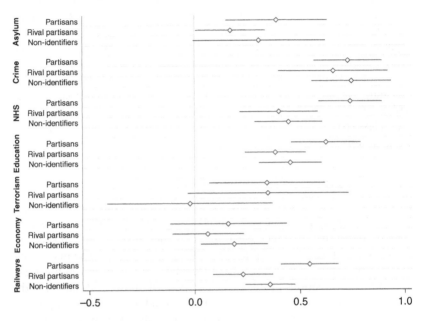

Figure 5.7 Subjective evaluations and party handling, by party identification, Labour government, UK, 2004–2010

Figure 5.7 presents the analysis for evaluations of issue handling by the governing Labour Party.

Figure 5.7 reveals that there are broadly corresponding effects of changes in perceived policy conditions and ratings of Labour's handling of the issue on all issues, irrespective of whether respondents hold an attachment to Labour, to the Conservatives or if they report no partisan attachment at all. Interestingly, Labour partisans exhibit stronger updating for those issues on which Labour tends to have its highest ratings: the NHS, education and railways; those issues which we would expect to be partisan priorities. It is also interesting that we observe no relationship on the economy except for non-partisans, particularly in the period when Labour suffered a significant loss of competence on the economic issue

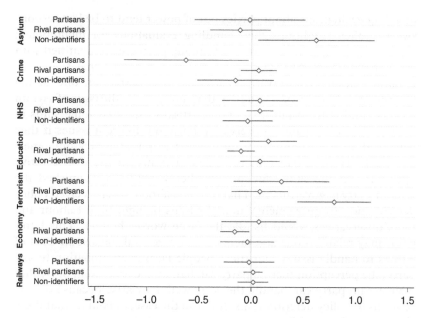

Figure 5.8 Subjective evaluations and party handling, by party identification, Conservative opposition, UK, 2004–2010

following the financial crisis.[16] These findings reveal that there is important variance in performance updating for incumbents, even among partisans (who may later revise their partisanship as a result), and that performance updating extends beyond the issue of the economy alone. Performance fluctuations are likely to be important drivers of party support for incumbents, net of prior partisan attachments. These findings are consistent with the findings in Chapter 3, where we observed public opinion updating, using a different specification, for partisans compared to independents.

In Figure 5.8, we plot the same estimates for the models for the relationship – or the lack thereof – between changes in aggregate perceptions of policy conditions and changes in evaluations of issue handling of the Conservative opposition between 2004 and 2010.

The results in Figure 5.8 reveal five points of note: (i) there is much less updating overall, consistent with Figure 5.6, such that party

---

[16] Our economic handling question ('best party on the economy') differs to the handling scales for other issues, which might therefore exhibit greater variance. It is also possible that the switching of the 'best party to handle' the issue of the economy in this period (from Labour to Conservative) might result in a null finding.

handling evaluations about parties out of power tend to be less responsive to policy conditions than handling evaluations for incumbents; (ii) there is no updating whatsoever among people who identified with the Labour Party (rival partisans); (iii) to the degree that there was updating among Conservative partisans, it occurred on one of the Conservative Party's 'best issues' in that time period (the issue of asylum seekers coming to Britain); (iv) non-partisans exhibited some shifts in their evaluations of the Conservative Party on different issues if they perceived a deterioration or improvement in public policy outcomes; and finally (v) non-partisans rewarded or punished the Conservative opposition in the same direction as they rewarded or punished the Labour Party in government. That is to say, if there was perceived policy deterioration (improvement), non-partisans thought both Labour and the Conservatives would handle the issue worse (better). This latter point may relate to our arguments about a general malaise in trust of parties to handle issues. For those people lacking an affiliation to any party, the perception that no party can handle the issue well, or neither mainstream party can handle the issue well, may arise because of perceptions of policy deteriorations. It is also the case, of course, that these citizens tend to exhibit less persistence in their evaluations, as we showed in Chapter 3.

Earlier in this chapter we revealed how there was a stronger correspondence between objective policy measures and the issue-handling evaluations of parties in power than there was for parties out of power. Our analysis provides insight into those stronger and weaker relationships. It appears that the public updates its performance ratings for the party perceived to be responsible: the incumbent – and this is true irrespective of partisanship. But there is also some updating for the party in opposition, although mainly (and then not on all issues) for those people who have no prior party attachment. This would account for strong exogenous performance updating for governing parties but weaker updating for oppositions.

One of the interesting aspects of Figure 5.8 is that the issues on which non-partisans relate perceived changes in policy outcomes with ratings of the party in opposition are those issues for which parties might not be viewed as directly responsible (i.e. terrorism and asylum seekers). A hypothesis might be that opposition parties can benefit on these issues from a perceived improvement in a policy outcome because any party would be recognised as able to handle the issue better, or conversely, opposition parties do not benefit from a deterioration under the government of a rival party because citizens believe no party or government can handle the issue better.

These observations have important implications for question design. Survey designers should include questions that allow respondents to rate different parties independently, rather than asking 'which party is best' which allows for no analysis or comparison between parties (alongside the problem of partisan priming).

It is useful to highlight that only on one issue, and among opposition party partisans, do we find an inverse relationship between a policy outcome or experience (on asylum seekers) and the ratings of the Conservative opposition. On this issue, for Conservative partisans, a perception that the asylum system got worse resulted in an improvement in Conservative party rating on the issue. There appears to be some tentative evidence that partisans are more likely to update their party positively on issues that party is better rated on, and likely a priority for those partisans. However, there is very weak evidence overall that improvement or deterioration in a policy outcome confers an advantage or disadvantage for the party out of power. The asymmetry of changes in performance evaluations appears to be a robust aspect of public opinion about performance.

Implications for Performance-Based Voting

We see no reason why opposition parties should not gain votes at the expense of governing party performance failures. This suggests that performance voting will be more symmetrical than public opinion about performance. Vote gains (and losses) between governing and opposition parties are more likely to involve direct switching, especially in majoritarian systems, whereas for evaluations of performance there is more scope for uncertainty (for example it is possible for there to be a sizeable proportion of 'don't knows').[17] Furthermore, challenger parties have strong incentives to prime or frame (Iyengar and Simon 1993) the vote choice on the basis of governing failures, and governing parties have strong incentives to prime or frame the vote choice on the basis of governing success. The final set of analyses in this chapter reveal the effects of issue performance updating upon vote choices for parties in and out of power.

In Figure 5.9 we plot the standardised coefficients from time series regression models of change in voting intentions for the incumbent Labour Party and opposition Conservative Party ($\Delta VOTE_t$) as a function of change in subjective evaluations of policy conditions

---

[17] The situation might be rather different for niche parties, though we would expect that they too might also benefit from performance failures of governing parties (such as how perceptions of government handling of immigration are linked to rises in support for populist-right parties, e.g. Evans and Chzhen 2013).

(ΔCONDITIONS$_{jt}$) – whether things are perceived as having got better or worse – for the (j) issues in Figures 5.6 to 5.8.[18] The time series regression model in first differences takes the general form:

$$\Delta VOTE_t = \alpha_0 + \beta_1 \Delta CONDITIONS_{jt} + \beta_2 \Delta PID_t + \varepsilon_t$$

In addition to subjective evaluations of policy conditions across six policy issues, the models test the effects of alternate measures of perceived economic conditions; whether the national economy has improved or got worse ('How do you think the general economic situation in this country has changed over the last 12 months?'), whether the respondent believes their own personal economic circumstances have improved or got worse ('How does the financial situation of your household now compare with what it was 12 months ago?') and whether the respondent believes their personal economic circumstances will improve ('How do you think the financial situation of your household will change over the next 12 months?'). Figure 5.9 presents the results in the form of standardised coefficients, as earlier.

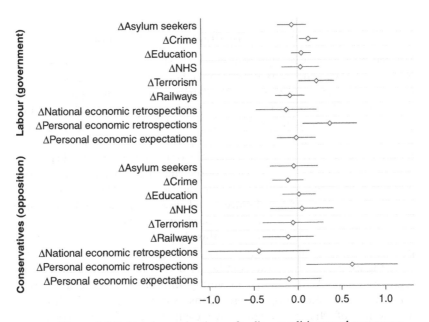

Figure 5.9 Subjective evaluations of policy conditions and party vote choice, Labour and Conservative parties, UK, 2004–2010

[18] Full results are reported in the Appendix, Table A5.3.

The effects of subjective evaluations of policy conditions in Figure 5.9 do not paint a compelling story of differences between the incumbent Labour Party and the opposition Conservative Party. While three issues show significant effects for Labour vote choice (crime, terrorism, personal economic retrospections), and only one issue shows a significant effect for the Conservatives (personal economic retrospections), the effect for the Conservatives on that issue is greater in magnitude. More striking is the absence of effects for both of the parties across the issues. This does not mean that performance voting is not important; it suggests it was not particularly important between 2004 and 2010, at the aggregate level. It is quite possible that performance voting is greater in other time periods.

We can also consider whether the observed patterns hold at the individual level, and in two countries: the United States and United Kingdom. For this we use data from national election studies carried out in the United States and United Kingdom between 2000 and 2015. Over this period, the British Election Study (BES) and the American National Election Studies (ANES) asked questions about perceived changes in policy conditions.

For the BES, we identified items in the 2005, 2010 and 2015 surveys.[19] These take the general form 'Do you think that the crime situation in Britain these days is ... ' with the possible options 'A lot better', 'A little better', 'The same', 'A little worse' and 'A lot worse'. Other policy domains include crime, immigration or asylum seekers, education, the cost of living, the risk of terrorism, the NHS and the economy. For each election we estimate a logistic regression model of vote choice for the incumbent and the opposition party (each time from the post-election survey). In 2005 and 2010 the incumbent is Labour, and in 2015 it is the Conservatives.[20] In all models we control for party identification and leader evaluations.[21] Our logistic regression models are as follows:

$$\text{Vote}_i = \alpha_0 + \beta_1 \text{Conditions}_{ji} + \beta_2 \text{PartyID}_i + \beta_3 \text{Leader}_i + \varepsilon_i$$

The results are reported in Table 5.2 and the full models can be found in the Appendix 5 (A5.4 to A5.7). The asterisks in Table 5.2 indicate whether or not the perceptions of policy conditions impacted on vote choice (and the level of significance). Effects that were not significant are marked with a '–'.

---

[19] The 2001 BES included various questions about party handling but none on the state of policy domains. The 2015 online survey was used because it included more policy conditions relative to the BES in-person survey.

[20] The dependent variable is a dichotomous variable of self-reported vote for the party, coded as equal to 1 where someone voted for the party and 0 where they did not.

[21] Party identification coded is as equal to 1 where the respondent is a strong, weak or close partisan for Labour or the Conservatives and 0 for non-identifiers or identifiers with other/minor parties. Leader evaluations are coded as equal to 1 where a respondent gives the party leader a positive rating on a ten-point dislike-like scale, and 0 where the evaluation is a negative rating or at the neutral mid-point.

Table 5.2 *Summary table of logistic regression models of vote choice in 2005, 2010 and 2015, UK*

	In-party			Out-party		
	2005	2010	2015	2005	2010	2015
Party identification	★★	★★	★★	★★	★★	★★
Leader ratings	★★	★★	★★	★★	★★	★★
Conditions: Crime	–	–	–	–	–	–
Conditions: Asylum/ immigration	–	–	★★	–	–	★★
Conditions: NHS	★★	–	–	–	–	★★
Conditions: Terrorism	–	–		–	–	
Conditions: National economic retrospections	–	★	★★		–	★★
Conditions: Education			★★			★★
Conditions: Cost of living			★★			★
Conditions: Economy			★★			★★

*p<0.05; **p<0.01

In Table 5.2, we see more variation by election in performance voting than variation by the party-in-power. In 2005, evaluations of the NHS impacted on Labour vote choice rather than Conservative vote choice, and in 2010 respective national economic evaluations show the same difference.[22] This is indicative of a marginally greater 'performance vote' for the Labour incumbent than the Conservative opposition. However, by 2015, the effects are observed across a wider issue set (where we have more measures) and equally so for the Conservative incumbent and Labour opposition. These effects may arise because the sample size of the BES post-election internet panel for 2015 is much larger (around 30,000), confirmed by results from the face-to-face survey for 2015 (reported in the Appendix, Table A5.7). Nevertheless, those results exhibit symmetric performance voting in the 2015 British general election.

We repeat the above analyses using the US data from the election studies for 2000, 2008 and 2012. There are some key differences in the models, due to the nature of these national elections. The biggest difference, of course, is that US voters are choosing a presidential candidate who represents a party. The other difference is that across the 2000, 2008

---

[22] Note the effect we saw for the economy on Conservative vote intention in Figure 5.9 used different data (monthly, aggregate) and model specification, and did not control for leadership ratings.

and 2012 elections some of the candidates had not previously served as president (Al Gore in 2000 and John McCain in 2008, though Gore had been vice-president for eight years). There may be weaker performance for these candidates, or they may be equivalent if the candidate is punished or rewarded for the performance of the previous incumbent president of the same party.

The post-election ANES in 2000 asked a series of questions concerning whether different policy outcomes got better or worse in the past eight years under the Clinton administration. Specifically, 'Would you say that compared to 1992, the nation's economy is better, worse, or about the same?', 'Would you say that compared to 1992, the United States is more secure from its foreign enemies, less secure, or hasn't this changed very much?', 'Would you say that compared to 1992 the nation's crime rate has gotten better, gotten worse, or stayed about the same?' and 'Would you say that compared to 1992, the nation's moral climate has gotten better, stayed about the same, or gotten worse?'. In addition to variants of the questions asked in 2000 (regarding whether the national economy was better or worse in the last year), the 2008 and 2012 pre-election ANES surveys asked whether unemployment or inflation had got better or worse in the last year, and if the US position in the world was weaker or stronger.[23]

The logistic regression models estimate performance voting effects for vote choices for the incumbent party's presidential candidate (2000 presidential vote choice for Al Gore, 2008 vote choice for John McCain, 2012 vote choice for Barack Obama) and the candidate of the out-party (2000 vote for George W. Bush, 2008 for Barack Obama, 2012 for Mitt Romney).[24] In all models, we control for presidential approval (PAPP) and partisanship (PartyID).[25] Our logistic regression models take the form:

$$\text{Vote}_i = \alpha_0 + \beta_1 \text{Conditions}_{ji} + \beta_2 \text{PartyID}_i + \beta_3 \text{PAPP}_i + \varepsilon_i$$

[23] Subjective policy evaluations are coded as equal to 1 where respondents think conditions have improved since 1992 and equal to 0 where they think they have got worse, remained the same or 'don't know'.

[24] The dependent variable is coded as equal to 1 where the self-reported vote is for the candidate (e.g. Al Gore or George W. Bush) and equal to 0 when a vote for one of their opponents (e.g. also including Ralph Nader, Pat Buchanan and 'other'), responded 'don't know' or refused to answer.

[25] Presidential approval is coded as equal to 1 where a respondent approves of 'the way [...] is handling his job as president', and equal to 0 for those who disapprove and don't know. Partisanship is coded as equal to 1 where the respondent is a strong, weak or close partisan of the incumbent party or the opposition party, and equal to 0 for independents and partisans of the rival party.

Table 5.3 *Summary table of logistic regression models of presidential vote choice in 2000, 2008 and 2012, US*

	In-party			Out-party		
	2000	2008	2012	2000	2008	2012
Party identification	★★	★★	★★	★★	★★	★★
Presidential approval	★★	★★	★★	★★	★★	★★
Conditions: Economy	★★	–	★★	–	–	★★
Conditions: National security	★★			–		
Conditions: Crime	★★			–		
Conditions: Moral climate	–			–		
Conditions: Unemployment	–	–		–	–	
Conditions: Inflation	–			–		
Conditions: US world position	–	–		–		★★

* $p<0.05$; ** $p<0.01$

Table 5.3 presents the findings and the full models can be found in the Appendix (A5.8 to A5.10). The asterisks in the table again indicate whether or not the perceptions of policy conditions impacted on vote choice (and the level of significance). Effects that were not significant are marked with a '–'.

The results in Table 5.3 reveal another mixed picture of performance voting. In 2000, there appear to be greater effects of performance assessments for the Democratic Party candidate Al Gore. Gore had, of course, served as Vice President prior to 2000, so this greater performance vote may reflect this key context. However, the same cannot be said for Barack Obama in 2012. Despite having been president for four years prior to the election, the effects of performance voting in 2012 are only visible on the economy – though this was a focal point of the election, in the context of the US recovery from the economic crisis and a campaign by challenger Mitt Romney which centred upon economic management. Our presidential approval measure may be soaking up a substantial portion of variance in presidential performance. In 2012, however, we see a greater impact of US world position on a vote choice for challenger Romney. The results for the 2000 presidential election are consistent with asymmetric performance voting, whereas those for 2008 and 2012 provide less support. Overall, the findings show more variation by election context, and potentially by candidate, than they do clear asymmetry between incumbent and opposition.

Our analyses of performance updating, and performance voting, demonstrate three clear findings. The first is that there is robust and repeated evidence of greater performance updating – in terms of public opinion – for incumbents than for oppositions. The second is that for some issues, and some periods, opposition ratings on different policy issues respond to evaluations of policy conditions under the current incumbent. These instances are rarer in our data, and opposition ratings do not always respond positively to negative performance, or negatively to positive performance. The final finding is of the absence of a clear asymmetry or symmetry in effects of performance updating between incumbents and oppositions. What appears to be the case is that different elections, and different candidates, lead to greater or lesser performance effects. This contextual explanation of performance voting is something we explore further in Chapter 7.

Conclusion

One of the implications of separating the basis of 'ownership' into long-term reputation and short-term changes in handling, or performance, is that the former can relate to any political party in a system, but the latter should realistically relate only to the party that has responsibility for governing. In this chapter we have demonstrated that public opinion about performance relates primarily to governing, not to opposition. However, while the fluctuations in public opinion about performance relate to the actions and outcomes of government, they may apply equally to vote choices for incumbents and oppositions. We suspect it is the context of the elections and the candidates that demonstrates the effects of policy conditions and performance on electoral choice. What is clear, however, is that there is no standard asymmetry in vote choice models in the same way as there is asymmetry in public opinion on competence. An incumbent party may or may not be punished for its performance; an opposition may or may not be rewarded.

There is a close correspondence between how governments perform and how the public updates its evaluations of the party-in-government's performance on many issues. This is not an obvious conclusion. We might assume that it is always beneficial for a government to perform 'well' and to deliver improvements in public services and conditions, but this only holds if voters notice, and then it may only hold if these assessments form the basis of electoral outcomes. Governments have incentives to pursue certain policy objectives such as balancing the budget, changing incentives in the market and improving public services, but do they have incentives for things to always be 'getting better' in the eyes of the electorate? Our analyses suggest that they do. That said, the degree of correspondence between performance and public opinion is by no means perfect. There is substantial opportunity for voters to not notice changes in performance, to not update their opinions of the performance of a political party, and therefore to not punish – or reward – that party at the ballot box. This chapter reveals the extent – and the limits – of the responsiveness of public opinion to good and bad performance on policy.

6 Generalised Competence and the Costs of Governing

When Thomas Dewey accepted the Republican nomination in 1944 he said, 'Does anyone suggest that the present national administration is giving either efficient or competent government? We have not heard that claim made, even by its most fanatical supporters. No, all they tell us is that in its young days it did some good things. That we freely grant. But now it has grown old in office. It has become tired and quarrelsome. It seems that the great men who founded this nation really did know what they were talking about when they said that three terms were too many.'[1]

Seasoned observers of politics will note how parties in government often struggle to renew themselves and their reputations in office. Parties exhaust themselves through policy activism, succumbing to sleaze, scandal or division, slowly leaking support, mismanaging public policies and projects, presiding over external shocks, and so it goes. A few parties find ways to periodically renew themselves, others stagger on against weak opponents, but the secular erosion of electoral support for parties in office is one of the seemingly unwavering laws of politics (Cuzán 2015). It is known as the costs of governing, or the costs of ruling.

Often, when voters make a judgement about a candidate or party's rating on one issue they 'transfer' that rating to other issues via transmission of useful and relevant information onto other issues, or via information short-cuts (Green and Jennings 2012a). This underpins the concept of generalised competence we outlined in Chapters 1, 2 and 3. Events and economic shocks can lead to changes in competence ratings across issues via this process of transfer (Green and Jennings 2012a), and incumbents may suffer general deterioration of their reputation for governing competence across the issue agenda. To the extent that voters form a generalised rating of party competence across many issues, this broad evaluation should have implications for vote choice. When we conceptualise

[1] www.presidency.ucsb.edu/ws/?pid=75627

competence as a generalised rating, we can understand the broader dynamics in evaluations of government competence over time. As Nannestad and Paldam wrote in 2002; 'Few facts are so robust – and so little discussed – in political economy as the one that it costs to rule' (p. 17). In this chapter we use our concept of generalised competence to analyse and explain one of the most significant and yet largely unanswered questions about politics and electoral support. Why do parties so regularly lose public support over their period in office?

The Regularity of Costs of Governing

Politics is said to exist in cycles (Merrill et al. 2008), whereby regular party alternation is explained by the return of vote choices to an equilibrium (Norpoth 2004). Such cycles have been argued to be so robust and predictable that they should be explained by a deep human instinct in political evaluations (Nannestad and Paldam 2002). Insofar as costs of governing have been examined, they have mostly been analysed in the United States, and then in relation only to presidential approval (rather than support for parties in the generic congressional ballot). The regularity of declines in incumbent popularity – or costs of governing – is matched by the regularity of honeymoon periods: a new president or government tends to benefit from an initial boost in public support (Sigelman and Knight 1983, 1985). This dissipates with varying speed (Dewan and Myatt 2012), but it frequently seems to dissipate. Declines over an incumbent cycle are sometimes marginally offset by upticks before elections, leading to the expectation of a parabolic curve in presidential approval or party support. Stimson (1976a: 1) observed 'the extraordinary fit of parabolic curves to actual presidential approval leads to the suspicion that presidential approval may be almost wholly independent of the President's behavior in office'. Similar parabolic curves have been identified in vote share trends, such that costs of governing are observed across presidential approval and party support, over long periods and in a range of country and political contexts (Campbell and Converse 1960; Mueller 1970; Miller and Mackie 1973; Stimson 1976a, 1976b; Kernell 1978; Rose and Mackie 1983; Ostrom and Simon 1985; Paldam 1986, 1991; Nannestad and Paldam 2002; Norpoth 2004; Dewan and Myatt 2012).

Figure 6.1 displays the pattern of costs of governing in 31 countries (see Table A6.1). The analyses use data on aggregate-level vote intention in legislative elections for the main party of government by period of government, drawing on a dataset of more than 17,500 polls from between 1942

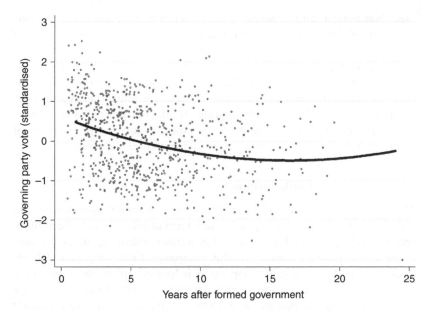

Figure 6.1 Vote intention for governing parties by length of time in government

and 2013 (Jennings and Wlezien 2016).[2] The governing periods shown vary in length considerably. Some are just for one election cycle when there is a change of president (and president's party) or a change in party-government following the next election. Some are for periods where a party-president remains in office over multiple election cycles.

Figure 6.1 fits a parabolic curve to the data, where the estimated R-squared is equal to 0.093. This is (only) a slightly better fit than with a linear relationship with an R-squared of 0.086. These are *not* strong statistical relationships, and there is interesting variation in costs of ruling and variation arising from the different time periods, data availability and the use of annual data; much more so than highlighted by other authors

[2] The vote intention data are standardised by governing period, which runs from the first calendar year of a government to its final year (ranging from 1 to 24 years). The standardised measure of vote intention is estimated as the raw value minus the mean for that period of party government, divided by the standard deviation. In instances of coalition government we code the governing party as the largest party in terms of overall vote share and legislative seats (i.e. in a few coalition governments the Prime Minister is from a smaller party). For example, the CDU/CSU is coded as the governing party for the German 'grand coalition' between the CDU/CSU and SPD over the period from 2005 to 2009. Similarly, the VVD is coded as the governing party for the coalition between the VVD and CDA in the Netherlands between 2010 and 2012.

(see Nannestad and Paldam 2002).[3] However, Figure 6.1 reveals a pattern of decline in vote intention for governments across a range of country and institutional contexts consistent with the widespread observation that costs of governing, or costs of ruling, exhibit a very important trend that we need to explain.[4] This pattern is a very important phenomenon for understanding political incentives and political behaviour, and, as discussed, one of the least well understood, considering its regularity. There are many existing theories for 'costs of governing' or 'costs of ruling' but little robust, compelling evidence that explains them.

Existing Explanations

Mueller (1970) accounted for declines in presidential approval by the inflation of support at the beginning of a term in office, which, he argued, was caused by 'weak followers'. This weaker following arises because a president promises more in the campaign than they can deliver. According to Mueller, initial popularity is 'puffed up' by those promises (or campaign 'myths') among bandwagon supporters whose fair-weather support quickly dissipates, and from 'excitable types' who quickly become bored. As presidential approval dissipates, opposition partisans are ready to join the aggrieved. This idea of the inflation of expectations is also consistent with arguments made by Stimson (1976a), who accounted for declines in presidential approval by the expectations gap that arises following campaigns. The simplicity of campaign pledges, combined with the absence of well-formed preferences among the majority of citizens, contributes to the 'spread of naive expectations', according to Stimson. Furthermore, '[b]ecause the public, and particularly the ill-informed, expects more than can possibly by achieved under the best of circumstances, it is always prone to great disappointment over what is achieved by mere mortal presidents acting under less than ideal conditions' (Stimson 1976a: 10). Stimson (1976b) provided evidence for his explanation pointing to greater declines in presidential approval following higher initial levels of support. Miller and Mackie (1973) also suggested that initial peaks in electoral support arise from temporary backing of uncommitted voters with weak party identification. Those voters tend to

---

[3] Some scholars have noted this variability, pointing to clarity of responsibility as an explanation for different rates (Palmer and Whitten 2000), and the enhanced costs of governing if anti-political establishment parties enter coalitions, and are punished more for cooperating with the establishment (van Spanje 2011). It is also widely known that junior coalition partners tend to bear more electoral penalty than senior partners, and Wlezien (2016b) points to important system differences between presidential and parliamentary systems.

[4] We see this further when we disaggregate all the data by country and governing period.

revert to their 'normal' identification over time. This was used to explain by-election results in Britain (pointing often, as they do, to support for the opposition party). However, attempts to further explore and validate the empirical implications of the expectation-disillusionment explanation resulted in little support (Sigelman and Knight 1983, 1985). Bigger declines in incumbent support have been found among partisans of the out-party but no differences were found as a function of sophistication, which might have been expected if citizens respond to information about performance (Presser and Converse 1976–7). Stimson (1976a, 1976b) found that greater declines in approval were found for incumbents with the highest initial ratings, but Sigelman and Knight (1983) noted that those relationships alone cannot explain parabolic trends.

An alternative explanation for cycles or costs of governing results from the concept of the importance and accumulation of 'coalitions of minorities'. Downs (1957) first described the process whereby a government may have majority support from the electorate on a given issue, but with every policy decision and/or action, a new minority bloc is alienated. If the minority feels sufficiently aggrieved about the policy that it cannot be placated by support from the government for policies it favours, a government will gradually lose support of sufficient minorities to be defeated. The opposition party has an opportunity to build a coalition of these minorities in order to overthrow the incumbent. This explanation was put forward by Mueller (1970) to account for cycles of presidential approval. Governing is ultimately about making decisions, and the more decisions a government or a president makes, the more people the government or president antagonises. However, difficulties arise in applying the 'coalition of minorities' explanation because (a) the explanation has not been empirically tested and (b) it has not been tested against a performance or disillusionment explanation for costs of governing trends, and hence the superiority of any explanation cannot be verified. It was also argued by Sigelman and Knight (1983) that this explanation relied too implausibly on the presence of a strong, clever and well-organised opposition and a minimal level of issue voting. Those preconditions are not sufficiently present to account for regular governing costs.

A further explanation for costs of governing was put forward by Ostrom and Simon (1985), who argued that political events, as well as economic distress, served to explain the reduction in support for a president over a period of office. Those events would combine to inform a largely visceral reaction to a president, especially where performance failed to match expectations, where there was a sudden or dramatic change in an outcome, growing media coverage of a particular performance 'dimension' or particular efforts by a president to focus on that dimension. These arguments suggest that dynamics of public opinion could vary according to the number of events and their nature. However, it is hard to understand these effects as explanations for the repeated patterns of presidential costs of governing across administrations. If events explain declines in support for the incumbent, we may need additional explanations for the honeymoon period, the systematic and regular declines in presidential approval or party support, and for the parabolic nature of minor increases in vote shares towards the end of a period in office.

Furthermore, Nannestad and Paldam (2002: 31) argued that costs of governing arise because individuals exhibit 'grievance asymmetry' in their reactions to economic performance: 'Consider the effect on the popularity of the government of a symmetrical change up and down of an economic variable. A grievance asymmetry means that the effect of the positive change is smaller than the one of the negative change.' They put this forward as the most convincing explanation for costs of ruling, and observed that the size of these costs had grown across Western Europe since the 1990s. However, while this theoretical explanation is compelling, and benefits from both parsimony and generalisability across party, country and institutional contexts, Nannestad and Paldam did not offer any direct empirical evidence in support of it. The literature on costs of governing has mainly eluded an empirical explanation, although we have a variety of intuitive explanations.

There is a risk that scholars continue to use time as the explanation of governing costs, rather than explaining the time-based phenomenon (Kernell 1978). As Sigelman and Knight (1983: 320) pointed out, 'It is one thing to know that a presidential unpopularity cycle exists, but it is something else to know why it exists ... The real problem is to determine why the reaction to the substance of presidential actions nearly always has a cumulatively negative impact on presidential popularity.' Sigelman and Knight (1983) conclude that declines in both expectations and popularity are outcomes of the effectiveness with which a president is thought to be handling his job. And yet those evaluations are also subject to the same unexplained governing costs. As Stimson (1976a: 10) suggested, it is as though presidents are 'passive observers' of their own sinking popularity. And as Nannestad and Paldam observed, since the cost of ruling is an unusually stable constant, it should be explained by something 'going beyond institutions, i.e. by a deep parameter of human behaviour' (2002: 19).

There is one study that *does* provide an empirical analysis in support of a theoretical explanation for costs of ruling, put forward by Wlezien (2016b). Wlezien builds on the Downsian explanation (developed by Paldam and Skott, and referred to as the 'median gap' by Nannestad and Paldam (2002)), and on his work on the public thermostat (Wlezien 1995, 2004), revealing that parties gradually move policy away from the average citizen when they are in power. This increasing policy divergence can account for a proportion (around 40 per cent) of the cost of ruling effect in US presidential elections. While not intended to provide a comprehensive model of costs of ruling, these findings suggest there is an important spatial story to the phenomenon, in the form of increasing policy distance between governing parties and voters. Wlezien also points to the economy as an important factor, although this perhaps begs the question as to why costs of ruling are expected to be so regular across governments within equivalent systems, as well as across system types.

All in all, we have some very compelling ideas about costs of ruling, and an empirically supported explanation for a portion of the costs of ruling in the US presidential system. However, there is still a substantial gap in understanding and in scope for testing existing and expanded theories using empirical measures. There is also little comparative evidence. In particular, the grievance asymmetry idea merits further development but we need an independent measure of public opinion about competence, alongside measures of policy distance. This is the contribution we now make.

Generalised Competence and Governing Costs

One reason for the unresolved nature of the costs of governing puzzle has been the absence of measures that allow researchers to analyse the effects of subjective evaluations of incumbent party performance independently of presidential approval and vote intention (Sigelman and Knight 1983). When analysed by governing period, generalised evaluations of competence reveal a systematic tendency of electorates to judge a party-in-government more harshly across issues over its period in office. This chapter puts forward such a measure of subjective competence ratings as a way to test an explanation for governing costs.

Figure 6.2 reveals how electorates rate the party-in-government when measured as a generalised rating of competence, exhibited by the shared variance in performance ratings on different issues: 'macro-competence'. Chapter 3 provided information on the underlying data and characteristics of this measure by country (specifically in Table 3.15), and the individual series are plotted separately in the Appendix, Figures A3.9 to A3.18. The construction of a subjective measure of party performance offers a unique way of estimating the dynamics and effects of competence in different time, institutional and country contexts.

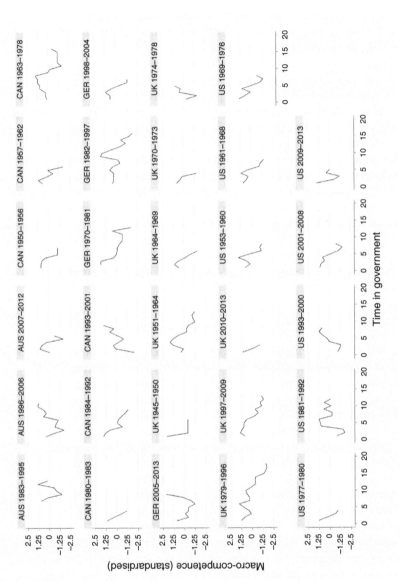

Figure 6.2 Macro-competence rating of governing parties by length of time in government

As discussed earlier, available survey data on issue handling enable us to calculate our measure of macro-competence for five countries: the United States, the United Kingdom, Australia, Canada and Germany. We plot the macro-competence score for the governing party for the duration of each party's period of office in Figure 6.2.[5]

The series of line graphs demonstrates that in the majority of cases – 22 out of 29 cases – the public comes to view the general competence of the party-in-government more negatively over time. Part of this will be due to the endogenous nature of public opinion about competence where competence evaluations follow losses in vote intention for a party. Some of this may also be due to the interrelationship between evaluations of competence and the distance between electorates and incumbents, the latter highlighted by Wlezien (2016b) and discussed above. However, we suggest that these declines in competence are also responsible for declines in party support.

A Theory of Costs of Governing: Time-Varying Attribution of Blame

Governments lose support over time because electorates judge incumbent parties' performance in predictable ways. If we consider a voter's experience of an incumbent administration, variation can be theorised in periods. These periods are defined by the way voters and electorates apportion blame.

We argue that governments experience a largely blame-free honeymoon period but then a period of blame and the accumulation of blame. These periods are outlined here in a theory of variation in attribution of responsibility and blame comprising four parts:

(i) Attribution of responsibility to the outgoing party in the first period of a new government;

(ii) When the in-party is blamed, there is negativity bias (negative evaluations of competence are weighted more than positive evaluations, akin to the 'grievance asymmetry' argument of Nannestad and Paldam (2002));

(iii) As negative information exerts an effect on performance evaluations, blame exhibits an accumulative effect (competence increasingly depresses support for the incumbent);

(iv) Accumulation of blame has an effect up to a saturation point, after which any additional information has weaker effects.

---

[5] The governing party is the largest party in the government or the party that controls the presidency in the United States.

We elaborate on each stage in turn, and consider evidence for each as we do.

Honeymoon Period: Attribution of Responsibility to the Outgoing Party

Citizens have very little information on which to judge the performance of a new government. They will rely on the heuristic of its leader, the performance of the outgoing government, optimism based on campaign promises or their underlying party preference to form their opinion. Before the change of government, citizens have to judge the opposition party on its likely performance, relying more on party identification in place of concrete performance information (Fiorina 1981; Green and Jennings 2012b). These differences arise because 'the information-seeking costs necessary to evaluate the past performance of an administration are far less than those needed to assess a set of future government policies' (Miller and Wattenburg 1985: 359).

A number of additional features should characterise the evaluations of a new incumbent.

The difference in support for a new incumbent before the election and afterwards may arise because voters use the election outcome – and the decisions of others – as a heuristic for the party or president likely to handle problems best. This outcome rationalisation explanation is similar to the bandwagon explanation offered by Mueller (1970). Weak partisans (and non-voters who take part in surveys) may join the crowd, or may simply provide top-of-the-mind responses to survey questions following news of an election winner.

Another feature is the likelihood that voters, and the mass media, tend to give the incoming administration the benefit of the doubt (Sigelman and Knight 1983). In the absence of any concrete information on performance, voters (and opinion formers) deduce that anything must be better than what has gone before. The very fact that the outgoing party has lost the election reflects a lack of trust in the past government's performance. A new party or president may be rewarded with an 'anything must be better' bonus.

Underlying both explanations, and building on these, is our prediction that an incoming government is judged by attributing responsibility for performance experiences and failures to the outgoing administration. This makes sense for three reasons. The first is simply that the new administration is not practically responsible for the results of policy decisions taken by the previous administration. The results of new government decisions have not yet had an effect on political and policy realities. Fiorina (1981: 5–6) argued that elections do not signal the direction in which society should be going as much as they convey an evaluation of where society has been. The voter judges whether an incumbent has done well or badly by changes in their own welfare. At the beginning of a term of office, this evaluation cannot be applied to the incumbent. The second is that the rationalisation of the result towards the incoming government will also apply to evaluations of the outgoing party. It is just as true that voters will jump on a bandwagon of support for the victor as a bandwagon of condemnation of the loser. This may even increase blame for the outgoing government. The third is that the political message that things are the fault of the previous government has greater organisation, conviction and weight. A new opposition party (the previous incumbent) cannot formulate a convincing political attack on the failure of a new government (their policy decisions are still the ones being felt), whereas the new incumbent, riding higher in the polls, has more opportunities to point to the previous administration to blame where things have gone wrong. These realities will also be reflected in mass media. They render the honeymoon period one in which 'normal' political competition is relatively absent. A recently defeated party will likely be in a state of flux. Recently defeated parties often experience changes of leadership, disunity, blame and internal questions over ideological direction as post mortems are carried out over the reasons for defeat. They are less able to organise themselves to oppose.

Whereas theories of government and opposition attribution generalise to the entire period of government, and the entire period of opposition, those theories make assumptions that the government can be judged for its failures and voters have little reliable information about the opposition. That cannot be true in the honeymoon period of a government. As such, we put forward a time-varying theory of attribution over a government cycle.

The honeymoon period should be characterised by performance attribution on the previous administration or president, represented by the new party or parties in opposition. As Iyengar (1989: 879) reminded us, 'Individuals tend to simplify political issues by reducing them to questions of responsibility, and their issue opinions flow from their answers to these questions.' The more unpopular the previous government, the bigger the honeymoon boost to the new government. Not only should the performance evaluations of the new government be predicted by the performance evaluations of the previous government, these effects should dissipate with time. This is because the memory of the performance of the outgoing government will likely wane, and also because the relevance of this evaluation on incoming government performance will decline. These expectations lead to Hypothesis 1, the *honeymoon hypothesis*.

Hypothesis 1 Incumbent performance evaluations are a function of outgoing government performance evaluations; these effects decline over time.

We expect the perceived competence of the incoming government to be an inverse function of the competence of the outgoing government. This should hold true controlling for other predictors of incoming party competence, namely party identification, leader evaluations and economic evaluations or conditions. We also expect the effects of outgoing party competence on incoming party competence to weaken over time so that the effect is large when the incoming party enters office, but it weakens over a period of government.

Hypothesis 1: Data and Evidence

Our measure of macro-competence provides an aggregate-level over-time measure of subjective performance evaluations of the party in government (the party of the president in the United States and the largest party in the government in the United Kingdom, Canada, Australia and Germany). We first calculated macro-competence for each party before creating a measure of generalised competence for the governing party for each governing cycle. The cycle length is determined by the number of years the party holds office.[6] The unit of analysis is party competence-year and our cases are 23 governing periods.

Time series cross-sectional first-order autoregressive, AR(1), models are estimated, with the governing cycles (i) as panels.[7] In order to test the impact of outgoing government performance evaluations on the performance evaluations of the newly elected incumbent, we model government party competence in year t, $MCOMP_{it}$, as a function of the ratio of the level of macro-competence of the incoming governing party to the outgoing government in its final year (carried forward as the same value in

---

[6] Macro-competence and our other variables (i.e. leader evaluations, macro-partisanship and percentage change in GDP) are standardised for each governing period by calculating the raw value of the variable minus its mean for that period of party government, divided by the standard deviation.

[7] Our models are estimated with panel-corrected standard errors (Beck and Katz 1995) which control for panel heteroscedasticity and contemporaneous correlations of the errors. The models are fitted using the Prais-Winsten method to test for serial autocorrelation (μ_{it}), with the *rho* estimated separately for each panel as the first-order autoregressive process: $\mu_{it} = \rho\mu_{it-1} + \varepsilon_{it}$. This allows the rate of persistence to vary across governing periods.

all years of the new government), MCOMP(OUT)$_{it-c}$. Higher values indicate a larger honeymoon effect (i.e. the less popular the previous incumbent was compared to its challenger in its final year of office, the higher the honeymoon bonus). The model also controls for the number of years that the new incumbent has been in office, GOVTIME$_{it}$.[8] Here a negative coefficient means that there is a decline in competence evaluations of the incumbent party over time. We also test the interaction of outgoing government party competence with that count variable for time in government, where the coefficient captures the annual rate of decline of the honeymoon bonus (i.e. of negative evaluations of the outgoing previous government), GOVTIME$_{it}$ × MCOMP(OUT)$_{it-c}$. A negative coefficient indicates that the effect of that honeymoon bonus declines over time.

For two countries, the United States and United Kingdom, we also have measures of macro-partisanship (MacKuen et al. 1989), presidential or prime ministerial approval and economic growth (year-on-year percentage growth in GDP).[9] These controls help isolate effects of MCOMP(OUT)$_{it-c}$ on MCOMP$_{it}$ to generalised policy performance evaluations rather than on other factors which also co-vary with macro-competence. The full model can be represented in the form:

$$MCOMP_{it} = \alpha_0 + -1 * \beta_1 MCOMP(OUT)_{it-c} + \beta_2 GOVTIME_{it} +$$
$$-1 * \beta_3 GOVTIME_{it} \times MCOMP(OUT)_{it-c}$$
$$+\beta_5 LEADER_{it} + \beta_6 MP_{it} + \beta_7 GDP_{it} + \mu_{it}$$

Table 6.1 presents the models using all five countries with only the macro-competence and time in government variables and interactions (Model 1(a)), with the same variables in the US and UK cases (Model 1(b)), and finally with all variables (including control variables) for the US and UK cases (Model 2).

Time in government has a strongly significant effect on incumbent macro-competence across all the models. This denotes that governing party competence declines over time, as costs of governing predict. The dependent variable is standardised such that the coefficient of −0.086 means that each additional year in office yields close to a 0.1 standard deviation decrease in governing party competence.

Competence evaluations of the previous government do not exert a significant effect on incumbent party competence in Model 1(a) for all

---

[8] In the first year of the government, this variable is equal to 1, in the second year it is equal to 2, and so on.

[9] We also compare (in robustness checks) each model using measures of subjective economic evaluations in the United States and United Kingdom, which reveal the same pattern.

Table 6.1 *Governing party competence as function of outgoing party competence*

	Model 1(a) (all countries)	Model 1(b) (US & UK)	Model 2 (US & UK)
Macro-competence(Out)$_{t-c}$	0.062	**0.158**	**0.059**
	(0.072)	**(0.036)**★★★	**(0.015)**★★★
Time in Government$_t$ × Macro-competence(Out)$_{t-c}$	−0.009	−0.032	−0.011
	(0.010)	**(0.007)**★★★	**(0.003)**★★★
Time in Government$_t$	−0.086	−0.146	−0.046
	(0.028)★★	**(0.040)**★★★	**(0.014)**★★
Leader(Gov)$_t$			0.550
			(0.076)★★★
Macro-partisanship(Gov)$_t$			0.216
			(0.077)★★
GDP$_t$			0.087
			(0.052)
Intercept	0.436	0.740	0.287
	(0.173)★	(0.305)★	**(0.094)**★★
R-squared	0.04	0.20	0.79
	23	13	13
N	204	93	93

★ $p<0.05$; ★★ $p<0.01$; ★★★ $p<0.001$ (standard errors in parentheses)

countries, but do show a significant positive effect in Models 1(b) and 2 for the United States and United Kingdom.[10] In substantive terms the coefficient for Model 2 (0.059) means that a one standard deviation increase in the generalised competence of the outgoing party leads to just over a five per cent decrease in the competence of the new incumbent.

Models 1(b) and 2 also reveal a statistically significant effect of the interaction of the previous government's competence with the period the new incumbent is in office. For each additional year the new incumbent holds office, the effect (in Model 2) of outgoing party competence decreases by a 0.011 standard deviation.

In Figure 6.3 we plot the marginal effect of MCOMP(OUT)$_{it-c}$ over time (years) based on Model 2, with 95 per cent confidence intervals indicated by the dotted line. Figure 6.3 demonstrates that the effect of out-party competence is stronger at the beginning of a new period of

[10] Jack-knifing the time series cross-sectional analyses for model 1(a) reveals that the honeymoon effect of outgoing party competence is weakly significant when Australia is excluded from the analysis, which is consistent with the trends observed in Figure 6.2 for two of the three government lifecycles (from 1983 to 1995 and 1996 to 2006).

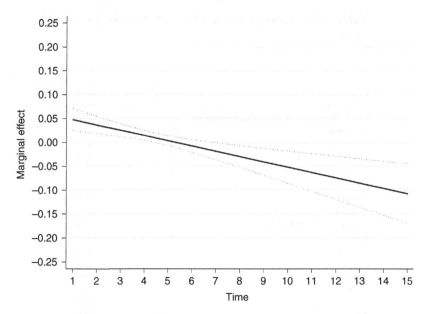

Figure 6.3 Marginal effect of outgoing government party competence on incoming government party competence

government and weaker over time, and has a significant effect, on average, for the first four years of a new government (on in-party competence).

These results reveal that a new government benefits from a competence boost due to the relative loss of competence of its predecessor. During this period, the previous government is blamed for its failings, and this out-party attribution effect is an important factor for incoming government competence. That boost lasts approximately four years, based upon data drawn from the United States and United Kingdom: countries in which a four-year period is the period of one presidential election cycle, and the average length of parliamentary cycle in the United Kingdom (elections are typically held every four or five years in the range of data).[11]

Honeymoons do not last indefinitely. From analysis of our monthly data on vote intentions we calculate the average period of time it takes for support for the governing party to fall to below the level of its support around the time of its election. This honeymoon period is equal to 3.4 months for the 79 governing cycles that we have data for (drawn from 20 countries), and equal to 2.7 months for 33 governing cycles in our five countries (the United States, the United Kingdom, Australia, Canada and

[11] The United Kingdom subsequently holds general elections in fixed terms of five years.

Table 6.2 *The average length of honeymoon period for governing parties*

Country	N of governing cycles	Average length of honeymoon period in months
US, UK, Australia, Canada, Germany	33	2.7
All countries	79	3.4
Australia	7	2.0
Austria	1	1.0
Bulgaria	1	2.0
Canada	7	1.6
Croatia	1	0.0
Denmark	5	10.6
Germany (Main party)	4	0.8
Greece	1	1.0
Iceland	1	2.0
Ireland	7	2.3
Japan	1	0.0
Netherlands	3	3.0
New Zealand	5	10.6
Norway	8	2.8
Portugal	4	1.5
Slovakia	1	2.0
Spain	2	2.0
Sweden	5	1.8
UK	7	6.6
US	8	2.0

Germany).[12] Table 6.2 summarises the average length of honeymoon by country. There is variation across governing cycles but these suggest that newly elected governments receive some sort of post-election boost. This can extend for quite some time, but it is temporary and typically dies out within a few months.

Incumbent Blame: Negativity and Accumulation

After a honeymoon period, a period of incumbent attribution should be expected. Partisans of the incoming government should be particularly

[12] The average honeymoon period is only tested for instances in which there are at least two polls in the first three months that a party holds office (i.e. interpolating party support over a long period of missing data carries the risk of inflating the estimated length of honeymoon if the interpolated trend is upwards). For cases where there is a poll in the month prior to the election, this value is carried forward as the baseline level of support for the incoming government. Note that our average honeymoon period is somewhat shorter than identified by Nannestad and Paldam (2002), who pointed to an average period of six months.

quick to attribute blame (Tilley and Hobolt 2011; Nawara 2015) and weak supporters should become relatively easily disillusioned, as predicted by Mueller (1970), Stimson (1976) and Ostrom and Simon (1985). The new incumbent makes their own policy decisions, which an opposition and critical media will be in a position to pinpoint. With time, voters experience the effects of policy decisions and they will be presented with a growing amount of negative information about the government. While direct experience of new policies may not be immediate, and experiences will not affect all citizens equally, the attribution of responsibility for negative policy experience – whether caused by the new incumbent or not – will be placed on the incumbent. As this continues, the opposition may have increasing credibility in apportioning blame.

Most of that information will likely be negative. Opposition and mass media have little incentive to publicise good news about government performance. While citizens update their evaluations of an incumbent based on policy experience, and that can be positive and negative, there are many reasons to expect citizens to be attuned more to negative rather than positive information. Insights from political psychology and political science tell us that citizens exhibit a negativity bias (Key 1966; Kernell 1977; Lau 1982; Fiorina and Shepsle 1989; Klein 1991, 1996; Soroka 2006, 2014).[13] This manifests itself in the retention in memory of bad news over good news, and a tendency to apportion blame greater than the tendency to apportion credit. These well-known tendencies have implications for governing costs, as argued by Nannestad and Paldam (2002). Ostrom and Simon (1985: 337) also argued that performance dimensions (i.e. particular issues) enter into the calculus of party support only if there is a reason for citizens to notice them. Such a reason might be the communication of negative news. While a government may plausibly deliver policy 'goods' over a period in office, and may even improve its performance against some metrics (Dewan and Myatt 2012), it should not be the case that public perceptions of performance improve. Every negative shock should result in a greater effect than every piece of good news, with the result being the greater sensitivity of party support to performance blame than credit. These mechanisms should, in part, account for systematic declines in party support observed in governing costs.

In summary, we expect negative information about government performance to be (a) more likely, given media and opposition attention and strategies during any period of government, and (b) more likely to

---

[13] Negativity bias is also manifested in the behaviour of policy-makers (Weaver 1986; Hood 2011).

influence party support than positive information. This is because negative information is more likely to be attended to and stored in memory; it is more likely to matter. We predict that performance effects on incumbent party choice will be stronger when performance evaluations are negative and weaker when they are positive, leading to Hypothesis 2, the *negativity bias hypothesis*.

Hypothesis 2 Incumbent performance evaluations have a significantly greater effect on party support when they are negative.

When an electorate is confronted with negative performance information about a government, every piece of bad news will gradually confirm what voters have come to believe. One bad news story will be followed by another, then another, and so on. We would not expect negative performance shocks to dissipate, returning to equilibrium, if they are stored in public memory in such a significant way and if negativity bias means they are more attended to and memorised. The accumulation of negative information will have an additional effect on incumbent party support. It is as though every piece of bad news reinforces what voters have previously heard.

As negative attributions accumulate, we should expect public opinion to become more resistant to change. If a voter has heard and been increasingly convinced by negative information, their attitudes will become more fixed over time. Zaller's (1992) research tells us that citizens notice information that fits with their existing opinions and discard information that challenges them. The oft-cited concepts of cognitive dissonance and motivated reasoning explain the tendency of citizens to discard or rationalise information that challenges a long-held opinion or affiliation. If presidential approval is based on cheaply acquired information (Brody and Page 1975), citizens are unlikely, in general, to expend effort in seeking out information once they have formed their opinions. As citizens form opinions about a government, those opinions may be increasingly resistant to change.

Any decline in government approval will be coupled by the potential for self-fulfilling prophecies. We can imagine the opposition becoming emboldened by the disillusionment of the electorate, to formulate political attacks and make challenges more effective. Members of the in-party may face incentives to distance themselves from the unpopular incumbent in order to gain local support or position themselves for the aftermath of expected electoral defeat. This may lead to factionalism and disunity among the governing party, causing further reputational damage. The media may become increasingly hostile, recognising that a positive message about a government will be unpopular with a readership that is favouring an opponent. This suggests that governments suffer something of a saturation point; the accumulation of blame denotes a crisis of confidence in the incumbent after which point a more positive assessment becomes unlikely. This is akin to a process described by Dewan and Myatt (2012: 123), who describe 'The presence of (perhaps small) random events that buffet the performance and popularity of a government is sufficient to pin down a unique equilibrium ... A crisis of confidence involving the rapid collapse of a government's performance is sparked when a sequence of negative shocks push the popularity of the government below a unique critical threshold.' Our theory of performance costs of governing suggests that this process will occur largely irrespective of the actual performance of a particular government. The process may vary in speed and extent, but it is likely that a crisis in confidence will arise with the passage of time. As governments experience a crisis of confidence, new information will have less effect on party support. Party preferences will be formed and will be more resistant to change, as summarised in Hypotheses 3 and 4: the *blame accumulation hypotheses*.

Hypothesis 3 The sum of negative incumbent performance evaluations will exert a significant effect upon governing party support.

Hypothesis 4 The sum of negative incumbent performance evaluations will exert a significant curvilinear effect upon governing party support.

Hypothesis 4 expresses the expectation that negativity effects will accumulate up to a certain point, and from thereon have a weaker effect once an incumbent's reputation becomes unredeemable. This expectation arises because in-party blame attribution is weak during the beginning of a period of government, as predicted by Hypothesis 1. If we find a curvilinear effect of performance evaluations on vote choice, this provides further evidence in support of the honeymoon period hypothesis, since effects of incumbent competence evaluations will be weaker at the beginning of a governing party period when the previous incumbent party is considered responsible. The effect of the negativity bias in Hypothesis 2 and the accumulation of blame in Hypothesis 3 mean that blame attribution will increase as a party or president governs. But the effect of this is to weaken the impact of new performance information once the public has reached a verdict on the incumbent. New information will have little additional effect beyond a certain tipping point, so that the effects of performance evaluations on party support will first increase and then diminish.

Negativity and Blame Accumulation: The Evidence

In order to test for negativity bias in the effect of performance evaluations on vote choice, we first model governing party vote intention, $VOTE_{it}$, as a function of its generalised competence (i.e. macro-competence), $MCOMP_{it}$, and whether the effect of macro-competence is greater when its value is negative (i.e. governing party macro-competence is below its average level for that government lifecycle), $NEGATIVE_{it} \times MCOMP_{it}$. The constitutive term, $NEGATIVE_{it}$, is coded as being equal to zero when macro-competence is equal or greater than zero and equal to one when it is less than zero. For the interaction, a positive coefficient indicates that the effect of macro-competence on vote is greater when the government party has a low competence rating.

In order to test Hypothesis 3 (the blame accumulation hypothesis), we include a variable, $MCOMP(SUM)_{it}$, which is the cumulative total of negative shocks (changes) to party competence within a government lifetime. This variable is multiplied by -1 so that higher values indicate a greater build-up of negative shocks to competence of the incumbent. A negative coefficient implies that support for the governing party declines as the cumulative total of competence shocks grows. We also include the squared cumulative total of negative shocks, $MCOMP(SUM)_{it}^2$, to determine if the effect decreases over higher values, which is a test of Hypothesis 4. Here a positive coefficient would mean that the effect of accumulated negative shocks decreases at higher values. The model used to test Hypotheses 2, 3 and 4 can be expressed in the form:

$$VOTE_{it} = \alpha_0 + \beta_1 MCOMP_{it} + \beta_2 NEGATIVE_{it} + \beta_3 NEGATIVE_{it}$$
$$\times MCOMP_{it} + \beta_4 MCOMP(SUM)_{it} + \beta_5 MCOMP(SUM)_{it}^2$$
$$+ \beta_6 LEADER_{it} + \beta_7 MP_{it} + \beta_8 GDP_{it} + \beta_9 MOOD_{it} + \varepsilon_t$$

Note that we also include public policy mood (Stimson 1991; Bartle et al. 2011) in order to control for the possibility that perceived negative competence shocks are endogenous to electoral policy shifts, and to assess our competence explanation against a policy-distance account (Wlezien 2016).

Table 6.3 presents the results using this model. We again present the results using all five countries without control variables, and then the results for the United States and United Kingdom with controls.

These results reveal fairly consistent support for our second hypothesis (i.e. the negativity bias hypothesis). The coefficient for the negativity bias variable (the interaction term for macro-competence when the governing

Table 6.3 *Macro-competence and governing party vote (negativity bias and accumulation)*

	Model 1 (all countries)	Model 2 (US & UK)
Macro-competence(Gov)$_t$	0.333	−0.076
	(0.131)*	(0.178)
Negative × Macro-competence(Gov)$_t$	0.337	0.490
	(0.200)+	(0.236)*
Negative	−0.040	−0.313
	(0.148)	(0.178)$^+$
Sum of Negative ΔMacro-competence(Gov)$_t$	−0.398	−0.499
	(0.127)**	(0.122)***
Sum of Negative ΔMacro-competence(Gov)$_t^2$	0.067	0.086
	(0.029)*	(0.025)***
Macro-partisanship(Gov)$_t$		0.234
		(0.079)**
Leader(Gov)$_t$		0.298
		(0.084)***
GDP$_t$		−0.037
		(0.049)
Mood(Gov)$_t$		−0.137
		(0.070)*
Intercept	0.490	0.791
	(0.166)**	(0.164)***
R-squared	0.45	0.77
N	248	99

$^+$ $p<0.1$; * $p<0.05$; ** $p<0.01$; ** $p<0.001$ (standard errors in parentheses)

party has a low competence rating) is positive and significant in Model 2, and weakly significant (at the 90 per cent confidence level) for Model 1. This denotes a stronger effect of macro-competence on party support at lower levels of macro-competence. Keeping in mind that the variables are standardised, the coefficient for the interaction means that when macro-competence is below its mean level for the governing cycle it has an additional 0.5 standard deviation effect on vote intention for the governing party (in the model for the United States and United Kingdom). This effect holds in the model for all five countries and in the model for the United States and United Kingdom including controls, although in the latter the base effect of party competence (i.e. when macro-competence is above its mean level) is no longer significant.

The results in Table 6.3 also reveal support for the accumulation hypothesis, both in the effect for the accumulation of negative changes in macro-competence (Hypothesis 3) and in terms of its curvilinear effect (Hypothesis 4). The sum of negative macro-competence shocks is strongly significant in each model (at the 99 per cent confidence level). The coefficient means that for every one standard deviation increase in the level of accumulated negative shocks to governing party competence evaluations there is a 0.5 standard deviation decrease in party support (in Model 2). Simply, the costs of governing are a function of the accumulation of blame for perceived poor performance. Note that this effect is significant in addition to the significant base effect of macro-competence (in Model 1) and the significant negativity bias interaction term. This means that governing party votes are lost due to changes in performance evaluations, they are especially lost when performance evaluations are at a low level and they are also lost when negative performance evaluations are treated cumulatively. The curvilinear term for summed negative competence ratings is significant and positively signed, as predicted by Hypothesis 4. The curvilinear relationship can best be interpreted when the marginal effect is plotted, as shown in Figure 6.4.

Figure 6.4 reveals how the addition of negative competence information increases the negative effect on vote. The largest gradient arises from accumulation of a one standard deviation negative shock to competence,

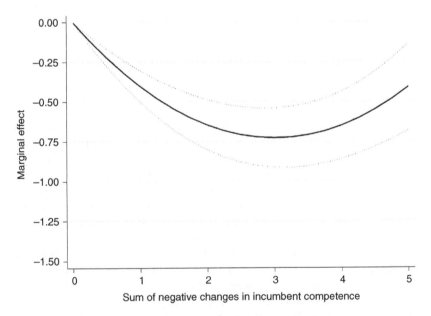

Figure 6.4 The curvilinear effect of blame on vote choice

followed by a further one standard deviation increase, where the addition of negative information increases the negative effect upon party support. However, after this point further negative shocks have no new effect upon vote choices, and the effect then begins to weaken once the sum of negative shocks exceeds four standard deviations. It is not the case that the effect returns to zero. The accumulation of negative performance information continues to exert a negative effect upon vote choice as we would imagine. However, it is largely new information that has the largest effect, with subsequent information having a reduced effect.

The Possibility of an End of Term Bounce

As noted at the start of this chapter, costs of governing sometimes follow parabolic curves whereby support for an incumbent president or party in government tends to increase at the end of a period of incumbency. These increases are not of a size to equal honeymoon periods; they reflect modest upticks in support just before the termination of a period of government. Some evidence for these upticks could be found in Figure 6.1, but recall that the curvilinear line of best fit was only marginally superior to a linear fit.

Providing a theoretically based empirical test for these upticks is problematic, and the use of annual data may obscure end-of-government or election year effects that happen over a period of months rather than years. One explanation for an up-tick prior to an election, or an end-of-government bounce, might be the notion of 'political business cycles', whereby governments are thought to make strategic spending decisions, and the timing of those decisions, to coincide with forthcoming elections (see Lewis-Beck 1990).[14] Governments who can decide the timing of elections may also time those elections to coincide with short-term recoveries in electoral fortunes. We modelled effects with a pair of dichotomous variables added to the models in Table 6.3, first testing for an election effect in an election year that does not lead to a change of party-in-government, and second testing for an election effect in election years in which the incumbent is defeated. An election year effect may denote an effect of campaigns, a return to partisan loyalties following a mid-cycle slump or the effect of political business cycles, whereby governments provide fiscal and policy incentives to the electorate preceding elections. A greater end-of-government election effect might denote a return to partisan loyalties given greater electoral certainty about an upcoming change of government, or it might reflect the weakening of performance

---

[14] The evidence for political business cycles is far from clear, however.

costs against the incumbent as revealed in Figure 6.3. We find that the effect of election years in which the incumbent is defeated is significant and positive, whereas the effect is not significant in election years that do not coincide with an end-of-government. However, these variables add less than 0.01 to the explained variance in the above models and as such offer only the slightest improvement in predictive power.

Evaluating Competing Explanations for Governing Costs

We opened this chapter with a summary of the existing explanations for costs of governing. We also highlighted the paucity of empirical evidence for them, in general, beyond the existence of a time trend.

Here we examine our time-based theory of attribution against a measure reflecting as best as possible the 'coalition of minorities' or 'median gap' explanation offered by Downs (1957), Mueller (1970) and Wlezien (2016b). We use a measure of the deviation of governing party policy from a measure of public preferences, and model the effects of this variable and our performance-based variables on governing party support. To test whether the effects of competence shocks on governing party support are robust to repeated deviation from public preferences for policy (i.e. a proxy measure for coalition-of-minorities), we include in our model an additive measure of the distance between government policy and public policy mood, $DISTANCE(SUM)_{it}$. We focus only on the United States and United Kingdom, where both measures are available (and also the controls). Government policy is measured with DW-Nominate scores of the legislature for the United States and the left-right position of the election manifesto of the governing party for each election cycle for the United Kingdom. This measure is equal to the cumulative total of negative changes (shocks) to this distance between government policy and public preferences (so this additive measure increases each time the distance between policy and preferences increases, but does not decrease when the distance contracts, in line with the coalition of minorities idea). The model takes the form:

$$VOTE_{it} = \alpha_0 + \beta_1 MCOMP_{it} + \beta_2 NEGATIVE_{it} + \beta_3 NEGATIVE_{it}$$
$$\times MCOMP_{it} + \beta_4 MCOMP(SUM)_{it} + \beta_5 MCOMP(SUM)_{it}^2$$
$$+ \beta_6 LEADER_{it} + \beta_7 MP_{it} + \beta_8 GDP_{it} + \beta_9 MOOD_{it}$$
$$+ \beta_{10} DISTANCE(SUM)_{it} + \varepsilon_t$$

The results are presented in Table 6.4.

A spatial measure of additive increases in distance between the incumbent party and public policy mood does not have a statistically significant

Table 6.4 *'Coalition of minorities' and governing party vote*

	Model 1	Model 2
Macro-competence(Gov)$_t$	−0.076	−0.078
	(0.178)	(0.182)
Negative × Macro-competence(Gov)$_t$	0.490	0.437
	(0.236)*	(0.235)$^+$
Negative	−0.313	−0.335
	(0.178)+	(0.168)*
Sum of Negative ΔMacro-competence(Gov)$_t$	−0.499	−0.480
	(0.122)***	(0.130)***
Sum of Negative ΔMacro-competence(Gov)$_t^2$	0.086	0.082
	(0.025)***	(0.026)**
Macro-partisanship(Gov)$_t$	0.234	0.248
	(0.079)**	(0.084)**
Leader(Gov)$_t$	0.298	0.307
	(0.084)***	(0.083)***
GDP$_t$	−0.037	−0.040
	(0.049)	(0.047)
Mood(Gov)$_t$	−0.137	−0.148
	(0.070)*	(0.068)*
Sum of Negative Δ(Policy-Mood)$_t$		−0.032
		(0.035)
Intercept	0.791	0.793
	(0.164)***	(0.164)***
R-squared	0.77	0.77
N	99	99

$^+$ $p<0.1$; * $p<0.05$; ** $p<0.01$; ** $p<0.001$ (standard errors in parentheses)

effect on incumbent party vote intention when the accumulation of competence information is used to model costs of governing (although the effect is in the expected direction). Only one variable, the interaction of negative changes and macro-competence, demonstrates a slightly weaker effect of (negative) competence (where $p=0.06$). Our competence-based measures of blame accumulation (the equivalent negative change measure to that used for coalition of minorities) and the curvilinear term both remain significant in the model, and also the sum of negative policy distances between the incumbent and voters (supporting Wlezien 2016). We suggest that there is as much if not greater support for negativity bias (Hypothesis 2) and accumulation of performance blame (Hypotheses 3 and 4) than there is for an explanation based upon the 'coalition-of-minorities' – in the form of the effects of increasing policy distance with the electorate.

Additional Explanations?

We still need to consider other explanations for the costs of governing. Could it be, for example, that governments simply make more mistakes the longer they are in office? Or that mass media coverage of governments becomes increasingly negative over time? If that coverage becomes increasingly negative over time, is this because performance deteriorates or because there is something intrinsic to media reporting that sides with the incumbent at the beginning of their term of office, but steadily turns against them over time? An increasingly hostile media would not be inconsistent with our theory of governing costs (and we expect it to occur as governing parties are increasingly blamed for their performance), but it is important to explore whether governing costs arise for reasons in addition to these explanations, not just because of them.

We note that costs of governing exist in countries with particularly combative styles of reporting, such as in Great Britain, and they exist in countries with less hostile more regional media coverage, such as in Canada. These costs are comparable in terms of vote intention trends and also in terms of declines in macro-competence.[15] While there is partial evidence that support for the governing party declines faster over time for individuals with higher media consumption, this is not always true.[16] These comparisons tend to suggest that costs of governing may not arise only as a direct result of increasingly negative media reporting.

Furthermore, we find no evidence of better performance with a longer duration of government, but instead we identify variation in indicators of exogenous policy performance over time. To test this, we gathered data for the United States and United Kingdom on economic evaluations, GDP, unemployment, inflation, recorded crime levels and immigration (as discussed in Chapter 5). In no instances did we find significant downward trends in these variables in either country over the course of the governing lifecycle. Finally, we replaced GDP in the reported models in this chapter with the measures of subjective economic evaluations in the

---

[15] The effect of media context remains a possibility; the fit of a linear regression of time in government on vote intention data produces an R^2 of 0.03 prior to 1980 and an R^2 equal to 0.12 afterwards (the root mean squared error provides a comparison of unbiased error estimates, and the costs of governing are again more striking in the later time period, with an RMSE of 0.92 for the period before 1980 and equal to 0.87 afterwards).

[16] We test this using aggregate data for the United Kingdom from the CMS between 2004 and 2013 on vote intentions for the governing party by newspaper readership and non-readership. The trends of governing party support for newspaper readers and non-readers track closely together for Labour under Blair and Brown between 2004 and 2010. In contrast, there is a much higher level of support for the Conservatives from newspaper readers starting in 2010, but this support declines much more quickly over time than for non-readers.

United States and United Kingdom, and found that all our substantive conclusions were unchanged.

What Explains Exceptional Cases?

Before this chapter concludes, we consider two final questions: when do governing costs *not* exhibit the declines that we have described in this chapter, and are there systematic country differences?

For our country data in the United States, United Kingdom, Canada, Australia and Germany there are 24 cases (periods of government) where we observe clear costs of governing in vote intentions, three cases where there are fluctuating levels of support for the incumbent which neither substantially increase nor decrease (Canada between 1963 and 1978, the United Kingdom between 1974 and 1979, and the United States between 1981 and 1993), and two cases exhibiting fluctuation but for which the period of incumbency for the governing party has not yet come to its conclusion (Germany from 2005 and the United States from 2009). These vote intention data are plotted in the Appendix Figure A6.1.[17] Together they represent only three cases across the five countries for which the incumbent party does not suffer a substantial loss of support over its period in office, with no pattern by country.

These cases for which governing costs are not clearly evident are not the product of shorter periods of government. Although the UK Labour government was in power for just five years (1974–1979), and for some of that period as a minority government, in Canada the Liberal governments of Lester Pearson and Pierre Trudeau survived for sixteen years and in the United States the Republican administrations of Ronald Reagan and George H. Bush held office for twelve.

The Canadian case can possibly be explained by the strong leadership ratings of Trudeau, and the fact that there was a change in leadership of the incumbent Liberal Party. The Liberal government between 1963 and 1979 saw the charismatic Trudeau succeed Pearson as Prime Minister in 1968, with the national mood of the time being labelled 'Trudeaumania' (a feat repeated by his son Justin Trudeau, around half a century later). Pierre Trudeau's popularity remained very high until the late 1970s, in spite of an economic recession between 1973 and 1975. High inflation, unemployment and budget deficits preceded the Liberals' loss of power in 1979.

The UK case, between 1974 and 1979, represents a decline in incumbent support, but only in the final months of the government and only by

---

[17] Because these data are annual they do not always capture the early or final months of a governing period. We therefore use these trends to detect broad similarities and differences, not granular ones.

a relatively small amount (our annual vote intention data run to the end of 1978, showing an upturn, but in the 1979 general election Labour's share of the vote fell by 2.3 per cent). This was an unusual period in UK politics. Labour formed the government in February 1974, securing a greater number of parliamentary seats in the election but not the most votes. One reason for the absence of clear governing costs in that period might therefore have been the unusually low starting position of the party-of-government. This may have created something of a floor effect in the popularity of the governing party: Labour went on to lose 2.3 per cent of its vote share in the 1979 election, whereas the Conservative opposition gained 8.1 per cent. Another reason may be the change of Prime Minister in 1976, with James Callaghan taking over after the unexpected resignation of Harold Wilson, and the signs of economic recovery during 1978, with falls in both inflation and unemployment and gains in living standards. There was then a drop in government support following the severe industrial disputes known as 'the winter of discontent' in the run-up to the 1979 general election.

The US case of the Republican administrations of Reagan and Bush Sr. between 1981 and 1992 is notable for the popularity of both presidents for most of their periods of office, a period of sustained economic growth under Reagan, the end of the Cold War and the successful Gulf War operations in 1991 under Bush. The United States suffered a recession at the beginning of Reagan's first term but for most of his presidency the economy was growing strongly. Reagan left office with high approval ratings, while George H. Bush's ratings were very high for his first three years of office (peaking at a record 89 per cent during the Gulf War, as a result of a 'rally-round-the-flag-effect') before falling sharply due to a struggling economy in 1992. The absence of governing costs for these Republican administrations notably occurred around a time when the party was making gains in Congress, climaxing in the mid-terms of 1994, on the back of its campaign against waste and ineffectiveness – ending 40 years of Democratic Congressional control.

In each of these three cases, the incumbent administration sees a change of leadership. There are plenty of other cases, however, where party support continues to decline across leadership changes for the incumbent (think of the Conservative government of Margaret Thatcher then John Major, and the Labour government of Tony Blair then Gordon Brown). However, it is possible that without a major economic downturn and other serious policy or political events, a change of leadership in the midst of a party's period in office may offer a chance to alleviate – if not avert – some governing costs under certain contexts.

There are two periods for which our cases have or had not yet run their full course at the time of analysis (Germany from 2003, and the United

States from 2009). There are, of course, many reasons for the popularity of a party and government, but in Germany one might point to the high approval ratings of the German Chancellor Angela Merkel, at least up until the refugee crisis of 2015–2016 – although the election of Martin Schulz as SPD leader in early 2017 coincided with a drop in support for the Merkel's CDU. The US presidential election of 2016 is interesting, coming after eight years of Democratic Party control of the White House since the election of Barack Obama in 2009. One reason that incumbents may gain support towards the end of a period of governing is the relative unpopularity of challengers – leading to a reappraisal of their time in office. President Obama's approval ratings rose near the end of his term, and support for the Democratic Party rose throughout much of 2015 and 2016.[18] However, the Democrat's popular support saw an overall decline over the whole period since the high water mark of 2009 (where the party won 53.2% of the national vote). These costs of ruling were one factor that enabled Donald Trump to win the presidential election in 2016, though he did so despite Hillary Clinton of course winning the popular vote by 2.1 points – making his victory all the more surprising.

If country differences in governing costs do exist, we would expect to find weaker declines in performance evaluations in cases with reduced 'clarity of responsibility' (Powell and Whitten 1993), potentially where strong leaders enable governing parties' support to be more buoyant, where opposition parties are especially disorganised, divided etc., and arguably in periods where major economic shocks are absent. These questions, and more, are ones we must leave for future analysis.

Conclusion

MacKuen (1983) argued that 'citizen evaluations are as heavily affected by the president's action in the symbolic political arena as they are by fluctuations in economic conditions ... A president cannot, and need not, rely on economic success to maintain his political support. A substantive understanding of popularity would seem to require serious attention to the nature of high symbolic politics.' This statement reveals the importance of performance, competence and the management of presidential reputations for handling these strong components of symbolic politics. An adept president may be able to signal competence and trustworthiness through the handling of political events. However, the regularity of costs of governing suggests that these political decisions may have only minor effects. A president or a party is

---

[18] http://elections.huffingtonpost.com/pollster/2016-national-house-race

unlikely to achieve trends in support which reverse, halt or undo the costs of governing.

We have argued in this chapter that (a) honeymoon periods arise because electorates base their evaluations of the new incumbent on the basis of their evaluations of their predecessor. This mechanism weakens as voters acquire new information about the current incumbent, and discount information about the previous one. It differs from the 'weak partisans' and 'expectations and disillusionment' explanations, but provides an empirical explanation for the peak in government support at the beginning of a period of government (which can also help account for the rise in expectations at the beginning of a cycle, and the dwindling of weaker partisan support). We showed that (b) negative performance information accumulates, such that a performance shock at the beginning of a cycle, after the initial honeymoon period, matters more than a performance shock at the end of the cycle. Once voters have made up their minds about an incumbent, they are increasingly unlikely to revise their opinion about the governing party. This means that positive information, if it exists, has little effect on incumbent popularity once governing costs have set in. Finally, we showed that (c) these trends in perceived incumbent performance explain losses in governing electoral support, and this is more important than the effects of measures designed to capture 'coalitions of minorities', namely, the positional differences between the incumbent party and the electorate, where those positional differences arise in a dynamic thermostatic fashion (Wlezien 1995, 2016; Soroka and Wlezien 2010). The combination of a 'performance accumulation' explanation and a 'coalition of minorities' explanation provides additional explanation of costs of governing in five countries.

These findings have important implications. Incumbents are not able to misrepresent their competence to voters when entering an election, at least not sufficiently to undo the consequences of a term in office. The timing of elections to coincide with improvements in economic conditions can only partially offset the effects of costs of governing over the preceding electoral cycle. Incumbents have little control over their reputation for competence, since it is established on the basis of the previous incumbent at the beginning of the period in office, and accumulates in a predictable fashion, somewhat irrespective of party, country or period, in the analysis of the data collected here. The regularity of costs of governing undermines the ability of governments to reverse public opinion about performance, or perhaps helps account for greater incentives of the incumbent to focus on trying to improve perceptions of performance with time. There is something systematic in public reactions to governments over time. This has critical consequences for the dynamics of public opinion and for electoral choice.

7 Ownership, Performance, Generalised Competence and the Vote

On their own, ownership, performance and generalised competence each have consequences for vote choice. Issue ownership shapes campaign strategies and election outcomes, performance voting extends to issues well beyond the economy, and generalised evaluations of competence give rise to costs of governing in the secular decline in support for parties in government over time. But do these different constructs jointly impact on vote choices and therefore on election outcomes? For ownership, performance and generalised competence to add meaningfully to our understanding of electoral behaviour, their effects should be observed individually and in combination. The final step in our analysis therefore demonstrates how the concepts in public opinion about competence together shape electoral choice.

Throughout this book we have argued that context matters. This is particularly important for thinking about competence, since competence may be especially influential and highly politicised when it is lacking. That is to say, when a political leader or party suffers a negative competence shock, we should expect competence to be seized upon politically, to be salient, and therefore most relevant to public opinion and vote choice. This takes us back to Stokes (1963), who argued that valence issues were those issues that shape political competition in a given period because performance and competence *become* the salient and most relevant political evaluation. Practically any issue can be a valence issue if political competition becomes about competence and delivery on that issue. Likewise, we know that issue ownership can be more salient in some contexts rather than others, when an owned issue is highly salient, or perhaps when ownership of an issue is lost. We also found in the previous chapter that generalised competence has a greater effect on party support when competence changes are negative.

In this chapter we argue that the effects of ownership, performance and generalised competence will be enhanced when symbolic performance events occur to shape the electoral salience of each of these competence judgements. We reveal how major political events, and some elections, strengthen (and weaken) the relationship between public opinion about ownership, performance and generalised competence and party support. This means that our three concepts are not necessarily important in explaining electoral support all of the time, or not always equally important over time, or equal in relation to each other; their influence depends upon the political context.

Aggregate- and Individual-Level Data and Analyses

This chapter provides analyses of vote choice at the individual and aggregate levels, and therefore measures of each concept at both levels. There are several reasons this is important. The first is that we provide greater insight into the contribution of these concepts. At the individual level we apply our concepts to micro-level evaluations; at the aggregate level we apply our concepts to dynamics in public opinion. The second motivation is more substantive. The concepts are not quite the same at both levels. Performance changes at the aggregate level will match imperfectly to changes in the policy environment, but they will be less prone to heterogeneity, which will much more strongly predict performance evaluations at the individual level. There we can capture the vast array of different perceptions – and much greater variance – but also more heterogeneity and potentially more bias. The concept of generalised competence (macro-competence at the aggregate level) has never (to the best of our knowledge) been applied in individual-level models. Here we can tap an underlying perception, which again should be much more prone to heterogeneity and bias. The third motivation is to assess whether there is the same degree of effect when other variables are controlled for, especially partisanship. If there were a problem with endogeneity in aggregate models of vote choice that was unidentified because of measurement differences, we would expect individual-level models controlling for the respondent's own partisan attachments to reveal this more strongly. Finally, it is important to model the effects across data type because we know that our aggregate data are of varying density, and are gathered in different time windows. Our aggregate-level data tend to be sparser, measured at repeated intervals and we are modelling change between one time point and the next. Our individual-level data are dense; we have large numbers of observations, and the survey measures of competence are observed fairly contemporaneously to vote choice.[1] Analysing our

---

[1] Where possible we take all explanatory variables from the pre-election wave of each election survey, and reported vote choice from the post-election wave.

concepts at both an aggregate and individual level allows us to more thoroughly examine their validity.

Measuring Ownership, Performance and Generalised Competence

In each of the preceding chapters we offered details about measuring concepts in public opinion about competence. We bring these together here.

Ownership

The measures of ownership used in this chapter's analysis of party support are:

Aggregate level: Proportion of responses naming a party as best at handling the MIP

Individual level: Survey responses of individuals naming a party as best at handling the MIP

Note that our ownership measures are different to those we used in Chapters 3 and 4. In those chapters we examined changes in aggregate survey data over election cycles and extended periods of time to better understand the characteristics of party reputations across many issues and their alternation. Here we need repeated measures in both time series and election studies. Survey questions asking about the 'best party' to handle particular issues are not perfect measures of ownership. However, they are available over time in aggregate-level survey data, and at the individual level in many election studies. They capture the idea of issue-publics since they require respondents to judge parties on the issue that they consider to be *most important*. They have a positional, competence and commitment component, because the idea of judging a party as 'best' on an issue is not confined to competence alone. They are very useful when researchers wish to match party ratings against the salience of issues to individuals (see, for example, Green and Hobolt 2008). The disadvantages of 'best party' measures are the likelihood that they prime on party and so therefore increase endogeneity, they relate to whichever issue is most important at the time, or for the individual, and, as discussed earlier, they offer a constrained choice comparison between one party and another. As a consequence, it can be difficult to parse out the effects of salience changes with the effects of ownership, and the effects of partisan support. In all analyses we use controls for partisanship and are mindful that best party measures are only proxies for issue ownership. These measures may not be appropriate in all situations; we have shown how the relative ratings of parties on issues reveals important variation in ownership, and where we model relative attention of parties in government to issues we advocate using this rank measure (see Green and Jennings 2017).[2] However, for modelling the effects of ownership on vote choices over time and across countries, 'best party' measures offer the most practical solution.

The 2015 BES fielded an alternative survey measure, asking respondents to select the issues they considered most important to different *parties* as a measure of those parties' priorities (for use of a related measure, see van der Brug 2004). These issues can be compared to the issues ranked most important to the respondent, allowing for a more direct comparison of the shared issue concerns of voters and parties, and a subjective assessment of party commitments. We offer analysis of these measures as a way of comparing and further validating our analyses.

Performance

The measures of performance are:

Aggregate level: Change in party handling ratings on three policy domains; economic, domestic, foreign affairs

Individual level: Mean evaluation of change in policy performance, all available issues

Performance measures should capture fluctuations: the short-term changes in assessments of performance that are not random noise. Are crime rates rising? Has the job situation improved? Is the economy getting better or worse? Ideally, performance measures will not prime 'party' handling but capture changes in policy conditions. Where the available data do prime on party handling of issues (e.g. 'How well is party X handling the issue of healthcare?'), it is *change* in party handling ratings which matters, not the level. Hence we model change in evaluations of performance across available issues, at both the aggregate and individual levels.

For our aggregate level analysis we need to measure change in handling for defined policy domains (i.e. economic, domestic and foreign issues) due to the sparseness of continuous data on specific objective policy conditions over time. At the individual level we use respondent

---

[2] There are other instances where a rank measure may be most useful too, such as analysing the impacts of changes in aggregate-level rankings as shocks to party support, and if sufficient data were available, analysing the relative rankings of issues at the individual level in models of party support.

evaluations of change in policy conditions for all issues included in each respective survey.

Generalised competence

The measures of generalised competence are:

Aggregate level: Macro-competence (estimated with the dyad ratios algorithm) using all issue-handling questions

Individual level: Mean evaluation of party handling across all available issues or, where possible, a factor score of party handling across issues

Generalised ratings of competence should capture an underlying factor in public opinion about party competence: the degree to which assessments exhibit common variation across the issue agenda. At the aggregate level we use Stimson's (1991) dyad ratios algorithm to estimate the underlying dimension in public opinion about competence from all available survey measures about party handling of issues to construct our measure of macro-competence. As discussed in Chapters 3 and 6, this is consistent with the concept of generalised competence and it also enables the estimation of a long running time series of public opinion where survey items have tended to be fielded irregularly and sometimes infrequently. At the individual level we use a factor score where there are sufficient survey items relating to party issue handling or the mean score where there are insufficient items to calculate a factor score.[3]

We compute each of the measures using available data in the United States and United Kingdom. As so often in this book, these countries allow the best over-time data.

Data

Ownership (aggregate level): We use a long-running poll series first asked by Gallup in the United States in 1943 and in the United Kingdom in 1968, and often asked in election surveys, 'which party . . . is best/better able to handle . . . the most important problem'. The measure provides an average rating across all possible 'most important issues'. The question about the MIP is a much-used measure in survey research in the United States and United Kingdom (see Jennings and Wlezien 2011, 2015). It is

---

[3] One or more factors may emerge depending on the survey question wording, which might relate to competence, position or other concepts. In our analysis, for BES waves from 2005, 2010 and 2014–15, we found that the responses typically loaded onto one factor which explained between 90 per cent and 100 per cent of the variance.

typically asked in the form: 'What do you think is the most important problem facing this country today?' This is often followed by a question asking respondents who they consider hold a relative advantage on that problem. In the United States, the wording is 'Which political party do you think could do a better job of handling the problem you just mentioned?' In the United Kingdom, it asks 'Which party do you think can best handle that problem?'

For our aggregate data, we have 296 survey items for the party considered best on the MIP in the United States (1943–2012) and 347 survey items in the United Kingdom (1968–2013). In the United Kingdom, where the survey items are drawn from just two polling organisations, we use the average rating, while in the United States, where there is a greater variety of data sources, we use the dyad ratios algorithm to construct a continuous over-time measure, calculated at quarterly intervals. The level of each measure is equivalent to the proportion of the public who rate a given party as best on the most important issue facing the country. We model the contemporaneous (short-run) and lagged (long-run) effects of party ownership of the MIP. This enables us to consider how ownership assessments are sustained over time and/or how quickly they dissipate in the face of shocks.

Ownership (individual level): The MIP and best party on the MIP questions are fielded in both the BES (2005, 2010 and 2015 waves) and ANES (2000, 2008 and 2012 waves) so we are able to use the same measure. This takes the form of a dichotomous variable equal to one if the respondent believes that a particular party is best able to handle the problem that they named as most important and equal to zero if they believe another party is best on the issue or if no party is considered best.

Performance (aggregate level): We aggregate the available survey data into three broad domains; economic, domestic and foreign issues. This allows us to estimate change in aggregate ratings of issue handling over continuous time series, which would otherwise not be possible due to the sparseness of survey data for specific issues. Using these three policy domains we can undertake time series analysis of performance effects on issues beyond management of the economy (advocated by Wlezien 2016a). The topics give us a tough test of performance effects, since within each domain there will be changes which are cancelled out by other issues. The economy domain comprises questions on the economy, business, trade, labour and employment. Domestic issues comprise rights and minorities, health, education, environment, law and order, welfare and housing, agriculture, energy, science and technology, and public lands. Foreign affairs comprise foreign policy, defence, security and terrorism. In the United States, we have 1,607 survey items on the economy, 1,511 on domestic issues and 792 on foreign affairs. In the United Kingdom we have 1,235 survey items on the economy, 1,577 on domestic issues and 442 on foreign affairs. We use the dyad ratios algorithm to construct continuous measures, at quarterly intervals, of the party considered best able to handle economic, domestic and foreign issues. Because our theoretical expectations relate to performance *fluctuations* our models consider change in party handling ratings, capturing their short-run effect on vote choice.

Performance (individual level): We use the respondent's evaluations of change in the policy environment. We again use the BES (2005, 2010 and 2015 waves) and ANES (2000, 2008 and 2012 waves). The number of questions fielded is sparser than for policy handling, and varies across countries.[4] In the United States, we have data for six issues (the economy, crime, the moral climate, inflation, unemployment and foreign affairs), though typically only a subset of these is available in each year. Examples of the precise wording are ' . . . would you say that over the past year the level of unemployment has gotten better, stayed about the same, or gotten worse?' (ANES 2000 and 2008). In the United Kingdom, the issues number ten, including the economy, tax, crime, asylum, immigration, the NHS, terrorism, education and the cost of living. The question asked in the 2010 BES was: 'Do you think that the crime situation in Britain these days is . . . a lot better, a little better, the same, a little worse, or a lot worse?' A score of one is awarded if the respondent thinks things have got better on a certain issue and a score of zero if the respondent thinks things have got worse or have stayed the same. Because the number of issues varies, we take the mean of all available assessments in each election year.

Generalised competence (aggregate level): We use the measure of macro-competence introduced in Chapter 3 and used in Chapter 6, estimated at the quarterly level. This extracts the shared variance in handling evaluations across all issues. In the United States, this is based on 5,436 survey items (between 1956 and 2013), and in the United Kingdom, it is based on 3,536 items (between 1945 and 2012), accounting for between 50 and 70 per cent of shared variance in handling ratings for the Democratic, Republican, Conservative and Labour parties (as presented in Chapter 3).

Generalised competence (individual level): The measures are constructed using all available handling evaluations for a given election study. We use the mean or factor score of evaluations of party handling of policy issues across all available issues for each respondent (the survey responses are

---

[4] It is for this reason we are unable to use the 2004 ANES, where there are no questions on retrospective evaluations of policy conditions.

assigned a value of 1 for positive assessments of policy handling by a party and a value of 0 for negative or neutral assessments). In the United States, where in some years we have party handling scores for just a single issue (i.e. the economy in 2008 and 2012), we use standardised handling scores.[5] In the United Kingdom, where we have evaluations of party handling for between six and nine issues in a given year (i.e. the asylum system, the NHS, terrorism, the economy, taxation, crime, education, immigration, Afghanistan, financial crisis, the cost of living), we take the underlying factor (from factor analysis) to capture common variation in competence evaluations.

Effects on Party Support: Aggregate-Level Models

We begin our aggregate analysis by focusing on the United States over the period from 1956 to 2012. Our vote measure is the generic Congressional ballot (based on 1,973 survey items). We transform the data to analyse incumbent and challenger parties. That is, whichever of the Republican or Democratic parties holds the presidency in a given quarter (in the UK analysis, this refers to vote intention for the main party that forms the government). This transformation allows us to assess the relative effects of governing performance in the classic reward-punishment way, and opposition dynamics in the reverse.

The dynamic effects of ownership, performance and generalised competence are estimated using a single-equation error-correction model (ECM).[6] We model changes in party support ($\Delta VOTE_t$) as a function of short- and long-run effects of the party best to handle the MIP ($\Delta BEST(MIP)_t$, $BEST(MIP)_{t-1}$), short-run effects of change in policy handling of domestic issues ($\Delta HANDLING(DOMESTIC)_t$), foreign affairs ($\Delta HANDLING(FOREIGN)_t$) and economic issues ($\Delta HANDLING(ECONOMIC)_t$), and short- and long-run effects of macro-competence ($\Delta MCOMP_t$, $MCOMP_{t-1}$). The lagged dependent variable ($VOTE_{t-1}$) measures the rate of re-equilibration in response to shocks to its long-run equilibrium. As controls, we include change in presidential approval ($\Delta PAPP_t$), public policy mood ($\Delta MOOD_t$) and

---

[5] This renders the dichotomous measures comparable with the factor score estimated for 2000 where there were two issues, i.e. the economy and keeping the United States out of war.

[6] There has been a debate over use of generalised error-correction models with stationary and non-stationary data (Keele and de Boef 2008; Enns et al. 2016; Grant and Lebo 2016). Augmented Dickey-Fuller tests reject the presence of unit root in our variables of interest. Fractional integration offers an alternative framework, though tests of the order of fractional integration can be quite unstable. We use the single-equation error-correction method, but confirm the robustness of our results for fractionally differenced data.

macro-partisanship (ΔMP_t), as well as a series of dummy variables (GOV_{it}) for each separate period of party control of the presidency (i), taking 1980–1992 as the base period.[7] The model takes the form:

$$\Delta VOTE_t = \alpha_0 + \alpha_1 VOTE_{t-1} + \beta_1 \Delta MCOMP_t + \beta_2 MCOMP_{t-1}$$
$$+ \beta_3 \Delta BEST(MIP)_t + \beta_4 BEST(MIP)_{t-1}$$
$$+ \beta_5 \Delta HANDLING(DOMESTIC)_t$$
$$+ \beta_6 \Delta HANDLING(FOREIGN)_t$$
$$+ \beta_7 \Delta HANDLING(ECONOMIC)_t$$
$$+ \beta_8 \Delta PAPP_t + \beta_9 \Delta MOOD_t + \beta_{10} \Delta MP_t + \beta_i GOV_{it} + \varepsilon_t$$

The coefficients for the effects of ownership, performance and competence for US governing parties are reported in Figure 7.1 and for opposition parties in Figure 7.2. Unstandardised estimates for all the models are reported in the Appendix, Table A7.1. Each figure below plots the effect of each measure when tested separately (alongside controls), and then for the full model including all measures (and controls). In the coefficient plots, the variables are standardised to enable direct comparison of the relative effect sizes (relative to variance of the measure). The coefficient is indicated by a diamond and the whiskers indicate standard errors where significant effects do not cross the zero line.

The results reveal, in different ways, explanatory effects for each of the concepts, robust to the inclusion of controls (i.e. presidential approval, macro-partisanship, public policy mood). In the full model, the lagged effect of generalised competence is positive and significant at the 95 per cent confidence level for both governing and opposition parties. The coefficients indicate that when the lag of macro-competence is one standard deviation higher, support for the governing and opposition party in the generic ballot is around 0.1 standard deviation higher. Short- and long-run effects of issue ownership are positive and

---

[7] Our measure of presidential approval is the percentage of respondents who approve of the job that the president is doing, calculated as the average of all polls in a given quarter (using 3,688 polls using the traditional approve/disapprove formulation of the presidential approval survey question). Our measure of macro-partisanship uses the method and data developed by MacKuen et al. (1989) and Erikson et al. (2002), calculated as the percentage of respondents identifying with the Democratic/Republican Party at a given point in time (the series is estimated using the dyad ratios algorithm to account for house effects of survey items). This is transformed to equate to the proportion of partisans for the governing and opposition party. Our measure of public policy mood indicates whether or not the public's liberalism/conservatism shifted in the direction of the party when it was in government or opposition (i.e. positive values indicate a conservative shift in policy mood under a Republican administration, a liberal shift in policy mood under the Democrats).

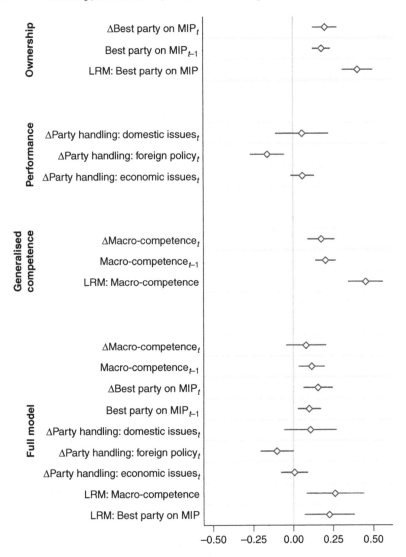

Figure 7.1 Competence effects upon governing party support, aggregate level, US, 1956–2012

significant in the governing party model (with a one standard deviation increase in the best party on the MIP rating leading to a 0.2 standard deviation increase in party support, and with the lag of the level of the variable associated with 0.1 standard deviation higher support), but not

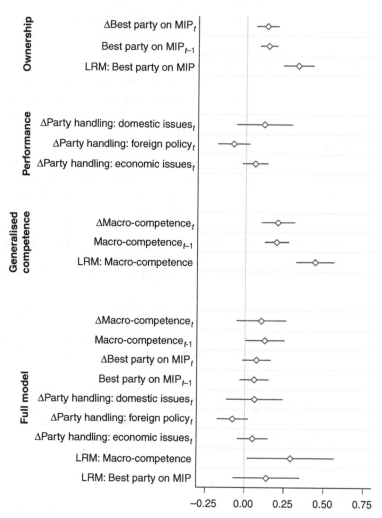

Figure 7.2 Competence effects upon opposition party support, aggregate level, US, 1956–2012

for opposition parties. Additionally, change in performance (on foreign affairs) has an independent effect for governing parties, though this is weakly significant and negative in the fully specified model.

Where we have both contemporaneous (t) and lagged ($t-1$) values of a variable in our model, the overall effect is given by the long-run multiplier (LRM); its total effect on party support distributed over future time periods.[8] This reveals substantial and strongly significant effects of ownership (i.e. best party on the MIP) and also for macro-competence in the fully specified model for governing parties, and a positive and significant effect for macro-competence for opposition parties. The addition of each of the measures to the base model improves the model fit (indicated by the adjusted R-squared reported in the Appendix, Table A7.1), and the fully specified model accounts for between 5 per cent and 8 per cent more variance in predicting party support.[9]

Overall, the aggregate level results for the United States reveal that these three concepts account for variation over time in vote choice, in particular for the party that controls the presidency. Issue ownership, performance and generalised competence all have significant effects when included in a model of party support.[10]

Figures 7.3 and 7.4 plot the comparable standardised effects in models of support for governing and opposition parties for the United Kingdom. Here the model specification is virtually identical but uses party leader approval ratings rather than presidential approval (the full results are reported in the Appendix, Table A7.2).[11]

The aggregate-level results for the United Kingdom further support the need for three concepts, but to a lesser degree. They show slightly different patterns compared to the United States. For the United Kingdom, we find positive and statistically significant effects of all three concepts in the

---

[8] The long-run multiplier (k_1) is calculated using the equation: $k_1 = \frac{\beta_1}{\alpha_1}$, where α_1 is the error-correction mechanism and β_1 is the long-run effect of the independent variable.

[9] Full details can be found in the Appendix, Table A7.1. The likelihood-ratio test of each model is compared to a base model with no predictors, confirming that the addition of each variable adds significantly to the explained variance. Note that we found a greater number of significant effects in the opposition model – specifically for change in generalised competence and domestic performance – when we dropped partisanship from that model, suggesting that partisanship may play a greater role in evaluations of oppositions with respect to competence, but competence exerts a stronger causal effect for the incumbent.

[10] There is a possibility, of course, that the effects of ownership, performance and generalised competence are partly subsumed into presidential approval, policy mood and partisanship. These models do not consider how our three concepts shape other predictors of party support. By controlling for them we offer a strict test of competence effects.

[11] The measure of party leader approval is taken as the proportion of respondents indicating that they approve or are satisfied in the Gallup (1951–2001) and Ipsos MORI (1977–2012) survey items on performance of party leaders. Historically, Gallup fielded the question 'Are you satisfied or dissatisfied with X as prime minister?', while Ipsos MORI similarly asks the questions 'Are you satisfied or dissatisfied with the way X is doing his/her job as Prime Minister?' For opposition leaders, Gallup used to ask, 'Do you think X is or is not proving a good leader of the Conservative/Labour Party' whereas Ipsos MORI ask 'Are you satisfied or dissatisfied with the way X is doing his/her job as leader of the Conservative/Labour Party?' These series are highly correlated (see Green and Jennings 2012a, 2012b) so we take the average for the overlapping period.

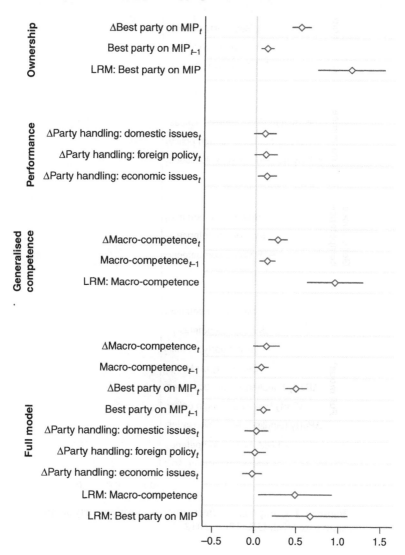

Figure 7.3 Competence effects upon governing party support,
aggregate level, UK, 1968–2012

models of governing party support, though the short-run effects of policy
handling drop out in the fully specified model. In the full model, the
short-run and lagged effects for macro-competence are very almost significant at the 95 per cent confidence level (and are significant at the

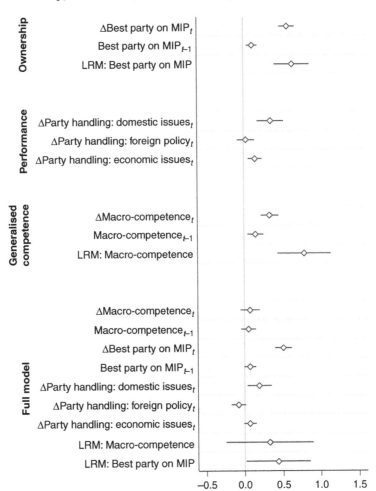

Figure 7.4 Competence effects upon opposition party support, aggregate level, UK, 1968–2012

90 per cent confidence level). A one standard deviation increase in macro-competence ($\Delta MCOMP_t$) results in a 0.1 standard deviation increase in support for the incumbent ($p<0.1$), while a one standard deviation increase in the best party on the MIP leads to a 0.5 standard deviation increase in support ($p<0.001$). The lagged level of both macro-competence and best party on the MIP is associated with a 0.1 standard deviation higher level of support. Importantly, the LRM for each measure

indicates that their combined short- and long-run effect is significant, at the 95 per cent confidence level (shown in Table A7.2).

In the model of opposition party support, issue ownership and performance effects remain robust to the inclusion of other predictors. Short- and long-run effects of macro-competence are only weakly significant ($p<0.1$), however.[12] The fully specified model accounts for between 12 per cent and 24 per cent more variance than for the base model with no predictors: substantially more than in the United States (where the range was between 5 per cent and 9 per cent). The likelihood-ratio test similarly confirms that each model adds significantly to the explained variance compared to the base model with no predictors. Overall, the findings suggest our three concepts provide substantial information to prediction of vote choices at the aggregate level.

By varying the country and data, we cannot make firm inferences about why we find differences in effect. There may be dynamics for governing and challenger parties that are specific to the United States and to the United Kingdom and contextual factors in each time period which may explain those differences, rather than institutional explanations, or simply data differences. Here we highlight the relevance of each concept in explaining party support across country and party contexts.[13]

Effects on Vote Choices: Individual-Level Models

We next consider vote choice at the individual level, using survey data from the ANES and BES, as described above. Our dependent variable is which presidential candidate or parliamentary party a respondent voted for. This is a dichotomous variable, indicating whether or not an individual voted for the incumbent or challenger party. The vote measure is taken from the post-election surveys in each case.[14] Party identification is

---

[12] Addition of each measure to the base model improves the model fit (indicated by the adjusted R-squared).

[13] As a robustness check we modelled the vote in both countries using fractional integration models. For US governing parties a fractional cointegration model of vote-macro-competence produces very similar results (without evidence of a long-run relationship between vote and best party of the MIP, but including a short-run effect of domestic policy handling), while for opposition parties there is evidence of a long-run fractional cointegrating relationship between vote and macro-competence with additional effects of short-run domestic policy handling. For the United Kingdom, fractional cointegration models find strong relationships for opposition parties (fractional cointegration of vote and macro-competence, plus fractional effects of best party on the MIP, domestic policy handling and economic handling at the 90 per cent confidence level), but weaker effects for governing parties.

[14] For the United States, we use all explanatory variables in the pre-election wave, the only exception being best party on the MIP where this is only available for the post-election

coded as equal to one if a respondent identifies with a particular party and zero if they do not.[15]

We model vote choice (Vote$_i$) as a function of party identification (PartyID$_i$), whether a party is considered best on the MIP or not (Best(MIP)$_i$), subjective evaluations of (good) policy conditions (Conditions$_i$), the average rating of party competence across all available issues (Competence$_i$). We control for presidential approval (PApp$_i$) and spatial distance between the respondent and the party (Proximity$_i$).[16] We also control for the year of survey, to capture the greater or lesser propensity to vote for a party at a given election. Our logistic regression models take the form:

$$\text{Vote}_i = \alpha_0 + \beta_1 \text{PartyID}_i + \beta_2 \text{Best(MIP)}_i + \beta_3 \text{Conditions}_i$$
$$+ \beta_4 \text{Competence}_i + \beta_5 \text{PApp}_i + \beta_6 \text{Proximity}_i + \varepsilon_i$$

Figure 7.5 plots the coefficients for the effects of ownership, performance and competence on US vote choice across the 2000, 2008 and 2012 presidential elections.[17] These are standardised effects from the logistic regression.

wave in 2008 and 2012. For the United Kingdom, the only exception is subjective evaluations of policy conditions which are from the post-election wave in 2010.

[15] Measures of party identification take the form of a seven-point scale in both the United States and United Kingdom but we prefer to use a dichotomous transformation to enable direct comparisons since we cannot be sure that the scales are equivalent (the US survey measure uses the terms 'strong', 'weak' and 'Independent-Democrat' or 'Independent-Republican', whereas the UK measure uses the terms 'very', 'fairly' and 'not very' strong Labour or Conservative.

[16] Presidential approval is coded as equal to one if the respondent approves of the job the president is doing, and zero if they do not approve or don't know. In our UK model this is coded as equal to one if the respondent offers a positive assessment of the leader (on a scale from 0 to 10, so any value of six or greater). In the United States, proximity is measured as the absolute difference between self-placement of the respondent on an ideological seven-point scale and their placement of the party on that same scale.[16] We recode any 'don't know' responses as the mid-point of the scale to avoid the loss of data. In the United Kingdom, proximity is the absolute distance between left-right self-placement of the respondent and their placement of Labour and the Conservatives in the 2005 and 2015 BES, and absolute distance between the tax-spend preferences of the respondent and their placement of tax-spend preferences of Labour and the Conservatives in 2010. In the 2005 and 2015 BES, the self/party-placement question was worded 'In politics people sometimes talk of left and right. Where would you place yourself on the following scale?' and ' . . . where would you place the following parties on this scale?' with the scale running from 0 (left) to 10 (right). In the 2010 BES, the tax-spend question took the form 'Using the 0 to 10 scale on this card, where the end marked 0 means that government should cut taxes and spend much less on health and social services, and the end marked 10 means that government should raise taxes a lot and spend much more on health and social services, where would you place yourself/party name on this scale?'

[17] The results are reported in full in the Appendix, Table A7.3.

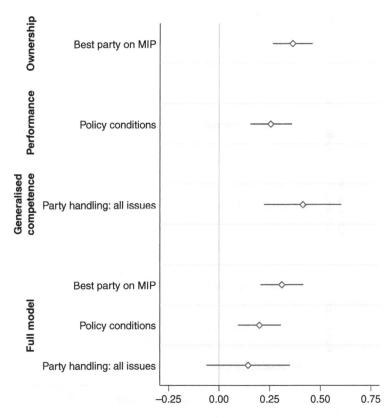

Figure 7.5 Competence effects upon governing party support, individual level, US, 2000–2012

Our individual-level models of vote choice find effects for all three concepts. These are observed consistently in the governing party and opposition party models, and when all three variables are included together, with just one exception where the effects of generalised competence (i.e. party handling across all issues) are not statistically significant at the 95 per cent confidence level in the full model for incumbents. Expressed as an odds ratio (as reported in Table A7.3), the increased likelihood of voting for the incumbent (1.918, $p<0.01$) is twice as high for those who consider policy conditions have got better compared to those who think they have not. The likelihood of voting for the opposition, in contrast, is reduced by two-thirds (0.342, $p<0.01$), if the respondent thinks things are going well. These effects are observed even when controlling for party identification, presidential approval and spatial

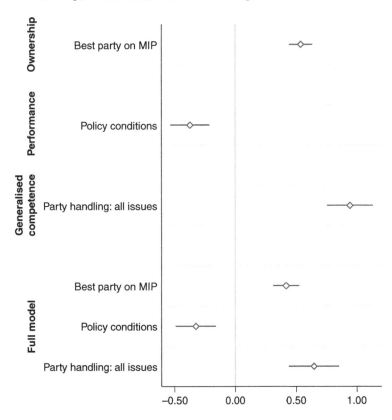

Figure 7.6 Competence effects upon opposition party support,
individual level, US, 2000–2012

proximity, all of which are important predictors of vote choice.
The inclusion of each variable in the model adds to the explained variance. We used the Wald test statistic to compare the fit of nested models
(see the Appendix, Table A7.3), adding one variable at a time.
The addition of each of the three variables leads to a significant improvement in the variance explained.

In Figure 7.7 we plot the coefficients for the equivalent models in the
United Kingdom, using data from the 2005, 2010 and 2015 BES.[18]

---

[18] Full results for the models are reported in the Appendix, Table A7.3. Results plotted in
Figure 7.7 include data from Waves 4 and 6 of the 2015 BES Internet Panel Study, rather
than the post-election face-to-face survey for 2015, due to the greater availability of
survey measures in that year.

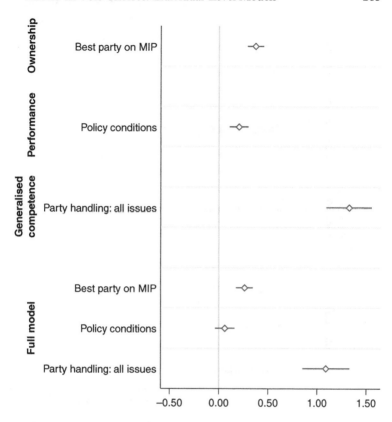

Figure 7.7 Competence effects upon governing party support, individual level, UK, 2005–2015

The results are consistent with those we show for the United States, providing support for all three concepts.

For our model of vote choice for UK governing parties we find positive and significant effects for both ownership and generalised competence in the full model, while the effect of performance (i.e. evaluations of policy conditions) is signed in the expected direction but not significant at the 95 per cent confidence level. The effect of generalised competence in particular is sizeable (Figure 7.7). In terms of the odds ratios (see the Appendix, Table A7.4), a one unit increase in the factor score (which ranges from −1.3 to 1.5) increases the likelihood of voting for the governing party by almost three times (2.982, $p<0.01$). For opposition parties, the effects of generalised competence, performance and issue ownership all remain significant in the fully specified model, including

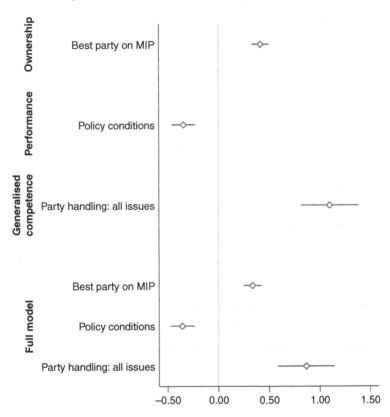

Figure 7.8 Competence effects upon opposition party support, individual level, UK, 2005–2015

controls for leader evaluations, party identification and spatial proximity. Wald tests reveal that the addition of each variable adds significantly to the variance explained.

At both the aggregate and the individual levels, in the United States and in the United Kingdom, our tests reveal the empirical significance of all three concepts for party support. The aggregate- and individual-level results are not mirror images of each other, nor are the US and UK comparisons. We are not testing the effects of the exact same concepts when we model them at the two different levels. In terms of dynamics, our concepts appear to be more substantively important for the vote shares of parties in power. At the individual level our concepts apply equally to parties in and out of power. This may arise because our aggregate models consider the effects of competence over the whole election cycle, and assess the temporal ordering of variables, whereas our individual-level models assess the effects at the time of elections.

Alternative Measure of Ownership

One of the reasons that ownership, performance and competence effects vary across contexts may simply be that the design of existing survey measures does not adequately capture their influence on vote choice. The 2015 BES fielded a number of questions that map directly onto our concepts, which provides an opportunity to explore the concepts further.

Ownership: respondents were asked whether they thought an issue was a priority for a party on a scale of 0 to 10. This enabled them to give an evaluation of the relative emphasis placed on issues by parties. Given that our concept of ownership in Chapters 3 and 4 is concerned with rank ordering of issues, this captures those issues associated with the party (and unlike the best party on the MIP, this is not constrained to a single issue and it is not a relative assessment between the parties: two parties could, in theory, both be associated with an issue).

Performance: respondents were asked whether they thought things had got better or worse in a particular policy domain. This again was coded as equal to one where it was believed things had got better and zero if they had got worse or stayed the same.

Generalised Competence: respondents were asked whether or not they thought a party had handled or would handle a particular issue very well, well, neither, badly or very badly (measured using a five-point scale). Our measure of generalised competence is here calculated as the underlying factor of handling scores across all issues (dropping 'don't know' responses).

We estimate a logistic regression model of vote choice, where our dependent variable is whether a respondent voted for the party or not, equal to one where an individual voted for the Conservatives (or for Labour) and zero where they did not. Standardised effects for the Conservative (incumbent) model are plotted in Figure 7.9.[19]

The full model demonstrates significant effects for each of our concepts, though not always in the expected direction. The effects of ownership (party priorities) and performance on the NHS – a highly salient issue in the context of recent elections in the United Kingdom and a focus of campaigning by parties – are particularly important. Rating

---

[19] The full model is provided in the Appendix, Table A7.5. Note that for the 2015 election the incumbent party also included the Liberal Democrats in a coalition with the Conservatives, but we omit this for the sake of brevity.

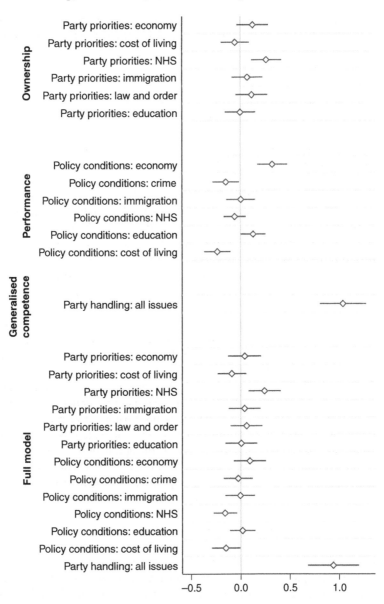

Figure 7.9 Competence effects upon governing party (Conservative) support, individual level, UK, 2015

the Conservatives as prioritising the NHS increases the likelihood of voting for the party, but evaluating the NHS as having got better has a negative effect on Conservative vote despite being the incumbent.[20] Alongside these effects, there is a strong effect of generalised competence on vote choice, in the factor score for handling across all issues. Recall that the full model includes the controls for party identification, leader approval and spatial proximity. In the performance model (not including measures of ownership or generalised competence), perception of improvements in the level of crime and cost of living have negative effects on Conservative vote in 2015, suggesting the incumbent party was not credited with improvements in these policy areas – or alternatively that respondents who believed these policy conditions had improved were more likely to vote for other parties.

The equivalent figure for the model of Labour vote choice is presented in Figure 7.10.

Once again, the full model offers support for all three concepts, with significant effects on Labour vote choice in 2015 on prioritisation of the economy (ownership, or the lack thereof), evaluations of whether the economy was getting better (with a positive view of performance having a negative impact on vote choice for the Labour opposition), and generalised competence via the factor score of party handling ratings across all issues.

The results offer further support for the relevance of all three concepts in models of vote choice. The Wald test reveals a significantly improved explanatory power when each additional variable is added (compared to a base model with party identification, leader approval and proximity as predictors), and in the fully specified model. These results are robust to the inclusion of controls for partisanship, leadership evaluations and spatial proximity measures, all of which are strongly significant. Given we believe spatial evaluations are part of issue ownership, and party-primed questions represent several aspects of party evaluations on issues, this offers a highly conservative test of the effects of ownership, performance and generalised competence.

When Competence Becomes Politicised

The preceding analysis takes a one-size-fits-all approach to the time periods covered. While we do this to demonstrate the value of each construct of competence, it is not an ideal way to think about the effects

---

[20] Voters may plausibly have credited Labour with any improvements in the NHS following previous Labour investment, or simply been unwilling to give credit to the Conservatives.

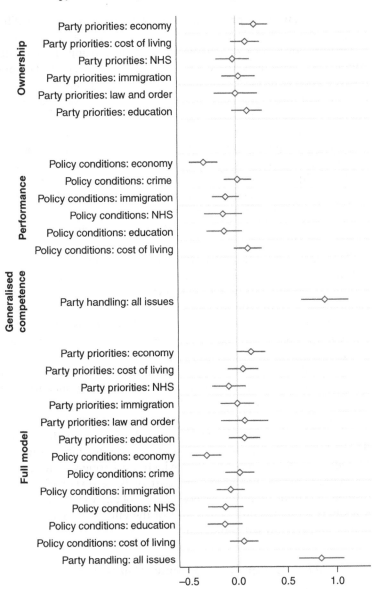

Figure 7.10 Competence effects upon opposition party (Labour) support, individual level, UK, 2015

of competence, drawing on the original concept of valence by Donald Stokes.

Stokes' definition of a valence issue was narrower than our three concepts, but the argument applies to each. Political context is critical. As discussed above, when political competition is framed as a competition based on competence, the political issue becomes a valence issue in nature.

We expect that when ownership is politicised its effects upon vote choices will be greater. The same is true for performance and for generalised competence too. Competence priming should be especially common where one party believes an opponent will be electorally damaged if the issue becomes central to party choice. But not all parties will be equally successful in priming performance on an issue, or in all contexts. When performance becomes *the* story in a political system it is much more likely to be associated with vote choice. This will most often arise because of a major political or performance-related shock or event. When a significant shock occurs to make an evaluation important, relevant and politically salient, we should witness that evaluation become a predictor – and/or a stronger predictor – of party support. Some election campaigns may also reflect greater framing of a choice based upon competence than others.

There are three ways in which competence might become more politicised and relevant to vote choices. The first is via high-salience performance shocks or high-salience events which politicise the handling of an issue and make managerial competence – or indeed issue ownership – more important and heavily weighted. An event – such as a scandal, a policy failure or a major international event – will not necessarily make that scandal, policy or event 'the most important problem facing the country'. However, it can frame the basis of party evaluation and support in the national media, political debate and, consequently, in party support. The second way is via issue salience. Competence might become more important to an individual voter simply because an issue is especially salient to them (Green and Hobolt 2008), and issues become more salient when they are considered to be problems (Jennings and Wlezien 2011). Issue salience effects should therefore be partly encapsulated by the effects of important political shocks and events. Finally, parties have incentives to frame an election choice as being about competence when they believe they will gain benefits from doing so; either because of a performance shock, or a salient issue, or simply because an incumbent is broadly perceived to be failing, or an opposition party is very weak. This strategy will not always be successful, but parties have the potential to help shape the basis of electoral choice under some contexts, aided by the wider media and policy context.

We expect major events or shocks to heighten ownership voting, performance voting or generalised competence voting. Given that parties have incentives to prime certain evaluations in campaigns, but are not always successful in doing so, we also expect election campaigns to exert an effect, in some instances.

Method of Analysis

Dynamic conditional correlations (Engle 2002) provide a framework for dealing with time-varying effects and volatility (Box-Steffensmeier and Lebo 2008), revealing when the relationships between variables are weaker and stronger. They offer a calculation of the current correlation between a pair of variables as a function of past volatility. This method involves a two-stage estimation procedure. In the first stage, univariate volatility parameters are estimated for each of the variables of interest using a generalised autoregressive conditional heteroscedasticity (GARCH) process, where variance at time t is modelled as a function of previous observations and previous variances.[21] At the second stage, standardised residuals from the first stage are used to estimate a time-varying correlation matrix.

For the purposes of our analysis, we model the first difference of each of our aggregate-level variables for governing and opposition parties (i.e. party support, macro-competence, best party on the MIP and party handling of domestic, foreign and economic issues) as a function of their past volatility, estimated as a GARCH(1,1) process. Here we are not interested in modelling predictors of each of the processes, but we use the univariate noise process as a benchmark against which the strength of association of ownership, performance and macro-competence with party support can be tested. These time series processes are modelled over the full time period for which we have reliable quarterly data (1956 to 2012 in the United States and 1968 to 2012 in the United Kingdom). These are the same time series data as used for Figures 7.1 to 7.4. Having estimated the underlying noise process behind each variable, we have an estimate of the dynamic conditional correlation between each variable and party support (DCC_t).

The dynamic conditional correlations for the US Democratic and Republican parties are plotted in Figure 7.11.

---

[21] For the variance of time series y, a GARCH(1,1) process would take the form:
$\sigma^2_t = \alpha_0 + \alpha_1 y^2_{t-1} + \beta_1 \sigma^2_{t-1}$.

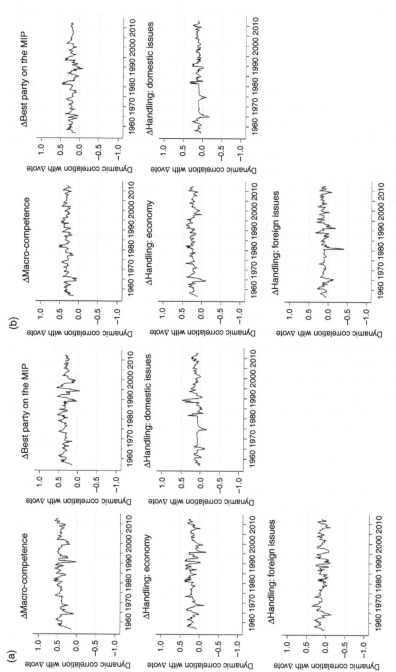

Figure 7.11 Dynamic conditional correlations between vote choice and measures of competence, US, 1956–2012 (a) Republican Party (b) Democratic Party

The dynamic conditional correlations in Figure 7.11 tend on average to be higher for change in macro-competence and change in the best party on the MIP, with weaker correlations observed for party handling on the economy, domestic issues and foreign affairs. This is as one would expect given the results from our earlier error-correction models. What is of particular interest to us is that the strength of the relationship between each of the measures and party support fluctuates over time, and undergoes a sudden upward or downward shifts at particular moments, reflecting a strengthening or weakening of the relationship between the variables before returning to a fairly stable mean in each case. This sort of re-equilibration in response to shocks is implied by the ECM framework used earlier, but here we are able to plot the process and then attempt, below, to model what drives these disturbances.

We plot the dynamic conditional correlations for the UK Labour and Conservative parties in Figure 7.12.

The correlation with change in party support, on average, tends to be higher for change in the party considered best on the MIP, with weaker associations for macro-competence, party handling on the economy, domestic issues and foreign affairs. This again is largely consistent with the results of our earlier ECMs and reveals interesting country similarities and differences with the United States. The performance measures are less strongly associated with party support in both countries, while the relationship with our measure of ownership is stronger in the UK.[22] The correlations between each of the measures and party support vary over time, often fluctuating noisily and sometimes undergoing sharp sudden movements, before returning to their long-run equilibrium.

The dynamic conditional correlations tell us that the relationship between ownership, performance, generalised competence and vote choice is time-varying. But what are the shocks and events that drive these fluctuations? We next model the effect of key events and shocks on each of the dynamic conditional correlation series as an autoregressive distributed lag (ADL) model. We expect that the effects of competence shocks/events will be temporary (we do not expect a long-lasting increase in, for example, the effect of performance ratings on party support). We therefore model each specific event, i, at time t as a 'pulse' intervention.[23] This model can be expressed in the form:

$$DCC_t = \beta_0 DCC_{t-1} + \beta_i Event_{it} + \varepsilon_t$$

[22] This may arise because we use survey data on 'best party' on the MIP.
[23] A pulse intervention indicates that the effect of an event (x) is temporary at time j, such that: $x = \begin{cases} 0, & t \neq j \\ 1, & t = j \end{cases}$.

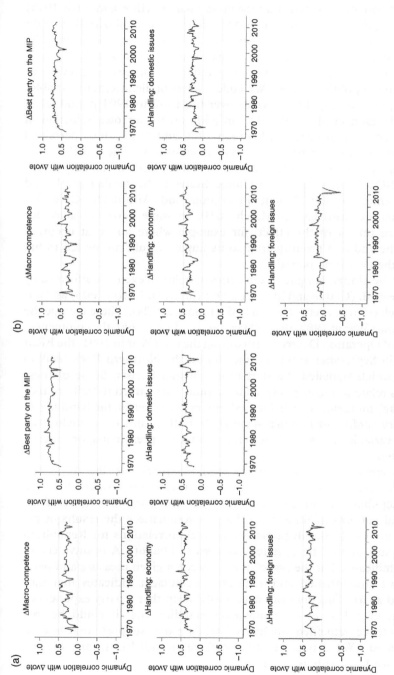

Figure 7.12 Dynamic conditional correlations between vote choice and measures of competence, UK, 1968–2012
(a) Conservative Party (b) Labour Party

This sort of time series intervention analysis (Box and Tiao 1975) requires prior expectations about the major events or shocks that might have impacted – positively or negatively – on the effects of ownership, performance and generalised competence on party support.

For the United States, we use a range of sources to inform our selection of political events. We code a series of dichotomous variables corresponding to political events over the 1955 to 1991 period taken from Erikson et al. (2002: 52), in addition to our own selection of major events that occurred between 1956 and 2013 which pertained to competence of parties in power or opposition. These include the federal government shutdown in December 1995 to January 1996, the Al-Qaeda attacks on the United States in September 2001, and the signing of the Patient Protection and Affordable Care Act 'Obamacare' into law in March 2010. In some cases we allow for a lag in timing of the effect, for example where an event occurred near the end of a given quarter so its impact would not be felt in full until the next time period.

For the United Kingdom, our series of political events is informed by Clarke et al. (Clarke and Stewart 1995; Clarke and Lebo 2003) and our own selection of events (Green and Jennings 2012a). These include the Falklands War in 1982, the poll tax riots in March 1990, the commencement of Operation Desert Storm during the Gulf War in 1991, the ERM crisis in September 1992 and the run on the Northern Rock bank in 2007 which signalled the start of the financial crisis. Some of these events relate to major policy failures, others are linked to 'rally-round-the-flag' moments which focused voters on government handling of military conflict or national security. In both countries we include an event variable corresponding to the quarter of (presidential or general) elections.

We report full results for UK and US parties in the Appendix, Tables A7.6 to A7.9, but here focus on those for the US Republicans and UK Conservatives, which are illustrative of the general patterns of findings. Table 7.1 summarises the results of the ADL models of the dynamic conditional correlations for Republican Party support (in the generic Congressional ballot). A positive coefficient indicates that the association between a given measure and party support strengthened and a negative coefficient indicates that they drifted apart. This does not necessarily mean that a party experienced a gain or a loss in its competence standing (i.e. it could be that competence remained unchanged while party support increased or decreased). We denote negative coefficients with '(neg)' and the significance level with asterisks.

Table 7.1 *Effect of events on dynamic conditional correlation with party support, Republican Party, US, 1956–2012*

	Macro-competence	Best(MIP)	Handling (economy)	Handling (domestic)	Handling (foreign)
1958-Q2: Civil Rights Act 1957 / Little Rock, Arkansas (t−2)	***				***
1964-Q2: Johnson SOTU sets out 'war on poverty' and civil rights legislation	(neg)		(neg)		(neg)
1965-Q2: Johnson begins bombing of North Vietnam			**		
1966-Q2: Johnson resumes bombing and increases troop numbers in Vietnam (Jan 31st) (t−1)			**		
1973-Q2: US involvement in Vietnam war ends with Paris Peace Accords (Jan 27th) (t−1)	*		***		***
1981-Q2: Iran hostage crisis end (Jan 20th) (t−1)	*		**		
1982-Q1: Economic recession/rising unemployment	**		***		**
1982-Q2: Economic recession/rising unemployment		**			
1987-Q1: Reagan apologises for Iran-Contra / Tax Reform Act of 1986 (Oct 22nd) – second of the two 'Reagan tax cuts'			**		**
1990-Q1: Bush/Gorbachev summit (Dec 3rd) / Fall of the Berlin Wall (Nov 9th) / Friday 13th crash (Oct 13th)			***	***	(neg)
1991-Q2: Gulf War (t−1)	***	**	(neg)	(neg)	(neg)
1992-Q3: Unemployment peaks at 7.8% (Jun 1992)	***	***	***		*
1993-Q4: US military operations in Somalia and Haiti (Oct 1993) / Air strikes in Ira-Q (Jun 1993) / Don't Ask Don't Tell legislation (Nov 30th) / Omnibus Budget Reconciliation Act of 1993 (Clinton's first budget raising taxes)	(neg)	(neg)	(neg)		*
1995-Q4: Shutdown of federal government	**	**	***		(neg)

Table 7.1 (*cont.*)

	Macro-competence	Best(MIP)	Handling (economy)	Handling (domestic)	Handling (foreign)
2002-Q1: September 11th $(t-1)$	***	*			
2003-Q4: Iraq War (Mar) – 80 fatalities of US troops in Nov (highest since start of conflict) / Bush tax cuts (May 28th)					**
2010-Q2: Obamacare signed into law (Mar 10th)	**		**		
1956-Q4: Presidential election	*				
1960-Q4: Presidential election		**		**	
				(neg) ***	
1964-Q4: Presidential election				(neg)	
1968-Q4: Presidential election		**	*** (neg)		***
1972-Q4: Presidential election					
1976-Q4: Presidential election					
1980-Q4: Presidential election	***	*	***		
1984-Q4: Presidential election	**	*	*		***
1988-Q4: Presidential election					**
1992-Q4: Presidential election					*
1996-Q4: Presidential election					
2000-Q4: Presidential election					
2004-Q4: Presidential election					
2008-Q4: Presidential election					

* $p<0.05$; ** $p<0.01$; *** $p<0.001$

In Table 7.1 we see that a few events had consistent effects across all measures. President Johnson's announcement of the war on poverty and civil rights legislation (landmark Democrat programmes) had a negative effect on the correlation between Republican competence, economic and foreign policy handling and party support. The end of the Vietnam War in 1973 – under President Nixon – was associated, in contrast, with a positive effect on the association between the same measures and party support. The Gulf War, once again under a Republican incumbent of the White House, President George H. Bush, was similarly associated with a positive effect on the correlation with competence, ownership and economic and foreign policy handling for the Republicans. The events of 9/11 and the response of the Republican administration of George W. Bush also had a positive and significant effect on the association between competence and ownership and party support.

Effects of bad economic news seem to vary in different time periods. In 1982, the onset of recession and rising unemployment rates under the Reagan Administration are associated with a strengthening of the link between macro-competence, ownership, economic handling and foreign policy handling. This suggests that competence became more salient to vote choice in this time period. In 1992, when unemployment peaked at 7.8 per cent, however, there was a weakening of the competence/vote connection for generalised competence, ownership and economic handling. We see similar sorts of effects for the Democrats (in the Appendix, Table A7.7), associated with critical events/moments relating to foreign policy and the economy, suggesting there is a general pattern whereby the effects of competence are amplified or reduced depending on the context. Note that a decrease (increase) in the dynamic conditional correlation between competence and party support does not necessarily mean that a party experienced a loss (gain) on the issue, but that the two variables diverged (converged) at that moment in time. In the case of an economic shock, this might occur because a large fall in party handling ratings translates into a smaller deterioration of party support. Or alternatively, it might be that a relatively small reduction of handling ratings has a disproportionately large impact on party support, due to the salience of the issue.

In the United Kingdom, too, it is possible to assess how the relationship between party support and each of the measures of competence varied over time. In Table 7.2 we present the results of the ADL model for the UK Conservative Party.

We see broadly similar patterns for the United Kingdom, of salient events strengthening or weakening the link between competence evaluations and vote choice, but far fewer effects for events, and no effects of

Table 7.2 *Effect of events on dynamic conditional correlation with party support, Conservative Party, UK, 1968–2012*

	Macro-competence	Best(MIP)	Handling (economy)	Handling (domestic)	Handling (foreign)
1974-Q1: Three Day Week / Oil Price Shock					*** (neg)
1979-Q1: Winter of Discontent		***			
1982-Q2: Falklands War ($t-1$)	*		*		
1990-Q2: Poll Tax riots			*		
1992-Q4: ERM ($t-1$)		**	***		**
2003-Q2: Invasion of Iraq				*	
2007-Q4: Northern Rock			*		
2008-Q1: Northern Rock	**	**	*	**	
1970-Q2: General election					
1974-Q1: General election					
1974-Q4: General election					
1979-Q2: General election					
1983-Q2: General election					
1987-Q2: General election					
1992-Q2: General election					
1997-Q2: General election					
2001-Q2: General election					
2005-Q2: General election					
2010-Q2: General election					

$+ p<0.1$; $* p<0.05$; $** p<0.01$; $*** p<0.001$

elections. For the Conservatives, a few events appear to have had consistent and substantial impacts on the association between our measures and party support. The Falklands War, a point of contention in the literature (Dunleavy and Husbands 1985; Sanders et al. 1987), strengthens the correlation of party support with best party on the MIP and economic handling. The other events with consequences for the correlation between competence and party support are the two major economic crises of the past 30 years in the United Kingdom – the ERM crisis of November 1992 and the run on the Northern Rock bank in 2007 (which signalled the onset of the global financial crisis). Each of these had positive and significant effects on the association between party support and four out of our five measures of competence; for ERM, there was no significant change in the correlation of party support and macro-competence, while for Northern Rock there was no significant change for foreign policy handling. It is interesting that none of the elections over this period were associated with an especially strong or weak relationship between each of the competence measures and Conservative support. This suggests that the effects of competence on Conservative support have tended to be stable across elections. By way of comparison, we find less evidence to suggest that particular events have altered the relationship between Labour support and any of our measures of party competence.

Overall, there are some interesting differences between the two country cases. In the United States, there is strong evidence of a conditional explanation of ownership, performance and generalised competence effects, with a series of major political and economic shocks disturbing the equilibrating relationship between each variable and party support. These shocks appear to be equally important for the series we examine for both parties. For the United Kingdom, the conditionality appears to be much weaker, pointing, perhaps, to the differences in party competition, in the importance of performance cues, or perhaps the nature of political debate, presidential campaigns and the nature of the US media. The differences do not denote stronger competence effects in the United States compared to the United Kingdom; the consistency of effects was evident in the general effects reported for the aggregate- and individual-level models in Figures 7.1 through 7.10. The differences are in the *volatility* of the relationships between ownership, performance and generalised competence, which appears to be more responsive to major shocks in the United States than in the United Kingdom.

The dynamic conditional correlations provide strong support for the importance of political context in shaping the effects of competence on party support, especially and very significantly in the United States. They provide support for a Stokes theory of valence and broaden that theory to the three concepts we identify in this volume: ownership, performance and competence. Ignoring political context when analysing and theorising about competence will miss an important aspect of the story. Furthermore, assuming ownership, performance and generalised competence to always be strongly associated with vote choices, or to always be equally associated in relation to the other concepts, will likewise overlook the electoral importance of political context.

Conclusion

We have shown that each of our three concepts – ownership, performance and reputation – matters for vote choice. Crucially, the effects that we observe are independent and robust to the inclusion of controls for other important political judgements, such as partisanship, leader evaluations and policy preferences. These concepts add significantly to explained variance in models of vote choice. We find comparable patterns at both the aggregate and individual levels, insofar as each of our concepts exhibits significant and substantial effects on party support, suggesting that our findings are not subject to an ecological fallacy in inference: the trends that we observe in long-term dynamics of party support, shaped by macro-level measures of ownership, performance and reputation, exhibit the same fundamental logics as cross-sectional models of individual behaviour.

In models of party support at the aggregate level in the United States and United Kingdom we see how the measures of best party on the most important problem (ownership) and macro-competence (generalised competence) have sustained effects on party support, especially for parties in government. The evidence for policy handling (performance) is weaker and inconsistent, but does highlight the distinct variance in specific policy domains – and how this can deviate from more generalised evaluations of parties.

In models of vote choice at the individual level, using US and UK data from recent election studies, we see stronger and even more consistent effects for each of the concepts. The stronger findings for evaluations of change in policy performance arguably reflect the superior measures of perceptions of policy conditions taken from the ANES and BES, compared to domain-specific measures of policy handling in our aggregate analysis. Indeed, the importance of measurement was discussed in our modelling of new survey instruments from the 2015 BES.

Alongside these models, which treat the relationship between competence and the vote as fixed in time, we considered dynamic conditional correlations of ownership, performance and generalised competence with party support. These provided support for the idea, first put forward by Stokes, that at certain moments in time competence can become politicised, as the defining dimension of political conflict and competition. Political events, landmark policies, policy failures, international events, scandals, policy crises and elections can serve to strengthen (or sometimes weaken) the degree of association between public opinion about competence and vote intentions.

These observations have important implications for the study of vote choice, campaigns and public opinion. They highlight that many existing studies miss out on focal criteria of political judgements: first, perceptions of the degree of a party's commitment to an issue, and its relative strength on that issue; second, attributions of responsibility for good or poor performance that most typically stem from responsiveness to the incumbent; and third, assessments of the overall competence or incompetence of parties. Each of these aspects of public opinion may sometimes be more important for party support, and at other times less so. The drivers of this importance appear to be shaped by major political, economic, policy and international events and the role of elections in establishing when vote choices are – or are not – more closely associated with issue competence.

8   Conclusion

Spatial models have dominated the issue voting literature, leading us to imagine political competition in ideological terms. Economic voting models have been equally dominant in the way we think about the effects of government performance. The literature on issue ownership, valence and policy competence has been relatively less well theorised and understood. And yet the politics of competence is omnipresent in campaign messages, in how entire periods of government are experienced and remembered, in how political leaders are selected and deposed, in how cabinet positions are filled, in the legislative priorities of governments and in the way voters assess who to place their trust in at the ballot box. Voters choose based on promises and also whether those promises can be or have been fulfilled, which party best represents their interests – not just in position, but also in trustworthiness, delivery and commitment – and whether a party looks fit to govern. There is relatively little theoretical and empirical work informing many of these competence aspects of politics. This book has not answered all of them, but it has offered a way forward to better understand how public opinion responds to party and government competence, and how competence and delivery matters across the policy agenda.

We have suggested three ways of thinking about public opinion regarding competence: through relatively stable issue strengths, or reputations on different policy issues (ownership), through short-term fluctuations in issue ratings (performance), and through the general way in which parties are rated to be competent, or incompetent (generalised competence). We offered insights into how each of these concepts in public opinion has important consequences. With respect to ownership, we revealed the frequency of issue ownership change and the causes of issue ownership change, and highlighted how our understanding of 'ownership' needs closer attention to its characteristics and measurement. With respect to performance, we revealed the dynamics and effects for governments versus oppositions, and with respect to generalised competence, we revealed the dynamics of costs of governing. All three concepts contribute to a fuller understanding of the electoral consequences of competence, and when those concepts matter. Competence is politicised and made more or less relevant to party support in response to events, and in response to some elections, particularly in the United States.

Each of the concepts fits with prevailing folk theories of what matters in elections in advanced democracies. Parties win elections because they are seen to commit to issues that voters consider important, and are trusted on. '24 hours to save the NHS', voters were told by Tony Blair's New Labour on the eve of the 1997 UK general election. Parties win elections because they are seen to have performed well on those issues in government and are trusted to deliver on them, or they win elections because other parties have failed to deliver on the issues that matter to voters. 'It's the economy stupid', the slogan famously used by James Carville in the Bill Clinton campaign for the US presidency in 1992, applies to a particularly salient policy domain. Parties also win elections because voters cast their ballots based on an overall assessment of who is most competent (and least incompetent) to govern. Setting out the decision facing voters at the 2015 general election, British Prime Minister David Cameron framed the vote around competence: 'Britain has a choice: between the competence that has got us this far or the chaos of giving it up, going backwards and taking huge risks.' The potential for the accumulation of information signals about performance to form into a generalised perception of party competence (or incompetence) can also shape the electoral future of parties. This updating of general perceptions of party competence was noted by another British Prime Minister, James Callaghan:

The serious and widespread industrial dislocation caused by the strikes of January 1979, short-lived though they were, sent the government's fortunes cascading downhill. Our loss of authority in one field leading to misfortune in others just as an avalanche, gathering speed sweeps all before it. (Callaghan 1987: 540)

The implications of the analyses in this book also challenge folk theories – and political science theories – about party competence. One of the most dominant assumptions in the literature on party competence is that parties can somehow shape their reputations on issues, and also shape the terms of the debate about competence. Scholars believe that party strategies alter the very basis of vote choices: either through long-term conflicts, polarisation, by setting the political agenda (Riker 1993) or by establishing what matters in the short-term decisions in election campaigns (Budge and Farlie 1983; Petrocik 1996; Petrocik et al. 2003). All of these assumptions may hold true. But the much bigger picture revealed in this book is that public opinion is very substantially shaped by major political or policy shocks, often outside the direct strategic control of any one party or government, and by predictable dynamics which seem almost impervious to control by governments.

We find that major changes in public opinion about party issue strengths and weaknesses arise when there are major performance shocks and when a policy conflict or issue is highly salient. Those performance shocks combine with party strategies of positional competition, but many of those shocks represent exogenous events in the wider policy environment. Likewise, when we analyse the factors which cause public opinion about ownership, performance and generalised competence to be more strongly associated with party support, it is the major events in political life, and in the economy and other policy domains which often coincide with a stronger 'valence' explanation of voting. Performance shocks can alter issue ownership and can also lead to downturns in generalised evaluations of competence. The story is one of parties responding to the wider policy environment and to what matters.

These insights run alongside our evidence for the costs of governing. The downward trend of generalised competence for parties in government is so regular that a view based on party agency bucking this trend must be viewed as an unusual exception. The way that blame accumulates over a period of office suggests that negative competence shocks have greater effects on vote choices towards the end of periods of office, largely irrespective of the performance and the strategies of those governments. None of these insights is directly tested in this book against the effects of political strategies. However, they should throw assumptions about party agency into new light. Public opinion about party competence is – to a great extent – the product of major shocks and predictable dynamics.

The remainder of this final chapter outlines how our findings on ownership, performance and competence contribute to understanding across a range of fields.

The Concept of Ownership

When we conceptualise issue ownership as the relative strengths of parties, we remove the short-term fluctuations that denote variation in performance, and the average rating of the party on all issues which denotes its generalised rating for competence. It was argued by Petrocik (1996) that parties hold long-lasting issue strengths, denoting associations and constituency representation. We support the idea that owned issues arise when parties are formed from constituency representation and associations, but we find little stability in 'ownership', even on the most classic issue-party associations (except in Australia). Hence, if ownership really is assumed to be a stable characteristic of a party's reputation, it is very difficult to find instances of it. All of the following insights are made possible because we allow one party's loss or gain of reputational assets on issues, its ownership, to be independent of the measurement of another party's issues; i.e. we do not compare the gap in ratings between two parties, but the relative within-party strengths and weaknesses. In the United States, the economy tends to be one of the Republicans' best or better issues, but the party was much more negatively rated on the issue in the years following the George W. Bush presidency, relative to other issues. Even the issue of defence became a weakness for the Republicans in our data (under the Obama administration). The Democrats tend to own 'rights and minorities' and 'welfare and housing' but those issues drop down their rankings considerably (during the 1990s and 2000s), for periods at least. Even if we categorised these issues as 'owned' they would constitute few examples of enduring ownership, and they would not constitute the parties' stable best issues. In the United Kingdom, the issue of health for the Labour Party is the only case where we see enduring, stable ownership in the period of our data, from 1955 to the present day.[1] Our analyses suggest that one reason this may be the case is that this ownership has been reinforced by the investments and disinvestments of Labour and Conservative governments, respectively. The wealth of our evidence suggests that it could be possible for this ownership to be lost if Labour ceased to invest in healthcare and if the Conservatives captured the issue. Our German data exhibits more variation in rankings; there is no issue where one of the parties holds a stable strength over the period since the 1960s. However, in Australia the stability of the party system is characterised by long-term ownership of several issues dating to the 1980s: the economy, defence and immigration for the Liberal Party; and labour and employment, housing and health for the ALP. There are also differences in the data availability and variability which might also account for these differences (our Australian data are taken from a single survey organisation using the same measure across a battery of issues, whereas the German data is sparser, drawn from a range of sources and using a number of variants of survey questions on issue handling), along with country differences (discussed below). What appears most convincing, however, is that stable issue ownership is a feature of Australian politics, but is not convincingly so for our other cases. Two of those cases, the United States and

---

[1] There are two election cycles for which we have no survey data on healthcare when we assume the party's ratings did not change. They were very consistently positive between 1970 and 2012.

United Kingdom, are countries in which the issue ownership literature was founded and remain the most common contexts in which the concept is applied. Ownership is not – in general – a stable feature of parties in these countries, except potentially on a very small number of issues, or if defined in an entirely different way – and then not consistent with the definitions used and applied throughout the existing literature.

Using our within-party measure of relative issue strengths we learn that issue reputations are not always symmetric: one party's issue strength is not always another party's weakness, and one party's weakness is not necessarily another party's strength. We find numerous instances where a party loses an issue – arguably because of the performance of its rival – but the rival never gains a relative strength on the issue. The Obama administration, for example, appears to have presided over the loss of Republican issues defence and foreign affairs, but without gaining issue strength on the same issues (the issues remain the bottom two Democrat issues). We find instances where a party gains an issue but the issue is not lost by a rival; but in all instances the rival's position remains unchanged as either a middle-ranked issue or a bottom-ranked issue. Only in two cases do we find one party's issue loss is another's gain, and vice versa: the cases we label as issue ownership realignments; the civil rights issue in the United States, which was an enduring change but so rare and important – and based on a constituency realignment – that it is almost a special case of its own; and the case of 'labour and employment' in the United Kingdom (associated with the miners' strike and Thatcher government), which saw the issue move from being a Labour issue to a Conservative issue, although never becoming one of Labour's worst issues, and the change being relatively short-lived. Hence, issue ownership need not be symmetric between parties, and issue ownership switching – or realignment – is practically absent.[2] These insights have important implications of analysing ownership as a relative issue strength of a party (relative to other issues), rather than as a lead of one party over another.

An implication of our findings is that ownership should be conceptualised differently. Rather than assuming, for example, that ownership implies a stable and commanding lead in public opinion, we might conceptualise it as a *tendency* for a party (or a candidate) to be better rated on an issue, a tendency for that rating to recover more quickly when its reputation deteriorates or an issue where a rival party never holds a positive rating. This would mean that parties could still, with a strict definition, own an issue on which they have lost a reputation for competence, and for a substantial

---

[2] One might argue that ownership is defined, then, by an issue being top-rated but never bottom-rated, but this would ignore very meaningful variation and the possibility of 'owned issues' not being near top-rated for prolonged periods of time.

period of time (two election cycles in our classification of ownership losses and gains). Our analyses of the characteristics of party reputations across issues, over time, across parties and for different countries, make possible these new potential directions in the conceptualisation of issue ownership.

The Concept of Performance

With respect to short-term variability in performance ratings, our analysis demonstrated that public opinion is more likely to update for the party in government than for the party-out-of-power. This suggests that there is a rational aspect to public opinion about performance given its responsiveness to the performance cues provided by governments. Even using exogenous policy performance indicators, which only loosely correspond to survey measures about party handling, we find a correspondence between performance and public opinion for governments, but not for oppositions. Despite this asymmetry, however, voters are as likely to cast a performance vote for a party-in-power as they are for the party in opposition. There remains a question regarding how those opposition performance judgements are made and updated (we control for partisanship in all our analyses), but their relevance is important.

Our asymmetric findings on updating of public opinion towards governing and opposition parties have implications for Petrocik's 'ownership lease' account of issue ownership. This explanation proposed that opposition parties gain a temporary lease, acquiring ownership of an issue because a governing party has performed badly on an issue. This may be true if we take a between-parties measure of ownership (which party is considered best able to handle an issue), but not if we analyse evaluations of parties' abilities to handle issues within party (i.e. the party's relative issue strengths). The fact that public opinion is less likely to update for the party without responsibility for an issue may help explain why issue ownership losses for incumbents, as we identify in Chapter 4, very rarely result in issue ownership gains for a rival party.

The Concept of Generalised Competence

In addition to within-party strengths and weaknesses on issues (ownership), and short-term variability in the ratings of governments on issues (performance), public opinion about competence exhibits shared variance across issues – reflecting a general sentiment about the competence of parties. A party that is considered to be performing well on one issue is more likely to be considered capable on others. This reflects an underlying factor onto which issues load from across the policy agenda.

Generalised competence ratings tend to deteriorate over time for parties-in-power, offering an explanation for why governments regularly lose support while in office (the 'costs of governing', or 'costs of ruling', phenomenon). We put forward a time-varying theory of blame attribution. At the beginning of a period of government, the new governing party's ratings are driven by those of the out-going party in government. As the incumbent governs, negative information counts more than positive information, accumulating in its effect - up to a saturation point.

The validity of these three concepts is demonstrated by the lack of conceptual overlap: a party can have owned issues, and non-owned issues, but public opinion will still exhibit short-term variance on both types of issue (for parties in power). The variability in performance ratings on different issues is parsed out in the extraction of the underlying shared variation in evaluations across issues. And the notion of generalised competence accounts for the overall level of party evaluations (on owned and non-owned issues) but not the variance which is distinct to each issue (performance). The empirical validity was further demonstrated by incorporating all three concepts and their measures in models of vote choice at the aggregate and individual levels, revealing their unique explanatory power. Each is needed for a broad understanding of the electoral politics of competence.

The term 'valence' has been loosely applied in the study of politics. Either scholars have tended to assign an issue with the labels 'valence issues' or 'position issues' – assigning static terms to concepts which might exhibit over-time variation and variation by survey measurement – or scholars have used the term 'valence' to encompass a wide range of electoral assets which have nothing or very little to do with policy competence. This book has sought to highlight the degree to which these literatures address different constructs, and the ways in which a clear framework for understanding public opinion about competence might yield interesting and important theoretical insights.

Competence and Partisanship

One of the longest running debates in political science concerns the question of whether people hold attitudes that lead them to form attachments to political parties, or whether people's attachments to political parties drive the attitudes they hold; i.e. whether attitudes have an exogenous effect on party support, or whether they are endogenous to partisanship. Clear conceptualisation of attitudes about competence makes possible three contributions concerning the relationship between party identification and the concept of party competence.

Public opinion about a party's *relative* strengths is not subject to substantial partisan effects. Partisans and rival partisans (and independents) tend to think the same issues are that party's best issues, and the same issues are that party's worst issues. This arises, we argued, because ownership relates to significant symbolic associations, and to trustworthiness on issues, which transcend partisan biases. The mean rating of any party on a given issue is substantially different for partisans, rivals and others, but the relative rating of any party is not, as we revealed in Chapter 3. This is one of the reasons we argue that we should focus on a party's relative issue strengths and weaknesses. We find greater consistency of party ratings among partisans and rivals in the United States than we do in the United Kingdom, but the overall pattern is consistent. We also find that there is no greater short-term volatility in mean ratings on owned issues relative to non-owned issues – providing further evidence that the concepts of ownership and short-term performance change are distinct.

When policy conditions improve or deteriorate, it is partisans who exhibit the greatest persistence in their opinions about party handling in response to shocks. This is a useful finding, since it means that changes in public opinion about party handling are not simply a function of partisanship (i.e. they are not purely endogenous). In the data we presented in Chapter 3 we found greater persistence in party handling measures for partisans and rival partisans in the United Kingdom than we did for partisans and rivals in the United States. In all the data we were able to examine, the greatest memory in performance ratings was among party identifiers.

One of the reasons it has been difficult to resolve the question of causation between partisanship and attitudes about competence (whether partisanship is a 'running tally' of performance), has been the absence of good over-time data on subjective assessments of competence. We resolved various difficulties using Stimson's (1991) dyad ratios algorithm to construct over-time measures of subjective competence (i.e. macro-competence). When we compared the direction of Granger causation between generalised competence and macro-partisanship in the United States, United Kingdom and Germany, we found a consistent picture of stronger Granger causation from macro-competence to partisanship than from partisanship to macro-competence, and evidence in both directions for the Republican Party ratings in the United States. While this does not rule out an endogenous relationship between public opinion about competence and partisanship, it suggests that the 'running tally' concept of partisanship also stands up to this kind of scrutiny.

Our subsequent models control for the effects of partisanship. Even when we do this, we find substantial and significant effects of issue competence upon electoral choice: as an issue ownership effect, as a performance effect for governments and oppositions, an accumulative effect where blame accumulation accounts for costs of governing, and in effects of all three concepts on vote choices at the individual level and at the aggregate level.

In future work about causation between attitudes and partisanship we suggest four considerations. The first, as we show in this book, is the importance of concepts and measures. Measuring public opinion about competence using average ratings on issues masks the identification of (a) cross-partisan distinctions on a party's relative strengths and weaknesses; (b) exogenous effects of *change* in performance; and (c) shared variance in public evaluations across issues – distinct from partisanship. The second consideration follows, and is: which measurement (and modelling) decisions impact upon the causal relationship between attitudes and party support? We strongly suspect that endogeneity is greater on questions that ask about the 'best party' than questions which ask respondents to evaluate the state of different policy conditions, and whether they have gotten better or worse. Models which take into account the possible causal sequence between measures will be preferable to cross-sectional data assuming causation in one time period. Learning from these points, the third consideration is: to *what degree* are attitudes endogenous? There is likely to be partisan bias in all attitudes, including about competence. But, as we show, this does not mean that there is not a substantial effect of competence on partisanship. Finally, we think this volume points to the importance of asking: under what conditions do attitudes have a greater exogenous impact on party support, and under what conditions are attitudes endogenous to partisanship? We point, for example, to the effects of government control, which clarifies the performance ratings of incumbents vis-a-vis oppositions (for partisans, rival partisans and independents), and the important policy shocks and events which (a) alter the associations of parties with particular issues; their owned issues, (b) move generalised evaluations of competence, and (c) strengthen the effect of public opinion about ownership, performance and competence on party support.

It is plausible that some political contexts will lead to stronger relationships between partisanship and performance assessments than others. Indeed, we expect that this contextual expectation of stronger or weaker partisan effects to be consistent with research investigating the contextual nature of the changing relationship between partisanship and positional voting. Analysis of elite polarisation in the United States by Carsey and Layman (2006), for example, found that under conditions of strong elite polarisation, when party differences are salient, policy preferences have a stronger causal impact upon partisanship, but when those policy differences are not present or salient, partisanship more often guides voter's policy preferences. Conversely, Milazzo et al. (2012) found that when the British parties depolarised during the 1990s, left-right preferences had a weaker effect upon partisanship. When there is strong party-based cueing of valence-based considerations such that parties are clearly differentiated on valence and when valence is high in salience, we might likewise expect the endogenous effect of one's partisan biases to be weaker. However, if a voter lacks information about the performance or competence of a party they may likely rely on their partisanship as a reliable heuristic. Hence, our earlier work (Green and Jennings 2012b), consistent with Fiorina's (1981) expectations, found a stronger relationship from vote choice to competence evaluations for parties in opposition (when voters have less reliable information about performance of a challenger party, and so make a hypothetical judgement) and a stronger relationship from competence evaluations to vote choices for parties in government (when voters can assess their experience of the governing competence of a party). For governing parties, and in periods where there are strong salient cues about competence for a party, these evaluations might exert a greater effect upon partisanship. Even a strongly aligned supporter of a party can recognise that their party has failed to be managerially competent.

Concepts and Their Consequences

Once we have clear concepts and measures it becomes possible to parse out clear explanations and consequences. This applies especially when we define 'long-term' ownership separately to a 'short-term lease'; i.e. we conceptualise ownership as a relative party strength and require substantial changes to indicate a change in issue ownership, rather than the short-term fluctuations in ratings which are associated with short-term variability in the performance of parties in government.

Measuring ownership as a relative strength across issues, and requiring a change in ownership to be a substantial shift in relative ranking and persist for two election cycles or more, we identify a large number of changes in party reputations on issues, as mentioned above. Identifying these changes means that we can, for the first time, offer an explanation for ownership gains and losses, in four countries and over consecutive election cycles. Our analysis reveals that ownership changes are associated with a precondition of salience or political significance. Only when an issue becomes one of the key issues of its time do we also witness a change in issue ownership. A further precondition that we identify is the presence of party supply. This can result in issue ownership loss when a new entrant party is present, or when an existing party is (or becomes) competitive on the issue. In terms of causal factors, in every case of ownership change, and in no case of ownership stability, we see the confluence of a significant change in performance and a significant change in policy (in emphasis, commitment or position). We cannot be sure about the causal direction of the factors; some positional shifts follow performance ones, and some performance shifts or shocks follow positional change. It seems most plausible that it is the confluence of these factors, or the conjunctive causation, that leads to the occurrence of ownership change, combined with the pre-condition of salience and/or significance and the pre-condition of party supply.

Short-term performance variation measures reveal that publics update performance ratings for governments much more than for oppositions. This finding holds when using exogenous data on policy performance, as well as using survey data on the short-term changes in handling evaluations of parties. As mentioned above, public opinion about performance exhibits incumbent-specific updating by the general public. However, and interestingly, performance ratings are as important in explaining governing party vote choices as they are for oppositions, at least in the country cases for which we were able to amass sufficient data to study parties in and out of power (the United States and United Kingdom.) Thus, whilst there is rational updating about the performance of governments, credit and blame models of vote choice across policy issues should not be confined to incumbents alone.

The concept of generalised competence opens up many analytic opportunities; it enables us to construct an aggregate-level subjective measure of party competence across time and countries that has not previously been available. We can show, for example, the dynamic interrelationship of competence with macro-partisanship, as we do in Chapter 3, and the nature of macro-competence for parties in government. Our aggregate-level analysis reveals that electorates tend to trust incoming governments but ratings of government competence decline throughout a period in office. This variation is not the same as party support, but the accumulation of negative evaluations accounts for declines in party support experienced by governments across their time in office. We test this mechanism in both the United States and United Kingdom, but the prevalence of governing costs in party popularity across time, country and institutional context (as revealed in Chapter 6) suggests this explanation has broadly generalisable implications.

By constructing new aggregate-level measures of public opinion on competence and issue handling, our study adds to the literature on 'macro-politics' (Stimson 1991; Stimson et al. 1995; Erikson et al. 2002; Bartle et al. 2011), incorporating competence into analyses that have traditionally focused on the public's left-right preferences, leader approval, partisanship and economic retrospections or prospections (e.g. MacKuen et al. 1989, 1992). We do not only measure generalised competence at the aggregate level. Using a factor score for party ratings at an individual level, our analysis of US and UK election study data reveals that this underlying factor in opinion about party competence has explanatory power in explaining vote choices across different elections.

The concepts, measures, theories and implications can be summarised here, in Table 8.1, which builds on Table 2.1 presented in Chapter 2.

The final empirical chapter of this book drew together the three concepts and revealed that all three add value via their explanatory power in models of party support. Not only this, we revealed how ownership, performance and generalised competence each have a greater relationship to party support when major events serve to politicise competence. That is to say, we offered insights into a Stokes-based theory of valence whereby the politicisation of competence occurs when major events in political life make vote choice more predominantly ones about valence. Stokes' theory applies to valence defined as ownership, performance and generalised competence.

Country Cases: Similarities and Differences

We have drawn on the largest amount of data available, always comparing results across at least two countries, and sometimes up to five. These countries were chosen because sufficient survey data are available given rich traditions of survey research and polling, but they also provide relevant institutional variation; the United States being a presidential-federal system, Germany being federal and comprised predominantly by coalitions and a greater number of parties, the United Kingdom, Australia and Canada being parliamentary majoritarian systems dominated by two parties, though with entrant parties, such as UKIP, in the United Kingdom. The question remains, then, whether there is an institutional story to the findings presented in this book.

We cannot systematically *test* institutional explanations with five or fewer cases, so any institutional implications must be tentative. What we tend to find, rather, throughout the volume, is that there is relatively little country-level variation in our findings. We find similar findings on partisanship in the United States and United Kingdom, for example, with relation to parity of issue ownership rankings, and with relation to Granger causation between macro-competence and macro-partisanship (also in Germany, as well as the United States and United Kingdom). We find a similar amount of issue ownership volatility, and the same characteristics in ownership (asymmetry in gains and losses, and very few consistently owned issues) in the US and UK cases, where we have most data and where the theory of issue ownership has been most commonly applied. There is a similar relationship between public opinion about party handling and governing party performance, and a similar lack

Table 8.1 *Summary of concepts, measures, theory and implications*

Concept	Measures	Theory	Implications/Why it matters
Ownership	*Individual level*: Party considered best on most salient issue to voter	Parties have relative issue strengths and weaknesses – which transcend partisanship	Less stability than traditionally implied Ownership is not symmetric
	Aggregate level: Rank ordering of perceived issue strengths and weaknesses of parties	Conditions associated with ownership gains, losses and realignments are (1) symbolic position shifts, (2) performance shock and (3) change of constituency representation	Policy position and performance shocks can lead to changes in ownership. There is often both a position and a valence component to political issues (the dominance of the 'valence model' needs to be treated more critically)
Performance	*Individual level*: Subjective evaluations of policy conditions in specific domains	Asymmetry of performance evaluations for parties in and out of government	Voters more likely to update evaluations for parties in government
	Aggregate level: Short-term fluctuations of issue-specific handling evaluations		Performance voting matters for incumbents and oppositions
Generalised competence	*Individual level*: underlying factor of party evaluations	Heuristics and issue transfer	Voters hold generalised views on the competence of parties
	Aggregate level: generalised competence of parties (shared variance over time)	Negativity bias Costs of governing	Explains why parties tend to lose support during time in office

of relationship for oppositions, notably in both the United States and United Kingdom. Our theory of governing costs is supported in our data and time periods for the United States, United Kingdom, Australia, Canada and Germany. When we model the effects on vote choices of each of the three concepts combined, we find similar results in our analyses of US and UK elections at both the individual and aggregate levels. We therefore suggest that competence effects are broadly general phenomena, at least with respect to the institutional variation that we have for our cases.

We find some country differences which appear to be reasonably clear-cut. One of the most obvious differences is the stability of issue ownership in Australia compared to our other cases, and the relative volatility in Germany. As noted above, this may arise because our survey data comes from a consistent source and question wording in Australia, unlike in Germany. However, these differences are also consistent with the highly stable two-party majoritarian system in Australia, and the stable political context and party constituencies, contrasted with the dramatic changes in Germany following reunification and the process of European integration since the 1990s, in a proportional system which allows for greater fragmentation of party competition. Some of these differences may arise because of shared responsibility in Germany, and by the presence of greater party supply, although the explanations we offered in Chapter 4 were consistent in nature with those we offered for our other country cases.

We also identify some more subtle differences between the United States and United Kingdom. We found, for example, greater persistence in performance ratings among partisans in the United Kingdom than in the United States. This is consistent with the strong nature of parties in the United Kingdom vis-a-vis the United States, although this may also have occurred due to the different time intervals of our US and UK data.

Finally, our models of ownership, performance and generalised competence voting revealed some small differences between the United States and United Kingdom. We observed many more event-induced effects on the association between competence and party support in the United States than we did for the United Kingdom. This may arise from the strong presidential nature of US vote choice and the particularly strong performance cues of the president, particularly given executive responsibility – rather than shared party responsibility – for major political, economic and other policy-based events.

Our analyses suggest that the main characteristics of competence politics are likely to be universal in advanced democracies, with some differences in ownership according to the party system, and potentially more persistence in performance updating depending on the nature of party attachments in a given national context. Our findings hint at some differences according to the clarity of responsibility. Assessing the institutional basis of any differences is a question for further investigation.

Future Research

As with any piece of work, there are limits to what is practically possible. Should more data become available, we would like to be able to analyse country and institutional variation. There are limits to the degree to which fine-grained analysis of short time periods and individual policy issues has been possible, even within the country cases for which we have data, and greater limits to the availability of individual-level data over time – especially panel data which would be helpful for disentangling the relationship between partisanship and competence. The politics of competence need not necessarily be analysed only using survey data. Understanding an individual's calculus could be achieved using experimental methods. Regression discontinuity designs could be used to assess the impacts of individual events. Qualitative methods could provide important insights into strategic incentives and insights of political actors. We have sought to highlight a number of important observations and findings to advance the research agenda in this field as well as adding conceptual and measurement clarity to a literature which has been characterised by fuzzy concepts, an absence of cross-fertilisation in concepts and theories, and a lack of clarity in measurement as a result. We hope that these measures, and their applications, can open up new directions for research.

One of the questions arising from our conceptual distinction is how political parties respond to different incentives arising from ownership, performance and generalised competence. Now that we know that parties cannot always count on their owned issues, we might view campaigns as a process of reminding voters of issue ownership, rather than simply priming or framing the issue-basis of the vote choice based upon issues already owned. Because we focus on within-party strengths and weaknesses, we find important asymmetry in changes in relative ownership. These differences may reveal new and important implications for party behaviour. Opposition parties may have incentives to highlight the performance failures of governments and to generalise those failures to the overall competence reputations of governing parties. The predictability of the costs of governing may result in particular performance incentives at the beginning of a period of office (perhaps taking more risks, doing unpopular things first) which do not exist at the end of a period of government, and greater competition about competence at the end of a period of government than at the beginning. Our study may help provide a basis for understanding popular concepts such as 'political capital'. Do unpopular governments work as hard to maintain their reputations when they have lost a reputation for competence, or do they work harder when faced with an imminent and competitive election? Fixed-term election cycles may change these incentives, as we know to be important in the United States.

Another question concerns the causal relationships between the three concepts we identify. It may be the case that the costs of governing are experienced more quickly when parties lose one of their owned issues (since this signifies a major upset in party reputation, cutting through partisan biases). Performance effects might be greater on owned issues than non-owned issues, or they may simply arise due to issue salience. We have not been able to incorporate separate measures of issue salience into our models, although we analyse the salience of issues in our owner-ship explanations and in our models of major events. This would be a useful area for further analysis.

Our theory of governing costs provides a new insight into a literature that has struggled to offer more than an empirical description of a widely observed phenomenon. We argue that these common governing cycles in popularity can be explained by the lack of attribution of responsibility to new governments, but subsequently by the accumulation of blame over credit. This macro-level theory might very usefully be tested at the indi-vidual level, as well as more extensively at the aggregate level.

Finally, there are additional concepts that may provide further oppor-tunities, particularly for more fine-grained analysis. We noted in Chapter 4 that we do not deal with the concept of issue neutralising, such as issues that are not owned but which become relatively more negative for a party or relatively more positive (see Holian 2004). We do not look at the extent to which a higher ranked issue is better rated than another issue, that is, the measure of the gap between best and worst issues (partly because this gap will be strongly endogenous). Nor do we focus on the absolute or relative *lead* of a party on an issue over its rivals, rather than its relative strength. Our measure makes it possible that an issue might be the best issue for a party but still lag behind its competitor – due to a poor reputation for competence overall. Parties could have bigger relative leads on some issues relative to others, and this could be important in some peripheral ways, increasing the incentives to prioritise some issues over others. Finally, it has been noted that 'negative issue ownership' can be a distinct concept focusing on the specific issue weaknesses of parties (Wagner and Meyer 2015). These are all interesting areas for future research, and we hope they are made more achievable as a result of the data and analyses we have outlined in this book.

Revisiting Theories of Ownership, Attribution and Valence

The theory of issue ownership expects voters to support parties who own the issues they consider most important, and parties and candidates to try to win support by placing their owned issues at the centre of electoral decisions. The implications of our analysis do not alter those expectations. But issue ownership theory has also implied a great deal of stability in long-term ownership, and much greater volatility in a performance-based lease (and for the most part confounded the two). The implication of stability in ownership is that we should be able to consistently predict those issues a party should emphasise in campaigns, and consistently predict the issues on which its voters will be most likely to cast a vote. Neither of those assumptions rings true against our evidence. The degree to which ownership changes in our data, and using our conceptualisation of ownership (as the relative party strengths and weaknesses on issues) suggests that parties should perhaps only try to focus voters' minds on their very strongest issues in a given time point, and those issues will be much less predictable than assumed. We should reconsider the degree to which parties hold stable 'issue publics' based on the issues a party owns, and instead consider the possibility that parties can lose issues without losing voters, or whether there is more flux in the issue-basis of party support than has been demonstrated. We would need long time series of panel survey data (and consistent questions about the same set of issues) to uncover this. Given that we show that ownership is not as stable as assumed we might also expect increasing volatility of ownership and greater influence of performance and position shocks in the restructuring of the issue-basis of party competition. A trend of increasing volatility in ownership would be consistent with accounts of the decline of parties and their growing disconnect from social interests and citizens (see, for example, Mair 2013). Indeed, volatility in ownership is the natural consequence of the hollowing out of parties so they no longer represent clearly defined issue publics. Since parties no longer have firm commitments to particular issues or social interests, the basis for issue ownership changes. This arguably is the crux of the issue around the decline of social democratic parties in Western Europe, and may even help explain the rise of anti-establishment voting and populism. As the social interests that parties once represented have declined (i.e. the old working class), and as globalisation has coincided with many mainstream parties forming some consensus on economic policy, their traditional ownership of issues has been undermined and space has been created to allow the emergence of new issues (such as immigration, most notably) which niche parties have taken up – eroding the basis of ownership and enabling party competition to cut across existing cleavages. One explanation for the rise in populist voting may therefore be the decline in association of left and right with their traditional issues.

One of the major gaps in the issue ownership literature has been the absence of systematic tests of an explanation of issue ownership. We do not provide an explanation of original issue ownership formation; our data do not go back far enough to assess it, and the variance we observe concerns change not formation. We argue that parties are formed along-side associations with issues and those issues can be enduring. Much more common is a substantial loss and gain in a party's issues over time. Our theory of ownership change relies on preconditions of issue salience and/or political significance and party supply, and the joint influence of performance changes and symbolic positional shifts. This fits with our assumption that ownership is not about competence alone, but about position and competence, and the issue associations derived from those factors and from the representation of constituencies.

Stokes' (1963) valence theory has been very widely used, but is rarely outlined in full. One aspect of Stokes' theory was to respond to the dominance of the spatial model. He argued that vote choices are not always about policy preferences on a distribution of opinion, but political competition and party support are frequently about matters of performance. The second part of his argument was that these issues – valence issues – were characterised by agreement about policy ends and means (but could also include good government, corruption, peace, etc.). The third and most overlooked aspect was that a valence issue is defined by its politicisation; it becomes the central 'dimension' of competition due to the significance of performance, corruption, peace etc., to the political climate of the time. This chimes with Converse's (1964) argument that many voters don't deal in ideology but in 'the nature of the times'. Watergate was a classic example; evaluations of Nixon and his government became primarily about trust. 9/11 might be another. Safety and security was undoubtedly the primary concern in politics and in political choice during this period. A major recession means that the party that is viewed as most capable of overseeing recovery is the party most likely to win an election, and competition becomes about blame for the state of the economy. This all means that there is a temporal definition of valence and valence issues. An issue or topic might become a valence issue for one period, but not be in another.

And there is often – if not almost always – a positional and valence aspect (or 'dimension') to every political issue, with the exception, perhaps, of those issues which relate to deeper values (abortion, euthanasia, same-sex marriage).

We suggest that owned issues can sometimes be more positional and sometimes more valence-based, and that performance has a positional element and a competence one (because individuals will rate performance better if they agree with a policy decision, a spending decision, etc.). Both can be valence issues when performance, governing capability, delivery becomes the central evaluation of public opinion. Major political events shape their relationship with vote choices.

Our findings shift attention away from party agency and strategy in establishing agendas to the external environment as a context, as discussed above. Riker's (1993) theory of heresthetics has become an established way of thinking about party strategies. Parties raise the importance of a conflict or a dimension of voting by their control of the political agenda. This party agency approach is also applied to shorter term strategies in campaigns (e.g. Budge and Farlie 1983; Petrocik 1996; Iyengar and Ansolabehere 1994). Our findings on the causes of ownership change, and on the determinants of ownership voting, performance voting and generalised competence voting, point to exogenous important 'events' – shocks to the economy, policy failures and so on. They point to how parties capitalise on these events via their policy competition, spending decisions and so on, but to a large degree there are external factors which realign issues with parties, which shape generalised competence and which provide a context in which competence is associated with vote choices. The regularity of governing costs – seemingly irrespective of government performance in many cases – will likely determine the tactics and bases of party competition in fundamental ways over the course of a party's period in power, and for its rival, and cause competence effects to accumulate towards the end of a party's period in government.

In terms of theories of attribution, and credit and blame, it is important that voters appear to only update their performance assessments of parties that provide information on policy performance (governments), but that performance voting seems to occur for governing parties and opposition parties alike; a finding that is robust to controls for leader evaluations and partisanship. This suggests that attribution is asymmetric, but the effects of credit and blame can be symmetric. Models of performance voting should not be applied to incumbent parties alone, and should not be applied to governing parties without taking into consideration the regular declines in support for a party in power. Our time-based theory of governing costs suggests that blame is more likely to be laid at the outgoing party's door at the beginning of a new government, and that blame then begins to accumulate for the new incumbent with negative shocks mattering more and more to party support than positive ones. Furthermore, our evidence suggests that attribution should not only be considered on the issue of the economy. Policy performance effects are found on a diverse array of issues and the degree to which voters form a generalised view of party competence relates to the issue agenda as a whole, not only to the economy. Indeed, issue ownership is a form of credit and blame, since it is explained by major changes in performance. A wider view of attribution is needed, which also has implications for the incentives facing parties and governments. Voters notice performance on a range of issues and reward or punish parties accordingly, but they do so in a range of ways. The concepts of ownership, performance and generalised competence might offer new ways of conceiving of the attribution of credit and blame. This is relevant to the literature on economic voting (e.g. Anderson 1995; Duch and Stevenson 2008). Alongside costs of governing, our theory of ownership losses and gains highlights how future major economic crises could lead to damaging losses of both generalised competence and specific ownership – depending on the arrangement of parties in office at the time and the public's view on who is responsible (or not) for shocks to national or global economies. Meanwhile, as globalisation increases the importance of non-economic issues to mass politics (Hellwig 2014), performance and ownership changes in other policy domains may have increasing consequences for electoral behaviour.

In an era where performance accountability systems have become ubiquitous in the organisation of government (Hood 1991, 1995; Hood et al. 1999), the ability of citizens to recognise improvements or deteriorations in policy conditions becomes central to democratic politics – and the awarding of credit and blame for the management of public services and public policies. Our evidence on the updating of performance evaluations for parties in and out of government are of consequence for debates around democratic accountability – where responsive citizens are able to hold government to account for good or poor performance (Holbein 2016). Our findings on governing costs are also very relevant here. There are important cycles in perceived government performance irrespective of levers of government control and objective measures of government performance. These findings speak to the literature on negativity bias in political evaluations and behaviour (Soroka 2014). They are also relevant to debates about the evolution of electoral preferences over time (Erikson and Wlezien 2012; Jennings and Wlezien 2016). Accounting for the dynamics behind the costs of governing, one of the perennial puzzles in electoral behaviour, we contribute evidence of asymmetric effects and accumulation in blame for parties in government. This offers insights that are consistent with studies of blame avoidance in public policy (Weaver 1986; Hood 2011; Hood et al. 2009, 2016) and observations in behavioural economics more generally (e.g. Kahneman and Tversky 1979), confirming why officeholders are more sensitive to blame than to credit.

Final Conclusions

This book has taken a broad view of decades of political events and changes in public opinion in order to elucidate these concepts, and their consequences. Because our theories relate to turning points in political life, and to the way mass publics respond to periods of governing, our focus has generally been on understanding change over time, also taking a cross-national view to enhance the validity and generalisability of our findings. We have amassed tens of thousands of survey items in five countries over as many as seven decades per country, as well as countless measures of subjective and objective policy performance. Using these unique data, we have been able to explore the time-varying dynamics and effects of competence, and have revealed how a contextual explanation is most appropriate when we are analysing a concept – competence – so integral to variation in government performance. We have also shed new light on decades of political history in our country cases.

We have extended the traditional focus on economic performance and credit and blame over management of the economy to a focus on the full breadth of policy issues. It has been one of the curious aspects of the lack of translation of the issue ownership and party competition literature – which recognises that parties strategise on any or all policy issues – that research on the attribution of blame has almost solely focused on the economy. We do not doubt that the economy is a 'super-issue' in many contexts, especially when there is a significant improvement or deterioration in growth, unemployment, the cost of living or other economic conditions that are consequential to mass publics. But party reputations and performance matter on other issues too. As governments are constrained by globalisation they are turning to other issues for strategic competition (Ward et al. 2015). It is only by combining public opinion across the issue agenda that we can account for the generalised sentiment about party trustworthiness in office. Combining the literatures on issue ownership, valence and economic voting enables us to provide new and more integrated insights.

We have developed a conceptual framework to make sense of the literature on competence and to offer a way forward in future research. Our evidence reveals numerous insights into the nature of ownership, performance and generalised competence. It provides explanatory theories for issue ownership change, the attribution of responsibility to governments, the phenomenon of governing costs, and it provides a more complete competence-based model of vote choices incorporating these insights. Our theoretical contributions and empirical findings have implications for a diverse range of fields within political science, ranging from those concerned with the study of public opinion, party competition, economic voting, blame avoidance, incumbency, public policy and governance, political institutions, partisanship, valence and government performance.

Competence is central to elections and it is therefore central to political elites. Competence matters because it decides the outcome of elections. Voters reward and punish parties accordingly for good government, trust, delivery, sound management and prudent steering of the ship of state. The performance of governing parties provides voters with a continuous stream of information that enables updating of evaluations of the fitness of parties to govern and deliver. Competence influences mass publics in a way that leaves a lasting impression of parties' reputations overall, and their commitment to specific issues – enabling parties to 'own' certain issues and use them to their political advantage. The politics of competence is not confined to ownership, performance and generalised competence. But these concepts help us understand public opinion about competence as it relates to political parties and to parties in government and in opposition.

Perhaps scholarship itself has been bound by the politics of its time. During the 1970s, 1980s and 1990s it seemed sensible to talk of parties of the right owning 'right' issues, and parties of the left owning 'left' issues, and to view politics in ideological terms. Those truths appeared to be the constants then. However, using a much broader time lens reveals that hardly any issues have been constantly associated with one party or another, and competence comes to matter more in some time periods than in others. What appears most true is that competence is a decisive characteristic of politics and we need to understand it far better.

Politicians have long understood the importance of competence. When Thomas Dewey accepted the Republican nomination for the US presidency in 1944 he spoke of efficiency and competence and the incumbent party growing old in office. When Ronald Reagan made his election eve address in 1980 he asked voters to focus on competence: 'If you feel that Mr. Carter has faithfully served America with the kind of competence and distinction which deserve four more years in office, then you should vote for him. If he has given you the kind of leadership you are looking for, if he instills in you pride for our country and a sense of optimism about our future, then he should be reelected.'[3] Reagan went on to list a series of evaluations of competence, and conditions, far beyond those focused only on the economy. When George H. Bush accepted the Republican nomination in 1988 he defined the key difference between the Democrats and Republicans as one of trust and record: 'There are those who say there isn't much of a difference this year. But America, don't let 'em fool ya. Two parties this year ask for your support. Both will speak of growth and peace, but only one has proved it can deliver. Two parties this year ask for your trust, but only one has earned it.'[4] Earning and losing trust – a reputation for governing competence – is fundamental to governing, party reputations and elections. This insight from the political world should have a greater impact on our political science understanding of public opinion, parties and voting: on the politics of competence.

---

[3] Ronald Reagan: 'Election Eve Address "A Vision for America",' November 3, 1980. *The American Presidency Project.* www.presidency.ucsb.edu/ws/?pid=85199.

[4] George Bush: "Address Accepting the Presidential Nomination at the Republican National Convention in New Orleans,' August 18, 1988. *The American Presidency Project.* www.presidency.ucsb.edu/ws/?pid=25955.

Appendices

Tables

Table A3.1 *Summary statistics for issue handling, US Democratic Party*

Topic	N	Mean	Max	Min	SD	Kurtosis
1: Economy, Business & Trade	63	37.10	55.33	20.50	7.40	2.76
2: Rights & Minorities	40	41.37	55.50	20.00	8.11	2.62
3: Health	35	42.76	57.27	24.00	8.41	2.69
4: Labour & Employment	43	42.60	54.25	27.00	6.92	2.59
5: Education	32	43.12	55.40	25.00	7.70	2.61
6: Environment	31	46.70	60.00	32.00	7.84	2.31
7: Law & Order	30	30.43	44.00	18.00	7.31	2.18
8: Welfare & Housing	35	47.21	62.67	24.00	8.73	2.98
9: Defence	39	29.10	45.28	15.00	7.71	2.16
10: Foreign Affairs	66	30.58	45.00	17.75	6.57	2.44
11: Government	43	32.39	46.67	17.83	7.61	2.21
12: Immigration	13	34.19	39.00	18.00	5.85	5.63
13: Morality	28	32.23	49.00	17.00	8.47	2.17

Table A3.2 *Summary statistics for issue handling, UK Conservative Party*

Topic	N	Mean	Max	Min	SD	Kurtosis
1: Economy, Business & Trade	58	31.64	45.00	17.00	6.00	3.08
2: Rights & Minorities	15	25.53	41.00	12.50	8.69	2.08
3: Health	43	21.91	35.67	10.00	6.68	2.16
4: Labour & Employment	41	29.10	47.60	11.00	9.48	2.48
5: Education	45	27.83	50.00	14.50	8.11	3.21
6: Environment	24	14.60	25.00	7.00	5.70	1.93
7: Law & Order	42	35.74	51.80	21.00	8.73	1.98
8: Welfare & Housing	47	25.10	47.00	12.00	9.62	2.60
9: Defence	38	35.49	63.00	16.00	10.97	2.53
10: Foreign Affairs	51	33.09	47.00	18.00	8.41	1.95
11: Government	10	16.47	19.33	13.00	2.15	1.82
12: Immigration	28	34.85	52.00	18.00	8.46	2.73
13: Morality	3	20.39	23.00	18.00	2.51	1.50

Table A3.3 *Ranking of ratings of Hillary Clinton by party identifiers, non-partisans and rival partisans*

Rank	Partisans	Non-partisans	Rival partisans
1	Healthcare	Healthcare	Healthcare
2	Economy	Economy	Economy
3	Homeland security	Homeland security	Homeland security
4	Taxes	Taxes	Taxes

Table A3.4 *Ranking of ratings of John Edwards by party identifiers, non-partisans and rival partisans*

Rank	Partisans	Non-partisans	Rival partisans
1	Healthcare	Healthcare	Healthcare
2	Economy	Economy	Economy
3	Homeland security	Homeland security	Homeland security
4	Taxes	Taxes	Taxes

Table A3.5 *Ranking of ratings of Barack Obama by party identifiers, non-partisans and rival partisans*

Rank	Partisans	Non-partisans	Rival partisans
1	Healthcare	Healthcare	Healthcare
2	Economy	Economy	Economy
3	Homeland security	Homeland security	Homeland security
4	Taxes	Taxes	Taxes

Table A3.6 *Ranking of ratings of Rudy Giuliani by party identifiers, non-partisans and rival partisans*

Rank	Partisans	Non-partisans	Rival partisans
1	Homeland security	Homeland security	Homeland security
2	Economy	Economy	Economy
3	Taxes	Taxes	Taxes
4	Healthcare	Healthcare	Healthcare

Table A3.7 *Ranking of ratings of John McCain by party identifiers, non-partisans and rival partisans*

Rank	Partisans	Non-partisans	Rival partisans
1	Homeland security	Homeland security	Homeland security
2	Economy	Economy	Economy
3	Taxes	Healthcare	Taxes
4	Healthcare	Taxes	Healthcare

Table A3.8 *Ranking of ratings of Mitt Romney by party identifiers, non-partisans and rival partisans*

Rank	Partisans	Non-partisans	Rival partisans
1	Economy	Economy	Economy
2	Taxes	Taxes	Healthcare
3	Healthcare	Healthcare	Homeland security
4	Homeland security	Homeland security	Taxes

Table A3.9 *Ranking of ratings of Fred Thompson by party identifiers, non-partisans and rival partisans*

Rank	Partisans	Non-partisans	Rival partisans
1	Homeland security	Homeland security	Homeland security
2	Taxes	Taxes	Economy
3	Economy	Economy	Healthcare
4	Healthcare	Healthcare	Taxes

Table A5.1 *Time series regression model of subjective and objective economic performance effects on handling of the economy, US, 1990–2013*

	Governing party handling: economy ΔHANDLING$_t$			Opposition party handling: economy ΔHANDLING$_t$		
ΔMISERY$_t$	0.066		0.226	0.113		0.076
	(0.282)		(0.285)	(0.301)		(0.308)
ΔICS$_t$		0.075	0.079		−0.020	−0.018
		(0.029)**	(0.029)**		(0.031)	(0.032)
ΔADMIN42$_t$	12.231	12.375	12.313	−14.985	−14.983	−15.004
	(2.019)**	(1.993)**	(1.996)**	(2.153)**	(2.151)**	(2.156)**
ΔADMIN43$_t$	12.994	13.451	13.268	−13.523	−13.524	−13.586
	(2.870)**	(2.827)**	(2.839)**	(3.060)**	(3.051)**	(3.066)**
ΔADMIN44$_t$	36.397	36.795	36.514	−35.548	−35.480	−35.575
	(3.527)**	(3.466)**	(3.486)**	(3.761)**	(3.740)**	(3.766)**
Intercept	−0.153	−0.150	−0.147	0.154	0.152	0.153
	(0.121)	(0.120)	(0.120)	(0.129)	(0.129)	(0.129)
N	279	279	279	279	279	279
Adjusted R-squared	0.38	0.39	0.39	0.35	0.35	0.35
Durbin-Watson statistic	2.414	2.422	2.423	2.718	2.714	2.715
Start	JAN 1990	JAN 1990	JAN 1990	JAN 1990	JAN 1990	JAN 1990
End	MAR 2013	MAR 2013	MAR 2013	MAR 2013	MAR 2013	MAR 2013

* $p<0.05$; ** $p<0.01$

Table A5.2 *Time series regression model of subjective and objective economic performance effects on handling of the economy, UK, 2003–2015*

	Governing party handling: economy ΔHANDLING$_t$			Opposition party handling: economy ΔHANDLING$_t$		
ΔMISERY$_t$	−0.899		−0.863	0.594		0.557
	(0.324)**		(0.317)**	(0.526)		(0.522)
ΔPEXP$_t$		0.052	0.045		−0.049	−0.052
		(0.023)*	(0.022)*		(0.036)	(0.037)
ΔPARTY$_t$	7.972	8.779	8.461	−8.105	−8.822	−8.675
	(1.226)**	(1.227)**	(1.219)**	(1.991)**	(1.959)**	(2.006)**
Intercept	−0.010	−0.030	−0.036	0.051	0.098	0.091
	(0.104)	(0.101)	(0.102)	(0.169)	(0.161)	(0.168)
N	138	144	136	138	144	136
Adjusted R-squared	0.27	0.26	0.30	0.11	0.11	0.12
Durbin-Watson statistic	2.003	2.161	2.055	2.478	2.502	2.540
Start	JAN 2003	JAN 2003	JAN 2003	JAN 2003	JAN 2003	JAN 2003
End	MAR 2015	MAR 2015	MAR 2015	MAR 2015	MAR 2015	MAR 2015

* $p<0.05$; ** $p<0.01$

Table A5.3 *Time series regression model of Labour and Conservative Party support, UK, 2004–2010*

	Labour Party $\Delta Vote_t$				Conservative Party $\Delta Vote_t$			
ΔConditions(Asylum)$_t$	−0.059 (0.186)	−0.114 (0.175)	−0.076 (0.184)	−0.131 (0.182)	0.003 (0.235)	0.003 (0.233)	0.049 (0.237)	−0.052 (0.235)
ΔConditions(Crime)$_t$	**0.246 (0.117)***	**0.248 (0.110)***	**0.251 (0.116)***	**0.248 (0.112)***	−0.201 (0.147)	−0.205 (0.146)	−0.210 (0.149)	−0.203 (0.145)
ΔConditions(Education)$_t$	**0.195 (0.116)+**	0.102 (0.103)	**0.186 (0.103)+**	0.127 (0.114)	0.062 (0.146)	−0.102 (0.135)	−0.024 (0.130)	−0.009 (0.149)
ΔConditions(NHS)$_t$	0.067 (0.115)	0.083 (0.109)	0.068 (0.114)	0.080 (0.110)	−0.007 (0.147)	0.015 (0.146)	0.002 (0.149)	0.007 (0.145)
ΔConditions(Terrorism)$_t$	0.048 (0.128)	0.107 (0.122)	0.067 (0.129)	0.116 (0.127)	−0.057 (0.164)	−0.035 (0.165)	−0.087 (0.168)	−0.005 (0.167)
ΔConditions(Railways)$_t$	**−0.200 (0.093)***	**−0.236 (0.086)****	**−0.224 (0.095)***	**−0.221 (0.092)***	−0.009 (0.120)	−0.068 (0.118)	−0.029 (0.127)	−0.016 (0.124)
ΔNREV(Econ)$_t$	0.006 (0.106)			−0.060 (0.110)	−0.165 (0.134)			−0.208 (0.142)
ΔPREV(Econ)$_t$		**0.326 (0.123)***		**0.354 (0.138)***		0.248 (0.164)		**0.355 (0.181)+**
ΔPEXP(Econ)$_t$			0.092 (0.116)	−0.020 (0.130)			−0.037 (0.150)	−0.090 (0.168)
ΔPtyID$_t$	−0.002 (0.032)	−0.002 (0.030)	0.001 (0.032)	0.001 (0.032)	**0.075 (0.034)***	**0.069 (0.033)***	**0.068 (0.034)***	**0.076 (0.034)***
Intercept	−0.001 (0.002)	−0.001 (0.002)	−0.001 (0.002)	−0.001 (0.002)	0.000 (0.003)	0.001 (0.003)	0.000 (0.003)	0.001 (0.003)
N	68	68	68	68	68	68	68	68
Adjusted R-squared	0.106	0.202	0.116	0.180	0.010	0.023	−0.014	0.041
Durbin-Watson statistic	1.838	1.743	1.895	1.735	2.301	2.320	2.351	2.290
Start	2004 M4	2004 M4	2004 M4	2004 M4	2004 M4	2004 M4	2004 M4	2004 M4
End	2010 M4	2010 M4	2010 M4	2010 M4	2010 M4	2010 M4	2010 M4	2010 M4

+ $p<0.1$; * $p<0.05$; ** $p<0.01$; *** $p<0.001$

Table A5.4 *Logistic regression model (odds ratios) of party vote choice, British Election Study, 2005*

	Governing party vote (Labour)	Opposition party vote (Conservative)
Party identification	29.711	28.108
	(7.158)**	(7.219)**
Leader	2.643	2.732
	(0.563)**	(0.728)**
Conditions: crime	1.389	0.493
	(0.399)	(0.231)
Conditions: asylum	1.209	0.659
	(0.399)	(0.244)
Conditions: NHS	1.881	0.677
	(0.405)**	(0.185)
Conditions: terrorism	0.945	0.827
	(0.273)	(0.322)
Conditions: taxes	0.586	0.853
	(0.289)	(0.399)
Conditions: national economic retrospections	1.199	0.785
	(0.306)	(0.247)
N	1,414	1,340
Pseudo R-squared	0.42	0.44

* *p*<0.05; ** *p*<0.01

Table A5.5 *Logistic regression model (odds ratios) of party vote choice, British Election Study, 2010*

	Governing party vote (Labour)	Opposition party vote (Conservative)
Party identification	66.221	67.054
	(15.912)**	(13.258)**
Leader	1.048	1.055
	(0.215)	(0.235)
Conditions: crime	1.575	0.675
	(0.383)[+]	(0.175)
Conditions: immigration	1.428	1.113
	(0.467)	(0.337)
Conditions: NHS	1.304	0.964
	(0.292)	(0.200)
Conditions: terrorism	0.971	0.812
	(0.233)	(0.218)
Conditions: national economic retrospections	0.591	0.868
	(0.144)*	(0.248)
N	1,452	1,470
Pseudo R-squared	0.47	0.50

[+]*p*<0.1; * *p*<0.05; ** *p*<0.01

Table A5.6 *Logistic regression model (odds ratios) of party vote choice, British Election Study, 2015 (Internet Panel Study, Wave 4 and Wave 6)*

	Governing party vote (Conservative)	Opposition party vote (Labour)
Party identification	**8.672**	**10.248**
	(0.442)★★	**(0.516)**★★
Leader	**3.900**	**3.290**
	(0.202)★★	**(0.165)**★★
Conditions: economy	**1.374**	**0.712**
	(0.094)★★	**(0.049)**★★
Conditions: crime	0.967	0.982
	(0.051)	(0.053)
Conditions: immigration	**1.361**	**0.782**
	(0.074)★★	**(0.042)**★★
Conditions: NHS	1.009	**0.618**
	(0.091)	**(0.101)**★★
Conditions: education	**1.230**	**0.631**
	(0.082)★★	**(0.062)**★★
Conditions: cost of living	**0.782**	**1.135**
	(0.037)★★	**(0.057)**★
Conditions: national economic retrospections	**1.486**	**0.716**
	(0.101)★★	**(0.050)**★★
N	30,273	30,046
Pseudo R-squared	0.39	0.35

★ $p<0.05$; ★★ $p<0.01$

Table A5.7 *Logistic regression model (odds ratios) of party vote choice, British Election Study, 2015 (face-to-face survey)*

	Governing party vote (Conservative)	Opposition party vote (Labour)
Party identification	24.931	22.783
	(3.894)★★	(3.563)★★
Leader	3.448	2.712
	(0.551)★★	(0.403)★★
Conditions: NHS	0.951	0.756
	(0.169)	(0.186)
Conditions: education	1.070	**0.611**
	(0.196)	**(0.118)**★
Conditions: cost of living	**1.921**	0.828
	(0.339)★★	(0.157)
Conditions: national economic retrospections	**1.439**	**0.685**
	(0.220)★	**(0.108)**★
N	2,580	2,521
Pseudo R-squared	0.48	0.38

★ $p<0.05$; ★★ $p<0.01$

Table A5.8 *Logistic regression model (odds ratios) of presidential vote choice, American National Election Study, 2004*

	In-party vote (Gore)	Out-party vote (Bush)
Party identification	**10.091**	**11.656**
	(1.828)★★	**(1.969)**★★
Presidential approval	**3.164**	**0.294**
	(0.655)★★	**(0.052)**★★
Conditions: economy	**3.956**	1.157
	(0.815)★★	(0.233)
Conditions: security	**1.562**	0.743
	(0.280)★	(0.152)
Conditions: crime rate	**1.661**	1.056
	(0.270)★★	(0.195)
Conditions: moral climate	1.032	0.601
	(0.287)	(0.201)
N	1,527	1,527
Pseudo R-squared	0.35	0.33

★ $p<0.05$; ★★ $p<0.01$

Table A5.9 *Logistic regression model (odds ratios) of presidential vote choice, American National Election Study, 2008*

	In-party vote (McCain)	Out-party vote (Obama)
Party identification	**19.720**	**10.426**
	(3.479)★★	**(1.648)**★★
Presidential approval	**3.780**	**0.266**
	(0.730)★★	**(0.059)**★★
Conditions: economy	0.984	0.899
	(0.420)	(0.596)
Conditions: unemployment	0.949	0.949
	(0.448)	(0.507)
Conditions: inflation	1.347	0.869
	(0.602)	(0.530)
Conditions: US world position	0.855	0.584
	(0.271)	(0.186)★
N	1,910	1,910
Pseudo R-squared	0.41	0.30

★ $p<0.05$; ★★ $p<0.01$

Table A5.10 *Logistic regression model (odds ratios) of presidential vote choice, American National Election Study, 2012*

	In-party vote (Obama)	Out-party vote (Romney)
Party identification	5.785	6.349
	(0.713)**	(0.770)**
Presidential approval	8.504	0.078
	(1.209)**	(0.013)**
Conditions: economy	1.558	0.615
	(0.204)**	(0.122)*
Conditions: unemployment	1.221	0.832
	(0.161)	(0.172)
Conditions: US world position	0.921	0.208
	(0.140)	(0.092)**
N	5,410	5,410
Pseudo R-squared	0.39	0.43

* $p<0.05$; ** $p<0.01$

Table A6.1 *31 countries used for analysis of costs of governing in aggregate-level vote intention in legislative elections*

Australia
Austria
Belgium
Bulgaria
Canada
Croatia
Denmark
Finland
Germany
Greece
Hungary
Iceland
Ireland
Italy
Japan
Malta
Netherlands
New Zealand
Norway
Poland
Portugal
Romania
Serbia
Slovakia
South Korea
Spain
Sweden
Switzerland
Turkey
UK
US

Source: Jennings and Wlezien (2016).

Table A7.1 *Time series error-correction model of competence effects upon party support, US, 1956–2012*

	Governing party ΔVOTE$_t$					Opposition party ΔVOTE$_t$				
ECM: VOTE$_{t-1}$	−0.245 (0.042)***	−0.446 (0.051)***	−0.440 (0.050)***	−0.210 (0.042)***	−0.437 (0.053)***	−0.252 (0.040)***	−0.447 (0.054)***	−0.428 (0.052)***	−0.224 (0.041)***	−0.431 (0.058)***
ΔMCOMP$_t$		0.355 (0.088)***			0.162 (0.131)		0.374 (0.099)***			0.187 (0.147)
MCOMP$_{t-1}$		0.412 (0.067)***			0.233 (0.085)**		0.359 (0.071)***			0.228 (0.115)*
ΔBEST(MIP)$_t$			0.300 (0.059)***		0.232 (0.071)**			0.182 (0.050)***		0.102 (0.064)
BEST(MIP)$_{t-1}$			0.268 (0.043)***		0.149 (0.056)**			0.195 (0.041)***		0.083 (0.066)
ΔHANDLING(DOMESTIC)$_t$				0.058 (0.087)	0.110 (0.087)				0.116 (0.091)	0.063 (0.092)
ΔHANDLING(FOREIGN)$_t$				−0.207 (0.070)**	−0.132 (0.067)+				−0.114 (0.077)	−0.112 (0.073)
ΔHANDLING(ECONOMY)$_t$				0.128 (0.082)	0.013 (0.094)				0.120 (0.086)	0.104 (0.102)
ΔPAPP$_t$	0.108 (0.022)***	0.069 (0.024)**	0.068 (0.023)**	0.110 (0.025)***	0.070 (0.025)**	−0.119 (0.022)***	−0.071 (0.026)**	−0.094 (0.023)***	−0.110 (0.025)***	−0.074 (0.026)**
ΔMOOD$_t$	−0.152 (0.282)	−0.172 (0.259)	−0.277 (0.257)	−0.012 (0.279)	−0.179 (0.256)	−0.209 (0.275)	−0.091 (0.259)	−0.059 (0.261)	−0.082 (0.275)	0.037 (0.262)
ΔMIP$_t$	0.692 (0.070)***	0.462 (0.078)***	0.477 (0.071)***	0.487 (0.111)***	0.265 (0.105)*	0.696 (0.065)***	0.512 (0.077)***	0.558 (0.067)***	0.472 (0.107)***	0.378 (0.107)***
GOV(1952/1960)$_t$	−1.759 (0.790)*	−1.502 (0.726)*	−1.922 (0.712)**	−1.465 (0.775)+	−1.502 (0.701)*	1.699 (0.771)*	2.440 (0.741)**	2.837 (0.768)***	1.551 (0.762)*	2.538 (0.765)**
GOV(1960/1968)$_t$	4.197 (0.803)***	6.270 (0.816)***	7.837 (0.943)***	3.532 (0.809)***	6.827 (0.963)***	−4.246 (0.773)***	−4.925 (0.738)***	−5.837 (0.799)***	−3.733 (0.793)***	−4.981 (0.859)***
GOV(1968/1976)$_t$	−1.472 (0.513)**	−0.402 (0.501)	−0.738 (0.475)	−1.278 (0.504)*	−0.291 (0.480)	1.553 (0.497)**	2.256 (0.487)***	2.640 (0.519)***	1.366 (0.497)**	2.322 (0.531)***

GOV(1976/1980)$_t$	4.344	7.142	8.171	3.839	7.585	-4.548	-5.598	-6.552	-4.099	-5.748
	(0.904)***	(0.953)***	(1.043)***	(0.895)***	(1.046)***	(0.862)***	(0.837)***	(0.913)***	(0.874)***	(0.964)***
GOV(1992/2000)$_t$	1.707	1.640	2.341	1.379	1.749	-1.745	-2.827	-3.609	-1.514	-3.049
	(0.531)**	(0.488)***	(0.490)***	(0.527)**	(0.499)***	(0.514)***	(0.527)***	(0.620)***	(0.518)**	(0.655)***
GOV(2000/2008)$_t$	1.330	0.760	1.053	1.163	0.705	-1.250	-2.380	-3.725	-1.155	-2.974
	(0.636)*	(0.591)	(0.574)+	(0.625)+	(0.567)	(0.621)*	(0.625)***	(0.776)***	(0.615)+	(0.835)***
GOV(2008/2016)$_t$	0.606	1.100	-0.291	0.538	0.304	-0.654	-2.997	-1.982	-0.624	-2.692
	(0.450)	(0.421)**	(0.428)	(0.440)	(0.470)	(0.439)	(0.622)***	(0.500)***	(0.434)	(0.641)***
Intercept	10.980	5.212	10.808	9.423	6.311	13.988	11.530	17.497	12.429	12.775
	(1.901)***	(1.972)**	(1.716)***	(1.912)***	(2.089)**	(2.213)***	(2.139)***	(2.204)***	(2.289)***	(2.878)***
N	215	215	215	215	215	215	215	215	215	215
Adjusted R-squared	0.648	0.704	0.715	0.665	0.730	0.665	0.705	0.701	0.674	0.710
Durbin-Watson statistic	2.052	1.860	1.870	2.111	1.880	2.021	1.814	1.899	2.085	1.918
Start	1956 Q3	1956 Q3	1956 Q3	1956 Q3	1956 Q3	1956 Q3	1956 Q3	1956 Q3	1956 Q3	1956 Q3
End	2012 Q3	2012 Q3	2012 Q3	2012 Q3	2012 Q3	2012 Q3	2012 Q3	2012 Q3	2012 Q3	2012 Q3
Long-run multiplier										
MCOMP	—	0.923***	—	0.533**	—	—	0.802***	—	0.530*	—
		(0.114)		(0.187)			(0.113)		(0.256)	
BEST(MIP)	—	—	0.609***	—	0.340**	—	—	0.455***	—	0.192
			(0.075)		(0.122)			(0.069)		(0.150)
Likelihood-ratio test statistic (nested)	—	38.99***	47.30**	13.71***	64.44***	—	29.14***	26.51***	9.39*	38.30***

+ $p<0.1$; * $p<0.05$; ** $p<0.01$; *** $p<0.001$

Table A7.2 Time series error-correction model of competence effects upon party support, UK, 1968–2012

	Governing party ΔVOTE$_t$						Opposition party ΔVOTE$_t$			
ECM: VOTE$_{t-1}$	−0.038	−0.151	−0.117	−0.038	−0.159	−0.115	−0.191	−0.178	−0.092	−0.162
	(0.026)	(0.045)***	(0.038)**	(0.024)	(0.047)***	(0.030)***	(0.044)***	(0.040)***	(0.028)**	(0.041)***
ΔMCOMP$_t$		0.344			0.176		0.506			0.112
		(0.076)***			(0.104)$^+$		(0.089)***			(0.098)
MCOMP$_{t-1}$		0.185			0.100		0.227			0.080
		(0.062)**			(0.056)$^+$		(0.080)**			(0.076)
ΔBEST(MIP)$_t$			0.432		0.398			0.497		0.445
			(0.047)***		(0.053)***			(0.046)***		(0.050)***
BEST(MIP)$_{t-1}$			0.108		0.086			0.099		0.062
			(0.033)**		(0.034)*			(0.031)**		(0.035)$^+$
ΔHANDLING(DOMESTIC)$_t$				0.116	0.025				0.290	0.159
				(0.073)	(0.076)				(0.073)***	(0.066)**
ΔHANDLING(FOREIGN)$_t$				0.119	0.008				0.032	−0.101
				(0.070)$^+$	(0.066)				(0.071)	(0.060)$^+$
ΔHANDLING(ECONOMY)$_t$				0.163	−0.028				0.246	0.114
				(0.070)*	(0.074)				(0.078)**	(0.070)
ΔLEADER$_t$	0.381	0.326	0.223	0.340	0.209	0.201	0.179	0.086	0.163	0.065
	(0.023)***	(0.025)***	(0.025)***	(0.027)***	(0.029)***	(0.028)***	(0.027)***	(0.024)***	(0.027)***	(0.025)**
ΔMOOD$_t$	0.702	0.963	0.161	0.733	0.350	0.153	−0.017	0.034	−0.105	−0.157
	(0.558)	(0.531)$^+$	(0.458)	(0.531)	(0.461)	(0.601)	(0.554)	(0.462)	(0.549)	(0.444)
ΔMP$_t$	0.080	0.044	0.075	0.043	0.056	0.442	0.351	0.308	0.301	0.220
	(0.064)	(0.061)	(0.052)	(0.061)	(0.053)	(0.069)***	(0.067)***	(0.055)***	(0.069)***	(0.058)***
GOV(1964/1970)$_t$	0.678	1.516	0.043	0.824	0.594	0.407	0.618	1.075	0.462	1.119
	(0.843)	(0.848)$^+$	(0.690)	(0.803)	(0.748)	(0.943)	(0.868)	(0.730)	(0.862)	(0.702)
GOV(1970/1974)$_t$	−0.197	−0.353	−0.497	−0.261	−0.548	0.266	1.588	1.213	0.096	1.195
	(0.610)	(0.578)	(0.498)	(0.580)	(0.498)	(0.664)	(0.746)*	(0.566)*	(0.606)	(0.606)$^+$
GOV(1974/1979)$_t$	−0.081	0.579	0.010	−0.025	0.336	0.743	0.245	0.854	0.573	0.603
	(0.545)	(0.552)	(0.444)	(0.518)	(0.474)	(0.571)	(0.534)	(0.466)$^+$	(0.522)	(0.480)

GOV(1997/2010)$_t$	−0.093	−0.483	−0.549	−0.062	−0.695	−0.915	0.056	−0.716	−0.750	−0.279
	(0.402)	(0.401)	(0.347)	(0.384)	(0.359)[+]	(0.488)[+]	(0.535)	(0.376)[+]	(0.446)[+]	(0.460)
GOV(2010/2015)$_t$	0.331	0.795	−1.457	0.624	−0.840	0.537	−0.200	0.152	0.477	−0.207
	(0.748)	(0.715)	(0.772)[+]	(0.725)	(0.824)	(0.815)	(0.789)	(0.642)	(0.751)	(0.638)
Intercept	1.482	−0.057	1.522	1.459	0.543	4.688	0.029	3.817	3.746	1.691
	(0.958)	(1.044)	(0.843)[+]	(0.910)	(0.996)	(1.293)***	(1.820)	(1.033)***	(1.193)**	(1.743)
N	176	176	176	176	176	176	176	176	176	176
Adjusted R-squared	0.676	0.711	0.786	0.709	0.789	0.475	0.557	0.690	0.567	0.718
Durbin-Watson statistic	2.170	2.155	2.261	2.232	2.261	2.064	2.179	2.012	2.274	2.080
Start	1968 Q3	1968 Q3	1968 Q3	1968 Q3	1968 Q3	1968 Q4	1968 Q4	1968 Q4	1968 Q4	1968 Q4
End	2012 Q4	2012 Q4	2012 Q4	2012 Q4	2012 Q4	2012 Q4	2012 Q4	2012 Q4	2012 Q4	2012 Q4
Long-run multiplier										
MCOMP	–	1.221***	–	–	0.630*	–	1.188***	–	–	0.494
		(0.221)			(0.289)		(0.274)			(0.445)
BEST(MIP)	–	–	0.918***	–	0.541**	–	–	0.555***	–	0.383*
			(0.167)		(0.187)			(0.105)		(0.190)
Likelihood-ratio test statistic (nested)	–	21.82***	75.00***	21.77***	82.53***	–	37.08***	94.93***	32.06***	116.92***

[+] $p<0.1$; * $p<0.05$; ** $p<0.01$; *** $p<0.001$

Table A7.3 *Logistic regression model (odds ratios) of vote choice, US, 2000–2012*

	Governing party candidate vote				Opposition party candidate vote			
Party identification	7.744	6.737	6.227	5.732	6.448	3.930	4.302	3.245
	(0.798)**	(0.765)**	(0.684)**	(0.669)**	(0.626)**	(0.429)**	(0.455)**	(0.372)**
Presidential approval	5.678	6.019	5.566	4.881	0.125	0.125	0.132	0.175
	(0.645)**	(0.675)**	(0.629)**	(0.577)**	(0.016)**	(0.016)**	(0.017)**	(0.024)**
Conditions (mean)	2.304			1.918	0.294			0.342
	(0.398)**			(0.344)**	(0.079)**			(0.095)**
Party handling: all issues (factor)		1.511		1.154		2.566		1.903
		(0.148)**		(0.122)		(0.247)**		(0.202)**
Best party on the MIP			2.152	1.926			3.052	2.383
			(0.228)**	(0.221)**			(0.317)**	(0.268)**
Proximity	0.837	0.841	0.849	0.850	0.789	0.788	0.794	0.810
	(0.028)**	(0.028)**	(0.028)**	(0.028)**	(0.027)**	(0.027)**	(0.027)**	(0.029)**
Year: 2008	3.316	2.425	2.418	2.684	0.386	0.584	0.377	0.376
	(0.671)**	(0.496)**	(0.500)**	(0.552)**	(0.102)**	(0.146)**	(0.093)**	(0.092)**
Year: 2012	1.413	1.337	1.207	1.244	0.414	0.474	0.449	0.399
	(0.259)	(0.247)	(0.228)	(0.229)	(0.104)**	(0.114)**	(0.106)**	(0.093)**
N	7,371	7,371	7,371	7,371	7,371	7,371	7,371	7,371
Pseudo R-squared	0.40	0.40	0.41	0.41	0.40	0.42	0.42	0.43
Wald test statistic	23.35**	17.75**	52.37**	68.42**	20.58**	95.71**	115.71**	165.05**

$* p<0.05$; $** p<0.01$

Table A7.4 *Logistic regression model (odds ratios) of vote choice, UK, 2005–2015*

	Governing party vote			Opposition party vote			
Party identification	8.222	6.777	5.867	10.824	8.804	8.317	7.020
	(0.825)**	(0.698)**	(0.619)**	(1.093)**	(0.920)**	(0.885)**	(0.761)**
Leader approval (like)	3.177	2.798	2.136	2.844	2.097	2.278	1.811
	(0.308)**	(0.277)**	(0.219)**	(0.272)**	(0.223)**	(0.231)**	(0.198)**
Conditions (mean)	2.425		1.304	0.223			0.212
	(0.523)**		(0.292)	(0.057)**			(0.056)**
Party handling: all issues (factor)	3.770		2.982		3.002		2.370
	(0.445)**		(0.366)**		(0.442)**		(0.344)**
Best party on the MIP		2.368	1.828			2.704	2.229
		(0.236)**	(0.188)**			(0.293)**	(0.248)**
Proximity	0.802	0.811	0.852	0.822	0.847	0.820	0.860
	(0.020)**	(0.021)**	(0.023)**	(0.019)**	(0.021)**	(0.019)**	(0.022)**
Year: 2010	0.993	1.048	1.000	2.320	2.311	2.134	2.681
	(0.137)	(0.143)	(0.141)	(0.302)**	(0.301)**	(0.285)**	(0.362)**
Year: 2015	1.367	1.752	1.413	2.434	1.655	1.855	2.503
	(0.155)**	(0.175)**	(0.161)**	(0.304)**	(0.180)**	(0.205)**	(0.326)**
N	8,218	8,218	8,218	8,218	8,218	8,218	8,218
Pseudo R-squared	0.38	0.39	0.40	0.38	0.39	0.39	0.41
Wald test statistic	16.85**	75.00**	160.98**	34.82**	55.71**	84.26**	164.84**

* $p<0.05$; ** $p<0.01$

Table A7.5 *Logistic regression model (odds ratios) of vote choice, UK, 2015*

	Conservative (incumbent) vote				Labour (opposition) vote			
Party identification	6.734	6.843	5.788	5.305	11.020	12.165	8.465	7.626
	(1.011)**	(1.007)**	(0.927)**	(0.848)**	(1.535)**	(1.711)**	(1.228)**	(1.152)**
Leader approval	3.372	3.807	2.371	2.245	3.749	3.801	2.298	2.109
	(0.500)**	(0.536)**	(0.373)**	(0.356)**	(0.524)**	(0.521)**	(0.376)**	(0.344)**
Conditions: economy	1.913			1.209	0.522			0.539
	(0.297)**			(0.203)	(0.078)**			(0.082)**
Conditions: Crime	0.726			0.949	1.040			1.047
	(0.110)**			(0.155)	(0.160)			(0.168)
Conditions: Immigration	1.011			0.991	0.798			0.856
	(0.165)			(0.168)	(0.122)			(0.134)
Conditions: NHS	0.795			0.531	0.588			0.606
	(0.185)			(0.131)*	(0.234)			(0.225)
Conditions: Education	1.438			1.059	0.715			0.695
	(0.263)*			(0.199)	(0.183)			(0.176)
Conditions: Cost of living	0.628			0.745	1.258			1.126
	(0.086)**			(0.110)*	(0.181)			(0.164)
Priority: economy		1.440		1.129		1.483		1.344
		(0.348)		(0.284)		(0.226)**		(0.211)+
Priority: Cost of living		0.881		0.811		1.218		1.127
		(0.152)		(0.145)		(0.180)		(0.177)
Priority: NHS		1.761		1.686		0.937		0.814
		(0.296)**		(0.301)**		(0.203)		(0.175)
Priority: Immigration		1.153		1.086		1.090		1.000
		(0.186)		(0.182)		(0.252)		(0.232)

	(1)	(2)	(3)	(4)	(5)	(6)	(7)	(8)
Priority: Crime		1.277		1.136		1.004		1.218
		(0.224)		(0.200)		(0.302)		(0.398)
Priority: Education		0.998		1.018		1.258		1.152
		(0.177)		(0.186)		(0.200)		(0.187)
Party handling: all issues (factor)			2.939	2.652			2.552	2.426
			(0.367)**	(0.364)**			(0.332)**	(0.302)**
Proximity	0.665	0.653	0.715	0.711	0.729	0.716	0.750	0.767
	(0.026)**	(0.024)**	(0.029)**	(0.029)**	(0.025)**	(0.025)**	(0.028)**	(0.030)**
N	4,359	4,359	4,359	4,359	4,359	4,359	4,359	4,359
Pseudo R-squared	0.53	0.53	0.55	0.55	0.49	0.49	0.51	0.52
Wald test statistic	51.93**	36.83**	74.55**	127.44**	42.54**	24.09**	51.91**	113.28**

+ p<0.1; * p<0.05; ** p<0.01

Table A7.6 Autoregressive distributed lag model of dynamic conditional correlations, Republican Party, US, 1956–2012

	Macro-competence	Best(MIP)	Handling (Economy)	Handling (Domestic)	Handling (Foreign)
DCC_{t-1}	0.802 (0.037)***	0.788 (0.040)***	0.751 (0.035)***	0.773 (0.045)***	0.768 (0.040)***
$Gov(Rep)_t$	−0.001 (0.007)	0.004 (0.008)	0.005 (0.007)	−0.004 (0.008)	−0.004 (0.008)
1958-Q2: Civil Rights Act 1957 / Little Rock, Arkansas $(t-2)$	0.070 (0.048)	0.095 (0.055)	0.046 (0.048)	0.048 (0.055)	0.090 (0.053)
1964-Q2: Johnson SOTU sets out 'war on poverty' and civil rights legislation	−0.185 (0.049)***	0.047 (0.055)	−0.134 (0.048)**	−0.009 (0.055)	−0.211 (0.053)***
1965-Q2: Johnson begins bombing of North Vietnam	0.066 (0.049)	0.072 (0.055)	0.073 (0.048)	−0.075 (0.055)	0.032 (0.053)
1966-Q2: Johnson resumes bombing and increases troop numbers in Vietnam (Jan 31st) $(t-1)$	−0.089 (0.049)	−0.109 (0.055)	0.132 (0.048)**	−0.018 (0.055)	−0.021 (0.053)
1973-Q2: US involvement in Vietnam war ends with Paris Peace Accords (Jan 27th) $(t-1)$	0.118 (0.048)*	0.083 (0.055)	0.202 (0.048)***	−0.016 (0.055)	0.178 (0.053)***
1981-Q2: Iran hostage crisis end (Jan 20th) $(t-1)$	0.115 (0.049)*	0.081 (0.055)	0.125 (0.048)**	0.017 (0.055)	0.104 (0.053)
1982-Q1: Economic recession/rising unemployment	0.137 (0.048)**	0.169 (0.055)**	0.172 (0.048)***	0.044 (0.055)	0.146 (0.053)**
1982-Q2: Economic recession/rising unemployment	−0.016 (0.049)	0.010 (0.056)	−0.056 (0.048)	0.005 (0.055)	−0.016 (0.053)
1987-Q1: Reagan apologises for Iran-Contra / Tax Reform Act of 1986 (Oct 22nd) – second of the two 'Reagan tax cuts'	0.039 (0.049)	−0.053 (0.055)	0.026 (0.048)	−0.022 (0.055)	−0.145 (0.053)**
1990-Q1: Bush/Gorbachev summit (Dec 3rd) / Fall of the Berlin Wall (Nov 9th) / Friday 13th crash (Oct 13th)	−0.092 (0.049)	0.088 (0.056)	−0.199 (0.048)***	−0.200 (0.055)***	−0.232 (0.053)***
1991-Q2: Gulf War $(t-1)$	0.217 (0.049)***	0.174 (0.055)**	0.216 (0.048)***	0.068 (0.055)	−0.116 (0.053)*

1992-Q3: Unemployment peaks at 7.8% (Jun 1992)	−0.229 (0.048)***	−0.199 (0.055)***	−0.242 (0.048)***	0.001 (0.055)	0.070 (0.053)
1993-Q4: US military operations in Somalia and Haiti (Oct 1993) / Air strikes in Iraq (Jun 1993) / Don't Ask Don't Tell legislation (Nov 30th) / Omnibus Budget Reconciliation Act of 1993 (Clinton's first budget raising taxes)	0.001 (0.049)	0.017 (0.055)	−0.031 (0.048)	−0.019 (0.055)	0.027 (0.053)
1995-Q4: Shutdown of federal government	0.026 (0.049)	0.183 (0.055)**	−0.433 (0.048)***	−0.018 (0.055)	−0.136 (0.053)*
2002-Q1: September 11th ($t−1$)	0.174 (0.049)***	0.140 (0.055)*	0.035 (0.048)	0.027 (0.055)	0.064 (0.053)
2003-Q4: Iraq War (Mar) − 80 fatalities of US troops in Nov (highest since start of conflict / Bush tax cuts (May 28th)	0.084 (0.048)	−0.042 (0.055)	0.051 (0.048)	0.070 (0.055)	0.141 (0.053)**
2010-Q2: Obamacare signed into law (Mar 10th)	0.136 (0.049)**	−0.011 (0.055)	0.130 (0.048)**	0.067 (0.055)	0.099 (0.053)
1956-Q4: Presidential election	0.018 (0.049)	−0.026 (0.056)	−0.025 (0.048)	−0.031 (0.055)	0.057 (0.053)
1960-Q4: Presidential election	0.117 (0.048)*	0.149 (0.055)**	0.027 (0.048)	−0.175 (0.055)**	0.102 (0.053)
1964-Q4: Presidential election	0.012 (0.050)	0.052 (0.055)	−0.009 (0.048)	−0.205 (0.055)***	−0.048 (0.053)
1968-Q4: Presidential election	0.072 (0.049)	0.148 (0.056)**	−0.260 (0.048)***	−0.028 (0.055)	0.244 (0.053)***
1972-Q4: Presidential election	−0.049 (0.048)	−0.038 (0.055)	−0.007 (0.048)	−0.003 (0.055)	0.014 (0.053)
1976-Q4: Presidential election	0.049 (0.048)	0.046 (0.055)	0.046 (0.048)	−0.003 (0.055)	0.071 (0.053)
1980-Q4: Presidential election	0.200 (0.049)***	0.113 (0.055)*	0.226 (0.048)***	−0.024 (0.055)	−0.087 (0.053)
1984-Q4: Presidential election	0.155 (0.048)**	0.137 (0.055)*	0.095 (0.048)*	−0.068 (0.055)	0.182 (0.053)***

Table A7.6 (*cont.*)

	Macro-competence	Best(MIP)	Handling (Economy)	Handling (Domestic)	Handling (Foreign)
1988-Q4: Presidential election	0.063	0.067	0.091	-0.024	**0.172**
	(0.049)	(0.055)	(0.048)	(0.056)	**(0.053)****
1992-Q4: Presidential election	-0.010	-0.006	-0.040	0.083	**0.123**
	(0.049)	(0.055)	(0.048)	(0.055)	**(0.053)***
1996-Q4: Presidential election	-0.009	-0.006	-0.007	-0.000	-0.019
	(0.049)	(0.055)	(0.048)	(0.055)	(0.053)
2000-Q4: Presidential election	-0.077	0.011	-0.005	-0.060	-0.020
	(0.049)	(0.055)	(0.048)	(0.055)	(0.053)
2004-Q4: Presidential election	-0.007	-0.018	-0.015	-0.002	0.005
	(0.048)	(0.055)	(0.048)	(0.055)	(0.053)
2008-Q4: Presidential election	0.068	0.060	0.041	0.105	-0.020
	(0.048)	(0.055)	(0.048)	(0.055)	(0.053)
Intercept	0.078	0.061	0.042	0.027	0.024
	(0.016)***	(0.014)***	(0.008)***	(0.008)***	(0.007)**
N	224	224	224	224	224
Adjusted R-squared	0.753	0.687	0.769	0.617	0.695
Durbin-Watson statistic	1.862	1.917	1.920	2.060	2.004
Start	1956 Q2	1956 Q2	1956 Q2	1956 Q2	1956 Q2
End	2012 Q3	2012 Q3	2012 Q3	2012 Q3	2012 Q3

* $p<0.05$; ** $p<0.01$; *** $p<0.001$

Table A7.7 Autoregressive distributed lag model of dynamic conditional correlations, Democratic Party, US, 1956–2012

	Macro–competence	Best(MIP)	Handling (Economy)	Handling (Domestic)	Handling (Foreign)
DCC$_{t-1}$	0.680	0.725	0.697	0.620	0.649
	(0.045)***	(0.045)***	(0.040)***	(0.050)***	(0.038)***
Gov(Dem)$_t$	−0.008	0.003	0.001	−0.001	0.003
	(0.007)	(0.007)	(0.006)	(0.006)	(0.007)
1958-Q2: Civil Rights Act 1957 / Little Rock, Arkansas ($t-2$)	0.112	0.132	0.042	−0.065	0.056
	(0.045)*	(0.048)**	(0.041)	(0.045)	(0.048)
1964-Q2: Johnson SOTU sets out 'war on poverty' and civil rights legislation	−0.090	0.214	−0.297	−0.055	−0.088
	(0.046)	(0.048)***	(0.041)***	(0.044)	(0.048)
1965-Q2: Johnson begins bombing of North Vietnam	−0.148	−0.174	−0.070	−0.084	−0.151
	(0.045)**	(0.048)***	(0.042)	(0.046)	(0.048)**
1966-Q2: Johnson resumes bombing and increases troop numbers in Vietnam (Jan 31st) ($t-1$)	0.166	0.176	0.158	−0.000	0.003
	(0.045)***	(0.048)***	(0.041)***	(0.045)	(0.048)
1973-Q2: US involvement in Vietnam war ends with Paris Peace Accords (Jan 27th) ($t-1$)	0.045	0.077	0.180	−0.032	0.116
	(0.045)	(0.048)	(0.041)***	(0.044)	(0.048)*
1981-Q2: Iran hostage crisis end (Jan 20th) ($t-1$)	0.204	0.253	0.128	0.018	0.035
	(0.045)***	(0.048)***	(0.041)**	(0.044)	(0.050)
1982-Q1: Economic recession/rising unemployment	0.109	0.098	0.146	0.188	0.082
	(0.045)*	(0.049)*	(0.041)***	(0.044)***	(0.048)
1982-Q2: Economic recession/rising unemployment	−0.071	−0.042	−0.133	0.027	−0.033
	(0.046)	(0.049)	(0.042)**	(0.046)	(0.048)
1987-Q1: Reagan apologises for Iran-Contra / Tax Reform Act of 1986 (Oct 22nd) – second of the two 'Reagan tax cuts' ($t-1$)	−0.123	−0.054	0.015	−0.019	−0.078
	(0.045)**	(0.048)	(0.041)	(0.044)	(0.048)
1990-Q1: Bush/Gorbachev summit (Dec 3rd) / Fall of the Berlin Wall (Nov 9th) / Friday 13th crash (Oct 13th)	−0.004	0.004	−0.028	0.212	0.039
	(0.045)	(0.049)	(0.041)	(0.044)***	(0.048)

Table A7.7 (*cont.*)

	Macro-competence	Best(MIP)	Handling (Economy)	Handling (Domestic)	Handling (Foreign)
1991-Q2: Gulf War ($t-1$)	**0.092**	**-0.125**	**0.124**	-0.031	**-0.332**
	(0.045)*	**(0.048)****	**(0.041)****	(0.045)	**(0.048)*****
1992-Q3: Unemployment peaks at 7.8% (Jun 1992)	0.014	-0.068	**0.102**	-0.076	**-0.134**
	(0.045)	(0.048)	**(0.041)***	(0.044)	**(0.048)****
1993-Q4: US military operations in Somalia and Haiti (Oct 1993) / Air strikes in Iraq (Jun 1993) / Don't Ask Don't Tell legislation (Nov 30th) / Omnibus Budget Reconciliation Act of 1993 (Clinton's first budget raising taxes)	0.011	0.006	-0.076	**-0.089**	-0.012
	(0.045)	(0.049)	(0.041)	**(0.044)***	(0.048)
1995-Q4: Shutdown of federal government	0.065	-0.004	-0.053	-0.029	**0.187**
	(0.045)	(0.048)	(0.041)	(0.044)	**(0.048)*****
2002-Q1: September 11th ($t-1$)	**0.205**	**0.170**	0.076	0.006	**0.189**
	(0.045)***	**(0.048)*****	(0.041)	(0.044)	**(0.048)*****
2003-Q4: Iraq War (Mar) – 80 fatalities of US troops in Nov (highest since start of conflict) / Bush tax cuts (May 28th)	**0.105**	-0.008	**0.110**	0.083	0.092
	(0.045)*	(0.048)	**(0.041)****	(0.044)	(0.048)
2010-Q2: Obamacare signed into law (Mar 10th)	**0.149**	0.032	**0.149**	**0.123**	**0.169**
	(0.045)**	(0.048)	**(0.041)*****	**(0.045)****	**(0.048)*****
1956-Q4: Presidential election	0.035	0.071	0.005	-0.028	0.025
	(0.046)	(0.048)	(0.041)	(0.044)	(0.048)
1960-Q4: Presidential election	0.065	0.075	-0.033	**-0.090**	**0.160**
	(0.045)	(0.048)	(0.041)	**(0.044)***	**(0.048)*****
1964-Q4: Presidential election	-0.077	-0.064	-0.073	**-0.276**	**-0.154**
	(0.046)	(0.048)	(0.042)	**(0.044)*****	**(0.048)****
1968-Q4: Presidential election	**0.128**	**0.118**	-0.040	-0.027	0.032
	(0.045)**	**(0.048)***	(0.041)	(0.044)	(0.048)
1972-Q4: Presidential election	0.004	0.006	-0.014	-0.003	0.009
	(0.045)	(0.048)	(0.041)	(0.044)	(0.048)

	(1)	(2)	(3)	(4)
1976-Q4: Presidential election	−0.007	0.014	−0.006	−0.066
	(0.045)	(0.041)	(0.044)	(0.048)
1980-Q4: Presidential election	0.074	0.057	−0.015	**−0.539**
	(0.045)	(0.041)	(0.044)	**(0.048)*****
1984-Q4: Presidential election	0.064	0.028	−0.087	**0.096**
	(0.045)	(0.041)	(0.044)	**(0.048)***
1988-Q4: Presidential election	0.058	0.076	−0.017	**0.098**
	(0.045)	(0.041)	(0.044)	**(0.048)***
1992-Q4: Presidential election	0.050	0.067	−0.020	0.015
	(0.045)	(0.041)	(0.044)	(0.048)
1996-Q4: Presidential election	0.013	−0.047	0.008	−0.023
	(0.045)	(0.041)	(0.044)	(0.048)
2000-Q4: Presidential election	−0.038	0.004	−0.037	−0.027
	(0.045)	(0.041)	(0.044)	(0.048)
2004-Q4: Presidential election	−0.008	−0.010	−0.008	0.005
	(0.045)	(0.041)	(0.044)	(0.048)
2008-Q4: Presidential election	−0.016	−0.018	−0.022	**−0.105**
	(0.045)	(0.041)	(0.044)	**(0.048)***
Intercept	0.099	0.069	0.045	0.040
	(0.015)***	(0.010)***	(0.007)***	(0.006)***
N	224	224	224	224
Adjusted R-squared	0.655	0.723	0.567	0.726
Durbin-Watson statistic	2.049	2.006	2.160	2.147
Start	1956 Q2	1956 Q2	1956 Q2	1956 Q2
End	2012 Q3	2012 Q3	2012 Q3	2012 Q3

* $p<0.05$; ** $p<0.01$; *** $p<0.001$

Table A7.8 Autoregressive distributed lag model of dynamic conditional correlations, Conservative Party, UK, 1968–2012

	Macro-competence	Best (MIP)	Handling (Economy)	Handling (Domestic)	Handling (Foreign)
DCC$_{t-1}$	0.790	0.728	0.735	0.707	0.644
	(0.047)***	(0.054)***	(0.050)***	(0.054)***	(0.054)***
Gov (Con)$_t$	-0.005	0.013	-0.002	0.004	-0.001
	(0.008)	(0.006)*	(0.007)	(0.008)	(0.009)
1974-Q1: Three Day Week / Oil Price Shock	-0.092	0.011	-0.069	-0.055	-0.266
	(0.053)	(0.037)	(0.045)	(0.053)	(0.055)***
1979-Q1: Winter of Discontent	0.051	0.019	0.032	0.055	-0.007
	(0.053)	(0.037)	(0.045)	(0.052)	(0.055)
1982-Q2: Falklands War ($t-1$)	0.028	0.152	0.094	0.040	-0.107
	(0.053)	(0.037)***	(0.045)*	(0.053)	(0.055)
1990-Q2: Poll Tax riots	0.140	0.031	0.115	0.072	0.072
	(0.054)*	(0.037)	(0.045)*	(0.052)	(0.055)
1992-Q4: ERM ($t-1$)	0.060	0.098	0.236	0.116	0.153
	(0.053)	(0.037)**	(0.045)***	(0.052)*	(0.055)**
2003-Q2: Invasion of Iraq	-0.014	0.011	-0.008	0.002	-0.005
	(0.053)	(0.037)	(0.045)	(0.052)	(0.055)
2007-Q4: Northern Rock	0.045	0.056	0.089	0.051	0.070
	(0.053)	(0.040)	(0.045)*	(0.052)	(0.055)
2008-Q1: Northern Rock	0.165	0.120	0.104	0.174	0.068
	(0.053)**	(0.038)**	(0.045)*	(0.052)**	(0.055)
1970-Q2: General election	-0.041	-0.007	0.015	0.008	0.006
	(0.053)	(0.037)	(0.045)	(0.052)	(0.055)
1974-Q1: General election	–	–	–	–	–

	(1)	(2)	(3)	(4)	(5)
1974-Q4: General election	-0.024	0.003	-0.016	0.004	-0.004
	(0.053)	(0.038)	(0.045)	(0.052)	(0.055)
1979-Q2: General election	0.024	0.048	0.072	0.068	-0.036
	(0.053)	(0.037)	(0.045)	(0.052)	(0.055)
1983-Q2: General election	0.015	-0.000	0.011	0.005	0.001
	(0.053)	(0.037)	(0.045)	(0.052)	(0.055)
1987-Q2: General election	-0.007	-0.006	-0.020	0.002	0.006
	(0.054)	(0.037)	(0.045)	(0.053)	(0.055)
1992-Q2: General election	-0.009	-0.026	0.004	-0.016	-0.015
	(0.053)	(0.037)	(0.045)	(0.052)	(0.055)
1997-Q2: General election	0.001	-0.073	-0.006	-0.020	0.006
	(0.053)	(0.037)	(0.045)	(0.052)	(0.055)
2001-Q2: General election	0.021	0.006	0.044	0.037	0.051
	(0.053)	(0.037)	(0.045)	(0.052)	(0.055)
2005-Q2: General election	0.068	0.037	0.041	0.043	0.025
	(0.053)	(0.038)	(0.045)	(0.052)	(0.055)
2010-Q2: General election	0.029	0.003	0.027	0.014	-0.042
	(0.053)	(0.037)	(0.045)	(0.052)	(0.055)
Intercept	0.064	0.191	0.111	0.110	0.110
	(0.015)***	(0.038)***	(0.021)***	(0.021)***	(0.018)***
N	176	176	176	176	176
Adjusted R-squared	0.627	0.629	0.598	0.519	0.508
Durbin-Watson statistic	1.798	2.164	1.998	1.887	1.845
Start	1968 Q2	1968 Q2	1968 Q2	1968 Q2	1968 Q2
End	2012 Q4	2012 Q4	2012 Q4	2012 Q4	2012 Q4

* $p<0.05$; ** $p<0.01$; *** $p<0.001$

Table A7.9 Autoregressive distributed lag model of dynamic conditional correlations, Labour Party, UK, 1968–2012

	Macro-competence	Best (MIP)	Handling (Economy)	Handling (Domestic)	Handling (Foreign)
DCC_{t-1}	0.719	0.793	0.778	0.672	0.796
	(0.050)***	(0.041)***	(0.045)***	(0.054)***	(0.048)***
Gov (Lab)$_t$	0.012	−0.006	0.010	−0.006	0.006
	(0.009)	(0.006)	(0.008)	(0.008)	(0.010)
1974-Q1: Three Day Week / Oil Price Shock	0.028	0.004	0.025	0.020	−0.007
	(0.054)	(0.034)	(0.049)	(0.050)	(0.060)
1979-Q1: Winter of Discontent	−0.059	0.004	−0.018	−0.044	−0.006
	(0.054)	(0.034)	(0.049)	(0.051)	(0.060)
1982-Q2: Falklands War ($t-1$)	−0.081	0.011	−0.066	0.038	−0.001
	(0.054)	(0.034)	(0.049)	(0.051)	(0.060)
1990-Q2: Poll Tax riots	0.019	0.029	0.044	0.021	0.045
	(0.054)	(0.034)	(0.049)	(0.051)	(0.060)
1992-Q4: ERM ($t-1$)	−0.045	**0.083**	0.083	−0.019	0.011
	(0.054)	**(0.034)***	(0.049)	(0.051)	(0.060)
2003-Q2: Invasion of Iraq	−0.039	0.018	−0.049	−0.012	−0.016
	(0.054)	(0.034)	(0.049)	(0.051)	(0.060)
2007-Q4: Northern Rock	0.082	0.036	0.035	**0.172**	−0.052
	(0.054)	(0.034)	(0.049)	**(0.051)***	(0.060)
2008-Q1: Northern Rock	0.058	0.038	0.062	0.041	−0.005
	(0.054)	(0.034)	(0.049)	(0.052)	(0.060)
1970-Q2: General election	−0.009	−0.009	−0.030	−0.001	−0.014
	(0.055)	(0.034)	(0.050)	(0.051)	(0.060)
1974-Q1: General election	–	–	–	–	–

	(1)	(2)	(3)	(4)	(5)
1974-Q4: General election	-0.051	0.023	-0.048	0.003	-0.063
	(0.054)	(0.034)	(0.049)	(0.051)	(0.060)
1979-Q2: General election	**0.204**	**0.095**	**0.182**	**0.286**	-0.015
	(0.054)***	**(0.034)****	**(0.049)*****	**(0.051)*****	(0.060)
1983-Q2: General election	**-0.109**	0.001	-0.071	**-0.145**	-0.078
	(0.054)*	(0.034)	(0.050)	**(0.051)****	(0.060)
1987-Q2: General election	0.046	-0.017	0.064	0.002	-0.008
	(0.054)	(0.033)	(0.050)	(0.050)	(0.060)
1992-Q2: General election	0.004	-0.007	0.018	0.018	0.028
	(0.054)	(0.033)	(0.049)	(0.050)	(0.060)
1997-Q2: General election	0.008	-0.001	-0.002	0.004	0.014
	(0.054)	(0.033)	(0.049)	(0.050)	(0.060)
2001-Q2: General election	-0.081	-0.034	-0.022	-0.033	-0.051
	(0.054)	(0.034)	(0.049)	(0.050)	(0.060)
2005-Q2: General election	0.001	0.005	0.003	0.017	0.006
	(0.054)	(0.034)	(0.049)	(0.051)	(0.060)
2010-Q2: General election	0.019	0.008	0.013	-0.016	-0.038
	(0.054)	(0.034)	(0.049)	(0.051)	(0.060)
Intercept	0.090	0.142	0.080	0.082	0.023
	(0.017)***	(0.029)***	(0.018)***	(0.014)***	(0.008)***
N	176	176	176	176	176
Adjusted R-squared	0.594	0.732	0.682	0.533	0.627
Durbin-Watson statistic	1.860	2.169	1.950	1.970	2.005
Start	1968 Q2	1968 Q2	1968 Q2	1968 Q2	1968 Q2
End	2012 Q4	2012 Q4	2012 Q4	2012 Q4	2012 Q4

* $p<0.05$; ** $p<0.01$; *** $p<0.001$

Figures

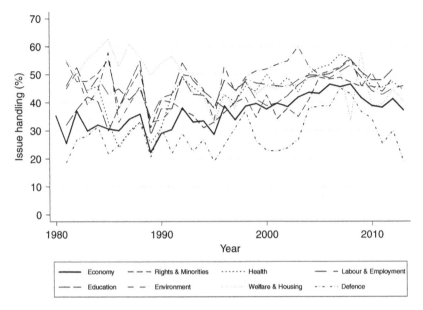

Figure A3.1 Public opinion about issue handling for the US Democratic Party, 1980–2013

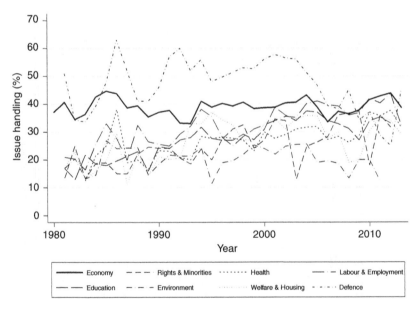

Figure A3.2 Public opinion about issue handling for the US Republican Party, 1980–2013

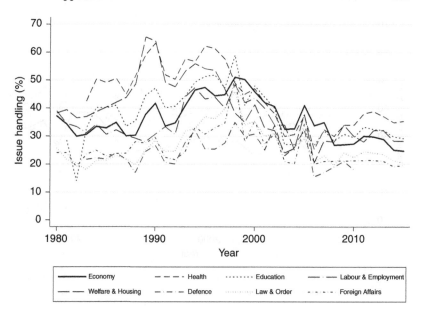

Figure A3.3 Public opinion about issue handling for the UK Labour Party, 1980–2015

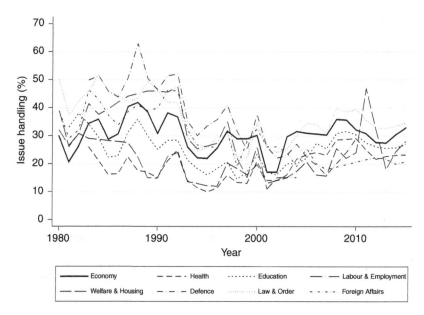

Figure A3.4 Public opinion about issue handling for the UK Conservative Party, 1980–2015

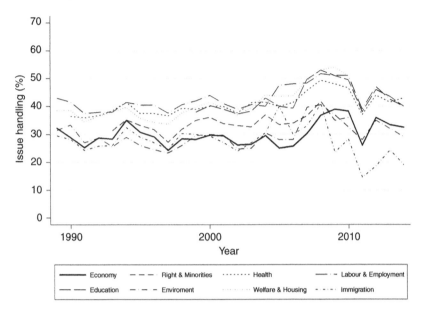

Figure A3.5 Public opinion about issue handling for the Australian Labor Party, 1989–2014

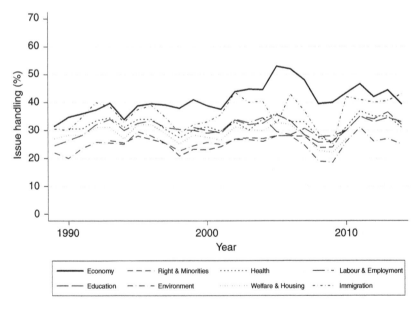

Figure A3.6 Public opinion about issue handling for the Australian Liberal Party, 1989–2014

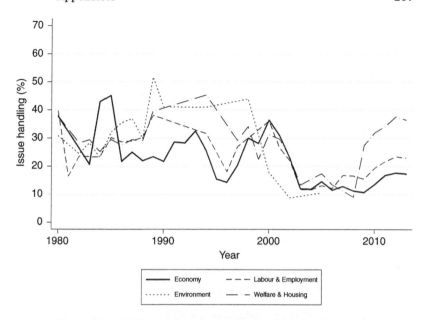

Figure A3.7 Public opinion about issue handling for the German Social
Democratic Party, 1980–2013

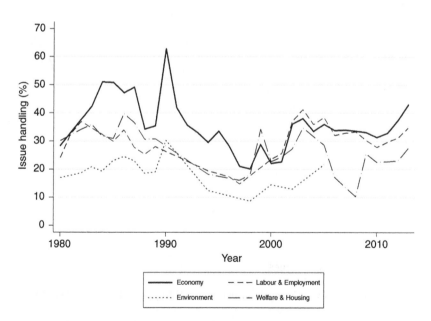

Figure A3.8 Public opinion about issue handling for the German
Christian Democratic Union, 1980–2013

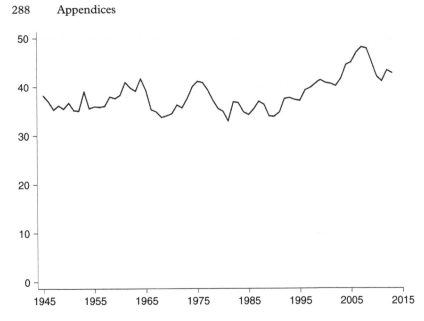

Figure A3.9 Macro-competence, US Democratic Party, 1945–2013

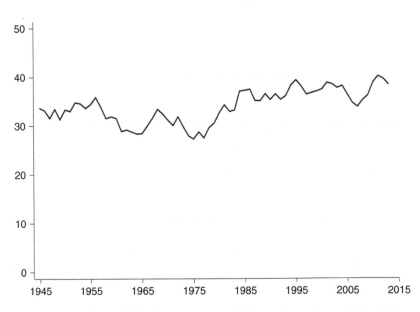

Figure A3.10 Macro-competence, US Republican Party, 1945–2013

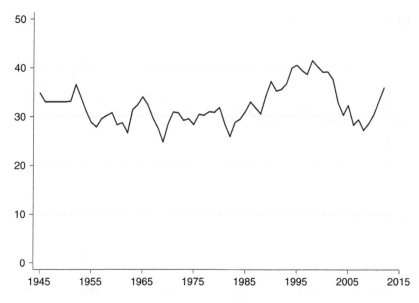

Figure A3.11 Macro-competence, UK Labour Party, 1945–2012

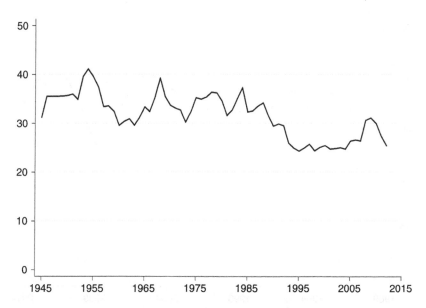

Figure A3.12 Macro-competence, UK Conservative Party, 1945–2012

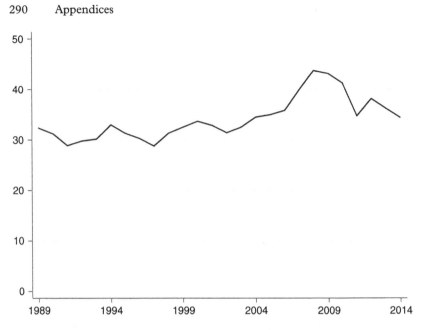

Figure A3.13 Macro-competence, Australian Labor Party, 1989–2014

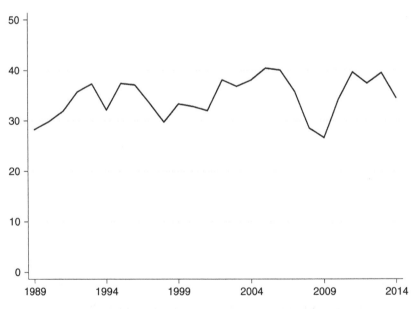

Figure A3.14 Macro-competence, Australian Liberal Party, 1989–2014

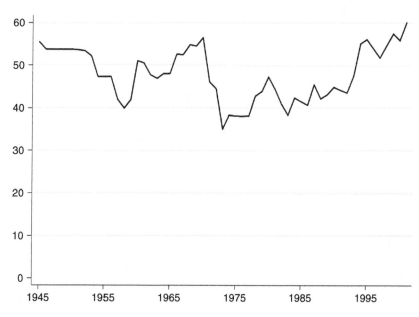

Figure A3.15 Macro-competence, Canadian Liberal Party, 1945–2001

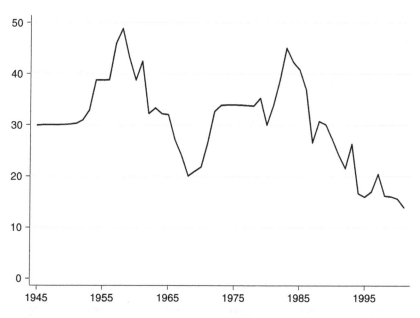

Figure A3.16 Macro-competence, Canadian Progressive Conservatives, 1945–2001

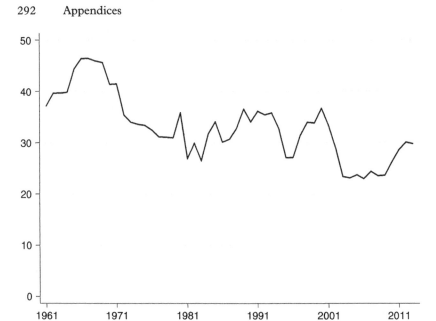

Figure A3.17 Macro-competence, German Social Democratic Party, 1961–2013

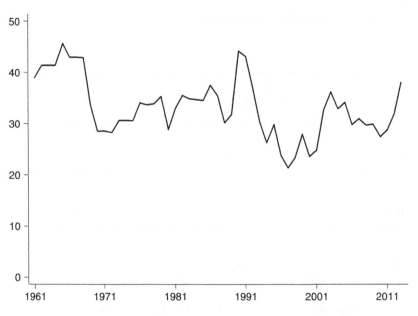

Figure A3.18 Macro-competence, German Christian Democratic Union, 1961–2013

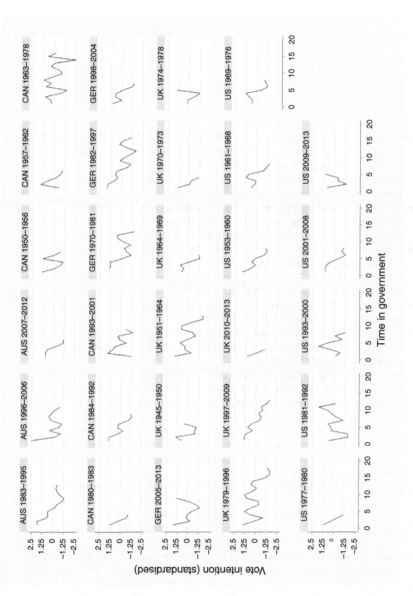

Figure A6.1 Vote intention for governing parties by length of time in government

Bibliography

Adams, J., S. Merrill, E. N. Simas and W. J. Stone (2011). "When candidates value good character: A spatial model with applications to congressional elections." *Journal of Politics* 73(1): 17–30.

Anderson, C. (1995). *Blaming the government: Citizens and the economy in five European democracies.* Armonk, NY: ME Sharpe.

Ansolabehere, S. and S. Iyengar (1994). "Riding the wave and claiming ownership over issues: The joint effects of advertising and news coverage in campaigns." *Public Opinion Quarterly* 58(3): 335–357.

Ansolabehere, S. and J. M. Snyder Jr (2000). "Valence politics and equilibrium in spatial election models." *Public Choice* 103(3–4): 327–336.

Austen-Smith, D. (1987). "Interest groups, campaign contributions, and pluralistic voting." *Public Choice* 54(2): 123–137.

Bartels, L. M. (2002). "Beyond the running tally: Partisan bias in political perceptions." *Political Behavior* 24(2): 117–150.

Bartle, J., S. Dellepaine-Avellaneda and J. Stimson (2011). "The moving centre: Preferences for government activity in Britain, 1950–2005." *British Journal of Political Science* 41(2): 259–285.

Bechtel, M. M. and J. Hainmueller (2011). "How lasting is voter gratitude? An analysis of the short- and long-term electoral returns to beneficial policy." *American Journal of Political Science* 55(4): 852–868.

Beck, N. and J. N. Katz (1995). "What to do (and not to do) with time-series cross-section data." *American Political Science Review* 89(3): 634–647.

Bélanger, É. (2003). "Issue ownership by Canadian political parties 1953–2001." *Canadian Journal of Political Science/Revue canadienne de science politique* 36(3): 539–558.

Bélanger, É. and F. Gélineau (2010). "Does perceived competence matter? Political parties and economic voting in Canadian federal elections." *Journal of Elections, Public Opinion and Parties* 20(1): 83–101.

Bélanger, É. and B. M. Meguid (2008). "Issue salience, issue ownership, and issue-based vote choice." *Electoral Studies* 27(3): 477–491.

Bélanger, É. and R. Nadeau (2015). "Issue Ownership of the Economy: Cross-Time Effects on Vote Choice." *West European Politics* 38(4): 909–932.

Bellucci, P. (2006). "Tracing the cognitive and affective roots of 'party competence': Italy and Britain, 2001." *Electoral Studies* 25(3): 548–569.

Benoit, W. L. and D. Airne (2005). "Issue ownership for non-presidential television spots." *Communication Quarterly* 53(4): 493–503.

Bernhardt, M. D. and D. E. Ingerman (1985). "Candidate reputations and the 'incumbency effect'." *Journal of Public Economics* 27(1): 47–67.

Bevan, G. and C. Hood (2006). "What's measured is what matters: Targets and gaming in the English public health care system." *Public Administration* 84(3): 517–538.

Blomqvist, P. and C. Green-Pedersen (2004). "Defeat at home? Issue ownership and Social Democratic support in Scandinavia." *Government and Opposition* 39(4): 587–613.

Box, G. E. and G. C. Tiao (1975). "Intervention analysis with applications to economic and environmental problems." *Journal of the American Statistical Association* 70(349): 70–79.

Box-Steffensmeier, J. M. and R. M. Smith (1996). "The dynamics of aggregate partisanship." *American Political Science Review* 90(3): 567–580.

Brasher, H. (2009). "The dynamic character of political party evaluations." *Party Politics* 15(1): 69–92.

Brody, R. A. and B. I. Page (1975). "The impact of events on presidential popularity: The Johnson and Nixon administrations." In A. Wildavsky (Ed.). *Perspectives on the Presidency.* Boston: Little, Brown, pp. 136–148.

Bruter, M., R. S. Erikson and A. B. Strauss (2010). "Uncertain candidates, valence, and the dynamics of candidate position-taking." *Public Choice* 144(1–2): 153–168.

Buchler, J. (2008). "The 'V' term: Unpacking the dimensions of valence and their policy consequences." Unpublished manuscript.

Budge, I. and D. Farlie (1977). *Voting and party competition: A theoretical critique and synthesis applied to surveys from ten democracies.* London: John Wiley & Sons.

(1983). *Explaining and predicting elections: Issue effects and party strategies in twenty-three democracies.* London: George Allen and Unwin.

Budge, I. (2015). "Issue emphases, saliency theory and issue ownership: A historical and conceptual analysis." *West European Politics* 38(4): 761–777.

Burden, B. C. (2004). "Candidate positioning in US congressional elections." *British Journal of Political Science* 34(2): 211–227.

Butt, S. (2006). "How voters evaluate economic competence: A comparison between parties in and out of power." *Political Studies* 54(4): 743–766.

Callaghan, James (1987). *Time and chance.* London: Collins/Fontana.

Campbell, A., P. E. Converse, W. E. Miller and D. E. Stokes (1960). *The American voter.* New York: Wiley.

Carmines, E. G. and J. A. Stimson (1989). *Issue evolution: Race and the transformation of American politics.* Princeton, NJ: Princeton University Press.

Carsey, T. M. and G. C. Layman (2006). "Changing sides or changing minds? Party identification and policy preferences in the American electorate." *American Journal of Political Science* 50(2): 464–477.

Clark, M. (2009). "Valence and electoral outcomes in Western Europe, 1976–1998." *Electoral Studies* 28(1): 111–122.

(2014). "Understanding Parties' Policy Shifts in Western Europe: The Role of Valence, 1976–2003." *British Journal of Political Science* 44(2): 261–286.

Clarke, H. D. and M. Lebo (2003). "Fractional (co) integration and governing party support in Britain." *British Journal of Political Science* 33(2): 283–301.

Clarke, H. D. and M. C. Stewart (1995). "Economic evaluations, prime ministerial approval and governing party support: Rival models reconsidered." *British Journal of Political Science* 25(2): 145–170.

Clarke, H. D., D. Sanders, M. Stewart and P. Whiteley (2004). *Political choice in Britain*. Oxford: Oxford University Press.

(2006). "Taking the bloom off new labour's rose: Party choice and voter turnout in Britain, 2005." *Journal of Elections, Public Opinion and Parties* 16(1): 3–36.

(2009). *Performance politics and the British voter*. Cambridge: Cambridge University Press.

Converse, P. (1964). "The nature of belief systems in mass publics." In D. E. Apter (Ed.). *Ideology and discontent*. London, ON: Macmillan, pp. 206–261.

Curini, L. and P. Martelli (2010). "Ideological proximity and valence competition. Negative campaigning through allegation of corruption in the Italian legislative arena from 1946 to 1994." *Electoral Studies* 29(4): 636–647.

Cuzán, A. G. (2015). "Five laws of politics." *PS: Political Science & Politics* 48(3): 415–419.

Damore, D. F. (2004). "The dynamics of issue ownership in presidential campaigns." *Political Research Quarterly* 57(3): 391–397.

(2005). "Issue convergence in presidential campaigns." *Political Behavior* 27(1): 71–98.

De Boef, S. and L. Keele (2008). "Taking time seriously." *American Journal of Political Science* 52(1): 184–200.

Dewan, T. and D. P. Myatt (2012). "Dynamic government performance: Honeymoons and crises of confidence." *American Political Science Review* 106(1): 123–145.

Downs, A. (1957). *An economic theory of democracy*. New York: Harper.

Druckman, J. N., C. L. Hennessy, M. J. Kifer and M. Parkin (2010). "Issue engagement on congressional candidate web sites, 2002–2006." *Social Science Computer Review* 28(1): 3–23.

Duch, R. M. and R. T. Stevenson (2006). "Assessing the magnitude of the economic vote over time and across nations." *Electoral Studies* 25(3): 528–547.

(2008). *The economic vote: How political and economic institutions condition election results*. Cambridge: Cambridge University Press.

(2010). "The global economy, competency, and the economic vote." *Journal of Politics* 72(1): 105–123.

(2013). "Voter perceptions of agenda power and attribution of responsibility for economic performance." *Electoral Studies* 32(3): 512–516.

Dulio, D. A. and P. F. Trumbore (2009). "Running on Iraq or running from Iraq? Conditional issue ownership in the 2006 midterm elections." *Political Research Quarterly* 62(2): 230–243.

Dunleavy, P. and C. T. Husbands (1985). *British democracy at the crossroads: Voting and party competition in the 1980s*. London: Allen and Unwin.

Edwards III, G. C., W. Mitchell and R. Welch (1995). "Explaining presidential approval: The significance of issue salience." *American Journal of Political Science* 39(1): 108–134.

(2008). "Issue ownership and representation: A theory of legislative responsiveness to constituency opinion." New York University.

(2013). *Partisan priorities: How issue ownership drives and distorts American politics.* Cambridge: Cambridge University Press.

Enelow, J. and M. J. Hinich (1981). "A new approach to voter uncertainty in the Downsian spatial model." *American Journal of Political Science* 25(3): 483–493.

(1982). "Nonspatial candidate characteristics and electoral competition." *Journal of Politics* 44(1): 115–130.

Engeli, I., C. Green-Pedersen, L. L. Thorup (2012). *Morality politics in Western Europe: Parties, agendas and policy choices.* Basingstoke: Palgrave.

Engle, R. (2002). "Dynamic conditional correlation: A simple class of multivariate generalized autoregressive conditional heteroskedasticity models." *Journal of Business & Economic Statistics* 20(3): 339–350.

Enns, P. K., N. J. Kelly, T. Masaki and P. C. Wohlfarth (2016). "Don't jettison the general error correction model just yet: A practical guide to avoiding spurious regression with the GECM." *Research & Politics* 3(2): doi: 10.1177/2053168016643345.

Erikson, R. S. (1989). "Economic conditions and the presidential vote." *American Political Science Review* 83(2): 567–573.

Erikson, R. S. M. M. MacKuen and J. A. Stimson (2002). *The macro polity.* Cambridge: Cambridge University Press.

Erikson, R. S. and C. Wlezien (2012). *The timeline of presidential elections: How campaigns do (and do not) matter.* Chicago, IL: The University of Chicago Press.

Evans, G. and R. Andersen (2006). "The political conditioning of economic perceptions." *Journal of Politics* 68(1): 194–207.

Evans, G. and K. Chzhen (2013). "Explaining voters' defection from Labour over the 2005–10 electoral cycle: Leadership, economics and the rising importance of immigration." *Political Studies* 61(S1): 138–157.

Evans, G. and K. Chzhen (2016). "Re-evaluating the valence model of political choice." *Political Science Research and Methods* 4(1): 199–220.

Evans, G. and P. Norris (Eds). (1999). *Critical elections: British parties and voters in long-term perspective.* London: Sage.

Evans, G. and M. Pickup (2010). "Reversing the causal arrow: The political conditioning of economic perceptions in the 2000–2004 US presidential election cycle." *Journal of Politics* 72(4): 1236–1251.

Fenno, R. F. (1978). *Home style: House members in their districts.* Boston: Little, Brown.

Fiorina, M. P. (1977). "An outline for a model of party choice." *American Journal of Political Science* 21(3): 601–625.

(1981). *Retrospective voting in American national elections.* New Haven: Yale University Press.

Fiorina, M. P. and K. A. Shepsle (1989). "Is negative voting an artifact?" *American Journal of Political Science* 33(2): 423–439.

Galasso, V. and T. Nannicini (2011). "Competing on good politicians." *American Political Science Review* 105(1): 79–99.

Gasper, J. T. and A. Reeves (2011). "Make it rain? Retrospection and the attentive electorate in the context of natural disasters." *American Journal of Political Science* 55(2): 340–355.

Gerber, A. and D. P. Green (1998). "Rational learning and partisan attitudes." *American Journal of Political Science* 42(3): 794–818.

Goodhart, C. A. E. and R. J. Bhansali (1970). "Political economy." *Political Studies* 18(1): 43–106.

Goodwin, M. and C. Milazzo (2015). *UKIP: Inside the campaign to redraw the map of British politics.* Oxford: Oxford University Press.

Granger, C. W. (1969). "Investigating causal relations by econometric models and cross-spectral methods." *Econometrics* 37(3): 424–438.

(1980). "Long memory relationships and the aggregation of dynamic models." *Journal of Econometrics* 14(2): 227–238.

(1988). "Some recent developments in a concept of causality." *Journal of Econometrics* 39(1): 199–211.

Granger, C. W. and R. Joyeux (1980). "An introduction to long-memory time series models and fractional differencing." *Journal of Time Series Analysis* 1(1): 15–29.

Grant, T. and M. J. Lebo (2016). "Error correction methods with political time series." *Political Analysis* 24(1): 3–30.

Green, D. P., B. Palmquist and E. Schickler (1998). "Macropartisanship: A replication and critique." *American Political Science Review* 92(4): 883–899.

(2004). *Partisan hearts and minds: Political parties and the social identities of voters.* New Haven: Yale University Press.

Green, J. (2007). "When voters and parties agree: Valence issues and party competition." *Political Studies* 55(3): 629–655.

(2011). "A test of core vote theories: The British Conservatives, 1997–2005." *British Journal of Political Science* 41(4), 735–764.

Green, J. and S. B. Hobolt (2008). "Owning the issue agenda: Party strategies and vote choices in British elections." *Electoral Studies* 27(3): 460–476.

Green, J. and W. Jennings (2012a). "Valence as macro-competence: An analysis of mood in party competence evaluations in Great Britain." *British Journal of Political Science* 42(2): 311–343.

(2012b). "The dynamics of issue competence and vote for parties in and out of power: An analysis of valence in Britain, 1979–1997." *European Journal of Political Research* 51(4): 469–503.

(2017a). "Party reputations and policy priorities: How issue ownership shapes executive and legislative agendas". *British Journal of Political Science*. Early View.

(2017b). "Valence." In K. Arzheimer, J. Evans and M. S. Lewis-Beck (Eds). *The SAGE Handbook of Electoral Behavior.* London: Sage., pp. 538-560.

Green, J. and C. Prosser (2016). "Party system fragmentation and single-party government: The British general election of 2015." *West European Politics* 39(6): 11.

Green-Pedersen, C. and P. B. Mortensen (2010). "Who sets the agenda and who responds to it in the Danish parliament? A new model of issue competition and agenda-setting." *European Journal of Political Research* 49(2): 257–281.

Grose, C. R. and S. Globetti (2008). "Valence voters: Images, issues, and citizen vote choice in US Senate and Gubernatorial elections." *SSRN Working Paper Series (2008)*.

Groseclose, T. (2001). "A model of candidate location when one candidate has a valence advantage." *American Journal of Political Science* 45(4): 862–886.

Heath, A. F., R. M. Jowell and J. K. Curtice (2001). *The rise of New Labour: Party policies and voter choices*. Oxford: Oxford University Press.

Hellwig, T. (2001). "Interdependence, government constraints, and economic voting." *Journal of Politics* 63(4): 1141–1162.

(2014). *Globalization and mass politics: Retaining the room to maneuver*. Cambridge: Cambridge University Press.

Hellwig, T. and D. Samuels (2007). "Voting in open economies: The electoral consequences of globalization." *Comparative Political Studies* 40(3): 283–306.

Hinich, M. J. and M. Munger (1989). "Political investment, voter perceptions, and candidate strategy: An equilibrium spatial analysis." In P. C. Ordeshook (Ed.). *Models of strategic choice in politics*. Ann Arbor: University of Michigan Press, pp. 49–68.

(1995). *Ideology and the theory of political choice*. Ann Arbor: University of Michigan Press.

Holian, D. B. (2004). "He's stealing my issues! Clinton's crime rhetoric and the dynamics of issue ownership." *Political Behavior* 26(2): 95–124.

Holbein, J. (2016). "Left behind? Citizen responsiveness to government performance information." *American Political Science Review* 110(2): 353–368.

Hollard, G. and S. Rossignol (2008). "An alternative approach to valence advantage in spatial competition." *Journal of Public Economic Theory* 10(3): 441–454.

Hood, C. (1991). "A public management for all seasons?" *Public Administration* 69(1): 3–19.

(1995). "The 'New Public Management' in the 1980s: Variations on a theme." *Accounting, Organizations and Society* 20(2): 93–109.

(2002). "The risk game and the blame game." *Government and Opposition* 37(1): 15–37.

(2011). *The blame game: Spin, bureaucracy, and self-preservation in government*. Princeton, NJ: Princeton University Press.

Hood, C., W. Jennings and P. Copeland (2016). "Blame avoidance in comparative perspective: Reactivity, staged retreat and efficacy." *Public Administration* 94(2): 542–562.

Hood, C., O. James, C. Scott, G. W. Jones and A. Travers (1999). *Regulation inside government: Waste watchers, quality police, and sleaze-busters*. Oxford: Oxford University Press.

Hood, C., W. Jennings, B. Hogwood, R. Dixon and C. Beeston (2009). "Testing times: Exploring staged responses and the impact of blame management strategies in two exam fiasco cases." *European Journal of Political Research* 48(6): 695–722.

Ingberman, D. E. (1992). "Incumbent reputations and ideological campaign contributions in spatial competition." *Mathematical and Computer Modelling* 16(8): 147–169.

Iyengar, S. (1989). "How citizens think about national issues: A matter of responsibility." *American Journal of Political Science* 33(4): 878–900.

Iyengar, S. and A. F. Simon (1993). "News coverage of the Gulf War and public opinion: A study of agenda-setting, priming, and framing." *Communication Research* 20(3): 365–383.

Jennings, W. and C. Wlezien (2011). "Distinguishing between most important problems and issues?" *Public Opinion Quarterly* 75(3): 545–555.

(2015). "Problems, preferences and representation." *Political Science Research and Methods* 3(3): 659–681.

(2016). "The timeline of elections: A comparative perspective." *American Journal of Political Science* 60(1): 219–233.

Kahneman, D. and A. Tversky (1979). "Prospect theory: An analysis of decision under risk." *Econometrica: Journal of the Econometric Society* 47(2): 263–292.

Kayser, M. A. and M. Peress (2012). "Benchmarking across borders: Electoral accountability and the necessity of comparison." *American Political Science Review* 106(3): 661–684.

Kayser, M. A. and C. Wlezien (2011). "Performance pressure: Patterns of partisanship and the economic vote." *European Journal of Political Research* 50(3): 365–394.

Kaufmann, K. M. (2004). "Disaggregating and reexamining issue ownership and voter choice." *Polity* 36(2): 283–299.

Kernell, S. (1977). "Presidential popularity and negative voting: An alternative explanation of the midterm congressional decline of the president's party." *American Political Science Review* 71(1): 44–66.

(1978). "Explaining presidential popularity. How ad hoc theorizing, misplaced emphasis, and insufficient care in measuring one's variables refuted common sense and led conventional wisdom down the path of anomalies." *American Political Science Review* 72(2): 506–522.

Key, V. O. and M. C. Cummings (1966). *The responsible electorate: Rationality in presidential voting 1936–1960.* Cambridge, MA: Belknap Press of Harvard University Press.

Kiewiet, D. R. (1981). "Policy-oriented voting in response to economic issues." *American Political Science Review* 75(2): 448–459.

Kim, K. (2005). "Valence characteristics and entry of a third party." *Economics Bulletin* 4(18): 1–9.

Kinder, D. R. and D. R. Kiewiet (1979). "Economic discontent and political behavior: The role of personal grievances and collective economic judgments in congressional voting." *American Journal of Political Science* 23(3): 495–527.

King, A. and R. Wybrow (2001). *British political opinion, 1937–2000: The Gallup polls.* London: Politico's.

Klein, J. (1991). "Negativity effects in impression formation: A test in the political arena." *Personality and Social Psychology Bulletin* 17(4): 412–418.

(1996). "Negativity in impressions of presidential candidates revisited: The 1992 election." *Personality and Social Psychology Bulletin* 22(3): 288–295.

Lanz, S. and P. Sciarini (2016). "The short-time dynamics of issue ownership and its impact on the vote." *Journal of Elections, Public Opinion and Parties* 26(2): 212–231.

Lau, R. R. (1982). "Negativity in political perception." *Political Behavior* 4(4): 353–377.

(1985). "Two explanations for negativity effects in political behavior." *American Journal of Political Science* 29(1): 119–138.

Lebo, M. J. and J. M. Box-Steffensmeier (2008). "Dynamic conditional correlations in political science." *American Journal of Political Science* 52(3): 688–704.

Lewis-Beck, M. S. (1990). *Economics and elections: The major Western democracies.* Ann Arbor: University of Michigan Press.

Lewis-Beck, M. S. and R. Nadeau (2011). "Economic voting theory: Testing new dimensions." *Electoral Studies* 30(2): 288–294.

Lewis-Beck, M. S. and M. Paldam (2000). "Economic voting: An introduction." *Electoral Studies* 19(2): 113–121.

Lipset, S. M. and S. Rokkan (1967). *Party systems and voter alignments: Cross-national perspectives.* New York: The Free Press.

Macdonald, S. E. and G. Rabinowitz (1998). "Solving the paradox of nonconvergence: Valence, position, and direction in democratic politics." *Electoral Studies* 17(3): 281–300.

Mackie, T. and R. Rose (1983). "Incumbency in government: Asset or liability?" In H. Daalder and P. Mair (Eds). *Western European party systems: Continuity and change.* London: Sage, pp. 115–38.

MacKuen, M. B. (1983). "Political drama, economic conditions, and the dynamics of presidential popularity." *American Journal of Political Science* 27(2): 165–192.

MacKuen, M. B., R. S. Erikson and J. A. Stimson (1989). "Macropartisanship." *American Political Science Review* 83(4): 1125–1142.

(1992). "Peasants or bankers? The American electorate and the US economy." *American Political Science Review* 86(3): 597–611.

Mair, P. (2013). *Ruling the void: The hollowing of Western democracy.* London: Verso Books.

Mayhew, D. R. (1974). *Congress: The electoral connection.* New Haven: Yale University Press.

Meguid, B. M. (2005). "Competition between unequals: The role of mainstream party strategy in niche party success." *American Political Science Review* 99(3): 347–359.

(2010). *Party competition between unequals.* Cambridge: Cambridge University Press.

Merrill, S., B. Groffman and T. L. Brunell (2008). "Cycles in American national electoral politics, 1854–2006: Statistical evidence and an explanatory model." *American Political Science Review* 102(1): 1–17.

Milazzo, C., J. Adams and J. Green (2012). "Are voter decision rules endogenous to parties' policy strategies? A model with applications to elite depolarization in post-Thatcher Britain." *Journal of Politics* 74(1): 262–276.

Miller, W. L. and M. Mackie (1973). "The electoral cycle and the asymmetry of government and opposition popularity: An alternative model of the relationship between economic conditions and political popularity." *Political Studies* 21(3): 263–279.

Miller, A. H. and M. P. Wattenberg (1985). "Throwing the rascals out: Policy and performance evaluations of presidential candidates, 1952–1980." *American Political Science Review* 79(2): 359–372.

Mueller, J. E. (1970). "Presidential popularity from Truman to Johnson." *American Political Science Review* 64(1): 18–34.

Nadeau, R. and A. Blais (1990). "Do Canadians distinguish between parties? Perceptions of party competence." *Canadian Journal of Political Science* 23(2): 317–333.

Nadeau, R. and M. S. Lewis-Beck (2001). "National economic voting in US presidential elections." *Journal of Politics* 63(1): 159–181.

Nawara, S. P. (2015). "Who is responsible, the incumbent or the former president? Motivated reasoning in responsibility attributions." *Presidential Studies Quarterly* 45(1): 110–131.

Nannestad, P. and M. Paldam (2002). "The cost of ruling – a foundation stone for two theories." In H. Dorussen and M. Taylor (Eds). *Economic voting*. Abingdon: Routledge, pp. 17–44.

Norpoth, H. (1987). "Guns and butter and government popularity in Britain." *American Political Science Review* 81(3): 949–959.

(2004). "Forecasting British elections: A dynamic perspective." *Electoral Studies* 23(2): 297–305.

Ostrom Jr, C. W. and D. M. Simon (1985). "Promise and performance: A dynamic model of presidential popularity." *American Political Science Review* 79(2): 334–358.

Ostrom, C. W. and R. M. Smith (1992). "Error correction, attitude persistence, and executive rewards and punishments: A behavioral theory of presidential approval." *Political Analysis* 4(1): 127–183.

Paldam, M. (1986). "The distribution of election results and the two explanations of the cost of ruling." *European Journal of Political Economy* 2(1): 5–24.

(1991). "How robust is the vote function? A study of seventeen nations over four decades." In H. Norpoth, M. S. Lewis-Beck and J.-D. Lafay (Eds). *Economics and politics: The calculus of support*. Ann Arbor: University of Michigan Press, pp. 9–31.

Palmer, H. D. and G. D. Whitten (2000). "Government competence, economic performance and endogenous election dates." *Electoral Studies* 19(2): 413–426.

Peffley, M. and L. Sigelman (1987). "Economic conditions and party competence: Processes of belief revision." *Journal of Politics* 49(1): 100–121.

Petrocik, J. R. (1996). "Issue ownership in presidential elections, with a 1980 case study." *American Journal of Political Science* 40(3): 825–850.

Petrocik, J. R., W. J. Benoit and G. J. Hansen (2003). "Issue ownership and presidential campaigning, 1952–2000." *Political Science Quarterly* 118(4): 599–626 (528).

Pierson, P. (1995). *Dismantling the welfare state? Reagan, Thatcher and the politics of retrenchment*. Cambridge: Cambridge University Press.

Popkin, S. L. (1991). *The reasoning voter: Communication and persuasion in presidential campaigns*. Chicago: University of Chicago Press.

(1995). "Information shortcuts and the reasoning voter." *Information, participation and choice: An economic theory of democracy in perspective*, pp. 17–35.

Powell Jr, G. B. and G. D. Whitten (1993). "A cross-national analysis of economic voting: Taking account of the political context." *American Journal of Political Science* 37(2): 391–414.

Presser, S. and J. M. Converse (1976–1977). "On Stimson's interpretation of declines in presidential popularity." *Public Opinion Quarterly* 40(4): 538–541.

Przeworski, A. and J. D. Sprague (1988). *Paper stones: A history of electoral socialism*. Chicago: University of Chicago Press.

Riker, W. H. (1986). *The art of political manipulation*. New Haven: Yale University Press.

(1993). "Rhetorical interaction in the ratification campaigns." In W. H. Riker, (Ed.). *Agenda formation*. Ann Arbor: University of Michigan Press, pp. 81–123.

Rittel, H. W. and M. M. Webber (1973). "Dilemmas in a general theory of planning." *Policy Sciences* 4(2): 155–169.

Robertson, D. B. (1976). *A theory of party competition*. London: Wiley.

Sanders, D., H. D. Clarke, M. C. Stewart and P. Whiteley (2011). "Downs, Stokes and the dynamics of electoral choice." *British Journal of Political Science* 41(2): 287–314.

Sanders, D., H. Ward, D. Marsh and T. Fletcher (1987). "Government popularity and the Falklands War: a reassessment." *British Journal of Political Science* 17(3): 281–313.

Schofield, N. (2003). "Valence competition in the spatial stochastic model." *Journal of Theoretical Politics* 15(4): 371–383.

(2004). "Equilibrium in the spatial 'valence' model of politics." *Journal of Theoretical Politics* 16(4): 447–481.

Seeberg, H. B. (2016a). "How stable is political parties' issue ownership? A cross-time, cross-national Analysis." *Political Studies*. Early view.

(2016b). "What can a government do? Government issue ownership and real world problems." *European Journal of Political Research*. Early view.

Serra, G. (2010). "Polarization of what? A model of elections with endogenous valence." *Journal of Politics* 72(2): 426–437.

(2011). "Why primaries? The party's tradeoff between policy and valence." *Journal of Theoretical Politics* 23(1): 21–51.

Sides, J. (2006). "The origins of campaign agendas." *British Journal of Political Science* 36(3): 407–436.

Sigelman, L. and K. Knight (1983). "Why does presidential popularity decline? A test of the expectation/disillusion theory." *Public Opinion Quarterly* 47(3): 310–324.

(1985). "Expectation/disillusion and presidential popularity: The Reagan experience." *Public Opinion Quarterly* 49(2): 209–213.

Simon, A. F. (2002). *The winning message: Candidate behavior, campaign discourse, and democracy*. Cambridge: Cambridge University Press.

Smith, J. M. (2010). "Does crime pay? Issue ownership, political opportunity, and the populist right in Western Europe." *Comparative Political Studies* 43(11): 1471–1498.

Soroka, S. N. (2006). "Good news and bad news: Asymmetric responses to economic information." *Journal of Politics* 68(2): 372–385.

(2014). *Negativity in democratic politics: Causes and consequences.* Cambridge: Cambridge University Press.

Soroka, S. N. and C. Wlezien (2010). *Degrees of democracy: Politics, public opinion, and policy.* Cambridge: Cambridge University Press.

van Spanje, J. (2011). "Keeping the rascals in: Anti-political-establishment parties and their cost of governing in established democracies." *European Journal of Political Research* 50(5): 609–635.

Spiliotes, C. J. and L. Vavreck (2002). "Campaign Advertising: Partisan Convergence or Divergence?" *Journal of Politics* 64(1): 249–261.

Stimson, J. A. (1976a). "Public support for American presidents: A cyclical model." *Public Opinion Quarterly* 40(1): 1–21.

(1976b). "On disillusion with the expectation/disillusion theory: A rejoinder." *Public Opinion Quarterly* 40(4): 541–543.

(1991). *Public opinion in America: Moods, cycles, and swings.* Boulder, CO: Westview Press.

Stimson, J. A., M. B. MacKuen and R. S. Erikson (1995). "Dynamic representation." *American Political Science Review* 89(3): 543–565.

Stokes, D. E. (1963). "Spatial models of party competition." *American Political Science Review* 57(2): 368–377.

Stokes, D. (1992). "Valence politics." In D. Kavanagh (Ed.). *Electoral politics.* Oxford: Clarendon University Press, pp. 141–164.

Stone, W. J. and E. N. Simas (2010). "Candidate valence and ideological positions in US House elections." *American Journal of Political Science* 54(2): 371–388.

Stubager, R. and R. Slothuus (2013). "What are the sources of political parties' issue ownership? Testing four explanations at the individual level." *Political Behavior* 35(3): 567–588.

Sulkin, T. (2005). *Issue politics in Congress.* Cambridge: Cambridge University Press.

Taylor, S. E. (1991). "Asymmetrical effects of positive and negative events: The mobilization-minimization hypothesis." *Psychological Bulletin* 110(1): 67.

Therriault, A. (2015). "Whose issue is it anyway? A new look at the meaning and measurement of issue ownership." *British Journal of Political Science* 45(4): 929–938.

Tilley, J. and S. B. Hobolt (2011). "Is the government to blame? An experimental test of how partisanship shapes perceptions of performance and responsibility." *The Journal of Politics* 73(2): 316–330.

Tresch, A., J. Lefevere and S. Walgrave. (2013). "'Steal me if you can!': The impact of campaign messages on associative issue ownership." *Party Politics* 21(2): 198–208.

Tufte, E. (1978). *Political control of the economy.* Princeton, NJ: Princeton University Press.

Van der Brug, W. (2004). "Issue ownership and party choice." *Electoral Studies* 23(2): 209–233.

Wagner, M. (2012). "When do parties emphasise extreme positions? How strategic incentives for policy differentiation influence issue importance." *European Journal of Political Research* 51(1): 64–88.

Wagner, M. and T. M. Meyer (2015). "Negative issue ownership." *West European Politics* 38(4): 797–816.

Wagner, M. and E. Zeglovits (2014). "Survey questions about party competence: Insights from cognitive interviews." *Electoral Studies* 34: 280–290.

Walgrave, S., J. Lefevere and A. Tresch (2012). "The associative dimension of issue ownership." *Public Opinion Quarterly* 76(4): 771–782.

Walgrave, S., A. Tresch and J. Lefevere (2015). "The conceptualisation and measurement of issue ownership." *West European Politics* 38(4): 778–796.

Walgrave, S., K. Van Camp, J. Lefevere and A. Tresch (2016). "Measuring issue ownership with survey questions. A question wording experiment." *Electoral Studies* 42: 290–299.

Ward, D., K. H. Kim, M. Graham and M. Tavits (2015). "How economic integration affects party issue emphases." *Comparative Political Studies* 48(10): 1227–1259.

Weaver, R. K. (1986). "The politics of blame avoidance." *Journal of Public Policy* 6(4): 371–398.

Whiteley, P., H. D. Clarke, D. Sanders and M. C. Stewart (2013). *Affluence, austerity and electoral change in Britain.* Cambridge: Cambridge University Press.

(2016). "Hunting the Snark: A reply to 're-evaluating valence models of political choice'." *Political Science Research and Methods* 4(1): 221–240.

Whiteley, P., M. C. Stewart, D. Sanders and H. D. Clarke (2005). "The issue agenda and voting in 2005." *Parliamentary Affairs* 58(4): 802–817.

Wittman, D. (2005). "Valence characteristics, costly policy and the median-crossing property: A diagrammatic exposition." *Public Choice* 124(3–4): 365–382.

Wlezien, C. (1995). "The public as thermostat: Dynamics of preferences for spending." *American Journal of Political Science* 39(4): 981–1000.

(1996). "Dynamics of representation: The case of U.S. spending on defence." *British Journal of Political Science* 26(1): 81–103.

(2004). "Patterns of representation: Dynamics of public preferences and policy." *Journal of Politics* 66(1): 1–24.

(2005). "On the salience of political issues: The problem with 'most important problem'." *Electoral Studies* 24(4): 555–579.

(2015). "The myopic voter? The economy and US presidential elections." *Electoral Studies* 39: 195–204.

(2016a). "On causality in the study of valence and voting behavior: An introduction to the symposium." *Political Science Research and Methods* 4(1): 195–197.

(2016b). "Policy (mis)representation and the cost of ruling: US presidential elections in comparative perspective." *Comparative Political Studies.*

Wlezien, C., M. Franklin and D. Twiggs (1997). "Economic perceptions and vote choice: Disentangling the endogeneity." *Political Behavior* 19(1): 7–17.

Zakharov, A. V. (2009). "A model of candidate location with endogenous valence." *Public Choice* 138(3–4): 347–366.

Zaller, J. (1992). *The nature and origins of mass opinion.* Cambridge: Cambridge University Press.

Zaller, J. and S. Feldman (1992). "A simple theory of the survey response: Answering questions versus revealing preferences." *American Journal of Political Science* 36(3): 579–616.

Index

September 11th, 110, 114, 128, 229, 251

Afghanistan, 110, 114, 123
American National Election Studies, 161
Armed forces. *See* Military
Asylum seekers, 153, 158, 159, 161
Australian Labor Party (also ALP), 117, 122, 125, 129, 132, 237
Australian Liberal Party, 56, 57, 126, 129, 132, 237

Black Wednesday. *See* Exchange Rate Mechanism crisis
Blair, Tony (also Blair government), 97, 114, 115, 123, 194, 235
Blame
  Blame accumulation, 184–185
  Blame attribution, 24, 25, 185
  Blame avoidance, 24, 254, 255
British Election Study, 48, 161
Budge, Ian and Farlie, Dennis, 27, 28, 30, 31
Budget, 50, 107, 165
Budget deficit, 31, 193
Bush, George H. (also Bush I administration), 128, 193, 194, 229, 256
Bush, George W. (also Bush II administration), 70, 71, 72, 78, 79, 108, 109, 110, 111, 123, 128, 150, 163, 229, 237

Callaghan, James, 194, 235
Campaigns, 28, 38, 170, 189, 222, 248, 250
Canadian Liberal Party, 193
Chernobyl, 119, 121
Christian Democratic Union (CDU), Germany, 49, 55, 68, 118, 119, 120, 121, 123, 124, 126, 130, 131, 144, 169
Civil rights, 50, 59, 68, 104, 105, 124, 229, 238

Civil Rights Act, 104
Clarity of responsibility, 149, 170, 195, 248
Clinton, Bill (also Clinton administration), 95, 104, 106, 107, 109, 121, 128, 131, 132, 150, 163, 235
Clinton, Hillary, 70, 195, 258
Coalition of minorities, 171, 190, 191, 196
Cold War, 50, 123, 128, 132, 194
Comparative Agendas Project, 50
Constituency representation, 13, 36, 38, 96, 98, 99, 100, 103, 104, 110, 131, 236, 246
Continuous Monitoring Survey (also CMS), 48, 72, 78, 81, 151, 153, 155, 192
Costs of governing, 17, 18, 25, 43, 93, 167–175, 179, 185, 188, 189, 190, 191, 192, 193, 195, 196, 197, 234, 236, 240, 242, 248, 249, 253
  Curvilinear relationship, 185, 188, 191
Costs of ruling. *See* Costs of governing
Crime (see also law and order), 31, 143, 153, 161
  Crime rate, 49, 103, 112, 121, 128, 142, 163, 200
  Homicide rate, 142

Defence, 50, 55, 67, 76, 110, 114, 118, 123, 124, 125, 128, 131, 132, 237, 238
Dyad ratios algorithm, 82, 83, 85, 150, 152, 201, 202, 203, 205, 241

Economy, 50, 67, 109, 112, 115, 116, 118, 119, 122, 123, 124, 125, 126, 129, 131, 132, 149, 153, 161, 194, 237
  Economic evaluations, 3, 143, 149–152, 162
  Economic growth, 9, 15, 109, 115, 129, 132, 139, 179, 194, 254

Economic voting, 6, 138, 139, 140, 149, 234, 253
Recession, 112, 123, 129, 132, 193, 194, 229, 251
Super issue, 16, 254
Education, 108, 114, 123, 124, 156
Edwards, John, 70, 258
Egan, Patrick, 9, 10, 30, 33, 34
Employment, 55, 67, 98, 109, 113, 115, 119, 122, 123, 124, 237, 238
Endogeneity, 6–7, 57, 69, 92, 142, 155, 198, 199, 242
Environment, 31, 54, 55, 76, 104, 107, 119, 120, 121, 123, 125, 127, 131
Exchange Rate Mechanism crisis, 42, 56, 115, 226, 231

Falklands War, 123, 226, 231
Fiorina, Morris, 140, 177, 243
Foreign affairs, 55, 67, 104, 111, 113, 118, 121, 123, 124, 238
Freezing hypothesis, 99

Gallup, 31, 48, 104, 108, 201
Generalised competence, 2, 7, 12, 14, 15, 16–17, 20, 21–23, 25, 43–44, 47, 48, 81–92, 144, 167–196, 197, 201, 203–204, 205, 208, 213, 217, 219, 221, 224, 226, 229, 231, 232, 233, 234, 236, 239–240, 241, 244–245, 247, 248, 252, 253, 255
Gingrich, Newt, 106, 107
Giuliani, Rudy, 70, 71, 258
Global financial crisis, 109, 110, 116, 123, 129, 231
Gore, Al, 104, 107, 163, 164
Granger causation, 48, 85, 89, 90, 91, 241, 245
Grievance asymmetry, 17, 172, 173, 175
Gulf War, 128, 194, 226, 229

Hawke, Bob (also Hawke government), 129, 132
Health, 31, 50, 55, 106, 111, 117, 121, 122, 123, 125, 126, 127, 131, 237,
Healthcare costs, 142, 146
Hospital waiting times, 142
Heath, Edward (also Heath government), 112, 121
Heuristics, 43, 44, 82
Honeymoon, political, 25, 168, 172, 175, 176, 177, 178, 179, 181–182, 185, 189, 196
Duration, 181–182

Howard, John (also Howard government), 117, 122, 130, 132
Howard, Michael, 114

Immigration, 68, 103, 112, 124, 125, 126, 129, 131, 132, 142, 161, 237, 251
Incumbency (also incumbents and oppositions), 124, 125, 137–141, 155, 158, 165–166, 175–178, 182–185, 196, 242, 244, 253
Asymmetry, 137–141, 146, 159, 165, 239, 245
Oppositions, 36, 124, 125, 138, 158, 176, 239, 248
Inflation, 193, 194
Ipsos MORI, 48
Iraq, 110, 111, 114, 123, 128
Issue competence, concepts of, 10, 12–15, 26, 27, 38–44, 47, 92, 93, 234–235, 243–245
Issue competence, measures of, 26, 32–33, 46, 243–245
Issue evolution, 34
Issue ownership, 2, 3–6, 13, 27–32, 34–36, 38–41, 44, 45, 46, 56–57, 92, 94, 135–136, 236–239
Associative, 39, 95
Lease, 4, 29–30, 31–32, 36–38, 39, 45, 96, 138, 140, 239, 243, 250
Losses and gains (also change), 47, 57–69, 96–100, 101–102, 134, 243
Neutralisation, 37, 38, 95, 113
Neutralization, 95, 122, 128, 130, 132, 249
Realignment, 15, 34, 41, 47, 57, 66, 67, 69, 93, 94, 95, 99, 101, 102, 104, 105, 124, 134, 238, 246
Stability, 125–133
Issue performance, 2, 13, 38–39, 40, 44, 45, 137, 200–201, 202–203, 239
Issue transfer, 41–43, 44, 81–82, 167–168
Issue-public, 2, 99, 199

Keating, Paul (also Keating government), 129
Kohl, Helmut (also Kohl government), 118, 119, 120, 130

Law and order, 21, 95, 112, 121, 125, 128, 131

Macro-competence (see also generalised competence), 23, 44, 81–92, 93, 173–175, 178, 201, 203, 232, 241, 244, 245

Macro-partisanship, 23, 85, 88, 89, 91, 93, 178, 179, 205, 241, 244, 245
Macro-polity, 20, 23, 44
Major, John (also Major government), 56, 112, 194
Manifesto Research on Political Representation, 103
McCain, John, 70, 71, 163, 259
Medicare, 31, 106, 117, 121
Merkel, Angela, 143, 144, 195
Military casualties, 12, 142
Misery index, 142, 150, 152
Mood, 47 (see macro-competence)
Morality issues, 115
Most important issue, 103, 123, 202
Most important problem, 103, 199, 201, 202, 221, 232

National Annenberg Election Study, 70, 72, 78, 79
National Health Service (NHS), 127, 132, 146, 153, 154, 155, 156, 161, 162, 203, 217, 219, 235
Negativity bias, 19, 24, 175, 182–184, 185, 186, 188, 191, 253
Newspoll, 48, 54, 117
Niche parties, 36, 37, 99, 159, 251
Northern Rock bank, run on, 42, 226, 231

Obama, Barack (also Obama administration), 70, 110, 111, 123, 132, 143, 150, 163, 164, 195, 237, 238, 258
Obamacare, 111, 122, 226
Operation Desert Storm, 226

Partisanship, 26, 47, 50, 96, 240–243
  Persistence in performance ratings, 79, 81, 241, 247
  Relationship with generalised competence, 7, 48, 85–92
  Relationship with issue ownership, 69–74
  Relationship with performance fluctuations, 76–81
Party supply, 25, 100, 105, 125, 126, 131, 132, 134, 243, 244, 247, 251
Patient Protection and Affordable Care Act. See Obamacare
Pensions, 50, 130
Performance shock, 15, 18, 23, 32, 33, 38–39, 40, 42, 43, 47, 48, 78, 81, 96, 97, 98, 99, 104, 121, 122, 133, 134, 184, 196, 221, 236, 252

Performance updating, 6, 7, 47, 81, 137, 139, 140, 141, 155, 157, 158, 165, 248
Performance voting, 159–165, 197, 222, 252
Petrocik, John, 3–5, 13, 24, 27, 29–30, 31, 32, 34, 35, 36, 39, 41, 45, 94, 95, 96, 98, 137, 138, 139, 140, 236, 239
Police, 143
Poll tax riots, 226
Populus, 48
Public policy mood, 20, 186, 190, 204, 205
Public spending (also government spending), 12, 32, 50, 97, 98, 100, 103, 106, 112, 114, 115, 116, 117, 122, 123, 127, 143, 189, 252

Railways, 153, 156
Rally-round-the-flag, 194, 226
Reagan, Ronald (also Reagan administration), 106, 108, 128, 193, 194, 229
Reunification of Germany, 68, 118, 119, 247
Riker, William, 18, 28, 252
Romney, Mitt, 70, 71, 111, 163, 164, 259
Roper Center for Public Opinion Research, 48
Rudd, Kevin (also Rudd government), 56, 117
Running tally, 2, 6, 7, 23, 48, 91, 93, 241, 242

Saliency theory, 27
Schröder, Gerhard, 119
Social Democratic Party (SPD), Germany, 118, 119, 120, 121, 124, 126, 130, 131, 133, 169
Social security, 31, 49, 50, 106, 107
Stimson, James, 82, 85, 168, 170, 172, 183, 201, 241
Stokes, Donald, 1, 7, 8, 9, 10, 11, 197, 221, 232, 233, 245, 251
Strikes, 113, 114, 122, 142, 146
  Miners' strikes, 122

Terrorism, 50, 72, 153, 158
Thatcher, Margaret (also Thatcher government), 112, 113, 114, 115, 123, 194, 238
Thermostatic model of public opinion, 173, 196
Thompson, Fred, 70, 71, 259
Trudeau, Justin, 193
Trudeau, Pierre, 193,
Trudeaumania, 193
Trump, Donald, 97, 195

UK Labour Party, 42, 57, 67, 72, 76, 88,
    97, 98, 115, 122, 123, 124, 126, 155,
    156, 158, 159, 161, 237
UK Conservative Party, 42, 54, 55, 56, 57,
    67, 68, 72, 76, 104, 112, 113, 114,
    115, 116, 121, 122, 123, 124, 125,
    127, 131, 132, 134, 154, 156, 158,
    159, 161, 217, 219, 226, 231, 237
UK Independence Party (also UKIP), 104,
    113, 124, 245
Unemployment, 109, 110, 112, 113, 118,
    119, 123, 132, 193, 194, 229

Valence, 7–11, 41, 122, 197, 221, 232, 240,
    245, 251–252
    Formal theories, 10–11
    Valence voting, 11, 236
Vietnam War, 229

Welfare and housing, 54, 55, 106, 112, 119,
    125, 131, 133, 237
Wilson, Harold, 194
Winter of discontent, 194

YouGov, 48, 151, 152